791.43                92-01547
LEI               15.00
         Leitch, Thomas M.

Find the director.

WITHDRAWN

Find the Director
and Other Hitchcock Games

Thomas M. Leitch

# FIND THE DIRECTOR

## AND

## OTHER

## HITCHCOCK

## GAMES

The University of Georgia Press

*Athens and London*

© 1991 by the University of Georgia Press
Athens, Georgia 30602
All rights reserved
Designed by Louise M. Jones
Set in 10½/14 Berkeley Old Style Medium
The paper in this book meets the guidelines for
permanence and durability of the Committee on
Production Guidelines for Book Longevity of the
Council on Library Resources.

Printed in the United States of America
95  94  93  92  91  C  5  4  3  2  1
95  94  93  92  91  P  5  4  3  2  1

*Library of Congress Cataloging in Publication Data*
Leitch, Thomas M.
Find the director and other Hitchcock games /
Thomas M. Leitch.   p.   cm.
Includes bibliographical references and index.
ISBN 0-8203-1294-0 (alk. paper)
ISBN 0-8203-1341-6 (pbk.: alk. paper)
1. Hitchcock, Alfred, 1899–
—Criticism and interpretation.   I. Title.
PN1998.3.H58L46 1991
791.43'0233'092—dc20   90-45353   CIP

*British Library Cataloging in Publication Data available*

To Lisa Elliott

# CONTENTS

*Acknowledgments*    ix

One    GAMES HITCHCOCK PLAYS    1

Two    FIND THE DIRECTOR    36

Three    GRAVE TO GAY    74

Four    ODD MAN OUT    106

Five    CAT AND MOUSE    136

Six    HOME FREE ALL    165

Seven    TAILS YOU LOSE    189

Eight    FILL IN THE BLANKS    222

Nine    ONLY A GAME    256

*Notes*    267

*Index*    287

# ACKNOWLEDGMENTS

Portions of this book were written under the auspices of a General University Research Grant from the University of Delaware; and portions have appeared in earlier versions as "Narrative as a Way of Knowing: The Example of Alfred Hitchcock," *Centennial Review* 30, no. 3 (Summer 1986): 315–30; "Murderous Victims in *The Secret Agent* and *Sabotage,*" *Literature/Film Quarterly* 14, no. 1 (Summer 1986): 64–68; and "Self and World at Paramount," in *Reader on Hitchcock's Rereleased Films,* ed. Walter Raubicheck and Walter Srebnick (Detroit: Wayne State University Press, 1991). I am grateful for permission to reprint and revise this material. I owe a more particular debt to colleagues and friends who read the manuscript in different guises or pieces; thanks to Leo Braudy, Pat Ferrara, Jim Welsh, and especially Charles Eidsvik. Don Crafton, Kim Carson, and Audrey Kupferberg of the Yale Film Study Center have all been generous with their help. Out of the many students at the University of Delaware and Yale University who have discussed Hitchcock's films with me, I am particularly indebted to Elizabeth Coute. Thanks, finally, to Gene Adair, Madelaine Cooke, Louise Jones, and Karen Orchard at the University of Georgia Press.

A more fundamental debt is not so easily acknowledged. A structuring absence in most studies of Hitchcock's career is Alma Reville, his wife and long-time collaborator. Hitchcock often cited his reliance on her contributions to his work—she began as a script girl, became a scenarist and adaptor, and took an active role in the casting, writing, and final editing of many of her husband's films—yet no one has yet considered the ways in which the films she worked on are hers. It seems clear that she helped Hitchcock establish his career largely by repressing, or suppressing, her own. Such enabling gifts are never truly repaid; they can only be acknowledged, as I here acknowledge the contributions of my wife toward making this book possible.

Find the Director
and Other Hitchcock Games

# ONE

## GAMES

## HITCHCOCK

## PLAYS

Ten years after his death, Alfred Hitchcock's genius for self-advertising ensures his continuing status as one of the best-known of all film directors. Audiences all over the world know what he looks like because they have seen images of him in most of his films and television shows. Hitchcock's introductions to *Alfred Hitchcock Presents* and *The Alfred Hitchcock Hour* made his persona as familiar to audiences as many star performers of fifties television. These introductions were so popular that they were later eerily resurrected for posthumous episodes of *The New Alfred Hitchcock Presents*. Hitchcock poses in each introduction as impresario who stands outside the frame of the story, free to comment ironically on the characters and events within the story, the conventions of commercial television ("And now for something *really* horrible" is a favorite lead-in to a commercial), and his own frequently ridiculous figure, tricked out as an elephantine archer or an overgrown baby.

This elaborately ironic pose is maintained in the trailers to *Psycho* and *The Birds,* in which Hitchcock the impresario gives a talk about the subject of his new film, taking the audience on a facetious tour of the Bates house and motel or discussing his forthcoming lecture on our friends the birds. But in each case the trailer ends with an unexpected segue to a shot from the film itself. Hitchcock draws back the shower curtain to reveal a closeup of Janet Leigh screaming or looks off-camera right to a matched shot of Tippi Hedren crying, "They're coming!" Each segue is a joke that blurs the distinction between the world of the story and the world outside, a distinction the trailer had begun by insisting on. The trailer to *Frenzy* confuses this distinction further by cutting Hitchcock's remarks to the audience into the continuity of several scenes of the movie. Retrieving what he tells us is his necktie from around the neck of a strangled woman, Hitchcock looks at the camera and asks, "How do you like my tie?" looks right and says, "How do you like it?" then cuts to a shot of Barbara Leigh-Hunt saying, "My God! The tie!" The trailer emphasizes the film's ghoulish humor by treating murder as a joke and the director as a naif who has wandered into his own movie.

But the most problematic of Hitchcock's public images are his celebrated cameo appearances—his brief unbilled roles—in virtually all his films. Even more perversely than Hitchcock's trailers or television introductions, the cameos pose serious difficulties for leading models of narrative by playing with the distinction between the world of the film (the diegesis, the world contained within the cinematic discourse, the world of the characters and their problems) and the world outside (the world of the filmmaker and the audience, who see the film as an artful fiction and so are able to adopt myriad perspectives on the diegetic world unavailable to the characters). Any audience that recognizes Hitchcock aboard Uncle Charlie's train in *Shadow of a Doubt* holding the world's best bridge hand or sitting in a Copenhagen hotel lobby in *Torn Curtain* distastefully raising a diapered baby from his knee will be reminded that the movie they are watching is only a movie, but this realization will not break the movie's spell; if it did, the audience would not be able to enjoy the rest of the movie. On the contrary, spotting Hitchcock's cameo provides an additional source of pleasure for sharp-eyed audiences, and both director and audience are called on to exercise considerable ingenuity in devising and recognizing these cameos. Hitchcock's best-known cameo, his appearance in *Lifeboat* in before-and-after newspaper photos for a weight-loss product called Reduco, suggests the nature of the relationship the cameos establish between the director and

his audience. Hitchcock told François Truffaut that he had great difficulty in coming up with a way he could appear in a one-set film with
so few characters but that he finally hit on the newspaper ad as a solution which would not only provide for his appearance but would also
memorialize his recent weight loss.[1] Evidently by 1943 Hitchcock considered himself honor-bound to appear in every one of his feature films,
even though his appearance might be hard to find. And the audience
was expected by now not only to be familiar with Hitchcock's profile but
to be interested in its changing shape as a personal revelation, as if the
film were a mass-produced Christmas card on which the cameo were a
scribbled personal message.

Hitchcock sometimes appears in costume in his cameos, but he never
plays a character; the whole point of each cameo is that this is no ordinary character but rather someone whose mode of existence is different
from that of every other character in the movie. Truffaut's remark that
his first appearance as part of a crowd in *The Lodger* helps to "fill the
screen" aptly implies that the passersby Hitchcock affects in his films
never have any function in the story, never interact significantly with
the principals (Hitchcock appearing in *Stage Fright* looking askance at
Eve Gill telling herself that she is Doris Tinsdale is delivering a judgment, not making any impression on her), and never even speak.[2] The
sole purpose of such apparitions—they cannot truly be called characters, for Hitchcock makes no pretense of playing a role shaped by the
requirements of the diegesis—is to be recognized. The exception that
proves the rule is Hitchcock's cameo in *Rope,* in which he appears briefly
in the background in the costume and attitude of Mr. Kentley. Mr. Kentley is a character, but Hitchcock is not playing this character, for he does
nothing in the role but walk away from the camera for a few seconds.
Hitchcock is merely impersonating Mr. Kentley, a character played by Sir
Cedric Hardwicke; if he is acting at all, he is playing Hardwicke playing
Mr. Kentley.[3]

Specifying the mode of existence of Hitchcock's cameos poses a stum-
bling block for dominant modes of narrative theory. Communications
models of narrative, in which stories are messages sent by their authors
to their receivers, are inadequate to describe the situation of a film director using his own image as a means to communication, both because

the image cannot be decoded according to a communications model—
"Look, there's the director!" is not a message communicated by the diegesis but a perception that requires the audience to assume a perspective
outside the frame of the diegesis—and because, as Edward Branigan
notes, the author of a text cannot simply appear within a text as the
author. Branigan, following Roland Barthes, observes that "the artwork
provides no context within which to locate the author," who "is located
in the text only as a *subcode* of the code of narration and not as someone
who speaks, expresses the codes."[4]

But Branigan's own empiricist model of narration, although far more
sophisticated than the communications model he is criticizing, does not
adequately describe Hitchcock's cameos either because it does not make
the kinds of distinctions that give the cameos a witty power unlike
that of other directors' appearances on film. When Branigan argues that
"Hitchcock appearing in his own film is not the director made manifest
but a figure trapped as an object of a film process," he is overlooking
the decisive ways in which Hitchcock's appearances are different not
only from the appearances of such director-stars as Chaplin, Keaton, and
Olivier, whose films are typically organized around their performances,
but from the appearances of other directors like Renoir, Welles, Huston,
and Truffaut, who take dramatic roles in their own, or other directors',
films.[5] Characters in fictional films, whether or not they are played by
the director, are functions of the discourse: their significance is established through the ways in which they participate in the diegesis (the
characters they play, their bearing on the plot, their interrelations with
other characters having a cognate diegetic significance). But the significance of Hitchcock's cameos is essentially that they make an image of
the director available for recognition. (Hence new audiences' inveterate
questions about where Hitchcock appears in *Rear Window* or *Dial M for
Murder*.) It is possible to speculate, as Maurice Yacowar has done, about
the thematic significance of the cameos, individually or as a group, but
simply recognizing Hitchcock can provide a characteristic pleasure even
for an audience who makes no attempt to connect his appearance to the
characters or story in a particular film or to a pattern of cameos in his
other films.[6] Unlike the fictional characters played by other directors,
Hitchcock through his cameos manages to appear in his films without

being constrained in at all the same ways by the requirements of their diegeses.

Although Hitchcock's introductions to his television program establish a clear distinction between the world of the audience and the world of the story, his cameos have the opposite effect, because they introduce a non-diegetic figure into the story without stepping unambiguously outside the frame of the diegesis. Nor is this figure some historical personage like Napoleon as played by Charles Boyer in *Conquest* or Benny Goodman appearing with his band in *The Gang's All Here* but the storyteller himself, the creator rather than a performer. In this regard it is quite unlike the figure of Somerset Maugham as played by Herbert Marshall in *The Moon and Sixpence* and *The Razor's Edge* or those of the other storytellers whose narrative activity Branigan analyzes in his discussion of cinematic point of view because it is only secondarily a mimetic figure, and never directly a figure for perception; that is, the audience is never encouraged to adopt the cameo as a guide for its own perceptions, a surrogate storyteller or audience. Instead, the joke behind the cameos—that the storyteller is presenting himself neither as the storyteller nor as a fully articulated character but as a figure on the margin of the fictional world—depends on a kind of double awareness Branigan's theory does not ascribe to the audience.

In other words, it is the audience's desire for pleasure (the pleasure of recognizing the director hidden in the discourse), not its desire for justifying particular narrative devices (cut-in close-ups or voice-over commentary that can be assigned to a narrator), that gives the cameos their point, since they constitute a device whose point is that it can be recuperated only as a device (to recognize the cameo is automatically to note its potentially disruptive force). The resulting effect cannot be explained by theories of narrative which depend on establishing a dualism between *histoire,* or story (the events of a narrative apart from any given representational form—for instance, the Cinderella story), and *discours,* or discourse (a particular narration of a given story—for instance, Charles Perrault's or Walt Disney's *Cinderella*). Even dualistic theories organized around the problem of pleasure (what makes this shot worth watching?) rather than Branigan's problem of narrative motivation (how can this shot be logically justified?) cannot account for the effect of the cameos. Consider the influential argument of Christian Metz that most audiences think of the movies they watch as stories, natural sequences of events that the camera just happened to capture; even though they know all along that what they are watching is just a movie, they react with anger or fear or exultation as if it were an unmediated story.[7] Sometimes, however, a movie will remind the audience that it is not a story by dropping its naturalizing devices and emphasizing the artifices that make it a discourse. At such times the audience has the exhilarating or disconcerting feeling of falling out of the story or otherwise having its attention drawn to a diegetic frame whose existence the audience usually chooses to ignore. Hitchcock's cameos have the effect of reminding the audience of the filmmaker's power and his film's status as an artifact, an artful discourse rather than a transparent story.

But Metz's account, like Branigan's, is inadequate to the effects Hitchcock's cameos actually produce. The audience's two kinds of awareness of *Lifeboat* as story and as discourse should, according to Metz, be perpetually at war with each other as the audience struggled to find some stable point of view from which to follow and interpret images on the screen; in particular, Hitchcock's cameos would operate as a distracting interruption, like the network logo during a late-night television screening that reminds the audience that this is only a movie. But audiences who recognize Hitchcock at all are not really distracted, even pleasurably, from the story because their experience of the film as story and discourse is not nearly so sharply split; in watching a Hitchcock film, they do not shuttle neatly back and forth between two kinds of awareness.

The problematic status of Hitchcock's cameos also challenges other psychoanalytically based theories of pleasure. Psychoanalytic theories using analogies between the movie screen and the dream screen of early childhood to argue that movies inscribe their audiences into a particular position by requiring them to adopt certain attitudes in order to follow and enjoy their stories fail to account for the fact that the cameos do not inscribe passive, unconscious audiences through cultural constraints but rather engage audiences on a conscious, contractual, elective basis by providing a distinctive pleasure for audiences who recognize Hitchcock's sly appearances and allowing audiences who do not do so all the other pleasures associated with Hitchcock's movies.[8] The example of

*Lifeboat,* whose cameo so taxed the director's ingenuity, suggests that the cameos are better considered as a contract equally binding on director and audience than as a means of inscribing either into the discourse on the basis of unconscious motives. If Gaylyn Studlar is correct in arguing that "cinema is not a sadistic institution but preeminently a contractual one based on the promise of certain pleasures," Hitchcock's cameos can serve as a paradigm for cinematic pleasure.[9]

A much more promising model for the relationship Hitchcock's cameos establish with their audience is the constructivist theory developed by David Bordwell. Agreeing with Studlar that it is unnecessary and misleading to theorize an audience inscribed by the cinematic discourse— "I see no reason to claim for the unconscious any activities which can be explained on other grounds," he remarks—Bordwell describes the audience for fictional films as actively engaged in a process of constructing a story, an activity directed by operational cues. "A film," argues Bordwell, ". . . does not 'position' anybody." Despite the advantages of this constructive model over psychoanalytic models of inscription, however, it cannot account for the quirky effect of Hitchcock's cameos because Bordwell is at such pains to banish the storyteller from his narrative theory, which "presupposes a perceiver, but not any sender, of a message," that he breaks the tie between the represented Hitchcock—the fat Cockney onscreen—and the putative storyteller, denying the very source of the cameos' power.[10]

If none of these theories of cinematic narrative adequately explains the effects of the cameos, is there a superior alternative model? Branigan observes that "narration has been analyzed . . . as a simple unrolling, a logical progression, a violation, a set of oppositions, a set of alternatives, a control on connotation, a logic of reading, a reconstruction of unconscious mechanisms, and as a literal telling."[11] This list omits another model that is still more promising: the conception of narration as a game between a storyteller and an audience. Like Metz's analysis of cinematic syntax and Branigan's of point of view, the analysis of narrative as a game is based on an analogy with language, but this analogy, based on the later work of Wittgenstein, emphasizes the point of cinema's rules rather than the ways in which they facilitate understanding.[12] In short, it treats films as objects of pleasure rather than as objects of knowledge, and considers their rules as defined by their purpose in promoting the goals of the players—filmmakers and their audiences—whatever role understanding plays in those goals.

Although formal game theory, first developed as a mathematical model for analyzing social strategies (generating predictive or prescriptive rules concerning the most efficient ways to submit a bid, cast a vote, or deploy a nuclear arsenal), has rarely been applied to the analysis of narrative and never, as far as I have found, to narrative cinema, theorists like Johan Huizinga and Roger Caillois have long recognized the affinities between storytelling and other games whose rules are designed to promote pleasure. Considering Hitchcock's cameos as moves in a game of hide-and-seek—or, more accurately, find the director—not only explains their narrative status more precisely but illuminates their special role in Hitchcock's films, revealing their exemplary status as patterns for the ways the director's films operate and the kinds of pleasure they are designed to provide.

Games provide an obvious model for the relations Hitchcock's films establish between the filmmaker and the audience because games serve so often within the stories of the films themselves as models of the diegesis, from the chess game between the Lodger and Daisy (a game punctuated by his playful remark, "I'll get you yet," and his picking up a poker while she bends over to pick up a fallen piece) to the game of blindman's buff at Cathy Brenner's birthday party, a game interrupted by the first mass attack of the birds. In between, Hitchcock's heroes and heroines play tennis (in *Easy Virtue* and *Strangers on a Train*), shoot skeet (in the 1934 *Man Who Knew Too Much*), dress up in masquerade (in *Blackmail, The 39 Steps, Rebecca, Stage Fright, To Catch a Thief*), and even play another game of blindman's buff (in *Young and Innocent*). Probably the most sustained use of a particular game to provide the controlling metaphor for the characters' behavior is Hitchcock's boxing film, *The Ring,* one of the few films in which he takes screen credit for the scenario.

More generally, games provide a frame which contains, defines, or sharpens the suspense evoked by a genuinely threatening situation in many films which present attempts to deal with serious problems as a variously successful game, from Gilbert's and Iris's idyll in the baggage car in *The Lady Vanishes* to Blanche Tyler's enthusiastic performances as a medium in *Family Plot*. The fact that most of these games— Ted Spencer's attempt to pass off his spying on the conspirators as a lark in *Sabotage*, Huntley Haverstock's escape from his hotel room to Carol Fisher's room in *Foreign Correspondent*, Alicia Huberman's theft of the key to her husband's wine cellar in *Notorious*, Michael Armstrong's tensely ritualized attempt to lose his pursuing watchdog in the museum in *Torn Curtain*—are considerably darker reveals the intimate connection between games and Hitchcock's brand of suspense, which typically quibbles on the diegetic distinction between playing and pretending to play a game—a figure for the characters' activity that has considerable relevance to the audience's activity as well.

Finally, Hitchcock has directed a number of films which seem, despite the absence of particular recognizable diegetic games like hide-and-seek and blindman's buff, to be developed in an unbroken skein of games. The nonsensical continuity of *Number Seventeen* makes a great deal of sense if the film is considered as a series of games (among the characters, and between the director and the audience) which are actually variations of a single game (invoking and exploding the conventions of the thriller for a cast of characters who never take these conventions entirely seriously themselves). One way to distinguish between the two versions of *The Man Who Knew Too Much* is to note the much greater dependence of the first version on ludic metaphors; the film might be described as dramatizing the liberation of the Lawrence family through learning to play better. The pattern is reversed in *Secret Agent*, which shows the disillusioning consequences of treating international intrigue as a game. Among Hitchcock's later films, *Strangers on a Train* is most clearly organized around the metaphor of a game—the resonances of Guy's status as a tennis player are economically indicated by the adventures of his cigarette lighter, with its crossed tennis racquets over the inscription "A. to G."—but *Rope* and *North by Northwest* are equally dominated by ludic patterns. "And now let the fun begin!" exults Brandon as the guests for his post-strangulation party begin to arrive; and Philip Vandamm greets Roger Thornhill's attempts to establish his own identity with the weary disclaimer—"Games? Must we?"—which establishes the ludic tone of the film from the beginning.

The point of listing all these incidences of games within Hitchcock's films is not to argue that games have a unique importance in Hitchcock's work. Games are common in commercial cinema, and it is hard to imagine Hollywood genres like the musical and the romantic comedy existing without them. Furthermore, games have a much greater diegetic importance in the work of a director like Howard Hawks, who uses games and play as a radical metaphor for all human action, than in Hitchcock's films. The importance of games for Hitchcock is not their significance within the diegesis but their role as a figure for the relation between the storyteller and his audience, a relation which not surprisingly is often imaged within the diegesis as a game. The games the characters play are most significant as a metaphor for the games Hitchcock plays.

One reason Hitchcock's cameos do not force his audience to reassess its attitude toward his films is that they are not isolated moments of self-consciousness; instead, they are quintessential examples of Hitchcock's ludic approach to storytelling. Quite apart from his cameos, Hitchcock's films are strewn with highly artificial set-pieces and stylistic exercises. In fact, the very first distinctive feature of Hitchcock's early films is their self-advertising style. In virtually all of Hitchcock's films, however, the flagrant self-consciousness typified by the cameos does not undermine the power of the films but defines it. As Lesley Brill has pointed out, "During sequences of greatest emotional torsion . . . the maker's hand and eye draw attention to themselves most insistently. . . . To emphasize either represented or imposed artifice does not create a devaluing implausibility but rather signals a concentration of significance."[13] The audience's experience of a game as purposeful and pleasurable within contractual limits to which the audience freely and knowingly subscribes accounts better than dualistic models demarcating story from discourse for the enjoyment of Hitchcock's films.

A ludic theory of narrative offers many advantages over alternative theories in analyzing the audience's experience of Hitchcock's films. The escape from a simple duality between story and discourse (or between two kinds of awareness of narrative, immersion and analysis, or between two discrete audiences, an undiscriminating mass audience that follows the story and a self-conscious critical or professional audience that is aware of its discursive practice) allows game theory to describe

Hitchcock's cameos more accurately as moves in a game whose effect depends on their simultaneous appeal to two apparently irreconcilable kinds of awareness. Psychoanalytic theories of narrative have typically treated this double awareness in terms of fetishistic disavowal, as in the model Metz borrows from Octave Mannoni: "I know very well, but all the same . . ."[14] The psychoanalytic basis of this disavowal is the construction and validation of the experiencing self as given, authentic, inevitable, through a denial of the mechanisms that make the self possible. The point of the analogy is that even audiences who are most aware of the technology and conventions that foster the illusions of cinematic motion and fictional narrative have the same interest in repressing their knowledge that they have in repressing the knowledge that their identities rely on fetishes (the substitution of a beloved doll for the absent mother, the sexual response to an object associated with the loved one). Such theories set the theorist's passion for analysis squarely against the audience's will to be deceived. But using the metaphor of a game for Hitchcock's cameos and the films in which they appear indicates instead that the experience of even the most naive audiences does not privilege illusion over self-consciousness. Movie audiences are perfectly aware that they are being fooled, submit to the illusions of cinema willingly because the cinematic contract promises them pleasures that make their interest worthwhile, and very often enjoy reminders (like Hitchcock's cameos, or such outrageously stylized set-pieces as the long takes in *Rope*) of generic convention or cinematic illusion. Indeed without the pointed assurances provided by generic markers (the casting of John Wayne as western hero, for example, or the shiftiness of Wayne's opponents), the audience would be unable to respond in ways (rooting for Wayne, mitigating grief when his opponents are killed) that would protect its investment in the film. The distinction between the cinematic illusion and jarring reminders of a film's artifice—a wristwatch worn by an extra in *The Viking Queen,* for example—is less important than the distinction between pleasurable and unpleasurable reminders—a distinction that emphasizes the primarily ludic nature of the movies.

A further advantage of game theory over communication, psychoanalytic, or mimetic theories is the emphasis it places on the audience's motives for watching movies. All too often theories of narrative either assume the audience's interest, attention, and cooperation or assign the audience a single position remote from the wide range of possibilities open to actual audiences. Bordwell, following a Gestalt model of perception, assumes that "although we know a film is only a strobo-scopic display of fixed frames, we *cannot fail* to construct continuous light and movement,"[15] and argues elsewhere that, even if the audience knows Hitchcock filmed the birds' attack on the gas station and Melanie Daniels's horrified reaction on different days at different locations, the power of the continuity editing which intercuts the two series of shots is so strong that "we are compelled to see Melanie as being across the street from the gas station."[16] The first of these statements may be true—there may be no human audience that can resist the illusion created by the cinema's technological apparatus—but not the second, since the class of audiences who are "compelled" to visualize Melanie and the gas station as occupying contiguous spaces does not even include Bordwell himself.[17] The fact is that the vast majority of devices and techniques—causal, expressive, or figural conventions—by which narrative cinema secures its illusions operate only with the cooperation of audiences who are motivated to participate in those illusions, an audience that does not, for example, include very young children or film teachers analyzing a continuity sequence from *The Birds*.

Emphasizing the central importance of the audience's shifting motivations for playing the cinematic game produces a rhetoric of cinema sharply different from those of Bordwell and Branigan. Branigan's analysis of point of view, for example, is based on the proposition that "the most general problem that a viewer must confront about film narration is how to justify successive spaces and new scenes." Since "the usual scene in a classical film is narrated as if from the point of view of an observer capable of moving about the room," Branigan wonders, "How is it that we are privileged to see Norman Bates in secret conversation with his mother?"[18] The obvious answer to this question is not that the audience postulates a surrogate observer or worries about whether the point of view is consistent with its own—audiences who asked these questions would be puzzled by the simplest shot-reversal sequences and utterly baffled by zoom-ins, which do not imitate any capacity of the human observer—but rather that the audience accepts many "impossible" views gratefully and uncritically because they allow audience members access to precisely what they want to see. Carol Reed does not have to provide an optical or spatial justification for showing the doomed miners in *The Stars Look Down* because the audience wants to see how they are; Norman's conversation with his mother gratifies the audience's desire to get confirmation of her existence after Sheriff Chambers has just denied it. In each case, as in the famous opening sequence of *Psycho,* in which the camera seems to enter a window to eavesdrop on Sam's and Marion's romantic tryst, the film satisfies desires it has aroused, and these desires, not their narrative justification, are properly the basis of its rhetoric—a rhetoric which takes on a correspondingly ludic cast.[19]

A ludic model of film narrative posits an audience whose moviegoing habits are dictated by choice and discrimination rather than compulsion. Psychoanalytic accounts of cinematic pleasure privilege Freud's *fort/da* game, which served as the basis for his theory of the death instinct, as the basis for all others.[20] And Tania Modleski's study of women's fiction makes a persuasive case for a pathological reading of the audience's need for and response to such fiction.[21] But even compulsive moviegoers, like compulsive game-players, do not watch just any movies whatsoever; the appetite is for certain kinds of fictive experience, not for the cinematic illusion as such. And the bond between the audience and the movies it chooses, like the audience's participation in the game of identifying Hitchcock's cameos, is contractual, rewarding, and elective. This last quality is especially important as a corrective to theories of a universal audience compelled to accept the cinematic illusion or the constraints of any particular genre or mode of narrative presentation. It is precisely because audiences have different desires, fears, and fantasies that so many different kinds of films have been made. The appetite for moviegoing, like the appetite for game-playing, cannot be used as presumptive evidence for an appetite for any particular experience of the general type or as a universal appetite common to all audiences. Indeed an important aspect of the appeal of many kinds of movies (the teen-bonding films of John Hughes, slasher films that other putative audiences are too scared to watch, audience-participation films like *The Rocky Horror Picture Show*) is the audience's sense of superiority to other audiences excluded by unworthiness.

Gaylyn Studlar, arguing against the inscription of the cinema audience through the mechanisms of fetishism and scopophilia, has described the audience's attitude as masochistic rather than sadistic: "On one level, the pleasures of narrative film depend upon conflict and narrative predicament. These can be compared to the masochistic masquerade that pretends to keep pleasure at bay to fool the demanding superego. The spectator suffers with the characters and braves plot predicaments because, like the masochist, he/she knows the 'painful' experiences are based on a contract guaranteeing pleasure."[22] This argument seems especially apt to Hitchcock's chosen genre of the thriller. Because the audience's pleasure in identifying with characters who are often placed under distinctly unpleasurable pressure is based on their anticipation of later rewards that will justify the audience's vicarious suffering, this anticipation allows them to explore new games whose operation they do not fully understand, to revise their expectations in the light of new evidence, and ultimately to master cinematic games.[23] An important, though neglected, implication of this insight is that an audience's experience of a given story or genre or narrative mode changes over time because its projections and expectations are defined by its members' experience. It follows that films can never position or inscribe the audience definitively, since an audience familiar enough with a work's enabling conventions and analytically enough disposed will always be able to escape inscription. Audiences are never required to assume any particular attitude toward cultural myths, as Roland Barthes recognizes in *Mythologies*[24]; they are merely encouraged to do so and rewarded if they do. Whenever the rewards of cultural inscription are outweighed by the rewards of resistance (an audience's insight into the operations of the cinematic apparatus or its own psychology, its awakened sense of social or institutional importance, its members' personal vanity), an audience can easily break the contract the film seems to offer in favor of another that seems more likely to be profitable, as when students at my home institution, the University of Delaware, roar with laughter at the revelation that Guy's intoxicated fellow-passenger in *Strangers on a Train* teaches at Delaware Tech—a response so predictable that naive observers at the university might say it was inscribed into the text—or when their teacher successfully resists the nightmarish spell of the shower sequence in *Psycho* by analyzing it shot by shot. In this analysis the pleasure contract is always projective, consensual, and subject to revision by either filmmakers and audiences who think they can increase their rate of return by doing so.

It is important to stipulate the changing nature of the audience's experience because theories of audience inscription preclude the audience's developing new positions or attitudes. Such theories emphasize their own futility—after all, what is the point of writing for an audience whose position cannot be improved by enlightenment?—and so annul the point of their own project in a kind of pedagogical bad faith. Bordwell contends that despite most audiences' lack of self-conscious stylistic awareness, "to a great degree spectators can learn to notice and recall stylistic features of any film,"[25] and George M. Wilson uses a similar argument against Stephen Heath's analysis in "Narrative Space" of the place inscribed for the spectator by the rules of linear perspective: "Learning to look at the painting with lateral focus in a new way, a person can achieve new satisfactions by shifting back to a centered position before it. The same is true of film goers whose focus has been too narrowly constrained along the path of the narrative. . . . It is a key role of criticism . . . to enable viewers . . . to shift for themselves."[26] Learning and playing a game provides a useful and precise analogy for the experience of learning and playing with new ways of watching movies.[27]

One particular context which changes a film audience's experience in important ways is the context provided by earlier experience of the film at hand, because an audience's experience of any story will always be different the second time around. The limiting case is probably *Psycho,* whose success in shocking audiences was so complete and influential that latter-day audiences for the film, prepared by its reputation and their exposure to scores of later films it influenced, are hardly ever shocked, even though essays on the film continue to analyze it as if its success depended on establishing a close identification between Marion and the audience—an identification which can hardly be an issue for an audience that sits through the opening scenes with ill-disguised impatience for Marion to get into the shower. Bordwell's constructivist theory allows for an audience's experience to evolve as it masters the codes of the film and makes more accurate and comprehensive projections of what is to come, but game theory allows a much more precise analysis of the audience's changing experience though the analogy with a game played repeatedly by the same two players. Since both players seek maximal rewards from each game, players with the ability to vary their strategy based on increased information about the other player's strategy will surely do so if it is to their advantage. Audiences watching *Psycho* for the second or tenth time will use their foreknowledge of its narrative development in whatever ways best accord with their interests: attending more closely to its striking visual design or its ironic in-jokes ("My mother . . . isn't quite herself today"), theorizing about its historical significance, nostalgically reminding themselves of the ways it once frightened them, congratulating themselves on their immunity to its funhouse terrors.

Hitchcock's films constitute a series of games according to the definition of Roger Caillois: they are an activity which is essentially free, separate from the activities surrounding them, uncertain (in the sense of not being absolutely predictable), unproductive, governed by rules, and make-believe ("accompanied by a special awareness of a second reality or of a free unreality, as against real life").[28] Despite Peter Hutchinson's objection that Caillois's definition is "not ideally suited to literary games," it applies as closely to Hitchcock's films as the alternative definition Hutchinson borrows from Bernard Suits: "Playing a game is the voluntary attempt to overcome unnecessary obstacles."[29]

Caillois distinguishes two primary impulses in game-playing, the anarchic tendency toward "carefree gaiety" or "uncontrolled fantasy" he calls *paidia* and the complementary tendency toward channeling and controlling *paidia* through arbitrary and elaborate conventions whose mastery requires "an ever greater amount of effort, patience, skill, or ingenuity" he associates with *ludus,* a desire to solve problems posed only for the challenges they offer.[30] In addition, he categorizes all game-playing under the headings of *agon* (competitive games like football or chess), *alea* (games of chance like lotteries or football pools), *mimicry* (role-playing games like masquerades and theatricals), and *ilinx* (games designed to produce momentary dizziness, disorder, or loss of self-control, like rides in an amusement park). It is clear from this analysis that Hitchcock's games tend toward the pole of *ludus* rather than *paidia,* since they are from all accounts obsessively planned to manipulate audiences with maximum efficiency to their own greater enjoyment, and since audiences increase this enjoyment by mastering their rules. In other fundamental ways, however, Caillois's terminology provides an inadequate model for analyzing Hitchcock's films. In the first place, Hitchcock's games combine Caillois's major categories in unexpected ways, even to combinations Caillois rules impossible. Just as the festive atmosphere of casinos from Monte Carlo to Atlantic City challenges Caillois's assertion that there can be no connection between *paidia* and *alea* on the grounds that players cannot be exuberantly passive—think of the ways the ritual of playing a slot machine combines the two impulses— Hitchcock's films challenge his denial of any "connection between *ludus,* which is calculation and contrivance, and *ilinx,* which is a pure state of transport."[31] It is not merely that the director coolly plans the circumstances of his audience's vertigo; audiences themselves, as Hitchcock's cameos suggest, are encouraged in their awareness of the circumstances of their manipulation, the rules of the game they are playing.

More important, Hitchcock's films provide kinds of ludic pleasure which Caillois's categories do not fully describe. As a group, they include in varying combinations all of Caillois's four game-playing impulses. Hitchcock's games at their most genial are always agonistic and competitive, as in the challenge to find the director. This emphasis on *agon* is linked to *alea,* in the combination Caillois calls the most "inextricable" of all, through the "degraded and diluted form of *mimicry*" provided by the audience's identification with a hero or heroine who, though no more gifted than the audience, manages to overcome obstacles with miraculous success, combining "merit such as each might claim . . . with the chance of an unprecedented fortune," and so allows everyone in the audience to enjoy a vicarious success while "dispens[ing] with the effort that would be necessary if he truly wished to try his luck and succeed."[32] *Ilinx,* the fourth of Caillois's terms, enters not only in the completeness with which audiences identifying with Richard Hannay or Roger Thornhill are swept off their feet but in the problematic nature of the identifications Hitchcock urges, which often involve the audience in the vicarious experience of such equivocal figures as Scottie Ferguson and Marion Crane. No matter how familiar they are with the rules of his games, Hitchcock's audiences spend a great deal of time as if falling through his films because he keeps changing the rules, and indeed be-

cause the rules themselves—the rules of the Hitchcock thriller—stipulate an irreducible combination of controlled competition, identification,
and vertiginous surprise.

But Caillois neglects another important aspect of pleasure in Hitchcock's films, the pleasure the audience derives from having followed the
director's lead in reconstructing a story, in identifying with characters
whose adventures will justify the identifications, in looking for patterns
of motive and imagery in the confidence that the patterns will be worth
the trouble. This impulse, though clearly allied to *ilinx* through the experience of submitting to a storyteller's spell secure in the assurance
that the story will justify submission, is more properly described as the
imperative to follow rules whose purpose is individual gratification. It is
the impulse behind children's play with jigsaw puzzles and adults' play
at solitaire or cryptograms or crosswords. In each case a player (typically, though not always, a solitary player) confronts an apparent void
or chaos and undertakes gratuitous obstacles to comprehension for the
sake of a promised revelation or reestablishment of order that could have
been achieved much more easily by ignoring the rules or cheating. The
pleasure associated with this experience, the submission to structuring,
alienating rules for the sake of the satisfaction of seeing those rules reaffirm a reassuring order, is the constitutive pleasure of the game of
storytelling from the audience's point of view, and so the characteristic
pleasure Hitchcock's films offer as exemplary narratives.[33]

In the more rigorous terms of game theory established forty years
ago by John von Neumann and Oskar Morgenstern for economic ap-
plications, a Hitchcock film is a two-person, non-zero sum game.[34] The
two persons, or players, are the filmmaker and the audience. Since both
filmmaking and film viewing involve many more than two persons, the
model is an abstraction, but one especially suited to the work of a director whose close attention to technical detail, determination to control
as many aspects of film production as possible, and widely remarked
thematic and stylistic consistency made his films a celebrated ground
for the early defense of the *politique des auteurs,* and to an audience that
is encouraged to share so many of the same reactions that its members often gasp or laugh as one. In an economic sense, zero-sum games
are purely competitive: since the net total of any payout is zero, one

player can win only what the other loses. Commercial filmmaking is never a zero-sum game, for both filmmakers and their audiences intend that enough audience members enjoy the movie at hand that they will recommend it to their friends instead of demanding their money back. But if Hitchcock's games with the audience are not purely competitive, they are not purely cooperative either, since the audience purchases its pleasures not only with the usual coin (paying money, of course, and submitting to all the social proprieties of going to the movies—though the ascendancy of videotape as the unmarked medium of cinematic presentation is bound to change this situation) but typically by entertaining challenges to its members' sense of secure well-being that are the hallmark of the thriller. Thomas Schelling has proposed the term "mixed-motive" to refer to games marked by "the ambivalence of [each player's] relationship to the other player—the mixture of mutual dependence and conflict, of partnership and competition," and this term seems especially apt for the cooperative/competitive relationship Hitchcock's films establish with their audience.[35]

Like other games, Hitchcock's films posit a world defined by rules governing the behavior of its players. These rules do not constrain the players except by prior consent (e.g., Hitchcock's self-imposed decision to film *Rope* entirely in long takes). To the extent that they inscribe or position the audience, they do so on a contractual basis, with the implied stipulation that observing them will increase the audience's pleasure and the director's success. Within these contractual boundaries, Hitchcock's games have three leading functions: to beguile audiences by domesticating or making light of potentially threatening situations, to administer salubrious shocks to audiences by outraging their sense of propriety or exposing them to exhilarating dangers, and to encourage them to fall into misidentifications and misinterpretations which have a specifically moral and thematic force. The first of these functions can be illustrated by *The 39 Steps, Strangers on a Train,* and *To Catch a Thief;* the second by *Rope;* and the third by *Psycho.*

The most general function of Hitchcock's games is by definition to amuse the audience, and the simplest effect of Hitchcock's most characteristic set-pieces is to encourage the audience to adopt a perspective more amusing and amused than that of the characters immersed in an action they take much more seriously. Descriptions of Hitchcock's mise-en-scène as a place in which threats are everywhere, nothing is necessarily what it seems to be, every friend is a potential enemy, and mystery lurks around every corner overlook a fundamental aspect of the films' appeal, for the Hitchcock world as seen by its characters (and aptly described by such a menacing formula) is very different from the Hitchcock world seen by the audience. To speak most generally, the audience sees that it is at the movies, the only place where every gesture has a meaning, where stylistic consistency is the basis of knowledge and pleasure, where the visual and auditory field becomes a world much more salient than the world outside. This world is far from being Hitchcock's exclusive domain: movies as different as *Gone With the Wind* and *Casablanca* and *On the Town* depend for their effects on invoking a world more amusing, more close-textured, more salient than the audience's own. This is essentially the world of the movies, a place which promises to be both more interesting and more coherent, more deserving of the name world, than the world outside the frame.[36]

Movie audiences are constantly supplying temporal, causal, and thematic connections the movie leaves implicit, as when a film cuts from a shot of the hero and heroine embracing by moonlight to a close-up of bacon and eggs cooking in a skillet to the accompaniment of offscreen whistling. Audiences work to supply such connections and to impute an implicit value to what they see and hear because otherwise movies would be literally pointless. The payoff of Hollywood movies, the reason so many audiences are motivated to play the games they offer, is the consequent ability to enter a world and follow a story more expressive, more dramatic, more stylish, more continuously interesting than their own. Hitchcock's ludic storytelling often has a more specific point, for audiences are not only required to supply the missing connections or the implicit point in order to follow the story but are repeatedly rewarded with a witty recognition of their astuteness, as in the famous moment in *The 39 Steps* when Hitchcock cuts from a shot of Richard Hannay boarding a train to Scotland to escape the investigation of a murder in his flat to a close-up of an old woman opening a door, seeing the shadow of a corpse, and turning toward the camera to scream, only to have the sound of the scream covered by the sound of a train whistle as the film cuts again to a shot of a train emerging from a tunnel. In return for the assumptions audiences make about the identity of the woman and her relation to the train, they are rewarded with an exhilarating sense of intimacy with the film's world as a place where such moments are common—and where it would not be surprising to see the director standing in a crowd. The episode assumes not only a certain degree of attention—many audiences will miss its significance—but an attention focused on the specifically discursive aspects of the film ('now what's *that* doing there?'). Hitchcock never affects the transparent camera style of Chaplin or Hawks. Such a style, which is designed to be seen through, to draw attention to the performers rather than the director, tends to establish the screen as a window rather than a painting, conflating the film's world with the audience's world.[37] But the Hitchcock world is always the world according to Hitchcock; it cannot be entered and enjoyed without some awareness of the rules that make it worth entering.

In Hitchcock's films as in games like tennis or Monopoly, the audience's pleasure is governed by rules which mark off a world which its members always know is not their own, but which is neither a self-enclosed alternative world nor an artificial world trying to pass itself off as real. A great deal of the audience's pleasure in Hitchcock's films is provided by moments like the director's cameos that ought, according to the traditional model of narrative, to disturb its sense of the film's coherence. Instead, however, these moments intensify the audience's pleasure in the film by establishing a unifying style that confirms a belief that this world *is* a world, not just a spool of images or a series of events strung together.

Even an audience that is watching Hitchcock's films just for the story is encouraged to take note of their discursive features and is constantly rewarded for doing so. This discursive awareness is hardly unique to Hitchcock's audience; the audience for films in any Hollywood genre could not enjoy *Rambo* or *Lethal Weapon* as an exercise in escapism if it were not well aware of the formulaic nature of the generic convention; otherwise the audience would feel unpleasurably threatened instead of protected by the nature of the predictable generic conventions.[38] Largely because the promise of commercial films depends so largely on the audience's cultivating a double awareness of cinematic images at once representational and formulaic, audiences typically develop the ability to take pleasure in the film's play with the line between story and discourse without thinking self-consciously about the director's technique or about the problems posed for narrative theory. When Guy goes to a tennis club in *Strangers on a Train* to get some practice for an upcoming tournament and to get his mind off his wife's murder by the ingratiating psychotic Bruno, Hitchcock cuts from a shot of Guy on the court to a long shot of the grandstand, with every spectator's head ticktocking in unison to follow the ball except for one, Bruno's, which stares straight ahead. This shot does not tell audiences anything they do not already know about the action and characters, since it has already been established that Bruno is obsessively attached to Guy and follows him everywhere. But it carries an additional potential to amuse them because of its audacity and witty economy, using their knowledge of the conventions of visual representation (the odd figure is the one to look at), tennis (to follow a game, you need to keep shifting your eyes back and forth), and Hollywood movies (would any audience outside the movies move their heads in such metronomic unison?) to draw them further into the story instead of keeping them at a distance.

Set-pieces like this one can draw audiences further into the story by making them more intimate with the world of the film. An audience who recognizes Bruno in the stands is invited to be delightedly appreciative of Hitchcock's artifice; the shot would fail with an audience whose reaction was 'Look, there's Bruno again' or 'Bruno sure is interested in Guy.' But the shot is not supposed to make the audience focus on the storyteller either. Like Hitchcock's cameos, it plays on the customary distinction between story and discourse to create a no-man's-land not adequately described by communication, psychoanalytic, or mimetic theories of narrative. The audience's self-conscious appreciation of this shot—it can hardly be appreciated unself-consciously—does not necessarily make its members more aware of Hitchcock the storyteller, but it does make them more aware of the narrative style that makes the film distinctive and amusing.

Hitchcock's stylized view of the cat-and-mouse game Bruno is playing with Guy gives the moment a different effect on the audience than it has on Guy (even though the view is presumably available to him as well, neither he nor any other character seems to notice the joke), but the two games—the characters' games with each other, and the director's game with the audience—are closely related. In general, Hitchcock uses diegetic games between his characters as figures for his own relation to his audience. Even the discovery of the body in Hannay's flat, whose wit depends on a conjunction of sound and image unavailable to any character, is prepared by Hannay's earlier and unexpectedly droll escape from his building in the guise of a milkman. But the relation between the games within Hitchcock's films and the games offered by those films, so straightforward in these examples, can be considerably more complex. *To Catch a Thief* offers a remarkable succession of games—the police officers' opening pursuit of retired cat burglar John Robie, his tense standoff with the staff at Bertani's, his pursuit first by Danielle Foussard and later by Francie Stevens, his masquerades as Oregon lumberman Conrad Burns and as Francie's black servant at the climactic costume ball, his final flight from Francie—which are in terms of the film's diegesis almost entirely inconsequential. The police finally catch Robie only to let him go; Bertani and Foussard are only pretending to be hostile to him, since they have planned the robberies he is suspected of themselves; Danielle flirts with him knowing very well that he is not the cat burglar, since she is; Francie is not fooled by his disguise, nor is it really necessary, since the insurance agent Hugheson could easily have arranged a meeting between them; even Robie's final flight is only a move in a game, since he asks Francie to leave only to take her hand in a gesture of commitment. But all these games, which mean so little to the characters, mean a great deal to audiences, for they tell them how to watch the movie, establishing the basis for a playful relationship between Hitchcock and his audiences that allows them to take this story of theft, suspicion, paranoia, betrayal, and sexual jealousy as a divertissement, a witty and romantic trifle whose suspense is defined precisely as the ritualistic suspense of light comedy.

These games I have been discussing in *The 39 Steps, Strangers on a Train,* and *To Catch a Thief* all have the effect of lightening the films' tone by creating a perspective that defuses the threatening potential of a dangerous situation. But games can serve more equivocal functions as well. In *Rope,* as in *To Catch a Thief,* the characters' games provide a figure for the director's games, but this figure takes on a much darker tone, since Brandon's cat-and-mouse game with the guests who do not know their dinner is being served from a chest containing the body of absent guest David Kentley—a game whose force will redound on Brandon when he becomes the mouse to Rupert Cadell's cat—is, like Hitchcock's game with his audience, essentially a sadistically playful tease. The sardonic sense of humor that makes Brandon such a good game player—he is the only character who repeatedly makes deliberate jokes about David's murder—has an underpinning of barely controlled hostility revealed by one exchange. When Kenneth doesn't want to bring Janet's drink to her in the bedroom because "you'd like David to come in and find us together," Brandon genially replies, "Oh, no, that would be too much of a shock." In killing David for a lark, Brandon has not only carried out the ultimate practical joke but has provided himself with a basis for a series of running dialogue jokes at the expense of his guests. He typifies the image of Hitchcock as a manipulative practical joker whose primary relationship to his audience is condescending and adversarial.[39] The game Hitchcock is playing in *Rope* is less condescending than the game Brandon is playing, since Hitchcock's audiences at least know they are playing a game; but the audacity of many of Hitchcock's images—the moment when the camera first pans to reveal the buffet table, or when it reveals Brandon dropping the murder weapon into a drawer in between swings of the kitchen door—seems intended to shock audiences into amusement rather than beguiling them.

Hitchcock plays an even more punitive game in the opening of *The Wrong Man,* based on the story of Manny Balestrero's false arrest for robbery. When Manny, having decided to pay his wife's dentist bills by borrowing on his life insurance, goes to his insurance company, Hitchcock frames him in a medium close-up from the teller's point of view showing him reaching with an all-too-familiar gesture into his inside overcoat pocket just as Bernard Herrmann's music swells ominously. Is Manny going to pull a gun and rob the office? Of course he doesn't; he just takes out his insurance policy, whose cash value he wants to determine. But the gesture has troubled the teller, who will proceed to identify Manny as the man who recently held up the office, and for a crucial second it troubles the audience as well. Hitchcock is teasing viewers by misdirecting them—one of his favorite moves—and the tease here implicates the audience, as it usually does in Hitchcock's films, in a moment of judgment that resonates through the film. For the rest of the film Hitchcock makes it impossible for audiences to feel superior to Manny's persecutors by punishing them for that moment when they thought he might be a thief.

The combination within game-playing of cooperation (agreement on rules and goals within the game, mutual desire to have the game succeed) and competition is closely connected to the thematic paradoxes of the suspense thriller Hitchcock chose as his genre. Consider for example the central importance in virtually all Hitchcock's films of the idea of home. Homes have many thematic associations Hitchcock routinely trades on: the safety of a place of shelter or refuge, the stability and security of longstanding assumptions, the basis for self-definition through family relationships and a genetic sense of identity. At the same time, home is a ludic topos in Hitchcock's work, a place like home in games of baseball or Parcheesi, a final goal the pleasurable lack of which makes play possible (so that arrival home is merely the signal for putting a new piece in play or starting the game over again). Hitchcock's heroes and heroines are nearly always strongly attracted to ideals of home, but their plots subvert these ideals by pulling them out of their safe homes, betraying the promise of home as a haven, even undermining the notion that a secure identity can be based on one's ties to one's home.

Home is thus a goal both desired and deferred as the end of narrative, and audiences' ambivalence toward this goal—they want the principals to arrive home safely, but not just yet—opens the space for a profoundly contradictory attitude toward home and its associations which develops in Hitchcock's work beginning, not surprisingly, with his departure from England to America in 1939. Hitchcock thereafter frequently invites audiences to endorse domestic values his films undermine comically (*Rear Window* and *To Catch a Thief*), melodramatically (*Rebecca, Suspicion, Shadow of a Doubt, Under Capricorn*), or ironically (*Rope* and *Psycho*). This ambivalence toward home and domestic values is at the heart of the games Hitchcock plays in his American films.

The audience's willingness to defer the principals' desired arrival home for the sake of their entertaining adventures along the way points to another essential paradox of Hitchcock's films. Thrillers entertain audiences by making them apprehensive, uncertain, or frightened. How can anyone enjoy a film that puts sympathetic characters in danger? A purely rational answer would begin with the observation that audiences' enjoyment of thrillers depends on their appetite for vicarious experiences that would be anything but appetizing in their own lives; they find them amusing in movies because of the assurances offered by the conventions of all stories (this is happening to someone else, not themselves), the more particular conventions of Hollywood movies (the story will proceed to an ending that settles the principal problems raised by the plot, reassuringly definitive hints will be given about the characters' future lives, everything on the image track and sound track will turn out to be worth their attention), and the specialized conventions of suspense films (the conflict between heroes and villains will always have some significant point, there is always a reason or pattern behind every threat, the ending will resolve the mystery). These conventions reassure audiences who understand them, and audiences who do not—small children, for example—do not usually enjoy suspense films.[40]

Once the reassuring conventions of the thriller have been established in a given film, audiences can endure a good deal of suspense, mystification, and anxiety with pleasure because they know that these feelings are only temporary and necessary to intensify their pleasure in the resolution; they know the world of the film is a place where many unpleasant things are possible but trust that their vicarious suffering will be worthwhile. The result is that their suffering does not feel like real suffering but like a teasing game, a necessary prelude to the pleasures they expect eventually and therefore a pleasure itself. In other words, the pleasure audiences take in thrillers, as in many other narrative genres, is essentially projective and anticipatory, a pleasure defined and guaranteed by the promise of what is to come. Audiences who feel sufficiently reassured by a thriller's generic conventions can enjoy what would otherwise seem like perversely violent, sensational, or shocking stories.

But this rational argument for audiences' self-interest is incomplete, since Hitchcock's audiences often pay an unexpectedly heavy price for their thrills. Since thrillers from *Dead of Night* to *A Nightmare on Elm Street* scare audiences by violating a reassuring convention of earlier thrillers (in both these cases, the suggestion that whatever you saw can't hurt you because it's only a dream), the history of the suspense genre is largely a history of successively broken taboos. A remarkable feature of Hitchcock's films is that they not only violate conventions established by other suspense films but systematically challenge their own conventions, the rules of Hitchcock's game, in what often turns out to be the basis of a new game. Sometimes these challenges merely confirm the audience's sense of the Hitchcock world as a place where unexpected things happen to the audience as well as the characters. The apparent death of Richard Hannay halfway through *The 39 Steps,* though it startles first-time audiences of the film, is not really unpleasant to audiences who assume that there's been some sort of mistake and that it'll soon be cleared up—as it is when Hannay reappears alive a minute later. But often Hitchcock goes further, threatening the rules that make his world a world audiences enjoy spending time in. When the apparent death of Marion Crane less than halfway through *Psycho* turns out to be the real thing, the audience needs to find a new way to enjoy the film, since the terms it seemed to project (a crime story about a woman who steals forty thousand dollars and runs away to her boyfriend, raising questions about what he'll say and how she'll get punished—since, given the conventions of Hollywood filmmaking in 1960, she *has* to get punished) become inadequate once the apparent heroine is dead. Marion's death does not make *Psycho* any more difficult to follow, but it does make it more difficult for first-time viewers to enjoy. In order to enjoy the film, they need to find a new frame of reference that will make her death worthwhile. The long sequence following Marion's murder offers one such frame—the film is really about Norman and the mystery of the Bates Motel—which uninitiated audiences eagerly adopt, since it is less painful to give up their identification with Marion than to persist in mourning her and give up the possibility of pleasure for the rest of the film.

If suspense films depend on the paradox of pleasure-in-fear but resolve it by their use of reassuring generic conventions which make the audience's fear pleasurable, Hitchcock adds the complication of always threatening to undermine those conventions, even those he has established himself. Hitchcock's stylistic games are different from the games of other directors like Lubitsch not only because the thematic material

they ritualize—the audience's fears and forbidden desires—is potentially more dangerous, but because the contractual rules that allow audiences to enjoy their fears are themselves more unstable. Critics have
often noted the way these rules are broken in *Psycho* and other late
films, but in fact they are always in danger of being broken, even when
they are actually reaffirmed. Once the bomb goes off on a crowded bus
in *Sabotage* in 1937, audiences can never be sure for the rest of Hitchcock's career that things will turn out all right for their identification
figures, and each happy ending is purchased with sharpened anxiety.
Nor is Hitchcock's challenge to his audiences limited to tricking them
into identifications that turn out to be equivocal. Subverting the audiences' identifications is only one aspect of a much more general pattern
in Hitchcock's work: a tendency to undermine the narrative conventions
that make his stories worth watching.

Hitchcock's challenge to narrative conventions, like his fondness for
encouraging equivocal identifications, depends on the fact that audiences' ability to perceive any series of filmed images as parts of a story
inevitably carries strong moral concomitants. Perceiving Bruno as the
solitary spectator who is watching Guy places them in Guy's position
of being spied on; realizing that Hannay's char has discovered the body
in his flat both intensifies their sense of his danger and confirms the
film's tensely comic tone, insulating them from the worst consequences
of that danger; laughing at Brandon's jokes about murder increases their
uneasy complicity with him. Audiences' involvement in any film melodrama depends on the moral attitudes they adopt toward its characters
and situations. In Hitchcock's films this involvement is always potentially equivocal even at its most straightforward. After establishing in the
opening scene of *Sabotage* that someone has caused a blackout in London
by pouring sand into an electrical generator, Hitchcock cuts from the
question "But who?" to a close-up of Oscar Homolka striding purpose-
fully toward the camera over the menacing title music. Although there
is no evidence apart from the conventions of film melodrama to assume
that this man is the saboteur, most audiences do assume it, adopting a
specifically moral attitude toward Verloc, Homolka's character, in order
to resolve the film's images into an intelligible narrative sequence. Eventually their suspicions are confirmed. After returning home and washing

sand off his hands, pretending to his wife that he has been napping all afternoon, and expressing private satisfaction with the blackout and annoyance when it ends, Verloc goes to a clandestine meeting where he takes responsibility for the incident. But for the first fifteen minutes of the film, audiences have the pleasure of inferring Verloc's guilt for themselves, coupled with the moral responsibility of condemning him.

In *Sabotage* this responsibility provides an additional source of pleasure. Since Verloc is as guilty—and as unattractive—as he seems to be, taking sides against him confirms all audiences' comfortable moral assumptions. But Hitchcock often uses similar narrative conventions to manipulate audiences into more equivocal moral judgments, as when he imputes the guilt of the Lodger or of Richard Blaney in *Frenzy* or the innocence of Norman Bates. In such cases audiences' pleasure at following the story is complicated by their having taken the wrong side.

Hitchcock's films are fun to watch largely because they abound in such casually witty moments as the shot of Bruno in the grandstand or the blending of the charlady's scream with the train whistle.[41] But the example of *The Wrong Man* suggests that this fun is often more equivocal than it appears; Hitchcock's narrative imputations typically involve audiences more deeply in his story by forcing them to resolve an obscure or ambiguous situation in order to follow the story. His choice of the thriller, with its emphasis on crime or espionage, as his preferred genre means that the audience's interpretation is never neutral, for it entails not only sympathy but apprehension, moral judgment, and the possibility of dangerous mistakes, as when audiences trust or condemn the wrong person, or when they identify closely with someone who turns out to be a victim or a criminal. Every story presents more and less sympathetic characters, but in thrillers these characters are innocent and guilty in a technical sense essential to Hitchcock's deceptively two-dimensional moral labels of good guys and bad guys. Throughout Hitchcock's films, every gesture offers an obvious interpretation, but every interpretation is suspect. Under these circumstances, interpretation itself becomes a game which pits wary audiences against the resourceful filmmaker, so that, as in the games of beguilement and outrage, audiences find intensified pleasure simply in following the story.

The fact that so many audiences enjoy Hitchcock's films shows the extent to which Hitchcock's world, like the world of Astaire and Rogers musicals or *Friday the 13th,* establishes rules which make it entertaining after all, but these rules could not be inferred from any single film because Hitchcock repeatedly changes them. In *Sabotage* the first man the camera follows after a crime has been revealed turns out to be the criminal, but in *Frenzy* he turns out to be innocent. *Psycho* begins as if it were going to tell Marion's story, but after her death audiences must recast it as the mystery of the Bates Motel in order to justify their involvement in it. Of course, the process of recasting the story after being deceived provides a new source of pleasure which can in turn be formulated and mastered. In other words, the hallmark of the audience's experience of Hitchcock's world is that its members are made to want to be challenged—to have called into question their expectations about what will happen next and how they should react to it and who is the guilty party and how it will all turn out—so that mastering the challenge becomes an additional source of pleasure, and the challenge itself, like Hitchcock's cameos, finally confirms their sense of each film as part of the Hitchcock world. Although Hitchcock consistently exploits the contractual basis of narrative conventions, the way they establish rules that will make the audience's experience of his films worthwhile, he repeatedly violates the terms of the narrative contract, redefining the terms under which his films are to be followed, understood, and enjoyed. This repeated and pleasurable challenge and redefinition of the narrative contract form the most distinctive feature of Hitchcock's films.

This analysis of Hitchcock's game-playing has ranged from relatively inconsequential throwaways to deeply problematic cooperative-competitive relationships between the director and his audience. Since even the most lighthearted of Hitchcock's games have some thematic import, and even the most problematic of them offer the promise of pleasure, considering Hitchcock games at greater length, as the rest of this book will do, raises two questions—how does Hitchcock charge his thematic material with a sense of fun, and what is at stake in the audience's enjoyment of his games?—whose connections are obvious. Generally speaking, Hitchcock's films are marked by a strongly contradictory attitude toward game-playing. On the one hand, Hitchcock's games can be seen as a vehicle for specific effects. The games he sets the audience in films like *The 39 Steps* and *To Catch a Thief* are largely rational, goal-oriented, and fairly direct in their appeal to the audience's self-interest, even if the pleasures they offer are indefinitely deferred. In this regard Hitchcock's attitude toward his games is socially meliorative, therapeutic, and fundamentally conservative: Games are important because they help the audience confront fears and desires that might otherwise be overwhelming. On the other hand, a more radical and subversive impetus is discernible even in Hitchcock's most ebullient games: Francie's keen-eyed pursuit of the man she is convinced wants to steal her jewels has a perversity sweetened but not banished by the comic mode in which it is presented. Films like *Rope* and *The Wrong Man,* which show Hitchcock's game-playing at its most adversarial and punitive, present games whose force is irrational, deconstructive, and ultimately annihilating. The purpose of these games is ultimately to have a kind a fun which does not lead and cannot be assimilated to any meliorative or therapeutic end.

The development of Hitchcock's career, I shall argue in the following chapters, is shaped by the shifting relations his films establish with their audience, and in particular by the contradictions implicit in his own attitude toward game-playing from his earliest films. But before turning to a closer examination of Hitchcock's career, let me make explicit several assumptions behind my perspective on Hitchcock's films. Since anyone who stipulates the audience's response to a story invites the reply that the audience at hand does not feel that way at all, how can generalizations about the audience be justified? The audience I postulate for Hitchcock's films is an audience whose responses I take to be invited, though not inscribed, by cues within the film, in the broader context of Hitchcock's career as informed by the social, cultural, and generic assumptions appropriate to each given film. Any attempt to generalize about the audience, of course, begins in one's own experience of the films, and I have generally taken my own reactions, which have often changed considerably over the years, as a starting point for my thinking about the audience's response. To protect my analysis from the most obvious kinds of subjectivity and solipsism, I have compared it to that of three other audiences: contemporary reviewers (who stand in for the films' first audiences), academic critics (who represent institutional opinion since the investiture of Hitchcock as an auteur thirty-five years ago first made it possible to generalize with confidence about his career), and students with whom I have discussed the films over a period of ten years. Although I pause to cite evidence from each of these audiences only when it seems necessary, the frequency with which all three audiences have differed with my own impressions has forced me to reconsider many of those impressions. My aim has been neither to reconstruct and privilege a contemporary audience's reaction to the films nor to predicate a superreader or narratee ascribed purely to the film's formal system but to postulate what Hans Robert Jauss has called a "horizon of expectations" appropriate to each film and to Hitchcock's career as a whole.[42] Although generalizing about pleasure itself may seem unduly subjective and impressionistic, there is no empirical basis for assuming that pleasure is any more private or resistant to analysis than the kinds of understanding that theorists constantly generalize about with complete confidence.[43]

Positing Hitchcock as a storyteller or game-player whose agency largely determines the conditions under which his audience enjoys his films involves making unfashionable assumptions about the authorizing power of individual directors. Why should I take *Suspicion* as a game of Hitchcock's when the original novel was written by an author with a different agenda, hundreds of technicians were responsible for the finished product, and the film was released with an ending that completely contradicted the director's wishes? Why assume a model that places the director in charge of the historical forces that shape a film rather than emphasizing the ways in which he is at the mercy of them? To be sure, the interplay between the director's designs and the requirements of his implication in a centralized industry—his acknowledgment that Cary Grant could never play a villain, RKO's insistence that the ending be changed—rather than Hitchcock's private opinions and desires ultimately determines the conditions of the game. Although I am interested in Hitchcock only insofar as his films establish a distinctive basis for the audience's enjoyment rather than as a private individual—my analysis of the films will not be biographical or psychological—it seems disingenuous to use the label "Hitchcock film" to refer to a discursive practice that just happens to be closely associated with the direction of a historical figure when it is Hitchcock's thematic and stylistic consistency, his long-standing association with a single popular genre, his acknowledged mastery of the techniques of film production, his determination to control every aspect of his films, and his status as independent producer on his later movies that brought him to the attention of film scholars in the first place.

Finally, it might be objected that a two-person game is not really a precise model for the relationship between films and their audiences because only one player in the game has the option of adopting different strategies. The audience can learn from its experience of a film and of films generally to anticipate likely developments and signficant connections more precisely, but the film cannot benefit from this experience. Hitchcock the storyteller can anticipate the audience's likely reponses and incorporate them into the design of the film, but as those responses are changed by time and experience, the director cannot change the features that predicate these responses. Bordwell's description of film as presupposing a receiver but not a sender accords here with the current tendency in film study away from auteur criticism, or with any criticism that emphasizes the authority behind the signifying codes of cinema.

But defining Hitchcock as a storyteller rather than a signifier and his films as games that offer enjoyment rather than as messages that await decoding does greater justice to the nature of the audience's relation to his films. Storytelling itself is at heart interactive, since oral storytellers, who have the advantage of an audience's presence, can not only anticipate likely reactions but can incorporate actual reactions into the story they are telling; and stage-trained performers like Chaplin often seem to be playing directly to an audience they wish they could see. Hitchcock is by design and preference an absent storyteller; even his cameos remind the audience of his absence. But his audiences, whether or not they are watching his films as Hitchcock films—and Hitchcock does everything he can to encourage them to do so—always watch them as intended, not found or naturally created, objects, and less as objects than as invitations to interaction. Because in any given film Hitchcock is not an interactive player but rather a designer of games (the funhouse architect he so often likens himself to), he cannot alter his strategy in response to an audience's reaction to that film. But observing and an-

ticipating the audience's reactions to each film allow him to alter his
game-playing strategies from film to film. Just as Hitchcock's ludic structures predicate but do not inscribe an audience, inviting a response by
a promise of pleasure that can always be overridden by a more compelling promise, the audience's expectations of any new film predicate but
do not inscribe a Hitchcockian storyteller who is likely to conform to
certain rules (suspense plot, innocent but morally complicit hero, playfully adversarial romance, increasing dramatic tension, hermeneutically
satisfying conclusion) he may well break instead.

Jauss, defining the horizon of expectations as an attempt to historicize
the terms under which literary texts are produced and consumed, contends that "the interpretive reception of a text always presupposes the
context of experience of aesthetic perception: the question of the subjectivity of the interpretation and of the taste of different readers or levels
of readers can be asked meaningfully only when one has first clarified
which transsubjective horizon of understanding conditions the influence
of the text. . . . The ideal cases of the objective capability of such literary-
historical frames of reference are works that evoke the reader's horizon
of expectations, formed by a convention of genre, style, or form, only
in order to destroy it step by step."[44] To show the possibility of establishing an objective horizon of expectations, Jauss cites the work of Cervantes, Diderot, and Nerval. He might well have added Hitchcock, since
the director's relation with his audience is so inveterately, if playfully, adversarial. And it is the very adversarial nature of this relationship which
permits the discussion of Hitchcock's career without limiting the term
"Hitchcock" to a historical person or the discursive practice of a single
film. Critics who regard the insights of auteur theory suspiciously overlook the extent to which it was developed as a specifically intertextual
theory, a way of grounding perceived connections among different films
historically. Just as Jauss uses generic norms and their transformations
to establish the horizon of expectations for a given literary work, game
theory proposes intertextual games—invitations to play and pleasure
based on the expectations aroused in the audience by earlier work they
recognize as the product of a given cinematic storyteller—as the norms
which locate a given film in the development of Hitchcock's career.

Hitchcock described this career to Truffaut as an alternation between experiments with new material and new approaches and periods of "running for cover" to safer, more commercially promising projects.[45] His relationship to the audience is governed by a similar alternation between films that recast that relationship by challenging the assumptions that make them entertaining—that is, by a kind of radical cheating on the rules—and films that explore the area that a preceding film has mapped out. His career thus assumes the shape of distinct periods, beginning with his silent and early sound films—the films Hitchcock directed before there was such a thing as a Hitchcock film, many of them taking deliberate steps toward creating the rules of the Hitchcock game. *The Man Who Knew Too Much,* the most subversive of Hitchcock's British films, is also the film which consolidates Hitchcock's career as a director of thrillers and the first film in which the relationship between the director and his audience is unmistakably governed by the figure of a game. Each succeeding period of Hitchcock's career is marked at the beginning by a film that breaks the contract established by his earlier films and proposes new rules for the game, and then by a series of films which confirm this new contract, often consolidating or retreating from the challenge of the initial film, before it is broken in turn by the films of the following period.

This book traces the development of Hitchcock's career by considering the ways the films of each period break the pleasure contract, subverting the rules of the game, in a way that becomes the basis for a new game, with new rules and a contract that promises new pleasures. Chapter 2 examines Hitchcock's early attempts to make what he later called "true 'Hitchcock movie[s]'" by using set-pieces and other directorial flourishes to establish his films as parts of a world with its own Hitchcockian rules and pleasures, and his experiments in using the conventions of the thriller as a basis for that world.[46] Each of the following chapters begins by analyzing in detail the challenges posed by the opening film of the period and the pleasures implied by these challenges and then considers the ways in which the films of that period confirm the new contract between storyteller and audience. My focus throughout, as I indicated earlier, will be not so much on what is happening in the films as on what kinds of pleasures they offer the audience and what implications underlie those pleasures.

# TWO

# FIND THE

# DIRECTOR

itchcock's cameos invite his audience to play the game of finding the director as early as his third film, *The Lodger,* in 1926. His early films, however, offer a more general and pervasive version of this game as well, for they call repeated attention to Hitchcock's status as storyteller, wit, and *metteur en scène.* The often gratuitous ways in which Hitchcock's silent and early sound films advertise their director's shaping intelligence contrasts sharply with the director's status as adapter or stage manager. The contrast is especially important because most accounts of Hitchcock's early years as a director single out his first thrillers—*The Lodger, Blackmail, Murder!* and sometimes *Number Seventeen*—as his most characteristic films, those that most clearly presage his later development. But Hitchcock's primary concerns in these early films do not clearly gravitate toward the suspense genre, and are themselves tangential to the two major and contradictory projects of his early career: to place his storytelling flair, his gift for narrative exposition, in the service of other people's stories, and to establish Alfred Hitchcock as a storyteller of genius himself.

The retrospective foregrounding of Hitchcock's thrillers is due in large part to his French defenders' search for thematic unity in his work, but the decisive and more general version of Hitchcock's early years comes from the director himself.[1] When Truffaut interviewed Hitchcock in 1962, the director's attitude toward his own early work was unmistakable. Besides telling most of his favorite anecdotes, Hitchcock was most interested in discussing particular technical problems and isolated bits of business in the films: the glass ceiling in *The Lodger*, the operator overhearing the wedding plans in *Easy Virtue*, the flat champagne in *The Ring*, the process shots in *Blackmail*. Hitchcock clearly takes a craftsman's pride in such original solutions to narrative problems—new ways of giving the audience information or representing dramatic events like the airplane crash in *Foreign Correspondent*—and is correspondingly laconic when the discussion turns to projects that allowed no opportunities for such originality. He grows particularly impatient when Truffaut asks about his adaptations of novels or stage plays. *The Farmer's Wife* "wasn't actually very cinematic" (55).[2] *Downhill* was based on "a rather poor play" whose "dialogue was pretty dreadful in spots" (51). Although it was based on "an excellent play," *Juno and the Paycock*, "from a creative viewpoint . . . was not a pleasant experience" (69). "There isn't much to be said about" *The Skin Game* (77). And *The Manxman* "was not a Hitchcock movie, whereas *Blackmail* . . ." (61). "A Hitchcock movie," he explains to Truffaut, is a film like *The Lodger* in which "the whole approach . . . was instinctive with me. It was the first time I exercised my style. . . . I took a pure narrative and . . . presented ideas in purely visual terms" (44).

What Hitchcock means by "pure narrative" has been the subject of lively debate. The early pictures Hitchcock remembers most fondly— *The Lodger, The Ring, Blackmail, Murder!* and *Rich and Strange*—are distinguished by the opportunities they gave him for innovative set-pieces and original cinematic techniques, and more generally by a tendency toward visual narrative exposition. A more striking similarity from Hitchcock's point of view, however, is their profusion of "interesting" but essentially detachable stylistic flourishes. *The Ring* has "all kinds of innovations . . . at the premiere an elaborate montage got a round of applause" (52). At Truffaut's invitation, Hitchcock talks in some detail about "sound innovations" and "trick shots" (64, 65) in *Blackmail*. *Murder!* was "an interesting picture" because "we did many things that had not been done before" (74). *Rich and Strange* "had lots of ideas" (78). In each case Hitchcock seems more interested in particular isolated bits of technical showmanship or narrative finesse, or in describing scenes that were not included in the release prints, than in describing "pure narrative" in more general terms. Even in discussing *The Lodger,* whose long opening sequence giving information about the murderous Avenger Hitchcock describes in detail, he turns to a particular shot, a visual pun in which a news van carrying two men is blocked and photographed to look like a face with rolling eyeballs. Despite Truffaut's dismissal of the "claim that your movies contain a great many gratuitous effects" and his contention that "your camerawork is becoming almost invisible" and Hitchcock's own assertion that "I am against virtuosity for its own sake" (47, 103), the director repeatedly returns to visual and auditory effects which are in some way self-advertising, either originally, by the way they call the audience's attention to themselves, or at the time of the interview, by Hitchcock's insistence on displaying them to the appreciative Truffaut. Hence the repeated emphasis on details the audience failed to notice—the shot of the news van in *The Lodger,* the new sign for round 2 in *The Ring,* the shadow-mustache on Cyril Ritchard's face in *Blackmail.*

What pleases Hitchcock most in reviewing these early films, it seems, are those aspects of them which most clearly reveal his shaping hand, his cinematic originality, his personality, as Andrew Sarris has said. Sarris and other critics have followed Hitchcock's cue, as Hitchcock had followed Truffaut's, in voicing reservations about the films in which Hitchcock's intelligence is subordinated to that of the author of the property on which the film is based.[3] Hitchcock himself revealingly explained to Truffaut that he would never film a "literary masterpiece" like a Dostoevsky novel "precisely because *Crime and Punishment* is somebody else's achievement" (71). Just as Sarris's position is a fundamental tenet of his defense of cinematic auteurs, Hitchcock's position is eminently reasonable for the self-created auteur of the thriller, the Master of Suspense.

The ascription of authorship to a film director was first conceived by Sarris, and by Truffaut before him, as an affront to critical assumptions that characterized studio directors as mere adapters or *metteurs en scène.* Today, when independent filmmakers typically contract with directors for one film at a time, it is easy to forget that at studios like Gaumont-

British or British International, the analogy between film directors and stage managers would have had considerably more currency than it does now. Indeed for years after Hitchcock's first films, many reviewers took only passing notice of his contributions to the films he directed, and others deplored his insistence in placing his own stamp on the films he directed.[4] Such critics would have found Hitchcock's directorial career much less typical than that of Rouben Mamoulian, a contemporary of Hitchcock's who came from stage direction to the early sound cinema and continued to alternate between stage and screen productions for the rest of his career. Although Mamoulian directed the American stage premieres of *Porgy and Bess* and *Oklahoma!* and although his staging of these plays presumably has great relevance to his career in Hollywood and would be of considerable interest to students of his work, still no audience except for those students would regard *Porgy and Bess* and *Oklahoma!* as by Mamoulian; they are by George and Ira Gershwin, or Rodgers and Hammerstein. Similarly, the opening credits describing *The Farmer's Wife* as "by Eden Phillpotts" or *The Skin Game* as "a talking film by John Galsworthy" are not simply to be dismissed from our perspective of Hitchcock's later eminence; these films and many others were what they seemed to be, stories "by" their screenwriters or the writers of the works on which they were based.[5] This idea of authorship, an idea Truffaut's *Hitchcock* clearly finds inimical, has obvious relevance to his position from 1925, when he directed his first film for Michael Balcon's Gainsborough Pictures, to 1934, when he returned to Balcon at Gaumont-British to make *The Man Who Knew Too Much*. For Hitchcock's first consistent success was as an adapter of material often more distinguished than he was.

This is hardly surprising in view of the fact that ten of Hitchcock's first sixteen films were made after Hitchcock left the congenial Balcon to work for British International Pictures, whose head, John Maxwell, assigned Hitchcock to projects irrespective of his enthusiasm for them. Nor is Maxwell's behavior surprising, since Hitchcock, as British International's star director, would naturally be assigned to many of its most prestigious projects without regard for their thematic relationship. To expect or desire thematic coherence from such a director would be as illogical as to expect it from a stage director, whose expertise is assumed

to be placed at the disposal of his or her properties. Because Hitchcock's early films do not have the thematic coherence of his later work,
they have been neglected by his critics and largely dismissed by the
director himself, who preferred in his later years to think of himself as
the independent producer-director to come, whose work was interesting
precisely to the degree that it was identifiably his.[6] Although Hitchcock
dismisses the image of himself as a mere adapter in favor of the image of
himself as creator of a cinematic world, his early films act out the conflict
between these two images in a far more complex and revealing way.

By the time he filmed *The Skin Game* for British International in 1931,
the contradiction between directing as stage managing and directing as
creation had become so well-entrenched that it generates two radically
different attitudes toward the material and the project of filmmaking
itself. Maurice Yacowar's essay on the film, which he calls "a balanced,
moving performance by Hitchcock," focuses on the changes Hitchcock
makes in John Galsworthy's play, even though he remarks that "only
the closest of comparisons reveals changes and shifts of emphasis."[7] But
what makes *The Skin Game* a successful adaptation is not any changes
which might intimate its director's own vision, a vision which would
emerge from his skill in competing with his property, but the fullness
and resourcefulness with which Hitchcock finds cinematic equivalents
for Galsworthy's theatrical conventions and original images for the playwright's own thematic material.

In dramatizing the conflict between the aristocratic Hillcrists and the
parvenu industrialist Hornblower (Edmund Gwenn) over the Centry, a
farm bordering the Hillcrist estate, Hitchcock reinterprets Galsworthy's
play without for the most part changing it. Although Galsworthy never
specifies the presence of any animals onstage, for example, Hitchcock
constantly shows the Hillcrists with horses or dogs to dramatize their
assumption of patrician superiority to the natural world they are defend-
ing and to suggest the link between Mrs. Hillcrist (Helen Haye) and the
beasts she will resemble in blackmailing Hornblower into giving up the
Centry—exactly the sort of business an audience would expect from an
intelligent stage director. This link is picked up by the leather coat worn
by her agent, who discovers that Hornblower's daughter-in-law Chloe
(Phyllis Konstam) was formerly a paid correspondent in divorce cases

and so gives Mrs. Hillcrist a threat to use against Hornblower. Hitchcock avoids melodramatic theatrics in Hornblower's dispossession of the
Jackmans, cottagers whose land he has bought (a scene Galsworthy's
play only alludes to), by showing Hornblower's chauffeur pacing back
and forth before a darkened doorway and so encouraging the audience
to supply their own staging of the offscreen conversation.

Hitchcock's pacing of the auction scene, in which Hornblower succeeds in buying the Centry through an intermediary, is a masterly combination of straightaway long shots of the crowd, swish-pans from one
bidder to the next, and medium close-ups holding on individual bidders
or the auctioneer, the close-ups becoming gradually shorter and tighter
during each round of bidding. The sequence, filmed like a Griffith rescue but with practically no movement within the frame, captures the
tension of Galsworthy's scene but again without changing it substan-
tively. After the auction, when Hornblower tells the Hillcrists that the
man who submitted the final bid was his agent, Hitchcock shows him
standing outside and to the left of their closed car, separated from them
by a hard vertical and by a repeated pan back and forth which never
frames them all together.

In the group shots which dominate the film, Hitchcock's blocking
and focus are often unobtrusively expressive. When the Jackmans come
to Hillcrist to ask his help against Hornblower, Hitchcock repeatedly
pans from the Jackmans and Mrs. Hillcrist to Hillcrist (C. V. France),
emphasizing the power other characters are ascribing to him. But later,
when Mrs. Hillcrist and Hornblower are taking turns baiting each other,
Hitchcock's camera holds on Hornblower, showing his assurance in the
face of Mrs. Hillcrist's offscreen remarks. A moment later Hitchcock
cuts pointedly but tactfully away from a shot of Hornblower's extended
hand—he is offering to give up his pursuit of the Centry if the Hillcrists will recognize his position by visiting his family—to a long shot of
the Hillcrists' daughter Jill (Jill Esmond) coming in through the French
doors. A reverse-angle shot from Jill's point of view shows Hornblower
in sharp focus, and her parents, flanking him, slightly blurred. Without
calling special attention to themselves, the visuals dramatize the passage
of power from Hillcrist to Hornblower.

Although the film features no music after the opening credits, Hitchcock's use of sound is equally expressive. From the first shot of Hornblower's factory, which follows a series of close-ups of bleating sheep and honking horns, Hornblower is associated with raucous and unwelcome noise. A few minutes later, as Hillcrist is looking through his windows to the hills outside, Hitchcock dissolves to a long shot of Hornblower's factories belching steam, accompanied by appropriate sounds. Hillcrist tells Jill, "You won't be able to live here unless we stop that racket," and Hornblower's arrival at the climactic scene is heralded by the sound of his car horn. The association of the Hillcrists with well-bred silence is ironic, since Mrs. Hillcrist uses the threat of disclosing Chloe's past to blackmail Hornblower, and since her agent Dawkins (Edward Chapman), unable to keep his mouth shut, tells Chloe's secret to her husband and provokes her suicide attempt, but an audience which misses this thematic implication will still appreciate the conflict between quiet and noise.

Hitchcock's inventiveness, however, is not subordinated entirely to Galsworthy's play. In his first scene with Hillcrist, Hornblower, responding to Hillcrist's complaint about the Jackmans, rubs his hand absently on a wooden knob on top of Hillcrist's chair. But the shot is blocked in such a way that Hornblower seems to be stroking Hillcrist's bald head. The conception is certainly original, and perhaps the shot belongs in an anthology of Hitchcock's most impudent images, but its impudence introduces a jarring note here—jarring not only to Hillcrist's sense of propriety, since it makes him look ridiculous to an audience who notices it at all, but to Hitchcock's generally self-effacing attitude toward his material, since it is sharply at odds with the tone of the play's criticism of the sympathetic but ineffectual Hillcrist. Nor is this jeu d'esprit, which seems to belong in a different film, an entirely isolated moment, for Hitchcock's technique sporadically erupts into such self-conscious displays. When Hornblower's son Rolf (John Longden) makes conciliatory advances to Jill, she responds by throwing what is apparently a series of balls offscreen left, turning away from him on the right. After Hitchcock has held the framing long enough for her to repeat this gesture three times, he pans left to show a dog returning the ball to Jill, indicating that all the balls have been the same and that Jill has been keeping Rolf at a distance by playing with this offscreen dog. This shot, like the shot of Hornblower patting Hillcrist's head, shows the director breaking out of

his self-imposed (or studio-imposed) fidelity to his property in a strikingly gratuitous way, as if he could not suppress his sense of fun for one
moment longer and needed to declare himself in a subversive game.

Even such moments as these are not purely gratuitous and irruptive.
Coupled with Hitchcock's more unobtrusively adaptive techniques, they
suggest that the hallmark of Hitchcock's early films is not suspense but
narrative wit, a way of establishing sequence, causality, or thematic connection which plays on the audience's narrativity, their ability to follow
and enjoy a story.[8] Despite some fondness for jokes in the intertitles of
his silent films—a reference in *The Pleasure Garden* to Hugh as Jill's
"fiasco," a series of three titles as late as the sound film *Rich and Strange*
drawing a parallel between the adventure of the Hills' crossing the chan-
nel and their tipsy crossing of their hotel lobby to get to their bedroom—
and despite Donald Spoto's observation that *The Lodger* was originally
prepared with three hundred title cards, which Ivor Montagu reduced
to less than eighty, Hitchcock clearly excels from the beginning in narrative exposition.[9] Even in *The Pleasure Garden,* his first film, his images
often carry rich narrative implications. A man at the eponymous night-
club watches the chorus girls through binoculars and a monocle. When
Jill (Carmelita Geraghty) and her friend Patsy (Virginia Valli) undress
for bed, the camera holds on the mounting piles of clothing in between
them. Later, as Jill kneels to say her prayers, Patsy's dog licks her foot.
In each case the image suggests more than it explicitly shows about the
character in question, and the wit is pointed by the way the audience's
expectations are undermined. Even in his first film, Hitchcock exploits
his audience's narrative expectations to give his exposition a witty edge.

Nor is this exposition limited to the opening sequences of a film.[10]
Hitchcock's inventive staging and framing, his use of silence and offscreen space, rewards the audience's attention over and over when he
is giving information about the characters and their story. He mentions
several examples to Truffaut: the telephone operator who overhears the
wedding plans in *Easy Virtue* (and whose eloquent expressions tell the
audience that Larita has accepted Whittaker's proposal), the brand-new
second-round placard in *The Ring* (indicating that One Round Jack has
never had to go into a second round before), the flat champagne later in
the same film (reflecting Jack's disappointment that Mabel has not come

home). Many examples could be added. When her estranged husband's lawyer asks Larita in the opening scene of *Easy Virtue,* "Mrs. Filton, do you ask us to believe the correspondent never kissed you?" Hitchcock shows her replying, but instead of giving a title card, cuts to a long shot of the gallery's hilarity. When Bob Corby takes off his coat to fight One-Round Jack in *The Ring,* Hitchcock holds on a shot of Jack's trainer holding his coat, as he had held the coat of a sailor who had left the frame to return almost immediately with an aching jaw, and first shows Bob's prowess in the trainer's amazed expression when he turns toward the ring. When Emily Hill and Commander Gordon prolong a romantic moment in *Rich and Strange* by walking toward the bow of the ship, Hitchcock tracks right with their legs, showing Gordon's formal trousers and Emily's trailing silk gown as they slowly step over the chains and tackle on the deck. When they return from a confused and unhappy kiss, Hitchcock's matching track left shows them walking more briskly.

This expertise in presenting story information through images is hardly unusual in an era which had already witnessed the innovative films of Griffith, Chaplin, and Lubitsch. Chaplin's 1923 film *A Woman of Paris* was particularly influential in its fluid exposition of narrative through deftly chosen images. For example, the heroine's old love realizes she is living with another man when she opens her dresser drawer and a man's collar falls out. In Griffith, this revelation would have had immediate consequences in the story; in Chaplin, it remains simply a revelation, a way of allowing the audience, and this time the characters, to infer the unseen from the seen. The so-called Lubitsch touch, an ability to suggest more than the camera actually showed (so that a film like *Rosita* could suggest a world of offscreen intrigue and romance by tracking in toward an invitingly closed door), was simply another name for imputing narrative developments through visual means. The great silent filmmakers were almost by definition united by their finesse in such narrative imputations.

In beginning his directorial career in 1925, however, Hitchcock did not choose the uninflected visuals of Chaplin or Lubitsch as models. His trip to the continent as assistant director on the German-British coproduction *The Blackguard* the year before had provided him with a much more compelling model: the brilliantly expressionistic F. W. Murnau, who was noted alike for his passionate and precise visual imagination, his sensitivity to lighting effects, and his lack of interest in looking through the viewfinder.[11] Murnau's latest film, *The Last Laugh,* reflected more clearly than any of his earlier work his dream of a moving camera unconfined by spatial boundaries, and he shared this dream with the younger filmmaker when Hitchcock visited the set of *The Last Laugh* in Berlin. From Murnau Hitchcock took not only the expressionist cast of his British films and the fascination with the moving camera that would culminate in the long takes of *Rope* and *Under Capricorn,* but more generally the ideal of the director as visual impresario, a showman whose camera-eye upstaged the performers and their material as the real star of the film.

Although Hitchcock's silent films depend no more completely on suggestions and implications than those of other silent filmmakers, they are distinctive from other silents, even those of Murnau, in their gratuitous outbursts, their inveterate and discordant tendency toward self-advertisement, as if the film were a home movie mockingly interrupted by the image of the director sticking out his tongue. The offscreen dog and the shot juxtaposing Hornblower's hand and Hillcrist's head are jeux d'esprit which contribute little to the story's development but compete with its exposition in creating shots memorable for their own sake—a competition that comes out in other films as well. In *The Lodger* Hitchcock poses Ivor Novello beneath a strategically placed flowerpot. In *Murder!* the eleven jurors unite against a twelfth, Sir John Menier, who is unconvinced of the heroine's guilt, by marshaling the evidence against her and repeatedly asking, "Any answer?" until their voices rise in operatic chorus: "Any answer? Any answer? Any answer to that, Sir John?"

Such episodes differ from the shot of the man's collar in *A Woman of Paris* in their gratuitousness. Most of them are not necessary to follow the story; instead, like the offscreen dog retrieving Jill's ball, they tend to interrupt the story with some tangential joke or thrill or revelation whose obvious status as a set-piece is essential to the pleasures they provide. The falling collar is effective precisely because it is an unobtrusive and plausible motion; since the audience picks up information from this shot in much the same way they might have done in the world outside the film, they accept the convention that the world of the film is essentially continuous with their own world. But Hitchcock's world is conceived in two contradictory ways: as the unobtrusively staged world of fourth-wall theater and its cinematic progeny, and as the world according to Hitchcock. Many of Hitchcock's effects are so patently calculated that they cannot simply be referred to the context of the film's story or the world beyond the frame; they are best appreciated as stylistic exercises, products of a gifted storyteller's restless imagination, or games to which Hitchcock is inviting his audience at the expense of the unwary characters and authors whom he is playfully undermining. Unlike the sequences showing Hannay's char discovering the body in his flat or Bruno watching Guy from the stands, these early flourishes maintain a sharp distinction between story and discourse because their effect is so clearly at odds with that of their stories that they force an awareness of a distinctly discursive level.

Hitchcock's self-advertising flourishes are distinctive in another way as well. Despite his fondness for images which carry the promise of narrative implications, his mastery of storytelling in these early films is limited almost entirely to individual images or brief, epigrammatic juxtapositions of images. Unlike stories whose effects depend on their unfolding over a period of time, the narrative impetus most characteristic of Hitchcock's early films operates within individual images ripe with the promise of narrative development; when it comes to development in the sense of change or ripening, Hitchcock's interest invariably flags. The first half of The Manxman is a model of pointed and suggestive exposition, as Hitchcock uses an expressive searchlight, an imaginative use of interior space, and the unsettling teasing of his heroine Kate (Anny Ondra) to intimate the fragility of her commitment to the fisherman Pete (Carl Brisson) and prepare for her romance with Pete's friend Philip (Malcolm Keen). Once this romantic triangle has been established, however, the characters undergo no further development; the complications of the plot (Pete, presumed dead at sea, returns to marry Kate, who keeps her affair secret, bears Philip's daughter, tries to drown herself, and comes before Philip for sentencing) merely overtake them.

But if Hitchcock does not indicate the ways in which his characters are changed by their changing situation, he repeatedly offers striking images which dramatize their emotions. After establishing an association between indoors and imprisonment, outdoors and freedom, he shows Kate rushing down a narrow stairway outdoors across a startlingly low horizon to a rendezvous with Philip, whose framing within an isolating rock formation portends Pete's imminent return. Later, when Kate runs away from Pete, she is shown in Philip's book-lined office and wandering along a street whose blocking suggests the claustrophobic corridors of *Vertigo*'s San Francisco. In an even more characteristic shot, Hitchcock shows Pete and Philip waiting for news about Kate's confinement (the baby she is carrying is actually Philip's) by playing checkers; Pete is so excited that he repeatedly misses the winning move. Shots like these show the essentially expository nature of Hitchcock's storytelling. Nearly every memorable shot in his early films stands on its own, like a narrative painting by Rembrandt or Norman Rockwell.

These shots often turn up in unlikely places, for Hitchcock seems as interested in transitions as in set-pieces; sometimes, in fact, his transitions become set-pieces. In *Easy Virtue,* Larita's remarriage is shown by a close-up of a luggage tag labeled "Mrs. John Whittaker." In *The Ring,* Hitchcock shows Jack's growing reputation by a montage of fight posters in which his name successively appears in larger letters closer to the top. In *Champagne,* the heroine's newly established poverty is dramatized when a bedsheet she is shaking out toward the camera becomes a tablecloth on which she sets the first food she has cooked herself. A few moments earlier, Hitchcock had briskly taken her from near-poverty to poverty in one faceless and wordless sequence. After she offers to sell her jewelry to support her father, who has apparently lost his money in a market crash, Hitchcock tracks in to the cosmetic case holding the jewels and then dissolves to a lateral tracking shot of her legs as she walks down the street carrying the case. A moment after she passes a pair of sneakered feet; the feet pursue and overtake her; the bag is snatched from her, taken away, and finally discarded. In *The Skin Game,* Hitchcock cuts from Hillcrist's vow to fight for his home to an exterior shot of a manor house, which he holds over a burst of rough laughter. A track-out reveals this shot to be a still photograph used to advertise the coming auction, which immediately follows this visual reduction of Hillcrist's way of life to a commodity.

These sequences and set-pieces suggest that Hitchcock's leading interest in his early films is in "pure narrative" in the specific sense meant by the cinematic exposition of narrative, in particular by devising ways of imparting information which are peculiar to film and which could not be duplicated in any other narrative medium. Whether he is adapting a well-known property which demands close fidelity or working on a project which offers more opportunities for inventiveness, the director establishes a relationship to the audience based on their intermittent awareness of a storytelling medium whose narrative devices—the manipulation of space and sound, the insistence on telling details accessible only in close-up, witty transitions that might be too abrupt or technically impossible on stage—would be unavailable in any other medium. Hitchcock is never happier than when he is reminding his audience that this absorbing story they are watching is only a movie.

Often, as in *The Skin Game,* such reminders are intermittently at odds with the director's material, and an otherwise faithful adaptation is enlivened or undermined by a few obtrusively witty shots he could not resist. The first two shots of Farmer Sweetland (Jameson Thomas) in *The Farmer's Wife* are not so much obtrusive as pointless. Both times he is shot in medium close-up from outside a window as he looks out with a neutral expression. Only after Hitchcock's camera has climbed the stairs to the room's interior does it become clear that Sweetland is standing in the room where his wife lies dying. The withholding of this information might have achieved a moving or ironic effect if Hitchcock had established a closer relation between Sweetland and his first wife, but since he never reacts to her with any emotion, and since the film never reveals anything about her except that she has always been devoted to him, the shots of him seem to promise more meaning than the film delivers.

*Champagne* is a virtual anthology of such portentously anticlimactic shots, a kind of extended joke whose point is pointless. After a brief prologue showing the heroine's millionaire father (Gordon Harker) furious because she has run away to join her lover, the film opens with a shot of a champagne bottle being opened. The cork pops toward the camera; the bottle fills a glass; the glass is lifted toward the camera; and it is drained to reveal through the bottom an image of a party of dancers. The point of view is that of a sinister-looking man (Theo Von Alten) who will follow the heroine (Betty Balfour) through most of the film before being revealed as a friend of her father's whom he has commissioned to spy on her. The film's final image, similarly framed in the bottom of this man's champagne glass, shows the lovers kissing, enclosing their story in a visual frame whose significance is entirely formal and aesthetic rather than thematic, like the arrival home of the winning player's last piece in a Parcheesi game. In between, *Champagne* presents an unusual number of point-of-view shots. When the millionaire catches up with his daughter in Paris, for instance, his arrival is marked by an extreme close-up of a door, which opens to reveal a maid answering the bell. A forward tracking shot establishes the millionaire's point of view without showing who he is. When the heroine sees him, she comes forward as if to kiss the camera lens, and a cut to a reverse track-out shows his own pucker and reveals, finally, that this is her father. Since the point of view in sequences like this so frequently changes—most often between the heroine's point of view and that of her father's agent—the issues commonly associated with point-of-view shots—the discrepancy between perception and reality, the suspense arising from restriction to a limited point of view—never arise. Twice in the film Hitchcock experiments with subjective fantasy sequences, representations of the heroine's fears, without first identifying them as such, so that the audience is led to think, first that the mysterious man of the champagne glass is kissing her over her protests in a private room of the club where she is working, and later that she has eloped to America with him. These sequences look back to the confusion between the fo'c'sle in which Roddy Berwick (Ivor Novello) is sleeping and the dance hall he is dreaming about in *Downhill* and ahead to the famous lying flashback in *Stage Fright* twenty years later. All three cases are designed as traps for the credulous audience. The jolt provided by the deceptively realistic fantasy sequence in *Champagne* suggests a director so frankly bored or irritated with his material that he is willing to go to unusual lengths to interest the audience, however briefly and inconsequentially, in his own pyrotechnics.

It is no wonder, then, that *Rich and Strange* is the older Hitchcock's favorite of his early films even though it does not portend his later emergence as Master of Suspense, for more than any of his other films it breaks down into a series of witty stylistic exercises. The film chronicles the comic decline of Fred and Emily Hill's marriage by showing their inability to adapt to the riches they have always dreamed of. When Fred's uncle makes them a gift that enables them to travel abroad, they find their assumptions about the good life unsupported by reality. Getting tipsy at the Folies Bergere simply makes them unable to negotiate their hotel lobby; taking an ocean voyage makes Fred (Henry Kendall) seasick and Em (Joan Barry) lonely; tasting forbidden romance makes Em feel guilty and Fred brutal and defensive. Their fellow passengers aboard ship are represented all too well by the wallflower (Elsie Randolph) who attempts to monopolize the chivalrous Commander Gordon (Percy Marmont), Em's admirer, and by the bogus princess (Betty Amann) who snares Fred, takes his money, and abandons him to Em's forgiveness. Returning home on a tramp steamer, they are shipwrecked, rescued by Chinese sailors, and led to watch the death of one of their rescuers and the drying skin of the cat they had earlier played with and unwittingly eaten. Deciding after watching a Chinese woman in childbirth that a child of their own will bring them together, they return sadder but wiser to their dreary flat in London but immediately fall into a household quarrel that makes it clear they have learned nothing.

The film is structured as a comedy. Each of the Hills' adventures revolves around their gradual revelation of their inadequacies, especially Fred's. Many of the scenes, especially in Paris and aboard ship, are disarmingly funny. The film's opening sequence, a mock-earnest representation of Fred's rush-hour commute from his office, turns the rituals of desk work, raising umbrellas, and riding the underground into the material of operetta. (Like the opening reel of Blackmail, this sequence was filmed without dialogue but with a music track.) But Hitchcock is not interested in the deeper comic implications of his story; instead he prefers, like an earlier Mel Brooks, to focus on staging the film as a series of skits. Since so much of the film's humor depends on the contrast between everyday life and the ritualistic emphasis imposed by the characters' illusions or the director's camera, the energy of the film is centrifugal, with individual contrasts upstaging Hitchcock's central premise instead of extending or deepening it. Fred Hill in particular behaves so unattractively that the audience has no reason to wish his reconciliation with his wife, who seems as if she could do much better.

One result of the film's centrifugal force is that although the funny sequences of the film are witty, the melodramatic sequences are simply painful. When the Hills' marriage encounters serious trouble, Hitchcock's narrative invention goes flat because its source is remote from their troubles; their quarrels are canned theater of a sort he avoids far more successfully in *The Skin Game*. And during the shipwreck and its aftermath, Hitchcock's tone is generally nasty without being witty. He allows everyone to escape from the steamer except Fred and Em; he holds on the spectacle of the dying Chinese without showing that the Hills have learned anything from watching him; and he shows Fred churlish and narrow-minded to the end. The film indicates more fully than any of the director's other work why Hitchcock, for all his narrative wit, did not really excel in comedy: the imputations which are his stock in trade require a narrative center, a leading situation which makes the audience eager for further developments. Lacking such a strong situation, Hitchcock's wit tends to interrupt rather than develop the stories he is telling. *Rich and Strange* shows Hitchcock's wit and his talent for narrative development essentially opposed to each other. Hitchcock's later blaming of the film's failure on the casting of Henry Kendall and Joan Barry, suggests that although he never repeated the mistakes he made here—his only later comedies, *Mr. and Mrs. Smith* and *The Trouble with Harry,* present situations whose narrative implications, especially in the form of threats to the principals, are much clearer—he never completely appreciated the way in which he had allowed himself to get carried away.

But Hitchcock's imputations do not always carry him away, even in these early films, for they can take very different forms. An audience who notices the placement of the Lodger's head beneath a flowerpot will be amused at the director's inventiveness, even if that amusement works against the film's tone and emphasizes the dissonance between the film's story and its discourse. But the famous shot of the Lodger seen pacing overhead from below a glass ceiling works to integrate the audience's awareness of story and discourse, for it implicates the audience further in the story by intimating the Lodger's mystery and menace and his landlady's apprehension in ways that are essential to the development of the story. Here one kind of narrative mastery, the ability to make audienceship fun by imputing relations without making them explicit, is subordinated to another, the ability to integrate particular imputations in a way that gives the audience's experience a narrative pattern. This integration of particular expressive or amusing shots and sequences into a narrative pattern is what most clearly foreshadows Hitchcock's later work. In a filmmaker like Bergman or Godard or the later Woody Allen this integration would be thematic, but thematic consistency is not at the center of Hitchcock's early films, even when they focus on his most pervasive thematic motif: the contrast between the official surfaces of public life and the tawdry or foolish or banal life beneath.[12]

This contrast often remains on the fringes of Hitchcock's silent films. Probably the most memorable shot in *Champagne* shows the heroine talking earnestly with a potential employer about a job in a toothpaste advertisement while another man behind her casually raises the hem of her dress with his foot. In *The Farmer's Wife,* Sweetland's abortive proposal to Thirza Tapper (Maud Gill), which shows his desire for a new wife unrestrained by any consideration for the feelings of the women he is considering, takes place during a tea party filled with other images of unchecked appetite. Sweetland's proposal is curtailed by the arrival of a family of four, including a young boy whose point of view is shown by a rapid track-in to a plate of cakes. Although he is prevented from grabbing the cakes, most of them are soon eaten by an old man who piles them on a bandanna spread on his lap and gobbles them up. Later, after the guests have strolled outdoors, Sweetland's farmhand, Churdles Ash (Gordon Harker), whom Thirza has pressed into service as a butler, makes himself comfortable at the refreshment table and gulps coffee unconcernedly from his saucer. Here as in *Champagne,* the contrast between social appearances and the appetites they mask is only tangential to the story.

But the contrast between public reputation and private life is at the heart of *Easy Virtue.* The ways in which Larita Filton's unjustly scandalous reputation—the artist with whom her husband suspected her of infidelity had killed himself—wrecks her remarriage into the country-genteel Whittakers is dramatized in ways that show Hitchcock's preference for developing playfully inventive images to following the lead of his original material, in this case the play by Noël Coward. The silhouette of a camera over the opening credits prepares for a story which is organized around cameras and eyes as offensive weapons. Throughout the film, Larita (Isabel Jeans) is defined by the gaze of others—the myopic judge who presides over her divorce proceeding, the alcoholic husband who accuses her of adultery, the jurors who conscientiously note the prosecutor's remarks about her feelings for the artist Claude Robson, who had left all his money to her ("Pity is akin to love 2000 a year," one of them writes on a pad), the lovesick Whittaker (Robin Irvine), who stares at her so abstractedly that he is unable to mix their drinks, and the rest of Whittaker's family, especially his mother (Violet Farebrother), who, despite being "all smile and sweetness to [Larita]—in public," schemes to find out her guilty secret. Eventually a group photograph of Larita and the Whittakers in the *Tatler,* identifying her as "the former Mrs. Filton," confirms Mrs. Whittaker's suspicions and leads to a second divorce.

Hitchcock ingeniously works the theme of the obtrusive public gaze—a theme quite absent from Coward's play, which begins with Larita's arrival at the Whittakers' home and focuses narrowly on her relations with the family—into the most unexpected places. Larita first meets Whittaker when his tennis partner hits her in the eye with a ball, indicating her inability to move from object to manipulator of the gaze. When she commends the view from Whittaker's horse-drawn buggy, he replies, "I'm afraid I've no eyes for anything but you, Larita." His proposal of marriage to her, represented by horses nuzzling as the carriage has come to a stop, is interrupted by the horn of an impatient motorist behind them. Later, Larita's acceptance of Whittaker's proposal is overheard by the telephone operator. After their trip from the south of France to the Whittakers' home, they will have only one short scene alone together; everything else will take place under the eyes of witnesses.

*Easy Virtue* is more successful as a foretaste of Hitchcock's characteristic thematic concern with reputation than as a cinematic transcription of Coward's play because although the effect of the play requires the audience to sympathize with Larita throughout, Hitchcock maintains this sympathy only through the first half of the film. Coward's Larita is a refreshingly direct, affectionate woman whose marriage is destroyed by the sanctimonious hypocrisy of her husband's family (except for his father, who openly admires her) and her realization that her marriage to weak-willed Whittaker is a sign of her own weakness. Hitchcock's Larita is finally less sympathetic despite the audience's experience of her degradation in court because, as the part is written and played, she comes across as self-absorbed and petulant rather than spirited and principled. It is no wonder Mrs. Whittaker condemns her, for her bad-girl image is not balanced by any signs of love for Whittaker. In her one scene alone with him, she begs him to take her back to the Mediterranean because his family hates her, but she says nothing of her feelings for him. Nor does she express those feelings to anyone else, for instance to the sympathetic Sarah (Benita Hume), to whom Whittaker had been engaged. When she tells Sarah that Whittaker "loves only his family," Sarah chides Whittaker for neglecting his wife and urges him to stand by her against his mother. But this scene makes Sarah more sympathetic than Larita herself, whose behavior is alternately pettish and coolly provocative. Since the audience never gets to see Whittaker's "charming young wife" (as one vistor calls her) act charming, as she does throughout Coward's play, the audience perceives the marriage as merely a refuge for her, not an expression of her affection for her husband, and so is less concerned when it comes apart.

Hitchcock, who was prone to blame his actors for his films' critical and commercial failures, might have blamed Isabel Jeans for her unaffecting portrayal of Larita, but any actress in the role would be hamstrung by the film's omission of any scenes which might give Larita and the audience a greater stake in the marriage and by his limiting her emotional range to alternating bursts of bravado and self-pity. (The absence of a final tête-à-tête between Larita and Whittaker suggests that she would rather shame his family than work out the problems in her marriage.) The film's scenario, by Eliot Stannard (who is credited with the screenplay for all of Hitchcock's first five films, as well as the later *Champagne* and *The Manxman*), creates a heroine who suffers more than Coward's heroine and is more completely destroyed—the film ends with her famous line to the press photographers, "Go ahead and shoot, there's nothing left to kill!"—yet whose ability to win the audience's sympathy is set against the director's more absorbing interest in the visual motif of the hostile public gaze and the leading actress's neutral performance. For all his visual inventiveness, the young Hitchcock is a generally inexpressive director of actors, as he demonstrates again in his handling of Ivor Novello in *The Lodger* and *Downhill* and Henry Kendall in *Rich and Strange*.[13] It is as if his narrative gifts were cinematic in such a narrowly technical sense that he was indifferent to the contributions actors could make to his films. Indeed, the most successful performances in Hitchcock's early films—those of Jameson Thomas and Gordon Harker in *The Farmer's Wife*, Sara Allgood in *Juno and the Paycock*, and Edmund Gwenn in *The Skin Game*—are all theatrical performances which the director obviously did little to shape. Without such performances, the films often collapse into a heap of brilliant images, narrative pretexts or thematic premises without the consistent emotional resonance that would make them an effective story. *Easy Virtue*, like several of Hitchcock's other early films, avoids giving the audience the opportunity for the straightforward emotional identifications that would make the characters engaging. The film seems organized less around its characters than around its leading theme and the devices which visualize that theme.

It might seem that Hitchcock's playful visual inventiveness would undermine the force of his material in the manner of Douglas Sirk's Universal melodramas unless the films provided both a strong narrative to unify the director's incidental games and strong performances which would give the audience an ongoing stake in the characters' problems. But in the most ambitious and original of his silent films, *The Ring*, Hitchcock triumphs over the limitations of the actors who play One-Round Jack (Carl Brisson), his sweetheart Mabel (Lilian Hall-Davis), and his rival Bob Corby (Ian Hunter), by placing games at the thematic center of the film instead of keeping them at its fringes. *The Ring* is as tightly and imaginatively organized thematically as *Easy Virtue*, but its choice of boxing, a ritualized ludic conflict, as its leading metaphor roots the games the director is playing with the audience in images of the games his characters are playing with each other.

Hitchcock told Peter Bogdanovich that his point of departure for *The Ring* was the contrast between the social rituals surrounding boxing matches (the spectators wore formal clothes, and champagne was poured over the heads of the fighters before the last round) and the brutality of the behavior within the ring.[14] Although this contrast is not expressed in these visual terms until the final scene, it is implicit throughout the film, which presents a series of oppositions produced by the ring, an arena of rule-governed or civilized savagery. The contrast is more complex than the simple opposition of public and private lives, for the boxing ring is both public (in the sense that the boxers are under continuous scrutiny) and private (in the sense that no one can interfere with their activity, which is thereby isolated from the spectators). The ring is able to release the most dangerous human appetites by containing them within a series of highly ordered rituals. The film works, as its critics have noted, by presenting a series of interlocking rings, each one exploiting the contrast between civilizing ritual and potentially destructive appetites. After the credits, which appear over a still photograph of a boxing match surrounded by crowds of spectators, the film opens on a fairground, amid images of regulated vertigo and hostility: a pounding drum, dizzying rides, a cut from a barker's shouting mouth to a mouth-shaped opening out of which patrons shoot targets. This setting, which emphasizes the importance of rules and rituals in curbing potentially anti-social impulses, introduces Bob Corby, not yet revealed as the heavyweight champion of Australia, and his manager James Ware, who first appear at the dunking concession; Mabel the ticket seller, who first appears in a long shot from Corby's point of view; and One-Round Jack, who is first shown in a close-up accepting a piece of gum from Mabel. Jack's fights appropriately take place inside a tent into which the crowd cannot see at all, or Mabel very well. Even the audience does not see them, for as Jack dispatches his first few opponents, the camera stays on the bored reactions of his trainer (Gordon Harker), and when Jack's and Corby's fight goes into extra rounds, its point of view is mostly that of Mabel, whose perspective is limited by the size of the square in the tent and the crowds who are clustered around the ring. Her anxiety, a function of her limited perspective, establishes the audience's identification with her and the importance of her relationship with Jack. Hitchcock gets his plot under way with a single image of Mabel wiping Jack's face after the fight while her eyes remain on Corby.

The resonance of the ring is deepened when Hitchcock dissolves from a close-up of Jack shaking Ware's hand, sealing his contract to act as Corby's sparring partner, to a matched shot of Corby's slipping a coiled serpentine bracelet, which he has bought with his winnings from the bout, over Mabel's wrist. Mabel first attempts to hide the bracelet from Jack by covering it with her hand and, later, sliding it up over her elbow, but when it slides off her arm into a brook, disturbing the reflections of herself and Jack there, and he retrieves it and asks where it came from, she tells him that since Corby bought it with Jack's money, it was really a gift from him. He replies by pinching a bit of it into a ring, placing it on her finger, and saying, "I gave it to you for this." Much later, the breakdown of Jack and Mabel's marriage reaches a climax when he tears the dress from her shoulder, sees the bracelet hidden beneath it, and pulls it off too. The ring, which ought to legitimize sexual desire within social institutions, has become a symbol of uncontrolled desire and social betrayal, just as Jack's fights against Corby become more and more direct expressions of his resentment of his rival.

Throughout *The Ring* Hitchcock remains more interested in playfully visualizing conflicts than in resolving them. Since Corby is never shown confiding in Ware, for example, he never emerges as clearly sympathetic or unsympathetic, and the film's climax, in which Mabel, overwhelmed by the beating her distracted husband is taking at the hands of her lover, comes to him and tells him, "I'm in *your* corner," giving him the strength to win both her love and the match, suggests that Hitchcock is more interested in setting up these battles than in settling them. If Jack's hallucinatory breakdown when he realizes the extent of Mabel's involvement with Corby—the montage sequence that won the applause of which Hitchcock was so proud—is still a detachable stylistic tour de force by way of the similar breakdown Murnau had shown three years earlier in *The Last Laugh,* the film's most extended set-piece, the wedding of Jack and Mabel, is a masterly example of Hitchcock's integration of symbol and narrative. Like the boxing ring, to which it is linked by Jack's telegram announcing that because he has won the trial fight establishing him as Corby's sparring partner he and Mabel can now get married, the church where the wedding takes place is an arena governed by rules which license potentially subversive desires. The scene proceeds by showing these rules gradually breaking down, dramatizing the conflict between public ritual and private behavior and disclosing the deeper conflicts between and within the principals which the wedding ritual does not acknowledge.

The scene begins directly after a long overhead shot of the fairgrounds shows that it is deserted. The following shot shows the reason why: The carnival workers have all come to the wedding. A pair of Siamese twins argues about which side of the church to sit on; Mabel's escort, the carnival barker, is so accustomed to the limelight that he repeatedly stops to greet his friends and show off his formal wear; when the minister asks everyone to rise, the barker and Jack's trainer, who is acting as best man, burst into applause. As the minister reads the marriage ceremony, Hitchcock cuts in a close-up of the trainer picking his nose, and when he is asked for the ring, he drops it, pops off a button from his pants in searching for it, and offers the button instead of the ring. At the reception afterwards, the trainer, quite drunk, watches Jack and Corby playfully square off over the table and, seeing the fight as real, stands up, takes off his jacket, and tries to rally the crowd to attention before his point of view gradually blurs to an indiscriminate gray. Nearly every shot in the sequence exploits the symbolic dimensions of the rituals connecting the three principals, and the sequence as a whole clearly portends the breakdown of the newlyweds' marriage, but Hitchcock's handling of visual metaphors is so deft and understated that the scene remains funny, its narrative logic clear throughout.

Perhaps the most remarkable feature of The Ring is its virtual exclusion of any visual representations of boxing. The audience never sees the bout which introduces Jack to Corby or any of the bouts that mark his rise to fame; even the climactic fight between Jack and Corby is shown largely indirectly; the tension in the scene, as in the film generally, does not focus on the question of who wins the match. Instead Hitchcock substitutes visual figures for competitive or ritualized fighting in order to show what issues and relationships depend on the fighting and to multiply perspectives on the metaphor of the ring. It is precisely this indirection and displacement, engaging the audience's imagination, that makes the picture fun to watch.

The Ring, with its melodramatic handling of a romantic triangle, is one of the rare early Hitchcock films based on an original screenplay, for which Hitchcock himself takes screen credit.[15] Yet it lacks any of the criminal suspense with which Hitchcock's name would become so closely associated. Its suspense, which is considerable, hinges on its method—the way it engages the audience's sympathy and apprehension—rather than its subject—the status of its principals as murder suspects or secret agents—to borrow Robin Wood's distinction.[16] If there had been auteur-watchers in 1927, they would have found the film perfectly consistent with the vision of a director who had already presented the melodramatic or triangular romances of *The Pleasure Garden, The Mountain Eagle, The Lodger, Downhill,* and *Easy Virtue.* Given the director's later career, however, *The Ring,* more than any of his other silent films, is a work which achieves, in its use of visual symbols to represent emotions motivated and developed by the story, a unity and richness unique among Hitchcock's early films.

In many ways it is a far more characteristic film than any of Hitchcock's first four thrillers. Despite their critical and commercial success—*The Lodger* was the film which launched its director's reputation—Hitchcock's early thrillers were clearly not made by a director who considered himself a Master of Suspense.[17] No one who has realized his vocation as a director of thrillers titles his third thriller *Murder!*—an immensely self-serious, and in effect wasteful, title—and runs the credits over themes from Beethoven's Fifth Symphony. Taken together, the first four thrillers are not especially thrilling. Although three of them employ a chase sequence as their climax, there is nothing in them to compare for wit or sustained suspense with Hannay's escape from the Scottish police in *The 39 Steps* or the Albert Hall sequence in *The Man Who Knew Too Much.* Except for the long chase that comprises virtually the second half of *Number Seventeen,* all the films are paced deliberately—indeed, *Blackmail* seems, up to its final chase, to get slower and slower as it goes along—and none is marked by the kind of quick visual wit characteristic of films as different as *The Ring* and *The Skin Game,* films in which the audience's pleasure depends to a great extent on the subtle ways in which the director allows the audience to infer relatively straightforward states of affairs (the hostility between Hornblower and the Hillcrists, Jack's jealousy of his wife's attachment to Corby).

This kind of wit, which depends on narrative imputations, reappears in the thrillers, but in striking new ways. In *The Lodger* it seems at first to be on the periphery of the film, in touches outside the main intrigue. The scenes involving Mr. and Mrs. Bunting (Arthur Chesney and Marie

Ault), their daughter Daisy (June Tripp), and her fiancé, the policeman Joe (Malcolm Keen), are blocked and shot in a theatrical way that leaves nothing to the audience's imagination. But the first of these scenes is preceded by a long introductory sequence which is a marvel of accomplished exposition. After the famous close-up of a screaming woman and a shot of a neon sign reading "TO-NIGHT GOLDEN CURLS," Hitchcock gradually reveals that the woman is dead, that she has been murdered by a madman who has killed several blondes, always on a Tuesday, leaving each time a note identifying himself as the Avenger. The audience learns this information bit by bit by watching the police question a witness who saw the muffled killer, reading a teletype message, seeing a boy selling newspapers, going briefly behind the scenes of the show "Golden Curls" (where brunette members of the cast are unconcerned but blondes cower in fear or poke dark locks of hair under their hats), and finally following Mr. Bunting home, where he discusses the case with his wife and Joe.

Although Hitchcock's exposition, in which most of the characters remain anonymous in long shot, is far more assured than his direction of the Bunting family, the story comes abruptly into focus with the arrival of the Lodger (Ivor Novello), who is first introduced by a point-of-view shot, a rare track-in to the Buntings' front door, number 13. Everything about the Lodger is suspicious. He arrives in a swirling fog (reminding the audience of the film's subtitle, "A Story of the London Fog") amid sinister portents: the lights dim, a passing vehicle makes crazy patterns on the wall, Mr. Bunting falls off the chair he has climbed on. As played by Novello, the Lodger looks like a killer: tall, spectrally thin, swathed in a scarf, and carrying what looks like a medical bag, he precisely fits the witness's description earlier. When he examines the room Mrs. Bunting has for rent, he turns the paintings of blonde women to face the wall and asks Daisy, who of course is blonde, to take them away. He is elaborately indifferent to the rent money but is anxious that he and his bag be left alone.

Maurice Yacowar aptly observes that "all of Hitchcock's bravura technical devices in this film . . . trick the audience into a judgment [against the Lodger] on quite circumstantial evidence." For in fact the Lodger is innocent, a brother of the Avenger's first victim who is now on the Avenger's trail, even though Hitchcock "so extravagantly rigs the evidence against the innocent man that the audience misjudges him."[18] The Lodger carries in his bag a map in which the scenes of earlier murders are marked with the Avenger's signature, a triangle; his scenes with Daisy teasingly emphasize potential threats to her from his knife or poker; he is out the following Tuesday night, when another murder is committed. Even more damningly, several shots (most notoriously the glass-ceilinged shot showing him pacing in his room above the Buntings' kitchen and the overhead shot of his hand gripping the railing as he descends the stairs Tuesday evening), although they depict nothing more than a man pacing or going downstairs, and although they are explicitly referred to other characters' perceptions—the ceiling shot is preceded by a shot of the Buntings looking up at the ceiling and the staircase shot by a close-up of Mrs. Bunting sitting up in bed—are composed in a way that constitutes an imputation of guilt.

This imputation resembles those of the eavesdropping telephone operator in *Easy Virtue* or the flat champagne in *The Ring*—images which allow the audience to guess the unseen from the seen by establishing causal or thematic connections which the story seems to require— but develops their pleasures in new ways. Hitchcock's hints about the Lodger invite the audience to make a specifically moral judgment about him. The Lodger is not just accepting a proposal or disappointing a spouse; he is being established as the villain, a role available in its menace and straightforwardness only to the thriller. Any movie can present more and less attractive characters, but only melodrama has good guys and bad guys, and only thrillers make the bad guys criminals and lawbreakers, confirming their wickedness by legal judgments. The thriller is vitally important to Hitchcock's development as a storyteller because it allows him a shorthand system of moral tags which may be used as points of reference for the imputations which are already his stock in trade, and because its conventions provide a link between narrative imputations (what's going on here, and where is this all headed?) and moral imputations (what sort of person is this, anyway?) that gives his films a new complexity and resonance.

The sign of that complexity and resonance in *The Lodger* is simply that the audience's identification of the Lodger as the film's villain, which every cue in the film seems to urge, is mistaken. Hitchcock does not tell the audience that the Lodger is the Avenger, but he makes it almost impossible for viewers to avoid that conclusion; if they did not draw it, most of the movie would seem pointless. (Imagine sitting down to *The Lodger* knowing in advance that the murderer would never be named or shown.) [19] This fusing of narrative imputations, which makes audience-ship amusing by encouraging viewers to make narrative inferences from visual cues, and moral imputations, which make audienceship problem-atic by encouraging viewers to apply moral labels which are always sim-plistic and often mistaken, is the feature that distinguishes Hitchcock's thrillers not only from his non-thrillers, whose narrative imputations do not have such a problematic moral dimension, but from the thrillers of other filmmakers. [20] It is the feature that allows him to undermine the audience's moral assumptions and to generate a surprising moral com-plexity from the two-dimensional moral categories of the thriller, while still providing a good time.

Hitchcock undermines the audience's pleasure in identifying the Lodger as the Avenger by allowing the characters (even the spectacu-larly obtuse Joe) to share their unjust suspicions, arresting the Lodger, handcuffing him, and pursuing him when he escapes until he hangs from an iron railing by his handcuffs as an angry mob attacks him. The game Hitchcock is playing with the audience is highly competitive—he is rigging the evidence against the Lodger in order to encourage his audience to misread his film—but it is confirmed as a game by a con-ventional happy ending, in which the Lodger survives, marries Daisy, and remains on cordial terms with the Buntings, and which resolves the conflicts raised by the plot, if not the issues raised by Hitchcock's decep-tive visuals. [21] In his second thriller, *Blackmail,* the happy ending itself is subversive, an appropriate conclusion to one of the director's most problematic films.

The film begins by showing the Flying Squad dispatched to arrest a criminal, who is taken to Scotland Yard, interrogated, booked, finger-printed, and locked in a cell. This sequence closely resembles the open-ing of *The Lodger,* which also introduces a story about the devastating effects of the characters' implication in a crime by providing a disinter-ested overview of the mechanics of investigation. Both sequences, by adopting a day-in-the-life method of presentation, turn on the paradox of unusual and even dangerous events which are perfectly normal to the people involved. This paradox would have been clearer in *Blackmail* if Hitchcock had ended the film as he wished, with detective Frank Webber (John Longden) arresting his girlfriend Alice White (Anny Ondra) for murder and putting her through all the same banal routines of arrest and imprisonment. This ending would have been grim enough, but the happy ending Hitchcock claimed British International imposed on the film (the police blame the crime on the man who has been blackmailing Alice and whom they have pursued to his death), although it allows Alice and Frank to leave the police station together, is even more unsettling because it leaves unresolved all the questions the film has raised about criminal and moral responsibility.

These questions are introduced gradually and almost imperceptibly when Frank and Alice, leaving the station together after the opening sequence, begin to quarrel. Alice accompanies Frank to a restaurant where, unknown to him, she is hoping to see another man, whose meeting with her will lead to disaster. Whose fault is that meeting? As Alice and Frank sit in the restaurant, separated by a table and a broad pillar in the middle of the screen, they take turns alienating the audience's sympathy. Alice, who has refused to go to a movie with Frank, is shown looking at a note asking if she will be there at 6:30. Suddenly she says—it is her first moment of tenderness or cooperation in the film—"I'll go to the pictures with you tonight." But Frank immediately swaggers: "Oh, changed your mind, have you?" At this point, however, Alice, seeing the man she has been expecting, changes her mind again, indicating that the meeting is her fault after all. But then Frank, determined to be churlish, tells her he's had enough of her and asks for the bill. Alice, urging him, "Don't let's have a row," seems once again more sympathetic, but Hitchcock has one last twist in store. Frank leaves the table, stands in the dining room doorway, and seems about to return, but then sees Alice leaving with the other man. These rapid shifts of sympathy, which seem inconsequential at the time, portend the way Hitchcock will undermine the opposition between good guys and bad guys on which public morality and legal justice depend.

The question of moral responsibility also shapes the following sequence, in which the artist whom Alice has met (Cyril Ritchard) takes her back to his studio. Alice's alternating avidity and coyness are represented by the spot of paint she accidentally makes on the artist's canvas, enlarging it into a face, and allowing the artist to guide her hand to complete a nude which she signs, and a minute later by the ballerina's tutu she changes into in order to imagine herself a model. In each case the initial suggestion is hers, but she expresses reluctance to act on it until her objections are overridden. If Alice both misleads and is misled by the artist—as he adjusts the straps on the tutu, she closes her eyes and tilts up her face, but then resists when he kisses her—the audience is given inconsistent cues about what will happen. The vertical crane shot up the stairs to the artist's flat[22] and a shot from Alice's point of view of the policeman on the beat outside portend sinister developments, but a shot of Alice eagerly changing into the tutu in the right half of the frame as the artist, separated from her by a screen, sits in the left half playing the piano and singing a song about "Miss Up-to-Date," uses the audience's voyeurism (they can see what the artist would like to) to promise further playful intimacy. When the artist tries to capitalize on this promise by withholding Alice's own clothes and forcing himself on her, she stabs him to death.

Whose fault is this death? Presumably Alice's only punishment if she went to the police would be the notoriety arising from the case (although her insensitive neighbor the next morning suggests how great that notoriety might be). But she conceals her involvement instead, painting over her signature on the picture and sneaking out of the flat, though leaving behind both her gloves. One is found the next morning by Frank, who immediately realizes whose it is, the other by the ex-convict Tracy (Donald Calthrop), who traces it to Alice. In the meantime Alice, wracked with horror and guilt, has wandered the streets all night, imagining a neon sign of a cocktail shaker turned into a stabbing knife and seeing everywhere outstretched hands recalling the artist's pose in death. Even so, she and Frank have committed no serious crime until Frank, learning that the police are looking for Tracy, threatens to give him up to the police and so provokes the flight that leads to his death.

Frank's smug vindictiveness, which seems calculated to appeal to the audience's worst fears about the police, has been suggested from the beginning. When he arrived at the restaurant with Alice and was told,

"Full up here, sir; there's more room upstairs," he replied threateningly, "Go on," and pushed in. Later, as he and Alice argued about whether to go see the film "Fingerprints," he had remarked that it would be amusing to see the film's inevitable mistakes in police procedure. Hitchcock described the basis of the film as the conflict between love and duty, and a good deal of its tension is generated by Frank's double position as police detective and Alice's lover, but Frank's insistence on presenting himself as The Police is doubly ironic since after the opening sequence he never does any legitimate police work for the rest of the film.[23] As soon as he finds Alice's glove in the artist's flat, he conceals it; he sets the police on Tracy, whom he knows to be innocent; and when Alice goes to the station to confess her guilt, Frank simply takes her home. Frank shows the power of the police divorced from its moral authority.

All this is clear from analysis, but just as Hitchcock had worked in the first half of the film to muddle the issue of moral responsibility for the artist's death, he works in the second half to undermine the audience's analytical powers by forcing the audience to side with Alice, who is virtually paralyzed by what she has done—the final chase intercuts shots of Tracy and the police pursuing him through the British Museum with close-ups of Alice sitting immobile as she struggles to decide what to do—and against the threatening Tracy. Even the title of the film poses his threats as the film's primary problem. (Consider how different the audience's experience of the film would be if it were reissued under the title *A Woman's Revenge*.) When he traps Alice and Frank in the telephone booth in her father's shop, when he takes two minutes of screen time to choose and prepare an expensive cigar for which Frank will pay, when he sprawls obscenely at the head of her family's breakfast table, Tracy seems an invader who must be repelled at all costs. And the final chase scene identifies him, not Alice, with the criminal Frank had begun the film by apprehending. The music from the opening reel returns with a reprise of the opening image, a close-up of a spinning wheel; the shots of the Flying Squad's car are similarly blocked and edited; and Tracy himself looks a great deal like the earlier criminal. Is the audience to take this chase as melodramatically satisfying (as the producers seem to have intended), enabling the obligatory happy ending, or as morally ironic (as most recent critics have argued), parodying the opening sequence but inverting its moral values? [24] Whereas Hitchcock's method in *The Lodger* had been to mislead the audience's perceptions, he is playing a deeper game in *Blackmail,* imputing moral stances and categories which the film's logic neither supports nor definitively reverses. The film is a meditation on guilt and responsibility which, like several of Hitchcock's later films, undermines the audience's moral assumptions without substituting any more authoritative beliefs, and which combines the pleasures of melodrama—as in the handsomely photographed chase of Tracy through the British Museum—with an invitation to consider the adequacy of the reassuring categories that make melodrama possible.

If both *The Lodger* and *Blackmail* establish frankly adversarial relationships toward their audiences, the first misleading their perceptions about the lodger and the second manipulating their sympathies toward all the principals, the relationship Hitchcock develops toward his audience in *Murder!* and *Number Seventeen* is more benignly playful, for Hitchcock is playing in both cases with the audience rather than against it. The model for human identity remains the same—characters present an almost uniformly deceptive exterior or public façade in striking contrast with their true nature—but Hitchcock tips his hand so often and sometimes so clearly that the audience no longer assumes the expressiveness of appearances and becomes eager to participate in the unmasking of each character. It is as if the director, holding the same paranoid view of human nature as divided and so untrustworthy, no longer wished to torment audiences with his superior knowledge but instead took them into his confidence as impervious to the deceptions the characters played so constantly on each other and themselves. The irony in both films thus tends to be comic rather than sadistic, as audiences are manipulated into accepting deceptions which they soon see through (in *Murder!*) or which turn out to be inconsequential (in *Number Seventeen*).

This is true even given the frequently somber tone of *Murder!*, which deals with the failure of Sir John Menier (Herbert Marshall), a juror in the trial of the provincial actress Diana Baring (Norah Baring) for the murder of another actress, Edna Druce, to convince his fellow jurors of her innocence and his attempt to save her after the trial by discovering the real murderer. *Murder!* is usually described as one of Hitchcock's rare whodunits. But like *Stage Fright,* it is a peculiar whodunit, since neither of these films focuses on the investigation into the facts of the case: less than a quarter of the film's running time is devoted to the inquiries which establish the guilt of Diana's fellow-actor Handel Fane (Esme Percy). What Hitchcock is primarily interested in is not illuminating the process whereby the truth is established but dramatizing the application of the metaphor of acting to normal human behavior. As in so many films beginning with *The Pleasure Garden,* Hitchcock's characters have a public side produced by acting, theatricality, or conscious misrepresentation, and a private side hidden beneath. As in *The Pleasure Garden* and as against *The Lodger* and *Blackmail,* Hitchcock makes his characters' doubleness obvious from the opening scene, in which a woman who casts an alluring shadow on a window shade turns out to be clumsy and squint-eyed, and another couple, the stage-manager Markham (Edward Chapman) and his actress wife Doucie (Phyllis Konstam), struggle to assume their public identities, she by pulling on her clothes, he by putting in the dentures that transform his mumbling into words.

The notion of identity as based on a split between public appearance and private desire runs throughout the film. Diana's defense at her trial is that she committed the murder while in a fugue or trance, indicating what one juror calls her "dual personality." One point of the jurors' debate is whether someone who looks like Diana could ever kill anyone. They decide that her looks cannot be trusted—a good decision, since their own public façades are not to be trusted. Even before calling for a vote, the foreman absently practices his capital G (for Guilty) on a pad. Two jurors who at first defend Diana mark their recantations by lighting cigarettes and staring fixedly away from their interrogators. When Sir John attempts to review the evidence, the jurors' voices gradually become an expressionistic chorus of accusation. Eventually, Fane's motive for the crime turns out to be his attempt to conceal his hidden identity— he is a half-caste—from "the woman he dared to love."

Yacowar has analyzed the ways in which acting serves as a metaphor for each of these splits between public and private identity.[25] As Diana sits in prison, imagining she hears her curtain call, a placard at the box office announces that owing to indisposition, the parts of Diana Baring and Edna Druce will be filled by understudies. The police question Markham and the troupe of actors in the wings of a theater as the actors run on and off the stage, leaping into and out of the roles in the farce they are playing; and Hitchcock shoots the entire scene from backstage, showing the interrogation in the foreground and the play in deep space behind. (As in *Stage Fright,* Hitchcock offers a play within a film while withholding any shot of the stage from the audience's point of view; either the actors or the audience appear in every shot, insisting on the artifice of the stage production.) Fane, who first appears in this scene dressed as a woman, assures Sir John, "I am not the other woman in the case," and then tells another actor, "Blood always makes me sick, even the mention of it," as he buttons himself into a policeman's uniform—the same uniform that served as his disguise when he escaped the murder scene. Sir John attempts to convince his fellow jurors that his artistic sense as actor and playwright is dissatisfied by the theory of Diana's guilt, and he tells Markham that actors and playwrights should be experts on abnormal and duplicitous behavior. After satisfying himself of Fane's guilt, he resolves to trap him by offering him a part in a play based on the case, a play he compares to "The Mouse-Trap" in *Hamlet.* Fane refuses to give himself away this time, but later, dressed as a woman, hangs himself in the middle of his circus trapeze act. As the watching crowd becomes hysterical, the band strikes up a brisk march. Finally, Diana's entrance to Sir John's drawing room is revealed in the track-out in the film's final shot to be a scene in the play he has written for her.

The acting metaphor may sound portentous and melodramatic, like the misleading behavior of Ivor Novello in *The Lodger.* But Hitchcock modulates the irony of this metaphor in new ways. He so emphasizes the staginess of his big scenes that the audience, instead of remaining a victim of the film's duplicity, joins the director in observing it from above, alert to the film's histrionic implications. The opening sequence introduces a motivic contrast between noise and silence, motion and immobility, as it proceeds from the exterior of the flats where the actors are lodged, an exterior alive with rising shades, peering faces, barking, and confused chatter, to the interior of Diana's flat, where the camera pans over the silent and frozen scene of Diana sitting over Edna Druce's body. The same contrast recurs in the jury scene, when the jurors' choral accusations subside into another silent tableau framing all twelve of them in which the only thing moving is Sir John's hand writing "Guilty"; in the scene in which Fane responds to Sir John's increasingly impassioned directions about his new play by falling into a glacial silence; and in the climactic scene at the circus, when the lugubrious music accompanying Fane's acrobatics falls silent just as he begins, slowly and abstractedly, to fashion a noose. In each case silence and immobility establish the scene as a theatrical tableau, a moment frozen in time like a still photograph, which alerts the audience to the histrionic dimension of every character's behavior.

Because the theatrical metaphor's implications—the assumption that everyone hides a secret self under a public disguise—are so transparent throughout *Murder!* Hitchcock's implications of hidden selves often have a comic edge. As the Markhams' landlady, with them in their flat, pointedly takes out a "Rooms to Let" sign, they pretend to have an offer of work with Sir John. Later, when their bluff comes true and they are asked to lunch with Sir John, they awkwardly pick up his cue by pretending to be convinced of Diana's innocence. Sir John's repeated charge to Markham—"Think it over, Mr. Markham"—echoes the jury's refrain, "Any answer to that, Sir John?" which had bullied him into submission, and a minute or two later, when Sir John, framed in a two-shot with Markham, asks, "Then you don't share *our* conviction that Diana Baring is innocent?" Doucie, off-camera, chokes on her drink. Sir John anticipates and reciprocates their assent to his theory by treating Markham as an equal (referring to the two of them as "we artists") and following Doucie in using the wrong spoon for his soup. Many of these details recall Hitchcock's comic business in *The Skin Game.* But now the comedy is integrated into the tone of the sequence instead of undermining it, and particular bits of business are motivated and strengthened by the central metaphor of social identity as performance.

Hitchcock insists on the universality of public roles as the product of acting by his emphasis throughout the film on changes of costume. In no other film approved by the National Board of Censors, it seems, does the cast spend so much of its time changing clothes or in undress. Hitchcock twice uses a rapid series of cut-ins to show the Markhams getting dressed. Sir John first becomes certain of Diana's innocence as he stands shaving in his dressing gown, and the following morning he is shown in his pajamas as the children of the house invade the room where he has slept. Fane, whose apparent innocence is based on his disguise as a policeman, is shown applying makeup before his mirror at the circus a few minutes before he kills himself. If every character is split, the film suggests, the greatest power belongs to those who are most aware of the inveterateness of acting.

*Murder!* focuses on the tension between immersing oneself in a role imposed from outside (by a playwright, social mores, or the law) and self-consciously leaving it, not for one's true self, but for a more expressive and freely chosen role. This tension develops not only the opposition between public and private lives central to so many of Hitchcock's early films but also the director's own ambivalent attitude as self-effacing adapter and self-expressive showman. The contradictions in this attitude reach a climax in Hitchcock's final thriller of the period, *Number Seventeen,* whose plot, revolving around a stolen necklace hidden in a mysterious house, invokes the same theme—the dependence of all public identity on acting—which it trivializes through parody. According to Rodney Ackland, a writer working with Hitchcock at British International, both he and Hitchcock were interested in making a film based on John van Druten's *London Wall,* and Thomas Bentley wished to make *Number Seventeen,* so John Maxwell assigned each to the other's pet project. In revenge, Hitchcock determined to make in *Number Seventeen* a burlesque of the thrillers it so closely resembled, but "so subtly that nobody at Elstree would realize the subject was being guyed."[26] Instead of erupting only in isolated naughty images like the shots of Hornblower patting Hillcrist's head or the Lodger posed under a flowerpot, Hitchcock's playful ambivalence toward his material is expressed throughout by his invitation to the audience to share the enjoyment of his joke on John Maxwell. J. Jefferson Farjeon's comic thriller was a promising target for Hitchcock's straight-faced parody because it already included an extraordinary number of disguises and false identities. Pointer (John Stuart), who seems to be entering the mysterious house number 17 on a whim after he has chased his hat to its front steps, turns out to be the detective Barton. The crook who first claimed to be another crook's nephew and later claimed to be Barton is actually Henry Doyle, still another crook. This crook arrives in the middle of the night with two other people, all pretending to be prospective purchasers who have an appointment with a realtor to look over the house. The man who claims to be the head crook Sheldrake is actually Mr. Ayckroyd, the father of Miss Ayckroyd (Ann Casson), who has been introduced by falling through the roof. The real Sheldrake first appears in a closet, choking the hobo Ben (Leon M. Lion), who alternates between pretending to be unconscious and mugging for the camera. Asked to give his last name, Ben announces that it is Lloyd George.

Hitchcock turns this farce into a parody partly by exaggerating its absurdities. The dumb heroine (Anne Grey) is for once literally dumb, although she too turns out only to be pretending. The villains make their escape aboard a train which runs under the house. The ensuing chase, which ends the play, becomes the ultimate chase, involving the train, a bus, and a ferryboat. Most of Hitchcock's parody, however, depends on the characters' self-consciousness about their roles. Pulling a gun on Pointer, one of Sheldrake's thugs says, "Do you mind?" "Hmm?" murmurs Pointer. "Hands up," explains the thug. Later, as the villains prepare to make their escape, one of them says, "Hadn't we better— mmm, I don't know what one does in these cases. Hadn't we better tie them up or something?" To Pointer he adds, "Hope you don't mind. Have to catch a train." When Pointer says testily, "Don't be so damned silly," he urges, "Oh, please, come on." After the bannister to which Pointer and Miss Ayckroyd are tied has collapsed, leaving them dangling in space, Miss Ayckroyd faints, says, "Oh, I fainted!", then looks down and faints again. Tricked once into preceding Pointer into what turned out to be a closet, a thug asks Sheldrake, "Is this the right way?" "Of course it is," says his boss impatiently, "straight on and down to the cellar." After a pause, the thug says, "Do you mind going first?"

Like most of *Murder!* the first half of *Number Seventeen* is deliberately stagey. After the opening shot outside the house, the rest of the first half takes place on one set, the three-story winding staircase inside the door. The pace is leisurely (except, for example, for Ayckroyd's improbably frenzied fistfight with Sheldrake), and the music, dialogue, and framing frequently isolate portentous moments. The film's second half is devoted to a single sequence, the extended chase after the train the crooks have taken. This sequence, filmed almost entirely with miniatures and laced with ludicrous situations, apparently should not generate any suspense, but it does. Hitchcock introduces the train with a shot of three pictures of the "Ferry That Carries Trains to the Continent"; he shows Pointer pursuing the train by commandeering a Green Line bus whose passengers do not even know it has been hijacked; his crooks scamper over the tops of railroad cars in pursuit of each other until their train crashes into the ferry and begins to sink underwater; Pointer leaps into the water to rescue the handcuffed heroine, who is in danger of drowning in a boxcar. Everything is absurd and unconvincing, but suspenseful nonetheless, and it is no wonder Maxwell and the other powers at British International did not notice they were being had. Hitchcock's parody of a D. W. Griffith chase sequence, for example, is an effective parody precisely because it manages to generate so much genuine suspense from such unrealistic premises. In most of his early films, Hitchcock's frequent intimations that this, after all, was only a film often undermined the narrative world upon which his effects relied. But the premises behind the chase in *Number Seventeen,* which keep the film within the boundaries of both the comic thriller and the aborning Hitchcock world, make it incredible without diminishing its suspense; indeed the absurdity intensifies and accelerates the suspense. *Number Seventeen* is usually dismissed as a marginal film, and it certainly is slight and carelessly made. But the combination of its thematic material—role-playing run amok—its witty and ironic attitude toward its preposterous situations, and its genuine suspense based on manipulating the audience's perceptions and sympathies looks forward directly to the work which was to follow.

*Number Seventeen* reveals, for example, just what the thriller did and did not give Hitchcock. It did not provide him with new thematic material (for the contrast between deceptive appearances and hidden reality is important to most of his early films) or with suspense as such (for *The Ring* is just as suspenseful as *Blackmail,* and more suspenseful than *Murder!* ). What Hitchcock found in the thriller was a genre which depended on the simplistic moral tags he could impute so adroitly and manipulate so cleverly and whose conventions of criminal intrigue raised the stakes for the deceptions that had already become his characters' stock in trade. Alicia in *Notorious* will face the same dilemma as Larita in *Easy*

*Virtue:* both are women who cannot live down their shady pasts. But the far greater threat to Alicia—death rather than divorce and social ostracism—binds the audience much more closely to her. The thriller automatically gives each witty imputation both moral implications (is the Lodger guilty or not?) and narrative promise (once the Lodger goes down that staircase, what will happen next?). Establishing a film as a thriller invokes a convention of universal suspicion, so that it becomes natural for the audience to watch each shot in a state of heightened awareness and heightened expectation. No longer is the audience asked to find the director only in his irruptions into his own discourse; instead the conventions of that discourse continuously express Hitchcock's ambivalence in a way that promises pleasure. The thriller's conventions, by turns threatening and reassuring, do not resolve the tension between self-effacement and self-aggrandizement, between public lives and private, between alienation and expressiveness, that motivates Hitchcock early films, but they regulate that tension by establishing game-playing as the radical metaphor for the characters' roles, and the director's as well, providing at once rules for Hitchcock's games and the promise that playing those games will be fun.

# THREE

## GRAVE

## TO GAY

The contradictory relationship Hitchcock had established to his stories and his audience takes on new life with his return to Michael Balcon at Gaumont-British for *The Man Who Knew Too Much*, whose success in 1934, together with that of *The 39 Steps* the following year, secured Hitchcock's reputation as the screen's foremost master of suspense. But this new life, reflected in the films' narratives by the rescue or redemption of the principals from intrigue by love, depends as much on the conventions of romantic comedy as on those of the thriller. An essay Hitchcock published during the first run of *The Man Who Knew Too Much* sets the terms for the new relationship his films establish with their audience. Complaining that British films "have maintained too level a style," appearing as "one solid chunk of drama or comedy and nothing else," the director calls for freer and more unexpected changes in tone from "grave to gay."[1] Each of the Gaumont-British thrillers is structured by a series of such changes. Hitchcock had been introducing shifts in tone into his melodrama at least since the flowerpot above Ivor Novello's head in *The Lodger,* but they had usually competed with his stories for the audience's attention by making an issue of his own playfully disruptive presence. Beginning with *The Man Who Knew Too Much,* however, shifts in tone are so incessant that they lose their individually disruptive force and become a distinctive feature of Hitchcock's witty game.

The films of the later thirties are not only the wittiest of Hitchcock's career but those in which the storytelling itself, the development of the narrative, is wittiest, so that simply following the story provides amusement. Hitchcock's wit, like his cameo appearances, marks out a paradoxical place for the director. It would be an exaggeration to say that the witty exposition of narrative implies a joke without a joker, and indeed the witty set-pieces and jeux d'esprit that abound in Hitchcock's earlier films typically obtrude the figure of the manipulative director into his stories; but the wit of the Gaumont-British films is more often ascribed to the principals (even the lead villain in *The Man Who Knew Too Much* is an inveterate joker) or presented as simply a feature of the diegesis. Edward Branigan has observed that "point of view . . . is neither a 'person' nor even a reference to a person" but rather "a linguistic and logical relation whereby one set of statements encloses another set of statements thus *limiting* their epistemological status."[2] Hitchcock's wit works by means of a similar process of embedding or enclosing, allowing the audience to adopt a broader perspective on the action, a perspective frequently unavailable to the characters, without explicitly identifying that perspective with that of a director who uses it to interrupt stories that apparently continue to tell themselves, however wittily. The director disappears as a privileged figure and becomes an immanent presence which can be inferred not from any particular perspective but from the motivic shifts in perspective.

The best-known films of this period, *The 39 Steps* and *The Lady Vanishes,* are generally admired because of their narrative construction: Hitchcock's wit accelerates the pace of his story, instead of retarding it, as in the case of *Murder!* These films, along with *Young and Innocent,* use comic disruptions to establish an essentially complicit relation with audiences, who are invited to enjoy their intimacy with a world they understand better than any of its principals. In two other films of the period, *Secret Agent* and *Sabotage,* Hitchcock's relation to his audiences is more complex, more openly adversarial, because his wit is exercised at their expense, as in *The Lodger,* excluding them from the intimacy which the Gaumont-British films invite. In *Secret Agent* and *Sabotage,* the games Hitchcock is playing with audiences turn into games played against them.

Except for *Number Seventeen,* Hitchcock had not made a thriller since the 1930 film *Murder!*—perhaps his least thrilling thriller. The most obvious difference between *The Man Who Knew Too Much* and the films immediately preceding it (*Rich and Strange* and the costume picture *Waltzes from Vienna*) was therefore its melodramatic plot, which takes Bob and Jill Lawrence (Leslie Banks and Edna Best) from Saint Moritz, where their daughter Betty (Nova Pilbeam) is kidnapped to force their silence about the coded secret discovered by their murdered friend Louis Bernard (Pierre Fresnay), to London, where their attempts to rescue Betty lead them to a dentist's office, a nonconformist chapel, and the Royal Albert Hall, where a foreign minister is to be assassinated by pro-vocateurs under the direction of the mysterious Abbott (Peter Lorre). The motivic split between public façades and private lives, which per-vaded most of Hitchcock's earlier work, is portended by the film's title and developed systematically through every scene of the film.

From the beginning of the film, however, this split is complicated and enriched by a new development: Hitchcock's abrupt switch within many scenes between melodrama and comedy. Like a comic nightmare, the film generates pleasure from the very developments that plunge the Lawrences deeper into trouble. Louis Bernard is shot in the middle of a flirtatious dance with Jill and in the middle of Bob's childish revenge— attaching the end of Jill's knitting to the button of Bernard's frock coat and watching with Betty as the couple dances across the floor, gradually entangling other dancers in the yarn and pulling apart the vest Jill had claimed she was making for Bernard. Bernard's death, which still takes first-time viewers by surprise, must have been a particular shock for audiences who did not yet identify Hitchcock as a director of thrillers, since nothing earlier in the story prepares for it except, characteristically, a joke Bernard makes following his near-collision with Betty during his ski jump: "My last night in Saint Moritz might have been the last night of my life."

Throughout the film, Hitchcock continues to encourage the audience to adopt the wrong expectations and so to misread the tone of particular scenes and the film as a whole. Bob's comically failed attempt to make a young Swiss police officer understand his English is interrupted by the news that his daughter has been kidnapped. When Bob and Uncle Clive (Hugh Wakefield) investigate a dentist's office in Wapping, all the cues— a disturbingly canted shot of the stairway, the absence of noise which troubles Bob, and the dentist's sinister appearance—imply a melodramatic sequel, and when Bob hears a scream from inside the dentist's office, he expectantly draws his pistol. But the dentist has merely pulled Clive's tooth. When Bob himself is cross-examined by the dentist and tripped up, he is threatened with anesthesia but manages improbably to overpower the dentist and administer the gas to him. By building on the audience's fear and hostility toward dentists, Hitchcock frightens viewers with a bogey-man dentist and then allows a comic reversal before returning to his melodrama.

Most of these twists or modulations of tone are so abrupt—Hitchcock delights in pulling the rug out from under his audiences, as he had in fooling them about the Lodger's guilt—that they provide witty surprises even as they increase viewers' helpless uncertainty, their inability to say what will happen next or how they should be reacting to what they are watching. This uncertainty reaches a climax in the first sequence in the Tabernacle of the Sun, whose tone changes with dizzying rapidity. The sequence begins outside the building, when Bob recognizes the symbol over the door from a note he had taken from Louis Bernard's shaving brush. But any initial expectation that this recognition will lead immediately to further revelations, and perhaps to Betty's rescue, is modulated by Bob's remark to Clive: "Sun worshipers. Probably got nothing on." The new, comic expectation this speech arouses is in turn thwarted when, after spending several shots on the men's entrance, Hitchcock shows a lower-middle-class congregation of profoundly British middle-aged women. But the audience's belief that this lead is only a red herring is in turn undermined when Bob recognizes Abbott's mysterious female companion from Saint Moritz. The threat she poses is both heightened and comically broadened when Bob, trying to warn Clive, who has never seen her before, sings his admonition to the tune the congregation is carrying.

Throughout the sequence, Hitchcock has interfused melodrama and comedy ever more closely, so that instead of providing relief from the tension of the situation, the audience's amusement actually increases its appreciation of the danger. This process continues when the mysterious woman advances to the head of the congregation and addresses its members in a deep, authoritative voice, asking for a volunteer to come forward and choosing the hapless Clive. As she hypnotizes him, Hitchcock's subjective camera shows her growing more menacing to Clive, but a cut-in of Bob shows that he considers Clive's predicament funny. When most of the congregants suddenly leave, Bob is awakened to his own danger, a danger whose ambiguous tone is summarized in a single shot of Bob standing uncertainly before the gate as a frowsy congregant says to him, "You're not going to leave your friend, sir, are you?"—the camera tilting down at the end of the sentence to show the gun she is pressing into his back. The camera holds on Bob as a pair of hands come from offscreen to chain the gate shut, emphasizing his sudden helplessness.

Again Hitchcock modulates the tone by introducing the offscreen sound of chiming, inviting the audience to identify Abbott, whose pocket watch had distracted Jill from her shot in the opening scene, as the source. When Bob turns to see Abbott checking his watch, he greets him with friendly familiarity, almost relief, and a moment later he is lighting the cigarette Abbott has offered as he asks if it's all right to smoke in the church. Abbott, as genial as Bob, suddenly remembers that no one has searched him, good-naturedly upbraids the frowsy Mrs. Brockett, who is still holding a gun on him, and takes his pistol, chiding him, "Dangerous," and putting it in the collection plate. This tone of civilized comedy is broken almost immediately, however, when Bob, learning that Betty is being held in the building, starts a fight. Abbott, afraid that the noise may attract attention from the policemen posted all over the neighborhood, orders Mrs. Brockett to play the organ, and the ensuing melee is staged over a liturgical soundtrack. When Bob, carefully throwing chairs at Clive, finally manages to wake him up, it looks as if the scene may end triumphantly, especially as Abbott is clearly furious when Bob sees a ticket to an Albert Hall concert in the assassin's pocket and tells Clive to call Jill and have her go there. But a moment after Clive escapes through a window, Bob is subdued. Abbott, in perhaps his most menacing moment in the film, grabs his face, then lets go, takes a step back, and apologizes courteously. The apology makes him seem even more mercurial, more dangerously out of control.

As the sequence progresses, Hitchcock continues to mix comic touches into his melodrama. When the invincibly commonplace Mrs. Brockett wants to leave because "My 'usband wants 'is supper. . . , I don't want to get mixed up in any nasty business," one of Abbott's confederates prevents her from going by confiscating her skirt, leaving her walking around the room in billowing bloomers. Clive, going to fetch the police, is himself arrested for disorderly behavior in a sacred edifice. As Bob sits eating a piece of celery with elaborate unconcern, a police whistle sounds, but Bob's hope of rescue is crushed by Abbott's return a moment later. Seeing one of the gang, who has also expected the police, pointing his pistol at the door, Abbott raises his hands in mock surrender before smilingly waving the pistol aside. When Hitchcock cuts to a final shot of Clive, he is sneezing in protest as he is led off to the police station. Only the reunion of Betty with her father resolves the tone into straightforward melodrama.

The comic moments here are amusing for any audience who picks them up but unsettling because each one arrives without warning, though the sequence as a whole establishes a rhythm that makes the audience expect the unexpected. Because Hitchcock refuses to telegraph his punches (the entire film contains, for example, no non-diegetic music that would cue the audience to be frightened or amused) and because the pace of the scene, like that of the whole film, is so rapid—shots are rarely held for more than a few seconds, and Leslie Banks is one of Hitchcock's fastest talkers—most audiences miss many of his funniest moments.

Even though the film's shifts in tone are often treacherously abrupt, they are integrated by the film's emphasis on family relationships, especially the relations between parents and children. The film's analysis of the Lawrence family is strikingly different from Hitchcock's more jaundiced examination of the McKenna family in his 1956 remake of the film, even though the relationships among family members portend trouble in both films. The Lawrences' loss of their daughter is prepared by their condescension to her—they call her "wretch," "trouble," and "horrible woman"—and their repeated wish that she would go away or keep her mouth shut.[3] Bob Lawrence, who has already seen Betty dash in front of Louis Bernard and ruin his last ski jump, tries in vain to keep her from interrupting Jill, who is competing in the finals of the clay pigeon shooting. When Jill misses her shot, she blames Betty and leaves her in Bob's care, announcing as she leaves with Bernard, "I'm going off with another man," and telling Bob that he can go to bed with Betty, to whom he has already twice said, "Yes, dear"—as if she were his wife.

From this summary, the Lawrence family may seem ripe for disaster because it is evidently torn by indifference, contempt, infantilism, and sexual rivalry; but these problems are quite rightly treated by the Lawrences as a joke. Hitchcock's film presents a normal British family, a brighter, more articulate, less proletarian version of the Buntings or the Whites; the film is not dramatizing family problems that were present all along (as in the case of the later version), but thrusting the Lawrences into a nightmare which draws on their own problems the way most nightmares draw on waking experiences, by distorting and exaggerating them. In particular, the Lawrences' attempts to rise above their daughter's childishness by rebuking it as authority figures, a favorite device of the policemen who bully innocent or sympathetic characters (Joe in *The Lodger*, Frank Webber in *Blackmail*, the foreign service agent Gibson in this film), leaves them at the mercy of the monstrously childish Abbott and forces them to act like children themselves.

Ever since seeing Peter Lorre in *M*, Hitchcock had been eager to cast him in a film. *M* had recently been released in an English language print, and audiences who associated Lorre with the role of the psychotic child murderer would find him menacing as Betty Lawrence's kidnapper no matter how he played the role. But Lorre's discovery of an unsettling and unpredictable humor in the character gave him a pivotal place in the film, which, like Abbott himself, veers from the ludicrous to the menacing.

Abbott is amusing because he is so childish, and his unsettling personification of irresponsible childhood and authoritarian adulthood reveals the coexistence of childish and adult impulses within every person that lies at the heart of the film, which presents one of Hitchcock's rare children, Betty Lawrence, and two displaced children, irresponsible

Uncle Clive, who is first shown playing with her electric train set, and menacing Abbott, whose sense of humor is consistently childish. Abbott is repeatedly associated with breaches of decorum, beginning with the moment when he distracts Jill from her last shot in the match by displaying his chiming pocket watch to Betty. In the following scene, he is shown briefly in the ballroom at the Lawrences' hotel, laughing drunkenly. Not until later does the film reveal that he had already ordered Louis Bernard to be executed in this very scene. When he appears in his hideout at the Tabernacle of the Sun, he is again a figure of fun and indecorum, a comically unlikely minister, who intermittently jokes with his prisoner Bob Lawrence.

Like Hitchcock's earlier policemen, Abbott masks his infantilism behind a façade of authority. He orders Louis Bernard's death and the assassination of the foreign minister without participating in either; when a fight breaks out in the Tabernacle of the Sun, he shouts directions without raising a hand; shortly before his death he demands that someone else go for more ammunition and orders a member of the gang at gunpoint to keep on shooting at the attacking police. Despite his air of brusque authority, he is helpless when his companion, ambiguously identified in the credits as "Nurse Agnes" (Cicely Oates) is killed. The more stridently he asserts his authority, his superiority to the peers he treats as children, the more clearly his own childishness is revealed.

Abbott is not only childish himself; he provokes childishness in others, especially in Bob Lawrence, who asks him if the back room in the Tabernacle of the Sun is where he writes his sermons and who celebrates a minor victory—Jill leaves to go to the Albert Hall before Abbott's gang can stop her—by blowing smoke in Abbott's face. More often, however, other characters' response to childishness is the same kind of authoritarian superiority Abbott shows to his own peers, or the Lawrences to their daughter. When Louis Bernard is shot, Bob Lawrence immediately sends Betty away to her room, from which she is kidnapped; later, the Foreign Office man Gibson complacently tells Bob and Jill that the scope of the problem is beyond their own concerns, as if he were lecturing a pair of selfish children, and that if anything happens to the diplomat Ropa, whose assassination is threatened, it will be their own fault. In posing as figures of parental authority, Hitchcock's characters, including Betty Lawrence's literal parents, are most decisively revealed as children. Although Bob loudly and self-importantly insists on seeing the British Consul after Bernard's death, he is confronted by a guard whose language he cannot speak, and the only result of his announcement is to warn the villains to shut his mouth. Later, when he is finally reunited with his daughter, Bob refuses to give Abbott the satisfaction of a touching scene by maintaining a stiff upper lip, but his attempts to make small talk about Betty's "awfully pretty" robe and school report card only aggravate her hysteria. In trying to suppress Betty's childishness, the Lawrences deny the children in themselves, children who will necessarily be instrumental in foiling the villains.

Betty's parents, who are impatient with her because she has indecorously interrupted a public event (first by trying to retrieve her dog from Louis Bernard's path, acting as a parent figure herself), ultimately attempt to resolve their problems by acting indecorously themselves, Bob by starting a noisy row at the Tabernacle of the Sun, Jill by screaming in the middle of a performance at the Albert Hall. The characters who act according to the Lawrences' strictures are the criminals, who shoot Bernard without interrupting the dance in progress, who cover up the sounds of the battle in the Tabernacle of the Sun, and who attempt to shoot the foreign diplomat without interrupting the concert—a gesture which Abbott thinks "the composer would have approved."[4] Jill Lawrence is finally able to defeat the villains by subduing the voice of parental authority that bids her be silent and obey. As she watches the assassin take aim in the celebrated sequence in the Albert Hall, Hitchcock's cutting emphasizes not only the conflict between love and patriotic duty he described as the film's focal point but also the stifling presence of so large an audience on so august a public occasion in such an intimidating place. Given the pressure on her to do nothing, Jill's scream becomes an act of heroic indecorum. Later, when a police officer refuses to endanger Betty by shooting at the assassin, who is pursuing her along the edge of a roof, Jill takes his rifle and shoots without a word. Unlike her own and the assassin's earlier shots, which were bungled because of childish interruptions, this one is successful because Jill has incorporated the interruption into her own shot, acknowledging the childish incompleteness that coexists with her own sense of parental authority.

Abbott's divided nature as authoritarian infant provides a touchstone not only for the thematic organization of the film but also for the director's relation to his audience. Lorre plays Abbott as a man barely in control of his emotions, so that his jesting manner is constantly giving way to brutality. Abbott is made up (with scar and lock of white hair falling over his forehead) and photographed in a way that alternates between the amusingly grotesque and the frighteningly grotesque. Like Abbott, the director may seem to have no control over the tone he wishes to present, since his story constantly veers without warning from melodrama to farce and back again. But Hitchcock's abrupt shifts of tone not only entertain the audience even during the most threatening situations but reflect the interactions between the normal, adult world of Bob and Jill Lawrence and the interruptions of childish figures, prefiguring the threatening interruptions of the criminals, since the childish interruptions are amusing but implicitly dangerous and the villainous interruptions, no matter how nightmarish, always have an element of childish impudence.

One reason the characters' attempt to silence or suppress childish impulses is so ill-conceived is that all the fun of the movie, for the characters as well as the audience, comes from childish behavior. When the child breaks out within the adult, however, its behavior can be threatening, destructive, and monstrously selfish. As Nova Pilbeam represents the innocence of childhood, Peter Lorre's performance dramatizes its destructive potential. Hence the fun of the film's exposition and development, in which characters repeatedly make light of threats by attempting to rise above them, is uneasily allied to a nightmarish sense of doom. This alliance is most economically suggested in the film's final sequence, when police officers surround and storm the Tabernacle of the Sun. The first policeman to approach the door of the building, who has just indicated his assessment of the situation as another day's work—"Looks like an all-night job to me"—is shot down before he can knock. After a long shot has shown a crowd held back by a police cordon, a postal worker, told by another officer, "I've got orders to clear this street," replies, "Well, I've got orders to clear my box." Hitchcock then cuts to a shot of the officer in charge pinching a piece of penny candy as a shopkeeper watches him doubtfully. As other officers take up their positions in a row of flats, the occupants complain about the inconvenience of being shoved aside and about not being able to stay and watch. Two young officers, placing a mattress against a window, joke about how warm it is; after a burst of gunfire, one of them lies dead. The attempt to rise above serious problems by treating them as potential sources of fun is both futile and necessary; joking about evil and menace fails to come to terms with them but is still the only response that allows the characters to maintain a sense of their own dignity. Even the Lawrences, who ultimately develop a more comprehensive sense of themselves as potentially childlike adults, survive precisely because they learn the best ways to act like children.

Hitchcock's wit is so inveterately disruptive throughout the film that it has a paradoxical effect of integrating the pleasures it offers. The pleasures of his earlier thrillers had been integrated by a leading concept rather than a leading tone. In *The Lodger* it is fun for audiences to condemn an innocent man; in *Blackmail* it is fun to have their moral sympathies manipulated; in *Murder!* it is fun to know that everyone is playing a role; in *Number Seventeen* it is fun to watch a story whose characters never take it seriously themselves. In *The Man Who Knew Too Much* Hitchcock makes it fun not to be sure, from moment to moment, how consequential are the games the characters play, or what sort of movie this will turn out to be. By dramatizing the unstable relationship between acting in jest and in earnest, between child's play and adult consequences, Hitchcock has devised a new way for the audience to enjoy being manipulated. And by refusing to establish any single normative tone for its own incessant games, *The Man Who Knew Too Much* paradoxically sets a new tone for the rest of the British thrillers. This deftly, treacherously understated film is Hitchcock's pivotal achievement of the thirties and the most subversive movie he ever made.

*The Man Who Knew Too Much* is crucial in Hitchcock's career not only because it marked his return, after several years of indifferent reviews and box-office receipts, to critical and commercial favor, or even because it defined him once and for all as a director of thrillers, but because its interweaving of tones establishes Hitchcock's characteristic relationship with the audience throughout his remaining British films: a game in which it is fun to be swept up despite, or because of, its constant challenges. But each of the Gaumont films that follows is less challenging than *The Man Who Knew Too Much*. It is not merely that these films mark the consolidation of a style and a world mediated by narrative wit, although they do; none of them is as radically or unobtrusively manipulative or as subversive in its mixture of tones as the earlier film. All of them are marked by the same flow of witty invention, but none establishes such an original and equivocal relationship with its audience. Each of them treats its intrigue as a game, but as a game whose rules are finally more narrowly specified than in the earlier film. It is as if the director, determined to give his audiences the pleasure they expected from a master entertainer, felt less justified in making untoward demands on them. Three of the thirties thrillers—*The 39 Steps, Young and Innocent,* and *The Lady Vanishes*—are straightforward comedies of suspense, and two—*Secret Agent* and *Sabotage*—are more equivocal; but even the most problematic of them mark a retreat from the ambivalence of *The Man Who Knew Too Much*.

The most obvious sign of this retreat is the addition to each of the film's literary sources of a comic romance, a romance based on opposition, by adding a character to or changing a character from the original source.[5] Without exception these comic romances, unlike the Lawrences' deceptively casual marriage in *The Man Who Knew Too Much,* domesticate the oppositions implicit in the films by establishing a reassuring frame (nothing terrible can happen to the romantic leads, who are clearly meant for each other) and a promised resolution of thematic tensions (unstable oppositions will presumably collapse in an all-encompassing union).

Romance assumes an especially important role in *The 39 Steps, Young and Innocent,* and *The Lady Vanishes,* all romantic comedies with mystery elements, since a great deal of the suspense in these films involves the resolution of the romance itself. *Young and Innocent,* with its plot showing Erica Burgoyne (Nova Pilbeam), daughter of the Chief Constable (Percy Marmont), helping the murder suspect Robert Tisdall (Derrick de Marney) escape from the police and clear himself, is particularly straightforward in its romantic structure. Thrown together with Tisdall by a combination of accident and growing sympathy, Erica shields him from her father's men, leading her father to tender his resignation, but is eventually able to vindicate Tisdall and ask her father, "Don't you think we ought to ask Mr. Tisdall to dinner?" The film ends with a close-up of Erica's beaming face turning from her father to her lover—a shot which echoes and answers the film's opening close-up of the murder victim Christine Clay, whose estranged husband had killed her following a quarrel about the "boys" whose interest she was cultivating. Erica's passage from her father's authority to Tisdall's love and companionship is thus presented as a corrective pattern of romantic development.

In *The 39 Steps* and *The Lady Vanishes* the lovers move similarly through conflict to love. Richard Hannay (Robert Donat), the innocent suspect in *The 39 Steps*, first meets Pamela (Madeleine Carroll) as he is fleeing the police on a train. He dashes into her compartment, kisses her violently, and begs her to shield him, but she refuses and denounces him to the returning police. Later, after many adventures, she again sees Hannay, now unwillingly masquerading as the speaker at a political rally, and again denounces him. But this time she ends up handcuffed to him and after he escapes again is forced to spend the night with him before getting proof of his innocence. The film's final shot, which shows Hannay's hand, an open handcuff still dangling from his wrist, grasping Pamela's, again provides a resolution of the romantic conflict. But from their first meeting, Hitchcock had taken care to defuse that conflict's subversive possibilities. The episode on the train, in which Hannay's aggression is strongest (Hitchcock includes an evocative close-up of Pamela's frightened face under his kiss) and Pamela's hostility is sharpest, is only one of many narrow escapes for Hannay; if Madeleine Carroll did not have second billing, there would be no reason to believe her character would ever return. When Hannay meets her again at the rally, their conversation is enlivened by barbed insults, and their handcuffing, which raises serious questions about their relationship, is repeatedly treated as a perverse joke. As soon as Pamela learns that Hannay is telling the truth, she creeps back into their room, and a swell of strings on the soundtrack shows her heart warming to him.

The initial conflict in *The Lady Vanishes* is still more clearly romantic and its subversive impications more reassuringly domesticated. An avalanche in the middle European country of Bandrika has stranded many travelers at a remote inn, placing rooms at a premium. Iris Henderson (Margaret Lockwood), on her way home to be married, is annoyed by the noise of Gilbert (Michael Redgrave), an impudent student of native music. She bribes the manager to turn Gilbert out of his room, but he appears in her own, threatens to share her bed, and locks himself in her bathroom until she reinstates him in his room. When Iris is befriended the next day on the train by the elderly governess Miss Froy (Dame May Whitty), whose disappearance leads everyone but Iris to deny she was ever on the train, only Gilbert takes care of her (again, as in *Young and Innocent,* filling the shoes of a parent figure) and helps her solve the mystery. Long before this, however, it is clear that the two are earmarked for each other, and not just because of the convention that heterosexual quarrels on film are invariably the prelude to romance. Iris's fiancé, Charles Fotheringale, derided by her companions as a "blue-blooded check-chaser," clearly represents the end of the line for Iris, who says she will be "a slightly sunburned offering in Hanover Square. . . . I've been everywhere, and done everything," she adds; "what more is there left but—marriage?" The pause seems to invite the alternate conclusion "death," since Iris clearly views marriage with a fatalistic lack of appetite. Her only hope is to be rescued from this fate by the romantic intrigue provided by Gilbert and Miss Froy.

In all three films romance provides not only a paradigm of formal resolution but an indication of the film's leading tone of high comedy. In each film it is fun to be in love; it is fun to be mystified and perplexed; it is fun to risk danger and possible death. It is especially fun in *The Lady Vanishes,* since the alternative life would be not worth living, but all three films establish the hero's or heroine's experiences as exhilarating and generally delightful by indemnifying them against threatened disaster in several ways that Hitchcock's earlier thrillers did not.

*The Man Who Knew Too Much* had methodically subverted its implied guarantees to the audience about what would happen next by changing tones in the middle of so many sequences. In *The 39 Steps, Young and Innocent,* and *The Lady Vanishes,* the tone changes much less often and unpredictably. After a threatening opening, *Young and Innocent,* the most modest of the three, establishes a tone of comic melodrama that it sustains with only minor variations throughout. In the other two films, Hitchcock plays with a wider range of tones but adopts a less adversarial stance than in *The Man Who Knew Too Much* by telegraphing his punches.[6] These films establish a tone at the beginning of each sequence which is maintained throughout the sequence unless a change is clearly indicated in advance. When the comedy of the opening music hall sequence of The 39 Steps is shattered by a close-up of a pistol firing twice, the change in tone, though sudden, is not subversive (a brawl has already broken out in the crowd, and Hitchcock is not trying to delude the audience into a false sense of security, as in the killing of Bernard) or consequential (no one is seriously hurt). The following scene at Hannay's flat, the most portentous and expressionistic in the film—the furniture is covered with sheets, light from the outside casts deep shadows, and Hannay's mysterious visitor Annabella Smith (Lucie Mannheim) speaks slowly and gravely throughout—clearly sets the stage for melodramatic intrigue. Hitchcock prepares more pointedly for the shock of Annabella's murder by the two spies who have been following her by presenting an ominously ringing telephone, having her tell Hannay about the men, and showing a shot of an open window just before Annabella pitches forward dead on the recumbent Hannay. Thereafter the film's alternation of tones is marked by an alternation of scenes: Hannay's encounter with the milkman who lends him his uniform and his escape aboard the train are tensely witty, with laughter serving as a relief from the tension; his adventures aboard the train are increasingly improbable and so comically paranoid; his stay at the crofter's cottage introduces a brief note of pathos; his pursuit across the highlands, accelerated by undercranking, carries suggestions of slapstick.

The 39 Steps does not lack for witty surprises—for example, Hannay's discovery that Professor Jordan is actually the short-fingered villain he is looking for, Jordan's shooting of him a few moments later, and the revelation that he has been saved because the bullet has lodged in a hymnal kept in the pocket of a coat the crofter's wife pressed on him—but these surprises have a different force than in Hitchcock's earlier thrillers because the relatively reassuring narrative structure seems to make them moves in a game. Just as Hannay, Tisdall, and Gilbert all treat their romantic relationships as games and so discover love by playing, they all treat mystery and intrigue as games to be played and won. Games abound within the framework of the stories themselves. Hannay begins his film by joining a crowd asking questions of Mr. Memory—questions designed not to elicit information but to pit the questioners against Memory—and proceeds to a series of increasingly intricate disguises. Since his sincere appeals to the milkman, Pamela, the crofter, Professor Jordan, and the police invariably fail, Hannay's success depends on playing roles. In the course of the film he pretends to be a milkman, a motor mechanic, a marcher in a parade, a political speaker, and finally (for the benefit of Pamela, whom he is trying to bully into submission) a hardened criminal. After he has pointed a concealed weapon (actually his pipe) at Pamela and forced her to conceal their handcuffs while registering with him at an inn (as "Mr. and Mrs. Henry Hopkinson, The Hollyhocks, Hammersmith"; when the landlady sees through this disguise, he tells her that they are a runaway couple, and she delightedly promises not to give them away), he tells her of his life of crime, warming to his outrageous string of clichés as she falls asleep. This succession of disguises begins by emphasizing the danger to Hannay—he borrows the milkman's outfit to escape two assassins just outside—but gradually subordinates Hannay's danger to his adaptability, inventiveness, and finesse; when he lies to Pamela, his preposterous improvisations are elaborated far beyond the demands of his actual danger, and by the time the scene ends, he has lost his audience and is just lying to himself.

The central game in *Young and Innocent* is blindman's buff, played by a group of children at a birthday party for Erica's cousin to which she brings Tisdall. Tisdall, unaware that Erica has described him as an advertising writer, picks up her aunt's cue about "striking the right note" by identifying himself as a musician named Beechtree-Manningcroft. When her aunt grows suspicious, Erica's uncle (Basil Radford) blindfolds her and allows the young couple to escape while she is hunting for them. The game not only emphasizes the youth and innocence of the principals—only three years earlier Nova Pilbeam had played the child Betty Lawrence—but satirizes the pretensions of would-be authority figures like Erica's aunt, who replies to Erica's brother's suggestions with a stiff "That's for me to decide" and is last shown with her party hat falling off, in favor of the wisdom of her uncle, who knows how to make sure that games are fun.

The blindman's buff sequence is slight and charming, like *Young and Innocent* generally. The corresponding sequence in *The Lady Vanishes* is equally charming but more pointed. Iris and Gilbert, finally convinced that Miss Froy has been kidnapped, decide to search the train for her and begin in the baggage car, which is littered with the props of sinister Signor Doppo (Emile Boreo), who shares Iris's compartment and who turns out to be a magician. Iris and Gilbert take turns disappearing inside a magic cabinet before they sit down to make a plan, Gilbert disguising himself briefly as an old English gentleman, Will Hays, and Sherlock Holmes before they are discovered by the magician and a comic-sinister fight ensues. Together the couple succeed in getting the Italian into a chest, but when they look again for the pince-nez they see that he has disappeared through a false bottom.

This sequence combines the metaphorical wit of the blindman's buff game in *Young and Innocent* with the rapid pace and changes in tone of *The Man Who Knew Too Much*. Despite the mystery and danger it incorporates, it remains essentially comic; the danger serves principally to make the game more exciting by increasing its stakes. Even as he is generating excitement, Hitchcock confirms the status of the sequence as a game by including such details as the unlikely animals (doves, rabbits, and a calf) in the compartment, the couple's impatience with one another's disappearance inside the magician's cabinet (while showing the audience clearly what has happened to each of them), and Iris's absurd but ultimately effective attempts to help Gilbert win his fight (after pummeling both men, she finally disarms Signor Doppo by standing on a stool and biting his hand). Like the corresponding scenes in *The 39 Steps* and *Young and Innocent,* this sequence not only shows the principals falling in love but serves as a means to their trying on roles that will allow them to establish a romantic relationship. If love is a game in these films, games are also a means to love.

The characters' games in these films reflect Hitchcock's own playful relationship to his audience, as he undermines their expectation of a single unmodulated tone by inviting them to a more active intimacy and complicity with his world. Even at its most menacing, Hitchcock's camerawork remains playful. It is appropriate that *Young and Innocent,* the most consistently comic film of this series, contains the single most threatening shot—a one-hundred-forty-five foot crane-in to the eyes of the drummer whose twitch betrays him as the murderer—because the power of this shot is emphasized further by the relatively uninflected visuals which have preceded it.[7] But although the shot establishes a sadistic power over its subject, who seems to be blinking uncontrollably simply because he feels the camera spying on him, its relation to the audience is anything but sadistic; the omniscient shot which begins as an overhead long shot of the crowd sitting and dancing in the ballroom and ends by unmasking the man Erica is seeking is a transparent piece of wish-fulfillment, as Erica indicates when, immediately following, she says impatiently to the crucial witness Old Will (Edward Rigby), "He must be here somewhere!" Although the drummer seems terrified by the camera's gaze, viewers whose primary identification is with Erica are elated, since they hope he will be identified and captured. Hitchcock intensifies this hope by having Tisdall surrender to the police, who are at the point of leading him out when a crane-out from the drummer's eyes reveals his incapacity not only to the audience but to the other characters. The director's sadistic game with his guilty character is therefore overlaid by a more benign game he is playing with his identification figure and his audience: will she spot the easily spotted murderer before her time is up? The relationship between these two games is complex—the audience can hardly help sympathizing with the wretched drummer, who has been kept offscreen since the opening sequence—but their final effect is tonic for any audience willing to sacrifice the drummer's fate to Erica's happiness.

Even when Hitchcock's games involve a more adversarial relationship to the audience, the opposition is playful. The shot of Hannay's charwoman discovering Annabella's body in *The 39 Steps* begins with her back as she opens a door to disclose the shadow of a horizontal form bisected by a short vertical line sticking up and ends as she turns to scream, revealing her face but making the shriek, thanks to a bridge to the following shot, of a train emerging from a tunnel. The audience must decide in just a few seconds (1) that the shadow is that of Annabella's body, (2) that the woman is discovering that body for the first time, (3) that the woman is therefore presumably Hannay's char, (4) that she was about to scream when the scene was cut, and that (5) that it is appropriate that her scream be replaced by the sound of a train whistle. It might be argued that Hitchcock, in setting such a puzzle for his audience, is demanding too much. But since the shot is not necessary to the story's continuity, audiences who miss its significance pay only the price of a few seconds' wasted time, and audiences who make the necessary connections are rewarded with a sense of complicity with the filmmaker, a greater intimacy with the world of the film, and—since the discovery of the body had already been portended as a threat—a lightening of the film's tension. If Annabella's body had to be discovered and Hannay jeopardized, the discovery might as well be playfully witty.

Later, when Hannay is supposedly shot dead by Professor Jordan, Hitchcock, in cutting abruptly to a shot of the crofter's coat peg, seems to leave him for dead and so challenge the audience even further. But the news that the crofter's hymnal was in the pocket of the coat that Margaret gave to Hannay is established so quickly and surely—since Margaret does not even appear in the shot, the audience is discouraged from taking the shot as bearing primarily on the crofter's home life— that the audience is prepared for, without quite anticipating, the following close-up of the hymnal penetrated by a bullet. Even if they were not sure that Hannay would survive by virtue of his position as the hero, Hitchcock does not leave Hannay's fate in doubt long—just long enough to justify his escape from the professor's house (where he had also been left for dead) and to allow appreciation of his joke. For this sequence is structurally a joke whose rhythm of apprehension and reassurance is essentially comic. The audience has been frightened only in order to be wittily reassured, and by this time in *The 39 Steps,* and in Hitchcock's career, most audiences would find their apprehension allayed by the assumption that they would be reassured.

Even in Hitchcock's romantic comedies, of course, there are moments when unexpected modulations can darken or complicate the film's tone. When the singer to whom Miss Froy has just been listening is strangled without her knowledge, the scene suddenly develops a sinister edge, the more disturbing for going unmentioned for the rest of the film. In general, however, such modulations serve primarily to increase the stakes for which the game is being played. When Hannay, on the run from the Scots police, is suddenly introduced into Professor Jordan's Sunday morning circle, his paranoia does not so much abate as reveal a comic side, for the sense of easy security the company imparts to him and the audience is clearly about to be reversed. Hitchcock's comedy and melo-drama again intensify each other when Hannay ducks out of a parade into an auditorium where he suddenly finds himself addressing a political assembly, and his fear of the police, instead of being resolved, is transformed into the comic fear of being watched by rows of expectant strangers and giving a speech on a subject he knows nothing about. His speech not only suggests that the most successful speakers are the least partisan but marks out a space and a status within which he cannot be threatened by the officers waiting in the wings. By capitalizing on his confusion and paranoia and making them the subject of his speech, Hannay makes his audience into his allies, actors supporting a performance on which his freedom depends. In every case Hitchcock confirms the comic sense of his wit by linking his threats to wish-fulfillment fantasies. Audiences that want Hannay not only to escape but to escape in style will relish the abrupt changes in tone and situation which make new demands on his resourcefulness and their understanding.

The most extended fusion of melodramatic threat with comic wish-fulfillment is the identification of Iris with the train in *The Lady Vanishes*. This train, which, like the train in *The 39 Steps,* sounds a great deal like a woman screaming, begins the film buried under an avalanche and so forces the travelers to stay at a remote inn; later, after Iris is struck on the head and cannot find Miss Froy, the train's constant movement sets the conditions of Miss Froy's disappearance. In fact the train, like Iris, is heading toward a destination from which it is repeatedly being sidetracked (ultimately, in the train's case, literally so). Iris, feeling her sanity threatened by the crew members and fellow-passengers who repeatedly deny Miss Froy's existence, thinks that her only hope is to stop the train and appeal to the authorities, even though the other passengers are anxious to reach their destinations. But Iris's real reasons for wanting to stop the train are deeper than she understands, since it is carrying her closer and closer to her stuffy fiancé, with whom her life would end. The story's most serious threat—the removal of a woman from the train before she can reach her destination—is therefore closely linked to its audience's longest-standing desire—that Iris be rescued from the fatal journey to Charles Fotheringale. The rescue is appropriately effected by the musician Gilbert, whose function, portended from their first meeting, gradually changes from Iris's adversary to her skeptical guide and helper to her accomplice and finally to her mentor, concluding his services to her by taking over as engineer of the train and arranging for it to be switched to a more promising track than that ordained by the local authorities. Every mystery threatening Iris's sanity becomes another occasion for her saving intimacy with Gilbert, increases her respect for others' judgment as well as her own, and provides another fortunate delay before she is railroaded into marriage. Throughout *The Lady Vanishes* it is not only fun to be in danger; it is also, as in Shakespearean comedy, a necessary means to the characters' knowing themselves more completely, to shaping a more generous society within the film, and to giving the audience what they most want.

Although *The 39 Steps,* which consolidated Hitchcock's British reputation, and *The Lady Vanishes,* which led to his departure to America under the aegis of David O. Selznick, seemed to confirm as his forte the comic-romantic thriller in which the director's wit invites the audience into an intimacy with the world of the film, Hitchcock's wit continued to show the sharper, more threatening edge foreshadowed by his earliest thrillers.[8] His two remaining films for Gaumont-British, *Secret Agent* and *Sabotage,* though just as witty as his romantic comedies—*Secret Agent* is perhaps the wittiest film Hitchcock ever made—are distinctly less funny. Hitchcock's wit operates differently in these two films, whose slower, more meditative pace precludes the development of the sort of momentum that makes *The Lady Vanishes* into a roller coaster ride for the audience. As in Hitchcock's silent films, the director's wit is again irruptive rather than integrative, breaking the films into a series of tableaux or set-pieces whose discreteness keeps the audience at a distance and encourages an attitude more analytical than delightedly accepting. Both films, like Hitchcock's other Gaumont films, operate as games, but games soured by the unjustified death of a sympathetic character, which turns the mere suggestion of game-playing into a scandal. Audiences laugh less often at both these films, especially at *Sabotage,* and their laughter is invariably punished by the ironic realization that Hitchcock's games here present a bleakly unfunny world, and that the very incidents which seemed most amusing have been used to trap the audience into a response which the films ultimately undermine. Both films end with con-

ventional happy endings, but these have none of the comic resonance of
the other films' endings because they simply rescue the principals from
their moral and political entanglements without resolving them.

The tendency to break into witty tableaux is most noticeable in *Secret
Agent*. Even more than in Hitchcock's other British films, the world of
*Secret Agent* is a place in which appearances are universally deceptive.
The solemnity of the opening scene, a soldier's funeral set in May 1916,
is undercut as soon as the mourners leave and the remaining figure, a
one-armed soldier, uses a funeral taper to light his cigarette, then pulls
the coffin roughly off its stand until it falls empty. The funeral, staged to
give the illusion that Edgar Brodie has died, takes Brodie himself (John
Gielgud) by surprise in the following scene, in which he is reincarnated
as Richard Ashenden, a secret agent sent to assassinate a German agent
working in Switzerland and attempting to sway Arab support to the
Germans. In Switzerland nothing is at it seems. A bearded man on the
street is identified as a German spy when he buys a slab of chocolate,
throws the chocolate away, and examines the wrapper for a message.
Having undermined the innocence of the chocolate tourists associate
with Switzerland, Hitchcock will later place a nest of German agents
inside a chocolate factory. Nor is he more respectful of the country's
ancient churches. When Ashenden and his colleague, a comic-sinister
agent nicknamed the General (Peter Lorre), arrive at the church whose
organist is supposed to identify the agent they are to kill, the droning
organ note they hear turns out to be produced by the dead informer
slumped over the keyboard. But as in *The Man Who Knew Too Much*,
Hitchcock now adds a disconcertingly comic touch. In their haste to
avoid detection, Ashenden and the General scramble into the church's
bell tower, only to have the discoverers of the body immediately ring a
loud peal on the bells which makes it nearly impossible for them to hear
each other and gives them a thoroughly anticlimactic headache.

The heroes' initial response to the duplicity of their world is to adopt
a duplicity of their own which combines playfulness and dread. When
Ashenden asks his superior, portentously called "R," what he should do
when he discovers the German agent who has been attempting to rally
Arab support, the man pauses and says: "That sounded just like a pistol
shot, didn't it?" Oblique references to the sordid necessities of espionage,

repeatedly using ellipses and metaphors as a way of avoiding the moral problems of spying by comparing it to something innocent or turning it into a game, recur throughout the film. Immediately after learning of his assignment, Ashenden first meets the General during an air raid. Hearing a girl scream, he thinks she is frightened of a bomb, but it turns out that she is running away from the lecherous General. "Ladykiller, eh?" asks Ashenden. "Not only ladies," replies R, referring to the General's constant use of sexual entanglements as a figure for his real mission of assassination. In fact the General, as critics of the film have noted, represents everything about spying that Ashenden most abhors, and his grotesque appearance, vulgar manners, crude sexual appetites, and lighthearted bloodthirstiness fill Ashenden with self-doubt.[9] The General's playful attitude toward killing is echoed by Ashenden's "wife" Elsa Carrington (Madeleine Carroll), another agent he unexpectedly finds waiting for him at the Hotel Excelsior in Switzerland. Ashenden is disgusted by her explanation that she has become a secret agent to get "excitement, big risks, danger—maybe even a little"—concluding her speech by cocking the fingers of her right hand as if shooting, and so echoing R's playful reluctance to say directly what it is that secret agents do.

Ashenden's own reluctance to carry out his commission is already explicit in Hitchcock's source, two stories from W. Somerset Maugham's *Ashenden, or The British Agent,* which presents the secret agent as a modern Hamlet by showing how morally equivocal, and how unglamorous, his job really is. Hitchcock follows Maugham in his anatomy of the moral contradictions in Ashenden's position, but for Maugham's gray and quotidian world he substitutes a pyrotechnical visual and auditory continuity. Hitchcock's lighting for Madeleine Carroll is so persistently glamorous that in shot-reversal sequences with Gielgud she seems to be in a different movie, and the soundtrack, which emphasizes subjectively distorted effects, is, as Elisabeth Weis has observed, Hitchcock's most expressionistic.[10] Even the film's most extended set-piece, the killing of Caypor (Percy Marmont), suspected as the German agent, is shot and edited like a game, so that instead of stopping the film's flow of wit, it turns it sour. After maneuvering Caypor into a climbing expedition with the General and himself, Ashenden suddenly suffers an acute revulsion from his plan to push Caypor from a cliff, urges Caypor and the

General to return with him down the mountain, and finally, powerless before the General's determination, waits for them at an observatory. Hitchcock thereupon cuts in accelerating tempo between shots of the German-born Mrs. Caypor (Florence Kahn) entertaining Elsa and her foppish admirer Robert Marvin (Robert Young) as her husband's dog begins mysteriously to whine and cry and shots of Ashenden watching the General and Caypor through a telescope. The murder is represented by the dog's rising whine heard over an image of Ashenden looking through the telescope and crying, "Look out, Caypor, for God's sake!"—but once again, like all previous references to murder, remains inexplicit.

Hitchcock's cutting of the murder scene is at once so witty and so harrowing that it establishes a dominantly—and punitively—depressive tone for the rest of the film. This tone of depression and disillusionment is only confirmed by Ashenden's discovery, in the following scene, that Caypor was not the agent he was supposed to kill, a discovery which leads to the hearty laughter of the General and the nightmarish breakdown of Elsa, who had from the beginning shown more enthusiasm for the job than Ashenden, and to her bitter accusations to him: "Isn't Switzerland fun? I don't think I've ever met so many charming people in one place. . . . I don't like murder at close quarters as much as I'd thought—or murderers either."

In this later phase of the film, the problems raised by the necessities of doing a dirty job on orders of authority—the problems involved in being a secret agent as such—continue to multiply. As a result, the film begins to equivocate between the conventions of psychological realism and those of melodrama. Instead of facing responsibility for her own assent to Caypor's murder, Elsa turns on Ashenden as more closely involved than herself, and then forgives him when she learns he was really "half a mile away, at the other end of a telescope." The scene that follows, in which Ashenden and Elsa laughingly plan to resign from the foreign service and go off together, seems to make light of the issues of moral responsibility the principals have been struggling to face. The continuity requires the lovers to make up their quarrel in preparation for the film's climactic sequence, in which Elsa leaves Ashenden because he is still interested in tracking down the German agent. But the scene jars with the somber tone Caypor's death has established, as if Elsa and

Ashenden were able to put his death behind them a little too easily. Such shifts in tone had been common throughout *The Man Who Knew Too Much*, even in its final sequence, but here the romantic scene is less authoritative, more tentative, and structurally more like the set-up line for a particularly nasty joke, as Ashenden's apparently serene resolution of his relationship with Elsa only sets him up for final disillusionment.

But the film's complex and shifting tone is finally resolved into melodrama with the revelation that Marvin is the German agent Ashenden has been hunting. The force of this revelation is punitive, as it shows that audiences who have laughed at Marvin's whimsical flirting have been deceived. The revelation simplifies the complex ironies the film has been playing with because unlike Abbott, whose humor was an unsettling part of his true nature in *The Man Who Knew Too Much* and who therefore dramatized the link between authoritarianism and childish irresponsibility, Marvin has simply pretended to a sense of humor. When Elsa, thinking that she can abandon political commitment by leaving Ashenden for Marvin, follows him on a train to Germany, he announces, "You're in my country now"; boasts that he has never loved her ("You know that, don't you?"); and kisses her with the air of revealing a disillusioning truth.

In the film's closing sequence, Ashenden and the General, learning that Elsa has left with Marvin, become convinced that she has spotted him as the German agent, and even though Elsa, preceding Marvin through the train where Ashenden and the General are hiding, seems to hear the wheels saying, "Save Ashenden!" she refuses to allow his "cold-blooded murder" of Marvin, dismissing his plea on behalf of "thousands of our forces in the East" with the reply: "What do I care about them? What do I care about him either?—It's us. . . . We're not going to have this on our conscience." This Hamletish speech is closer than anything else in the film to the tone of Maugham's stories, and if *Secret Agent* were simply about the tragic necessity of killing the German agent, the speech would be the climax of the film. As it is, however, Caypor's death has made the film's earlier comedy seem so darkly ironic in retrospect that audiences who have no sympathy for the real German agent may wonder why Elsa is acting so petulant. Hitchcock has used Caypor's death to undermine the conventions of the comically glamorized spy story (a technique to which he will return in his last espionage films, *Torn Curtain* and *Topaz*) without undermining the conventions of the melodramatic spy story. Comic and melodramatic conventions clash far more discordantly here than in *The Man Who Knew Too Much*, in which they are evenly matched, and *The Lady Vanishes*, in which one has been subordinated to the other from the beginning; and it is no wonder that the film can be concluded only by a deus ex machina: a fortuitous British bomb wrecks the train, kills Marvin (and allows him to kill the General before he dies), and takes the hero and heroine off the hook. The film's closing image, a superimposition of Ashenden's and Elsa's smiling faces on a postcard to R reading "Home safe but never again" and signed "Mr. and Mrs. Ashenden," is as ironic as the happy ending of *Blackmail*, for the Ashendens, in treating their adventures as suitable material for a postcard, seem to be forgetting the more radically disillusioning implications the film has been insisting on.

The contradictions and abrupt modulations that make *Secret Agent* so like a parody of *The Man Who Knew Too Much* are more tightly controlled in *Sabotage*, the melodramatic complement to the straightforwardly romantic *Young and Innocent*. Throughout the film, even in its most unsettlingly comic episodes—the first appearance of Stevie (Desmond Tester) breaking a plate and hiding the pieces in a drawer, the visit to a pet shop which adjoins a bomb factory, Stevie's enforced toothbrushing and hairdressing by a street vendor hawking cosmetics—the predominant tone remains threatening. Louis Levy's growling music, Oscar Homolka's sinister performance as Stevie's brother-in-law, the movie exhibitor and political agitator Verloc, the pathos evoked by Sylvia Sidney's victimized heroine Mrs. Verloc (compare the wittier and more spirited heroines in the other Gaumont films), and Hitchcock's portentous intertitles marking each day of the week until "Lord Mayor's Show Day," the day Verloc plans to blow up Piccadilly Circus, all combine to establish a lowering tone, and apparent scenes of comic relief—the conductor on the tram joking with Stevie about the film he is carrying, or Stevie's sitting and playing with a dog moments before his package blows up the tram—seem ill-fated from the beginning and cruelly outrageous in retrospect. *Sabotage* is Hitchcock's most austerely dramatic film for Gaumont, and his most punitive as well, because the audience is manipulated into an identification even more devastating than their identification with the unwilling assassin in *Secret Agent*. After Verloc recruits unwitting Stevie to carry a bomb to Piccadilly Circus and inadvertently kills him when delays in Stevie's journey cause the bomb to explode before he has reached his destination, Mrs. Verloc learns of Verloc's involvement in Stevie's death and kills him. But her crime is concealed by the fortuitous return of another conspirator who, terrified of the police surrounding Verloc's theater, blows up himself and the building.

The pivotal event in the story, and the one over which the director lingers longest, is Stevie's journey across London with the bomb. As he is delayed first by the street vendor who presses him into service to demonstrate his toothpaste and hair tonic, and then by the Lord Mayor's parade, which he watches at first reluctantly but then with rapt pleasure, Hitchcock repeatedly cuts to an animated shot representing the mechanism of the bomb and a clock face whose hands are moving toward 1:45, the time the bomb is to explode. But it seems highly unlikely, especially after Stevie begins to play with the puppy next to him on the bus, that he will actually be killed, and when Hitchcock shows a close-up of a clock's hands moving to 1:46 the audience is ready to believe the bomb will not go off at all. Hitchcock repeatedly denounced his handling of this scene as a mistake—"the boy was involved in a situation that got him too much sympathy from the audience"—even after he had killed off a similar identification figure in *Psycho*.[11] But the two deaths are different in important ways. Marion Crane's death comes as a surprise (at least it did for the original audience), whereas Hitchcock works to generate considerable suspense over the question of whether or not Stevie will be killed, and therefore risks the pleasure contract more directly. But since the audience's identification with Marion is morally problematic, the basis for an undermining of the audience's complacency, whereas the identification with Stevie is straightforwardly pathetic because he is never presented as anything other than a victim of Verloc's plot—he exists only to be sacrificed—his death seems more clearly portended, especially since, unlike Marion, he is not the audience's primary identification figure, and when he is killed viewers can identify with the grief and shock of his sister, whom they remain close to throughout the film.

In one sense the novel on which the film is based, Joseph Conrad's *The Secret Agent,* is more "cinematic" than Hitchcock's film, for in the novel every character is seen with coldly dispassionate irony, whereas the film makes Mrs. Verloc and Stevie much more sympathetic and close to the audience and keeps Verloc at a distance as their nemesis.[12] Conrad's title applies not only to Verloc but implicitly to every character in the novel, for each of them, from the anarchists themselves to Verloc to Stevie to Winnie Verloc to Chief Inspector Heat to the Assistant Commissioner, is in some way a secret agent, an agent for whom the idea of rational and autonomous action is fatally compromised. In acting, Conrad's characters are inevitably estranged from themselves; they act out the desires of others, or act without knowing what they are doing, or act without compassing their desired ends. All action, Conrad suggests, is reaction; purposive, consequential action is a contradiction in terms. The question of moral innocence and guilt is therefore beside the point, for everyone who attempts to act is thereby complicit and alienated.

As in *Secret Agent,* Hitchcock intimates this pessimistic view of human action within the framework of a melodramatic narrative whose conventions militate against it. Unlike Conrad, Hitchcock presents the audience with clear heroes and villains. He replaces Conrad's equivocal Chief Inspector Heat with the untarnished, albeit callow, police detective Ted Spencer (John Loder), who is repeatedly set against the sinister Verloc and who will ultimately justify Mrs. Verloc's killing and rescue her from its consequences. Mrs. Verloc herself, another innocent victim of her husband's sabotage, becomes the audience's primary identification figure.

Despite the ironic potential of his material, Hitchcock's visual wit works to a great extent to reinforce rather than challenge the audience's moral assumptions. After the film's opening sequence broadly hints that Verloc is the man who has poured sand into a generator in order to shut off the power, and Hitchcock follows by showing Verloc sneaking into his house, washing sand off his hands in the sink, and expressing pleasure when he cannot turn the light on, he waits fifteen minutes before explicitly identifying him as the saboteur. But this witty tease is never reversed, as in the corresponding exposition of *Frenzy*[13]; the audience is convinced, and rightly so, that Verloc is the saboteur. Hitchcock is using a device appropriate to Conrad's critique of melodrama and individual identity while still retaining the moral categories of melodrama and identity.

Intermittently, however, Hitchcock develops the multiple ironies of his material further along Conrad's lines. When the power failure at the beginning of the film shuts off the film at Verloc's theater and the patrons demand their money back, Ted routs them with a nonsensical speech in which he calls the power failure "an act of providence" and then goes on to define an act as "any activity actuated by actual action"—a speech surely recalling the Second Gravedigger's equally circular definition in *Hamlet* and emphasizing, as that speech does, the potentially problematic nature of action. The title of the movie in Stevie's murderous package, *Bartholomew the Strangler*, attenuates the connection between ridiculous agents and their catastrophic actions, an irony reinforced by the identification between Stevie and Bartholomew (he tells Ted he has seen the movie fourteen times, and when he leaves home with the film and the bomb, Ted says, "So long, Bartholomew").

The ironic disparity between innocuous agents and their murderous actions is dramatized more fully in the film's major group of images. When Verloc goes to meet his employer at the aquarium of the Regent's Park Zoo, he is upbraided for the failure of the blackout to inspire public unrest. ("London Laughs," reads one newspaper headline.) As Verloc and the other man stand talking in front of a tank of giant sea turtles, the turtles seem both threatening and powerless, like Verloc himself, the would-be saboteur whose wrist is being slapped. The image of creatures simultaneously helpless and threatening returns powerfully later, when the bomb arrives at Verloc's home in a birdcage with a note reading, "DON'T FORGET THE BIRDS WILL SING AT 1:45."

Birds provide a new image of helpless violence first presented at the establishment of A. F. Chatman, the shopkeeper whose storefront is a pet shop and whose back room "other department" a bomb factory. Hitchcock first shows Chatman attempting to placate a customer who complains that the canary she bought from him will not sing. Chatman whistles to the bird, provoking a chorus of answering tweets from all over the store, though the customer remains skeptical. When Chatman repeats the performance and admonishes her to whistle to the bird at home, she replies: "Me whistle? Perhaps you'd like me to sit in the cage and him do the housework." This comic scene, which underlines the problematic nature of responsibility (which bird is doing the singing?) and the interchangeability of people and birds, ends with another image of lethal irresponsibility, when Chatman, having almost knocked a dangerous explosive off a high shelf, tells his granddaughter to "slap Grandpa hard," just as Verloc had been chastised earlier for his bad behavior.

The connection between birds and people as helpless agents of violence, once established, runs through the rest of the film, linking Verloc's impotence to Stevie's childish carelessness. Unable to leave his house because it is surrounded by suspicious policemen, Verloc watches the birds Chatman has sent with a clear sense of their analogy to himself, helplessly caged creatures who will be destroyed unless he can send the bomb with someone else. In asking Stevie to deliver the bomb, however, Verloc confirms Stevie's own identification with birds, which was established in an earlier scene which began with a shot of him feeding pigeons on the street and proceeded to Simpson's, where he and his sister were in turn fed by Ted. Later, Hitchcock places the back of a chair in the center foreground of several shots of the Verlocs' sitting room, re-creating the suggestion of prison bars he had used in one interior shot in the crofter's cottage in *The 39 Steps,* with the additional visual overtone here of the bars of a cage. Finally, he cuts the climactic scene in which Mrs. Verloc kills her husband in a way that heightens its moral ambiguity. Throughout the scene Mrs. Verloc seems an unwilling murderer, terrified of touching the knife she will use, and Verloc himself, as he realizes his danger, becomes as threatening as she is. She does not grab the knife until he makes a move for it; she stabs him below the bottom line of the frame, so that viewers cannot see her hand strike the blow; and as he begins to fall, she tries to hold him up.

All these images of passive agents and murderous victims undermine the moral framework—the assumption that people can choose how to act and, in choosing, define their own identities—in much the same way Hitchcock had explored the problematic nature of action through the figure of the secret agent Ashenden. But the films' revulsion from their heroes' unwilling implication in killing overpowers and eventually chastises their sense of play. The scene in which Elsa, having forgiven Ashenden his part in Caypor's murder, laughingly prepares to go off with him in *Secret Agent* is answered in *Sabotage* by the scene in which Mrs. Verloc, having stumbled through the streets seeing Stevie's face repeatedly appear in the middle of crowds, goes into her husband's movie theater and is briefly distracted by the Disney cartoon "Who Killed Cock Robin?" Responding to Cock Robin's antics as he serenades a bird voiced by Mae West, she begins to smile and laugh; but when Cock Robin is killed by an arrow, the parallel between this last bird and Stevie overwhelms her with grief, and she goes into the dinner she still does not know will end with her killing her husband in a final murderous game. In both films the form of the game is preserved only to heighten the irony of its fatal consequences.

Throughout the Gaumont films, Hitchcock's wit characteristically operates as a basis for the audience's intimacy with the world of the film —an intimacy most often figured by the metaphor of games. Whether their principals are players whose innocent games drop them into the middle of nightmarish intrigues, as in *The Man Who Knew Too Much*, or who treat the intrigues in which they are caught as games, as in *Secret Agent*, these films are organized around ludic figures which repeatedly cast menace and enmity as games. In *The 39 Steps, Young and Innocent*, and *The Lady Vanishes*, these games proceed to a happy ending; in the other films they are variously and ironically complicated.

In his romantic comedies at Gaumont—*The 39 Steps, Young and Innocent*, and *The Lady Vanishes*—Hitchcock uses games to domesticate his characters' conflicts and defuse the threats they face, containing potentially disturbing conflicts within a framework that reassures the audience that the heroine and hero will eventually resolve their differences and be reintegrated into the society from which they have become estranged, and allowing viewers to enjoy the thrills of conflict while protecting them from deeper anxieties. Already in *The Man Who Knew Too Much*, however, he had used games more subversively, to link the normal rituals of the Lawrences' family conflicts (the assumed domestic intrigue between Bob and Jill, the disruptions of Betty's childish behavior) and the monstrous threats of the conspirators, and to establish a narrative convention of rapidly shifting tones which gave no reassurance about his story's direction or outcome. *Secret Agent* and *Sabotage,* which show the fatal consequences of game-playing, return to the punitive mode of *The Lodger* and *Blackmail;* their distinctly less comic mode is less subversive than the shifting mode of *The Man Who Knew Too Much* precisely because it is signaled so much more clearly in advance.

The myth of the ludic metaphor, that conflict is cooperative, amusing, and rewarding, governs the relationship between Hitchcock and his audience throughout these films. The range of the characters' reactions, from the nervous tittering of Bob and Clive in the Tabernacle of the Sun to the horror and self-loathing of Ashenden and Elsa after Caypor's death to the growing trust and respect of Iris and Gilbert as they search for Miss Froy, reflects the range of relations between Hitchcock and his audiences. The films themselves are organized as games which establish a relationship between director and audience at once adversarial and cooperative. Just as it is fun, despite the danger, for Hannay to trade places with the milkman and run from the police, it is fun for audiences to allow themselves to be manipulated by the film, whose cinematic exposition offers constant challenges to their attention and rewards them with a sense of community and complicity if they are able to follow the story. In his earlier films, Hitchcock made it fun to follow particular scenes because of his innovative storytelling techniques. In the series beginning with *The Man Who Knew Too Much,* he makes it fun to follow the story as a whole by encouraging closer identification with the principals as well. Although all Hitchcock's pursued or lethally active innocents, however impressive their panache, play on the audience's innate paranoia, the thrillers of the late thirties manage to turn that paranoia into exhilaration by the suggestion—subversive in *The Man Who Knew Too Much,* romantic in *The 39 Steps, Young and Innocent,* and *The Lady Vanishes,* ironic in *Secret Agent* and *Sabotage*—that everyone among the characters and audience needs to learn to play.

# FOUR

## ODD

## MAN

## OUT

By 1939, audiences everywhere were familiar with the rules of the Hitchcock game. Hitchcock's films were fast-paced thrillers whose velocity, brio, and wit constantly kept his audience pleasurably off-balance, uncertain what to expect but certain that each film would move from grave to gay with variously amusing or disconcerting, but always piquant, results. Each film worked like a game between director and audience, challenging the audience by the means Hitchcock found to relate his story, so that following the story automatically implicated the audience in the game and insured the pleasure the film had contracted to deliver.

But by 1939 Hitchcock was already changing the rules of that contract—a transformation signalled, appropriately enough, by the signing of another contract the previous June with the Hollywood producer David O. Selznick. In March 1939 Hitchcock left England for America. His departure had an immediate impact on his filmmaking which has typically been ascribed to the influence of Selznick and Hollywood conventions generally. Ironically, the wit that had been the hallmark of the Gaumont-British films disappeared immediately and almost completely upon Hitchcock's arrival in America. Instead, Hitchcock's forties films are longer than his British films, more slowly paced, more expensively mounted, with more impressive set-pieces and a greater psychological weight, an emphasis away from particular situations toward the characters who are placed in those situations, and a corresponding lack of interest in the kinds of play with the audience suggested by the games so prominent in the thrillers since *The Man Who Knew Too Much*. The forties films take themselves far more seriously than Hitchcock's earlier work, especially his Gaumont-British thrillers, as stories.

There is no doubt that working with the technical resources of Hollywood studios, especially for Selznick, whose tradition of quality culminated in *Gone With the Wind*, played an important role in changing Hitchcock's approach to filmmaking and his relation to his audience. Just as working in Hollywood had a decisive impact on the films of such émigré directors as Murnau, Lang, Lubitsch, and Renoir, the resources of mammoth American studios and the tight control of studio chiefs were bound to change the nature of Hitchcock's games.[1] The wealth of published material on the production history of *Rebecca* makes it clear that Hitchcock first approached the project as another exercise in mixing grave and gay—beginning, for example, with a scene in which the hero enlivens a sailing trip on the Riviera by making his fellow-passengers violently ill.[2] In refusing to tolerate such whimsical departures from Daphne Du Maurier's best-selling novel and demanding a new, more faithful treatment, Selznick set the tone for Hitchcock's first decade in Hollywood.

Not all the changes in Hitchcock's forties films can be attributed to Selznick alone, since he produced only three of Hitchcock's American films—*Rebecca, Spellbound,* and *The Paradine Case;* all Hitchcock's other films of the period—*Foreign Correspondent, Mr. and Mrs. Smith, Suspicion, Saboteur, Shadow of a Doubt, Lifeboat,* and *Notorious*—were made for other studios to which Selznick had loaned Hitchcock. But all these films share so many characteristics, breaking in such similar ways with the pleasure contract of the Gaumont films and offering such a consistent new contract, that the period from *Rebecca* to *The Paradine Case,* the last time Hitchcock worked for any producer besides himself, might just as well be called Hitchcock's Selznick period.

As the series of films beginning with *The Man Who Knew Too Much* illustrates, Hitchcock's games had already relied from the beginning on the promise of disruption within a conventional contract. The Gaumont films all use witty, sometimes shocking surprises to sharpen or undermine the force of their conventional promises; the promise of surprise, even outrage, is as important to them as their more reassuring promises. Hitchcock's games are always ripe with the promise of change; if that change had not come at the hands of the American studio system, it would have come from somewhere else, since Hitchcock's games cannot be sustained without periodically cheating against their own rules. Indeed a primary sign of this revisionary cheating in Hitchcock's American films, rooted presumably in Hitchcock's impending departure for America, appears while he is still working in England: the emergence of a new fascination with homelessness and exile. In each film he directed through *The Paradine Case*, Hitchcock focuses on homeless principals, exiles from nowhere, people who can't go home again, or homebodies whose homes turn into traps and prisons. Like the director himself, the principals of his first American films are alienated from their homes; their films are skeptical about the values associated with home and finally about the very possibility of a stable home.

This shift produces new challenges for Hitchcock's audience as well as his characters, for it deprives the audience of the stability and security provided by the sense of home. The homelessness of Hitchcock's heroes calls into question the sense of personal identity that might be based on one's home, leading in turn to a breakdown of social or genetic conceptions of the self and defining Hitchcock's heroes by pairing them with enigmatic or malignant doubles and finally to a paranoid suspicion of family ties. In changing the rules of his game so dramatically, Hitchcock imperils the pleasures of witty exposition and high-spirited play the Gaumont films had offered, substituting the promise of new kinds of fun: the pleasures of close identification with a sympathetic principal, of dramatic pathos, of the illumination offered by psychological perspectives, and of the equivocal challenges posed by the principals' subversive doubles, who appear with startling frequency in the films of this period. Hitchcock's doubles pointedly illustrate the characteristically duplicitous pleasures of his forties films, since they endanger the heroes' and heroines' sense of security in their own homes and identi-

ties while promising the intoxication of exciting plot developments. The
films typically isolate their leading characters—and, through the identifications they encourage, their audience—from their sense of themselves
as self-controlled agents with a secure home in a social community as
completely yet as entertainingly as in a game of odd man out—a very
different kind of entertainment from that offered by the whirling tonal
modulations of the Gaumont films, but still a game after all.

*Rebecca,* the film which launched Hitchcock's American career, presents in its central figure the paradigm of the homeless hero: a heroine
without a family, a home, a place in the social order, or even a name.
*Rebecca* has often been called a British film because most of it takes place
in England and most of the actors are British. But it would be equally
true to call the immediately preceding film, *Jamaica Inn,* Hitchcock's first
American film for several reasons. Although the film was set and shot in
England for Erich Pommer's Mayflower Productions, it has less in common with the series of thrillers since 1934 than with Hitchcock's early
American films; it is more slowly paced, elaborately staged, and nearly
humorless. Hitchcock's critics have agreed with the director himself that
his having by this time signed a contract with Selznick prevented him
from taking much interest in the picture, but in one respect it is mark-
edly original: it is the first of Hitchcock's films to take homelessness as
its subject, and so looks forward not only to his following film, *Rebecca,*
also based on a Daphne Du Maurier novel about a homeless heroine, but
to the whole series of films which followed.

The world of *Jamaica Inn* is based on the systematic perversion of
hospitality, a condition announced in the film's opening shot of a manuscript page which begins, "O Lord, we pray thee not that wrecks should
happen—but if they do happen, guide them to the coast of Cornwall."
Hitchcock's villains are a gang of Cornishmen who get information about
when ships will pass, put out their beacon light, causing the ships to
crash, and then slaughter the survivors. This perversion of hospitality
is picked up in the two homes shown in the film, the rough tavern of
Joss Merlyn (Leslie Banks), leader of the gang, and the estate of the
local magistrate, Sir Humphrey Pengallan (Charles Laughton), its secret
head and informant. The arrival, immediately after the opening wreck,
of Mary Yellan (Maureen O'Hara), the orphaned niece of Merlyn's wife

Patience (Marie Ney), reveals the inadequacies of these two homes and emphasizes their systematic opposition. When the coachman carrying her refuses to stop near Jamaica Inn for fear of highwaymen, she walks instead to Squire Pengallan's, thereafter oscillating between the homes of Merlyn and Pengallan and the domination of these two men for the rest of the film.

Merlyn's home is clearly no place for Mary. On her arrival there, he demands to know her business, asks for a kiss, and only then reveals that he is the uncle she is seeking. His gang torments Mary by threatening her, insulting her sexually, and later pursuing her after she has freed their colleague Jem Trehearne (Robert Newton) from hanging and escaped with him. The contradictory attitude of the gang toward women is indicated by Merlyn's refusing to let Mary carry her own luggage box but insisting that Patience carry it instead.[3] Since women in Merlyn's world are both more and less than ordinary people, it is impossible for Mary to find a home there or a community that accepts her.

Throughout the film, the brutish world of Merlyn's seaside den is set against the ordered, cultivated world of Pengallan's home. Merlyn's house is rough, dark, noisy, crowded, and disordered; Pengallan's is polished, bright, quiet, and as well-ordered as the compass rose on the floor of his front hall. The contrasts are especially striking in a series of crosscuts between Mary's and Jem's escape from a cave to the rocky sea and the magistrate's court at Pengallan's. When Merlyn appears in Pengallan's house, Pengallan demands, "How dare you come here to me?" When Pengallan comes to Merlyn's, he too is out of place. On his first visit, he must sneak down the back stairs to escape detection. On his second, he must pretend to Jem, who has revealed himself as an officer of the law, that he wants to arrest the criminals and at the same time reassure Joss that he has not betrayed him. On his third, he shoots Aunt Patience, watches Merlyn die of his wounds, and kidnaps Mary, gagging and binding her as he expresses solicitude for her loss and reminds her of her dependence on him: "You're all alone now. You have no one but me."

Raymond Durgnat and others have pointed out the perversity of this scene, but no one has observed how logically it follows from everything that preceded it and how perfectly it encapsulates the nature of Mary's homelessness throughout the film.[4] Pengallan has been established from early on as a man who cares more for objects than people (he tells one of his guests, "That statue's more alive than half the people here"), more for women than men (he is first described to Mary as "partial to young women," and he tells Merlyn, "I'd transport all the riffraff in Bristol to Botany Bay to save one beautiful woman a headache"), and more for himself than anything. Pengallan's veneer of culture, though it seems to offer a contrast to Merlyn's brutishness, is only a mask and a pretext for his own brutality, as he shows when he introduces a horse into a dinner party and tells Mary that he shot her aunt because "she was going to tell you about me. I didn't like that; I wanted to tell you myself." Although Mary tells her uncle that "Sir Humphrey . . . knows how to behave to a woman," it becomes clear that Pengallan's refinement is a refinement of appetite, and that his rituals of hospitality are a prelude to possessing Mary himself. In short, he is simply a more plausible version of the men of Merlyn's gang, who use the forms of courtesy in order to demean Mary sexually.[5]

After showing Mary homeless at the beginning and offering her the choice between two false homes—and it is her attempt to be loyal to both homes, to her loyalties to both her aunt and the law she thinks Pengallan represents, that produces the catastrophe—the film provides her with a happy ending in the form of a romantic union with Jem Trehearne. But the film's closing minutes emphasize not Mary's restoration to Jem, but her rescue from Pengallan (who was attempting to take her to still another foreign land) and Pengallan's theatrical death (he jumps from the mast of a ship after announcing to the crowd below, "Tell your children how the great age ended!"). Presumably Jem, who mediates between the coarse brutality of Merlyn's gang and the refined brutality of Pengallan by loving and respecting Mary, will offer her a home more truly hers than anything she has seen so far. But only the conventions of romantic melodrama encourage this belief, because the film has so little interest in establishing Jem's love for Mary or in rooting him in any more stable sense of home. The film emphasizes Mary's peril rather than her eventual rescue because Hitchcock, as usual, is more interested in the narrative exposition of Mary's homelessness than in either rooting that homelessness in her personality or resolving the problems her situation raises. Since the juvenile leads are the least interesting or personable characters in the film, perversions of the home they might make become more interesting than that home itself. The audience can take pleasure in exploring these perversions with only the most perfunctory sketch of a happy ending because the conventions of romantic melodrama themselves imply such an ending so broadly from the moment Mary first rescues Jem.

The fun of *Jamaica Inn* comes from seeing Mary gradually isolated from both the homes she depends on while cherishing the certainty that the hero—or more properly the formal conventions of the plot—will rescue her from an alienation that would otherwise be deeply disturbing. In *Rebecca* Hitchcock works more subversively to make the exposition of alienation amusing on its own terms. Instead of enjoying a sense of homelessness that will surely be only temporary, the audience is invited to entertain the radically equivocal fantasy of gothic romance: that the murderous pursuer and the loving rescuer are the same.[6] Hitchcock's attitude toward the alienated heroine of his first American film seems far more gratuitously sadistic than his attitude toward Mary Yellan because throughout *Rebecca* he offers so much less assurance that the fantasy will have a happy ending. The audience enjoying the spectacle of the heroine's abasement and loneliness is subtly invited to take sides against the very figure its members are identifying with.

The first thing *Rebecca* says about the heroine, in a voice-over passage based on the opening chapter of Du Maurier's novel, is that she has no home: "Last night I dreamt I went to Manderley again. . . . We can never go back to Manderley again"—though this passage, unlike Du Maurier's, does not make it clear that the reason we can never go back is because "Manderley was no more"; it simply establishes the heroine's inability to return to her home.[7] As the story reveals, the heroine (Joan Fontaine) is homeless in other ways as well. Her mother has died many years ago, her father the summer before the story begins; she serves as a companion to the snobbish Mrs. Van Hopper (Florence Bates), who spends her time touring Europe, and whose constant complaining and petty tyrannies provide a perfect contrast to Hitchcock's earlier homes away from homes. The story begins when the heroine first sees Maxim de Winter (Laurence Olivier) staring down over the edge of a cliff in Monte Carlo, apparently about to jump. Although the hero and heroine seem to have nothing in common, they are actually well-matched, because de Winter is also homeless. He describes Manderley as "just the place where I was born and spent my whole life. Now I don't suppose I shall ever see it again." Even though Mrs. Van Hopper insists that "if I had a home like Manderley, I should never come to Monte," de Winter's memories, which he calls "demons," prevent him from returning home.

The heroine's romantic attachment to de Winter, which takes the form of a series of excursions during which he speaks to her often with kindness, but never with love or respect or reassurance, makes her relatively stable position with Mrs. Van Hopper impossible. When the exiled hero finally proposes marriage to the homeless heroine—just as Mrs. Van Hopper is about to take her away to New York—he frames his proposal in terms of an offer to take her to Manderley—"Which would you prefer, New York or Manderley?"—as he stands offscreen. Even though what he is offering is a home which should offer her security and stability, these qualities are precisely what their relationship lacks; they are never framed together in repose throughout the entire film.

Mrs. Van Hopper indicates the reason for the heroine's future discomfort when she receives the news of de Winter's proposal with condescending incredulity: "Mrs. de Winter indeed!" Can the heroine really take the place of Rebecca de Winter, who drowned a year before, and to whom de Winter is apparently obsessively attached? The first two-thirds of the film are a catalog of the ways she cannot. Everyone, including herself, considers her a visitor, a child, and a prisoner who is unequal to the demands of her home, its staff, and her place as the second Mrs. de Winter. De Winter and her in-laws, the Laceys, repeatedly refer to her as a child, and she acts like a child in her awe of the house and its servants, especially the housekeeper Mrs. Danvers (Judith Anderson). When she accidentally breaks a statue of Cupid, she hides the pieces in a drawer, just as young Stevie had done with the broken plate in *Sabotage,* and when she confesses the accident to de Winter, he tells Mrs. Danvers that his wife "was afraid you were going to put her in prison."

But Manderley is already a prison, as Hitchcock's visuals make clear. His camera lingers more often on large public rooms and spaces—the corridor connecting the east and west wings, the banquet hall, the formal staircase—than on the more intimate rooms which would not so completely dominate his heroine. The first shot of the newlyweds eating dinner together begins as a close-up of a napkin embroidered "R de W" before the camera cranes slowly around, up, and back along the length of the table to a point which dwarfs both living de Winters and emphasizes the space between them.[8] The only bedroom the camera lingers on is Rebecca's own, which has the character of a museum or another public place. Mrs. Danvers shows the heroine not only the view of the sea from its enormous windows but also Rebecca's clothes and furs, even the chair she used to sit in when she came in from parties, as if displaying sacred mysteries to the uninitiate. The heroine, who ought logically to feel that Manderley is her home, thus constantly feels that she is an intruder in the home of the dead Rebecca. Even the sinister Jack Favell (George Sanders), whom she overhears talking to Mrs. Danvers and then sees looking in through a window, makes her feel like an interloper.

It is shortly after she meets Favell, while de Winter is away in London and just after Mrs. Danvers has shown her Rebecca's room, that the heroine begins to assert herself by discarding the monogrammed stationery, telling Mrs. Danvers that she is Mrs. de Winter now, and asking her husband if they can have a costume party of the sort she has heard used to be given at Manderley. But following Mrs. Danvers's suggestion that she dress in the costume of one of the paintings in the hall, a painting of one of de Winter's ancestors, the heroine unwittingly poses for the last time as Rebecca, copying the dress she wore at the last ball given at Manderley. De Winter, shocked and furious, orders her upstairs to change.

The party's sequel, in which a ship run ashore proves to be carrying Rebecca's body below decks, explains de Winter's agitation. He had put the body there himself after a quarrel which led to Rebecca's accidental death, the last of many such quarrels, since the two of them secretly detested each other. (In Du Maurier's novel, he had shot her to death.) Evidently the woman whom the heroine has associated so persistently with de Winter's home and her own hopes of home was herself only an interloper whose spell can now be exorcised, and although de Winter cannot offer his wife the stability of a home, she offers him a haven from his guilt through their relationship, not through their relation to any particular place.[9] The substitution of a romantic pairing for the stability of a homesite, a staple of romantic comedy since Shakespeare, will become a leading motif in virtually all the Selznick films. *Rebecca* develops this pattern first by de Winter's narrative of that last night, which is accompanied by a tracking shot which inscribes Rebecca's absence as a defining feature of his home, and later by a sequence during the inquest on Rebecca, when shots of de Winter, irritated and progressively losing the coroner's sympathy, are intercut with tighter and tighter close-ups showing his wife's anxiety for him, until her faint seems a defensive weapon to prevent him from making matters worse. On the whole, however, the news that Rebecca was a monster, though it brings the de Winters closer together, does not allow them the luxury of a home because it simply defines homelessness as the normal human condition. The woman de Winter had deliberately misidentified as Rebecca the previous year was "some unknown woman, unclaimed, belonging nowhere"; the heroine wonders why the divers who found Rebecca's boat "couldn't . . . have left it there—at the bottom of the sea," especially as Rebecca's affinity for the sea has been a leading motif of the film. But the sea is no home for Rebecca living or dead, since it is eternally in motion and keeps bringing everything to the surface. Only the fire Mrs. Danvers sets can fix Rebecca's identity by destroying Manderley for good.

This destruction, however, only confirms the rule of homelessness. Rebecca will now be eternally misremembered, de Winter separated from his ancestral home, and the heroine without any home at all. Although the de Winters are finally united, Hitchcock seems less interested in ensuring their happiness than in emphasizing their permanent alienation from the home on which both of them have repeatedly and unsuccessfully attempted to base their identities.[10] His ending resolves the film's plot without abating the tension generated by the problem of homelessness. Far more subversively than *Jamaica Inn, Rebecca* invites the audience to savor the exposition of a homelessness that can never truly be resolved.

*Rebecca* illustrates the intimate connection between Hitchcock's preoccupation with homelessness and his conception of personal identity as a problem to be resolved. His concentration on this problem is unprecedented because his earlier films, although many of them consider it in some way, all tend to keep it at arm's length, on the fringes of the set-pieces or games that provide these films' principal pleasure. The pleasure audiences took in Hitchcock's British films depended primarily on the unexpected ways in which they manipulated and satisfied the storytelling requirements of the cinema. In his Selznick films, by contrast, the audience's pleasure depends on a much closer identification with the principals; when Hitchcock works to complicate or undermine the audience's reponse to his fictive situations, he works within his stories, emphasizing the mysterious nature of his heroes' and heroines' identities most pointedly by depriving them of their homes or creating mysterious doubles to challenge their sense of themselves, rather than by disrupting the diegesis itself, as he had done so persistently in the films that followed *The Man Who Knew Too Much*. It is in this sense that the Selznick films are Hitchcock's most homogeneous and least formally adventurous, for virtually all their complications operate within the diegesis, not in the director's play with the discourse. For this reason, too, the identifications the Selznick films urge on the audience are more powerfully straightforward than the identifications in any of Hitchcock's other films: the relationship between Hitchcock and the audience is represented more clearly than at any other time by the characters' own evolving perceptions of themselves.

Human identity in Hitchcock's American films, beginning with *Rebecca,* is conceived in terms of a conflict between one's perceptions of oneself and one's perception by other people. The heroes and heroines of these films think of themselves as having a stable, knowable, rational identity but are caught up in events which lead others to impute an incompatible identity to them; the function of the plot is to generate the conflict which calls their identities into question and to resolve it by mediating between the claims of their private and public selves. Hitchcock's earlier films contain obvious portents of this conflict. In *The 39 Steps* and *Young and Innocent,* the police impute a criminal identity to a hero who knows himself to be innocent. *The Lodger* and *Blackmail* explore in greater depth the incongruity between private and public selves in terms of guilt and innocence: the lodger is more innocent than he looks (though there is no sign until nearly the end of the film that he is aware of how guilty he looks, or of how he looks at all), and Alice White is more guilty. *Easy Virtue* considers the difficulty of attempting to maintain one's conception of oneself in the face of unanimous public ostracism; *Secret Agent* and *Sabotage* examine the banal private lives of government agents and government informers; *The Man Who Knew Too Much* is a virtual catalog of the ways private lives and public actions can influence each other; and *Murder!* uses the theater as a metaphor for the net of deceptions involved in constructing any public identity whatsoever.

Of all the British films, however, the one which most clearly integrates the problem of identity with the sort of plot characteristic of Hitchcock's work, and therefore the film which most clearly looks forward to his later work, is *The Lady Vanishes,* a film ostensibly organized around the figure of its eponymous lady and focusing on the questions of what has happened to Miss Froy and what sort of person Miss Froy is but actually organized around another figure, its heroine Iris Henderson. When Iris insists in the face of mounting opposition, first that Miss Froy was indeed on the train, and later that the woman produced as Miss Froy is an imposter, the pivotal question of the film becomes whether Iris, who was knocked on the head just before boarding the train from which Miss Froy vanished, can vindicate her perceptions and indeed her sanity by convincing her fellow passengers to look for Miss Froy. Each of these passengers has reasons for ignoring Iris: the lawyer and his mistress because they do not want to be found out, the two Englishmen because they do not want to make a fuss which might delay the train, the political conspirators because they are conspirators. Only the musician Gilbert, after duly expressing skepticism, accepts Iris's story and thereby her account of herself, helps her find Miss Froy, and proves himself a suitable mate for her. As in *The 39 Steps* and *Young and Innocent,* the film ends with a reassuring triumph of the private self over an oppressive and mistaken court of public opinion. But this triumph has been portended from the beginning by the sunny tone of the prologue at the inn, which even the murder of the singer does little to darken. This sequence establishes the comic basis of the film securely, and even when Iris is later ready to doubt her own sanity, Hitchcock reassures the audience with shots of the cricket fans and the unmarried couple acknowledging Miss Froy's existence to themselves. All these signals frame the story of Iris's alienation comically, promising a satisfying resolution.

Hitchcock's forties films are seldom able to provide such clear-cut and affirmative portents of resolution because their conception of identity is more problematic. The police are seldom simply mistaken, as they are in *The 39 Steps* and *Young and Innocent;* characters like Maxim de Winter in *Rebecca* and Charlie Newton in *Shadow of a Doubt* really do have something to hide. The private self is less solid and confident than in the British films, and the claims of public identity more pressing. *Rebecca* indicates the ways in which identity becomes more tenuous and problematic because of the weakening of the private self's primary source of power, stablity, and renewal: the home which first fosters the idea of a self apart from the opinion of others. The principals of Hitchcock's forties films are for the most part heroes without homes, men and women deprived or estranged from the homes, and often the ideas of home, that would enforce their own ideas of themselves.

The absence of homes has several obvious visual implications for Hitchcock's forties films. In *The Lodger,* the Buntings' home is frequently represented or introduced by the same shot of their basement kitchen, looking across the room toward the iron staircase outside. The shot provides an unmarked or zero-degree representation of the world into which the lodger has come. In Hitchcock's American films, however, there are no such unmarked shots because home as either a place or a sense of stability is not something that can be taken for granted; the hero's identity is always under examination, precluding even the temporary retreat of Erica Burgoyne into her father's house in *Young and Innocent* or Alice White back to her family's home in *Blackmail.*

Hitchcock's critics have often noted his relative lack of interest in the close observation of social reality in his later films.[11] But the displacement of the sharply observed interiors of *The 39 Steps* and *Sabotage* by the classless worlds of *Spellbound* and *Torn Curtain* does not simply indicate snobbery or withdrawal from social reality, but more fundamentally a loss of the conviction that characters can define stable identities within a given social context. Like the later work of Ibsen and Henry James, Hitchcock's American films dramatize their principals' psychological conflicts in terms of symbols and formal conventions rather than social minutiae. In later films like *Vertigo* and *North by Northwest,* the plot dictates its own world and confers on the hero an identity with which he must come to terms; in forties films like *Spellbound* the principals move from one set of handsome, nondescript rooms to the next without ever finding an environment which will confirm their sense of themselves. When the environment is important, as in the long shots of the tiny crowd surging through the huge doors in the aircraft assembly plant at the beginning of *Saboteur* or in every shot of *Lifeboat,* it pointedly fails to provide any stable context for the characters' conceptions of themselves. No matter where they go, most of these characters remain homeless.

It is hardly surprising that Hitchcock, himself an exile during this period, should make his heroes and heroines exiles.[12] This development, coupled with his long-established interest in stories involving innocence and guilt, releases a question which will overshadow all his later work: How is it possible for the hero or heroine deprived of the reassurance of a stable home to conceive an identity which would be confirmed by an essentially hostile world? For a time this question, by far the most ambitious theme Hitchcock had considered, threatens to overpower his work; films like *Suspicion, Spellbound,* and *Under Capricorn* labor under its burden without resolving or even fully articulating it. For this reason the forties are for Hitchcock an uneven period, a time of exploration rather than mastery.

In Hitchcock's British films, the hero's or heroine's home is taken for granted as a source of identity in the genetic sense popularized by Alex Haley's *Roots.* Home is a stable resting place for the heroes and heroines, a repository of moral value which provides them with an unmarked identity, an identity which can be assumed instead of having to be resolved. When Roddy Berwick, unfairly accused of seducing a waitress, leaves his family's home in *Downhill,* he enters what an intertitle calls "the world of make-believe," and his return to home and forgiveness at the end of the film is nothing less than a return to his true identity. In *The Manxman,* Hitchcock reserves his most emphatic pathos for Pete's desolation at finding his home shattered and for Philip's and Kate's final departure from their home. The Buntings' home in *The Lodger,* the Whites' home in *Blackmail,* and the Kendalls' home in *Rich and Strange* all provide a similar sense of rootedness and stability for their principals. When the heroes of *Downhill, Champagne,* and *Rich and Strange* leave home deliberately, they are marked for misadventures and can only hope for a return to the stability they left behind. The greatest menace in the British films comes from threats to the home, for instance by Ivor Novello's lodger or Tracy's blackmailer; and one reason that *Sabotage* is the grimmest of the British films is that the Verlocs' home does not embody any of the values normally associated with home: Verloc's movie theater is only a front for a nest of provocateurs, Mrs. Verloc is an American who has never become completely at ease in London, and the tension among the Verlocs, which is felt most acutely in the domestic scenes in their rooms, leads them to murder. In a more typically transitory threat to domestic values, Erica Burgoyne's only moment of real unhappiness in *Young and Innocent* comes when she feels alienated from her father in their home, and the secret arrival of Robert Tisdall outside her bedroom window a few moments later signals a conventionally romantic threat to Colonel Burgoyne's home. The film appropriately ends with a shot of Erica framed between the two men she loves, joined to her lover without having to give up her father's home.

Hitchcock's heroes are often shown separated from their homes in the Gaumont-British films. But their sense of homelessness is typically defused by providing a substitute home within which life can go on normally. In *Secret Agent* the Ashendens' hotel is defined as their home base, a setting exempt from danger and characterized by a tone of domestic comedy. Even the Caypors' home is a place of safety and security, from which Caypor must be lured by the General. *The Lady Vanishes* similarly uses its hotel as a stable point of departure for its principals' adventures and its heroine's conception of herself. Although the hotel is overcrowded, the only people who are shown unaccommodated are the two Englishmen, and their discomfort at having to share the maid's room is treated as a joke. Iris, who is installed as queen of the hotel in the opening scene, finds her sleep and her privacy comically threatened by Gilbert as a rehearsal to the far more serious threats to her testimony and her sanity aboard the train, where all the conspirators make their first appearance. Even when the principals are far from home, there is usually a home away from home at their disposal; the danger is simply transferred to departing from this surrogate home, which anchors the reassurances of pleasure the earlier films had anchored in home itself.

The situation is more complex in *The Man Who Knew Too Much* and

*The 39 Steps.* In the former, the stability of the Lawrences' home is shattered by the abduction of their daughter, so that they seem out of their
element for the rest of the film. Bob Lawrence's inability to speak German in Saint Moritz suddenly becomes urgently important; Hitchcock
treats not only Switzerland but the London neighborhood of Wapping
as a foreign landscape; and the harmony of the Lawrences' home life is
disrupted by the arrival of the police, who cross-examine them about
their daughter. Only the recovery of Betty in the last shot of the film
can restore the Lawrences to the domestic stability they had begun by
taking for granted. *The 39 Steps,* by contrast, presents a hero pointedly
without a home, takes him through a series of parodies of home life,
and provides him with a happy ending independent of any home at all.
Hannay is established in the opening scene as a Canadian who is staying temporarily in London. His flat, with its sheet-covered furniture and
expressionistic lighting, is the opposite of homey; even the placard outside the door is temporary. After Hannay leaves London, he travels to
the crofter's cottage, where a grim placidity barely conceals the conflict
between the crofter and his wife; to Professor Jordan's home, where the
professor's wife entertains luncheon guests while he shoots his latest arrival; and to an inn where he and Pamela pose as young lovers without
revealing that they are handcuffed together. This last version of home,
however, establishes both a resolution to the film's tension—Hannay
will never be in serious danger after this—and a ludic figure for his relationship with Pamela, since all their behavior, private as well as public,
is perfectly consonant with their being romantically attached to each
other. If the episode begins as a parody of domestic life because of the
handcuffs, it ends by suggesting that handcuffing lovers together is as
reasonable as any other away of getting them acquainted.[13]

The difference between Hitchcock's interest in the comedy of homelessness in *The 39 Steps* and the pathos of homelessness in the forties
films is indicated by the departure scenes in *The 39 Steps* and two later
films which use essentially the same plot: *Saboteur* and *North by Northwest.* All three films depend on the heroes' estrangement from their
homes, but the three estrangements are treated very differently. In *The
39 Steps,* Hannay's homelessness is so complete—he is forced from a flat
which did not seem like his home in the first place—that it is paradoxi-

cally prevented from becoming an issue; the audience perceives Hannay as a man on the run, but not particularly as a man alienated from his home, for he has no home to lose, no stable past identity to be called into question by the police.[14] In *North by Northwest,* Roger Thornhill's home, which is never seen, is instead incarnated in his mother, and his departure from her, and from the Manhattan crowds in which he has been used to operating, is treated comically. (As he dashes out of the elevator in which he has been confined with a crowd including her and two murderous thugs, she calls after him, "Roger! Will you be home for dinner?") Only in *Saboteur* is the departure of the hero treated as a true alienation, a serious estrangement from a source of moral value and genetic identity. The farewell scene of Barry Kane (Robert Cummings) is played not with his own mother but with the mother of Ken Mason, the friend Barry is accused of having killed. The Mason home is presented in only a few shots, a straightaway long shot isolating it from other houses nearby (a shot Hitchcock echoes in showing the Hubermans' house in *Notorious*) and a few interior two-shots which have room for only a few background details, most of them (e.g., the framed picture near the front door, the unlit candles on the dinner table) emphasizing Ken's absence. Even though Hitchcock reveals no more about Barry Kane than about Richard Hannay, his departure is presented as a wrenching loss not only of the stability of his home but of his assumption that others will accept his innocence, since Mrs. Mason, even though she does not give him up to the police, replies to his protestations of innocence with a weary "I don't know. . . . You'd better go." The danger the returning police represent to Barry is dramatized without any of the wit informing Hannay's escape from his flat disguised as a policeman or Thornhill's final telephone conversation with his mother; the pathos depends on the loss of home itself.

*Rebecca* is the seminal account of homelessness in Hitchcock's work because of its use of the theme to link the motifs of instability, alienation, and the loss of identity. But images of homelessness or estrangement from home abound in the films which follow. Even when the orphanhood of the principals is not stressed, as it is in *Jamaica Inn* and *Rebecca,* they are isolated from their homes, as in *Saboteur,* or in *Lifeboat,* in which the status of the characters aboard the boat is repeatedly set against their customary status in the world they have life behind—so that the wealthy C. J. Rittenhouse (Henry Hull) carries less weight than the proletarian Kovac (John Hodiak)—or in *Spellbound,* in which the hero's childhood memory of accidentally killing his brother is so traumatic that another fatality has led him into complete amnesia. Several of the forties films besides *Saboteur* contain scenes showing the principals' departure from homes to which they will not return. Hitchcock told Truffaut that his leading interest in *The Paradine Case* was reflected in the opening scene, in which the evening routine of the cultured Lady Paradine (Alida Valli) is interrupted when she is taken from her home by the police and arrested for her husband's murder.[15] And *Foreign Correspondent* is filled with departure motifs having little to do with the film's intrigue: the changing of the hero's name, in the opening scene, from Johnny Jones to Huntley Haverstock (creating a dissonance or doubleness for Joel McCrea's character that the film continues to insist on, even though he is one of Hitchcock's least problematic heroes); a scene aboard the ship at which the Jones family has gathered to say good-bye; and several episodes in which the hero loses the bowler hat that represents his new European identity.[16]

The homes that do appear in the forties films can never maintain their innocence for long. *Mr. and Mrs. Smith,* Hitchcock's atypical domestic comedy, is precisely a comedy of homelessness. David Smith (Robert Montgomery) and his wife Ann (Carole Lombard), though they are constantly fighting, have preserved their marriage by the simple expedient of agreeing never to leave their bedroom during a quarrel, even though this policy sometimes leads to week-long vigils. When David finds out about a legal flaw in his marriage to Ann, he plans to sleep with her before he tells he that they are not legally married, but she finds out anyway, locks him out of their apartment, and resumes her maiden name. The film thereupon gravitates away from the Smith, or Krausheimer, apartment, and over a range of locations including David's club (where the film emphasizes his humiliating need to take a room by repeated shots of the desk attendant taking down a key), a restaurant to which both David and Ann go with their dates, the office David shares with Jeff

Custer (Gene Raymond), who is pursuing Ann, a Ferris wheel on which Jeff and Ann are trapped, and finally a ski resort where David reclaims Ann by tricking her into taking him into her cabin.

A more serious critique of the home as a source of family identity is *Shadow of a Doubt,* in which the innocent world of Charlie Newton (Teresa Wright) and her family, focusing on their home in Santa Rosa, California, is gradually overshadowed by the news that her beloved Uncle Charlie (Joseph Cotten), who has come to stay with them, is fleeing from the police, who suspect him of being a murderer of rich widows. The film begins by setting up a contrast between the seedy boarding house in Philadelphia where Uncle Charlie has been staying and the wholesome, sunlit town of Santa Rosa, but defines this contrast in such schematic terms (e.g., Uncle Charlie and his niece are both first seen lying in bed, he facing left, she facing right) that the opposition is tantamount to an ironic equivalence. This opening sequence, which is not in the least funny, shows the new uses Hitchcock has found for the expository wit that marked his British thrillers; its point is now its mordant aptness rather than its velocity or its humor. Throughout the Selznick films, as in *Secret Agent* and *Sabotage,* Hitchcock will divorce wit repeatedly from humor.

Just as *Rebecca* turns on the relation between the two Mrs. de Winters, *Shadow of a Doubt* doubles the hypernormal teenager Charlie Newton with her psychopathic uncle by allowing him to invade and, in her eyes at least, gradually corrupt the world she has taken for granted. Hitchcock's uncharacteristic use of deep focus throughout the film, whose visuals seem strongly influenced by those of William Wyler's *The Little Foxes,*[17] begins by placing the Newton family in an unusually detailed visual field, gradually develops a greater interest in shadows (most notably in the shadow Charlie casts before her as Uncle Charlie, who has just heard the news that the police no longer suspect him, watches her from the top of the stairs), and ends by representing her home as a prison, so that as she frantically attempts to telephone the detective Jack Graham (Macdonald Carey), she is shown through the bannister as if through bars. She is correct in feeling her home to be a prison, for her initial sense of the confining limitations of her small-town milieu is ironically confirmed when Uncle Charlie turns the familiar accoutrements of home against her, trying to kill her by sabotaging a stair tread and locking her in the garage with the car's engine running. Home, which Charlie first considers stifling in its limitations, finally becomes useless even as a refuge from the world Uncle Charlie describes as "a foul sty," the world which Charlie must face in all its ugliness.[18]

Charlie begins by bewailing the constrictions of her family's sheltered life, gradually realizes that Uncle Charlie's challenge to the values of home and family is devastating, and finally feels trapped in her home by that very challenge. The conception of home as a trap, which receives its definitive statement years later in *Psycho,* first appears during Hitchcock's forties films. When Alice was threatened by Tracy in *Blackmail,* the most unpleasant image in the film showed the blackmailer making himself comfortable at the family table. But the family group itself still represented an inviolable system of values, a potential, albeit endangered, refuge from Tracy's threats. When Charlie discovers Uncle Charlie's secret in *Shadow of a Doubt,* she feels that not only her own safety but all her assumptions about her life, everything that her home and family represent, are imperiled, for Uncle Charlie's invasion of her world is far more comprehensive. Many homes in the films of this period turn out to be traps of one sort or another. In *Rebecca,* all of Manderley, from Rebecca's bedroom to her cottage by the sea, becomes a trap for the second Mrs. de Winter. In *Suspicion,* Lina Aysgarth, another unprepossessing heroine played by Joan Fontaine, moves out of her parents' staid and reassuring home into the house her impecunious new husband Johnnie (Cary Grant) has rented only to find that it too is a trap—a point confirmed by repeated shots of shadows forming a spider-web pattern behind Lina or Johnnie, for example as he ascends the stairs with a glass of milk that may or may not be poisoned. In *Notorious* another new bride, Alicia Sebastian (Ingrid Bergman)—although the audience significantly continues to think of her as Alicia Huberman, and winces when the American agent Captain Prescott (Louis Calhern) calls her "Mrs. Sebastian"—is poisoned by her husband (Claude Rains) and mother-in-law (Leopoldine Konstantin) and confined by her illness to her home, her room, and finally the bed which she has violated in marrying Sebastian.

In another sense, Alicia is not confined to her home at all, since a home which is used to imprison her can hardly be her home. Hitchcock emphasizes Alicia's homelessness in *Notorious* by providing her with too many homes, none of which is truly hers. She is repeatedly put under stress in public places: the courtroom where she first hears her father sentenced to prison, the airplane where she gets the news of his death, the racetrack where she meets her lover Devlin (Cary Grant) as Sebastian watches them through field glasses, the park bench where she and Devlin meet secretly. But the private places, the potential homes which ought to offer a refuge from the publicity that follows her, turn out to be equally public. A government agent crashes her party in Miami, stays with her after her friends have all passed out, and next morning shows her that her house has been bugged. The intimate dinner she tries to cook at her hotel in Rio de Janiero is ruined first by a phone call Devlin insists on making to Prescott and then by the news that the Americans, including Devlin, are trying to get her into bed with another man. Devlin turns what should be their most private moment, a kiss in the wine cellar after they have just discovered Sebastian's secret, into public theater by playing to Sebastian as an audience. Even her final escape from her husband's house is made possible only by Devlin's ability to turn her departure into a public event which Sebastian dares not disrupt because of what the witnesses, his fellow conspirators, would do to him.

Which home is truly Alicia's? She moves through several homes— the house in Miami, the hotel in Rio de Janiero, the Sebastians' house— but is never at home herself. She simply moves from her father's house, where she clearly does not belong, to her husband's house, where she is equally an outsider. The film charts a movement away from a home and the apparently (but only apparently) stable identity it confers to a series of places which cannot serve as homes. Devlin himself has no home; after he turns up without preparation or introduction at Alicia's party, he is never associated with any particular place other than the park bench. (The film never even shows his hotel room in Rio.) He spends the entire film taking Alicia out of other people's homes without providing any home of his own. The only homecoming the film's conclusion shows is therefore ironic: Sebastian's return, in the film's final shot, to his house, whose door shuts before revealing the death that surely awaits him and his mother inside.

In Hitchcock's British films, the hero's or heroine's initial departure from home had typically been followed either by an ultimate restoration to home or by the creation of a new home defined by marital rather than parental bonds, on the traditional model of romantic comedy; *Young and Innocent* manages to combine both patterns by uniting its heroine with both father and lover. Already in the early films, however, there are suggestions of a departure which is not completed by a homecoming. *The Pleasure Garden* moves from London to the tropics, from a decadent civilization to the breakdown of civilized behavior, without a corresponding return. *The Manxman* ends with the departure of the heroine with her lover from her husband and the significantly named Isle of Man; *The 39 Steps* concludes as it began, in a large, noisy public hall, its final image emphasizing Mr. Memory's death as much as Hannay's union with Pamela; *Sabotage* concludes with the explosion of the Verlocs' house; *The Lady Vanishes* takes Iris from betrothal to a man she does not love through a series of detours to a reunion with Miss Froy at the British Foreign Office. In each of these films, however, the sense of departure is complemented by a romantic resolution which will presumably establish a new home somewhere. Only in two films, *Easy Virtue* and *Juno and the Paycock,* are the values and the very possibility of any home decisively undermined.

The endings of the forties films are much more problematic. Even those whose conclusions are most straightforwardly affirmative are complicated by their pace, setting, or visual design. In *Spellbound* the mysterious J. B. (Gregory Peck), nameless after his unwitting imposture of Dr. Anthony Edwardes is unmasked, is restored to his true identity as John Ballantine, cleared of any criminal complicity, and reunited with Dr. Constance Petersen (Ingrid Bergman). This affirmative conclusion is qualified, however, by the film's final scene, which shows the principals repeating an earlier scene by kissing each other good-bye in a train station and then getting on the same train, leading a conductor to wonder whether they are crazy, or he is. In *Lifeboat* the community of bickering survivors on the boat finally demonstrate their unity—though the black pullman porter Joe Spencer (Canada Lee) tellingly abstains— by killing the U-boat captain Willie (Walter Slezak). In *Saboteur,* Barry Kane's pursuit of the saboteur Frank Fry (Norman Lloyd) ends abruptly with Fry's fall from atop the Statue of Liberty; the film ends seconds later as Barry is pulled back to safety. In both cases the audience is invited to enjoy the villain's punishment rather than the hero's homecoming or the community's solidarity.

A few films have endings which are more clearly inconclusive. *Foreign Correspondent,* which piles climax upon climax—the rescue of the Dutch statesman Van Meer (Albert Basserman), the airplane crash, the scene aboard ship in which Haverstock finally sends in his story—until the scenes lose their terminal force, finally ends with a cliffhanger: Haverstock and Carol Fisher (Laraine Day) are broadcasting home from London when the blitz puts out the studio's lights, and Haverstock concludes, "Keep those lights burning, America! . . . They're the only lights left in the world!" This ending is a deliberate non-ending; like the ending of Dickens' Christmas story *The Chimes,* it addresses the complications of its plot not by resolving them within the frame of the story but by taking up a collection in order to forestall them.

*Suspicion* avoids terminal resolution still more completely. Hitchcock claimed that he would have liked the film to end, like the novel on which it is based, with Johnnie's murder of his wife, perhaps with a scene in which he poisons her and then posts a letter to her mother without realizing that it reveals him as her killer. But the studio chiefs at RKO, objecting even to the suggestion that Cary Grant's character might be a murderer, cut the picture, according to Hitchcock, from ninety-nine to fifty-five minutes before allowing him to reassemble it. Differences of opinion within the studio eventually led to an unusual degree of indecisiveness about the film's ending and the scripting of several widely differing conclusions.[19] The ending with which the film was finally released, in which Johnnie confesses his earlier sins to Lina but reacts with outrage and hurt to her accusation that he killed Beaky Thwaite (Nigel Bruce) and is trying to kill her, is the most inconclusive of all, since it fits equally well the belief that Johnny is innocent—a belief which was unanimously adapted by contemporary reviewers and has prevailed among critics ever since—and the belief that he is guilty. After all, Johnny is behaving in this scene precisely as he has always behaved in covering up his guilty secrets: admitting offenses for which Lina has evidence, insisting that he has turned over a new leaf, indignantly denying her accusations of serious wrongdoing. When the film's final shot shows the Aysgarths' car turning in a loop and going back to their house, it is possible to predict with equal confidence that now they will finally be united or that now Johnny will go on trying to kill Lina.

An ending which supports two such dramatically opposed readings of the entire film—of Johnny's character and all his actions, of Lina's suspicions of him, of their marriage and future prospects, of the deaths of Beaky and Lina's father, of Lina's relation to her home, or any home she might have with Johnnie—indicates, at the very least, a cavalier attitude toward resolution generally. Hitchcock is more interested in complicating the relationship between Lina and Johnnie than in resolving it; he would rather generate suspense through Lina's suspicions about her husband than reveal exactly what these suspicions tell us about Lina and Johnnie. Hitchcock's project in this film is simply to take Lina out of her parents' home and isolate her in her husband's home, to what final end it hardly matters, because the focus of the film is on Lina's loss of her home as a metaphor for her loss of identity as she becomes obsessed with a mysterious figure who, whether or not he is guilty of murder, is far stronger than she is.

Johnnie is not only stronger than Lina; he is more charming, more attractive, more interesting, a figure of infinitely more narrative promise. Without him Lina, however contented she might be with her life, would have no story to tell, just as Charlie Newton would have no story without her Uncle Charlie and the second Mrs. de Winter would be boring without the threats posed by the first. The presence of these enigmatic doubles, who force their heroes and heroines into games of odd man out, reveals at the same time the new kinds of pleasure Hitchcock's latest games offer the audience. As *Rebecca* and *Saboteur* show, an important aspect of this pleasure is the pathos Hitchcock had sought in such earlier films as *The Manxman, Juno and the Paycock,* and *The Skin Game,* now intensified by a more clearly psychological orientation. Hitchcock's overt emphasis on the psychology of his troubled principals suggests that another promise of pleasure is in the films' ability to illuminate the mysteries of the human mind so portentously indicated by the opening titles of *Spellbound.*[20] More than any of Hitchcock's other work, the Selznick films pose as self-serious explorations of the human psyche. Yet this promise of illumination, of some sort of residual knowledge of the world and its people, is less consistent than the promise of pleasure in the witty and visually precise ways psychological states are imputed—in the acts of implication rather than in the nature of what is implicated.[21] Hitchcock's divided and isolated principals, whether or not they are threatened by sinister doubles, carry within themselves the promise of teleology, of narrative development, that makes their doubles so dangerously attractive.

The range of pleasures Hitchcock generates from his game of odd man out can be illustrated by the progress from *Spellbound* to *Notorious,* a pair of films whose relation strongly resembles the relation between *Jamaica Inn,* which marks a new point of departure for Hitchcock thematically in its presentation of homelessness, and *Rebecca,* which emphasizes the equivocal pleasures to be teased out of this material. *Spellbound* and *Notorious,* both written by Ben Hecht, both starring Ingrid Bergman, both initiated in Selznick's studio (though Selznick ultimately sold *Notorious* to RKO) in successive years—Hitchcock began work on the later film immediately after completing the first[22]—make a matched pair for several reasons, but their treatment of the mystery implicit in their principals' personal identities marks a contrast more interesting than all their similarities. It is easy to see what attracted Hitchcock to the story of the nameless amnesiac impersonating a psychiatrist, for it incorporates the perfect MacGuffin[23]: the unconscious mind of a man whose alienation is so complete that he can serve as both subject and object of its investigation. *Spellbound* is conceptually the most ambitious film Hitchcock had made so far, and his most determined attempt to employ the jargon and images of psychoanalysis, from its immensely self-serious prologue to the famous superimposition of a series of opening doors over Dr. Petersen and the apparent Dr. Edwardes as they kiss. Hitchcock is so determined to penetrate the mysteries of his hero's troubled mind that for the only time in his career he takes the MacGuffin as seriously as his characters do, and the film, which Hitchcock later described as "just another manhunt story wrapped up in pseudo-psychoanalysis," is complicated by pretensions to be something more.[24]

*Notorious* is conceptually a far more modest film because it poses its central question—who is to determine Alicia's identity?—in terms of the heroine's reputation and the development of the plot, using its Mac-Guffin as a pretext for the human relations that develop around it and not as a conceptual focus for the film. Instead of as a quest into the true identity (that is, the authentic unconscious) of its heroine, *Notorious* is organized as a study of diverse aspects of her reputation. The revelation of Alicia's true nature is wholly subordinated to the multiplication of situations which display or develop her attempt to escape her notorious reputation. This relatively superficial model of human identity frees Hitchcock from the psychoanalytic focus of *Spellbound* and allows him instead to focus on imputations of psychological states whose point is not their profundity but their ironic wit. In the central party sequence, when Devlin, having just received Alicia Sebastian's key to the wine cellar, remarks that he hopes the champagne holds out so that Sebastian won't have to go down to the cellar for more, suddenly Alicia, whose notoriety has consistently been associated with drinking, realizes that she can protect Devlin, and her own reputation in her husband's eyes, only if everyone at the party drinks more slowly. The following shots—Alicia distractedly refusing a glass of champagne, the other guests helping themselves, the diminishing supply at the bar—create a romantically witty nightmare, as the dreamy waltz music of the party contrasts ironically with Alicia's panic even as it sets the stage for her big scene with the man she loves. The appearance of Hitchcock himself as one of the guests whose drinking further imperils his heroine dramatizes the way the scene is suspensefully witty without being funny: Once Hitchcock has established drinking as a threat to Alicia's reputation, every intensification of that threat carries an ironic aptness that gives it a pleasurable edge. And this particular threat is so understated visually—what could look more innocuous than people drinking champagne at a party?—that the audience's intimacy with Alicia, tightened by their perception of the threat, carries a double excitement because of the secret they share with her. Hitchcock has made it fun to watch the revelation of Alicia's character by involving her in a promisingly dangerous situation while adumbrating the danger with such authority and wit that following the continuity provides the same perverse pleasures as identifying Hannay's char and the body she discovers in *The 39 Steps*. What is revealed about Alicia is much more commonplace than the exotic revelations of John

Ballantine's unconscious in *Spellbound;* the ways in which it is revealed have become far more important in establishing the revelation as a game.

The pleasures of narrative exposition so important in *Notorious* account for Leonard J. Leff's remark that "Hitchcock conceptualized films outside-in; he built his scripts on neither character nor plot but setting and object."[25] Even when a producer or screenwriter provides a Hitchcock film with a strong narrative premise, as in most of his forties films, the director's overriding interest is still in the exposition of conflict rather than its resolution. A character like Johnnie Aysgarth, however, shows Hitchcock turning a convention of melodrama, the enigmatic villain, into a touchstone for the heroine's identity and a narrative premise, a pleasurable promise of further development, himself. Enigmatic figures like Johnnie take center stage throughout Hitchcock's forties films. In dramatizing the plight of the second Mrs. de Winter, *Rebecca* revolves around a still more problematic figure, the first Mrs. de Winter herself. What sort of person was Rebecca de Winter? From the moment when Mrs. Van Hopper first tells the heroine, "I suppose he can't get over his wife's death. They say he simply adored her," and the elevator doors slide shut behind them, Rebecca's personality is offered as the key to the mystery surrounding Maxim de Winter and to the problem of her successor's happiness. Everything in the film depends on what kind of person she was, even though most of the characters are completely mistaken about her, some of her motivations remain obscure, and the film ends without her true nature being made public. In Hitchcock's earlier films, only Ivor Novello's lodger had cast anything like the same portentous shadow. But the films that follow are repeatedly built around enigmatic central characters: Johnnie Aysgarth, Uncle Charlie, John Ballantine, Alicia Huberman, and Lady Paradine.

Lina Aysgarth's movement from her parents' home to her husband's home, like Alicia's movement from her father's home to her husband's home, is a metaphor for the loss of any identity that could be taken for granted. What sort of identity replaces this comfortable genetic identity, what sort of identity could possibly replace it, is exactly the question these films pose. Stranded, like Connie Porter (Tallulah Bankhead) in *Lifeboat,* in a situation which her previous social status and sophistication has no power to control, or beguiled, like the heroine of *Rebecca,* into a magical world in which her life is run by other people, each of Hitchcock's heroes and heroines during this period ends by defining himself or herself in terms of an enigmatic Other, a shadow-self which can never, even after the final revelation, restore the initial sense of security the films had worked to undermine. This pattern is clearest in *Shadow of a Doubt,* but it operates as well in *Suspicion, Spellbound,* and *Notorious.* When Anthony Keane (Gregory Peck) realizes the folly of his infatuation with Lady Paradine and goes home to his wife Gay (Ann Todd), her acceptance of him provides a happy resolution to *The Paradine Case,* but that resolution is much more tentative than Tony's original sense of right and wrong, and the apparent security of his home with Gay, had seemed to promise. Even when the enigmatic figure who doubles the hero or heroine is identified with a home, that home is not felt as the hero's or heroine's home; it is some other home, the home as trap, like the imprisoning Sebastian house.

It is not only homes which can no longer be trusted, but the mothers within them. The mothers and mother-figures in Hitchcock's early films nurture and support the identities of their children, or, at their most problematic (in *Blackmail* and *Saboteur*), remind the children ironically of the stable identities their implication in crimes has cost them. Throughout his British films, Hitchcock's maternal figures are loving, sympathetic, and attractive, even when they are slightly ridiculous. The first indication of any change comes in *Rebecca,* in which the heroine's sympathetic older sister-in-law Beatrice Lacey (Gladys Cooper) is overshadowed by the threatening Mrs. Danvers. In *Mr. and Mrs. Smith* Hitchcock presents a whole series of equivocal or childless mothers, from Ann Krausheimer Smith (whom her husband repeatedly calls "Mother") and Mrs. Custer (Lucile Watson) to the "Mamma Lucie" who reputedly owns the restaurant at which the Smiths eat their memorial dinner but who turns out to be a mustachioed man.

Dr. Petersen, almost the last of Hitchcock's sympathetic maternal figures, is neatly balanced by Madame Sebastian, the first of his truly malignant mothers. Although Constance Petersen is in love with the nameless man who has impersonated Dr. Edwardes, she treats him like a child, shielding him from the police and holding him up when he blacks out, as she takes him to her own father figure, Dr. Brulov (Michael Chekhov), for help in ascertaining his identity. She functions as both mother and lover: as mother, she helps the imposter discover who he really is by opening the doors that lead back to his childhood; as lover, she accepts and completes him as an adult. Madame Sebastian's function is exactly opposite. By chiding her son for behaving as a schoolboy in falling in love with Alicia (a judgment in which he eventually concurs), she serves notice that she does not accept the links between his childhood and his adult identity; she prefers to keep him forever a child under her control rather than see him as the child of another woman. But Madame Sebastian's lack of acceptance is focused on Alicia, whom she insists on seeing first as her father's daughter, later as her father's betrayer. Instead of opening doors, as Constance does for John Ballantine, she keeps the keys to the house, refusing to give them up without a fight. If Constance Petersen, the sympathetic doctor to many irresponsible patients, is everybody's mother, Madame Sebastian is nobody's mother. She marks a transition from representations in Hitchcock's work of the mother as a source of stability and reassurance to the mother as nemesis because she is someone else's mother rather than one's own, the mother seen only from outside, as Hitchcock's heroes and heroines see their false homes and enigmatic doubles only from outside.

Seen from outside, Hitchcock's mothers become sinister for the same reason they used to be reassuring: because they represent the hero's or heroine's rootedness, a rootedness which is now profoundly dangerous. Madame Sebastian refuses to see her son as an adult because she wants to keep him (and Alicia, whose adult sexuality she rightly perceives as a threat to her authority) a child forever. In Hitchcock's later films, the pattern continues with dotty Mrs. Anthony in *Strangers on a Train,* neurotically possessive Lydia Brenner in *The Birds,* and Mrs. Bates in *Psycho.* Even Hitchcock's comic mothers follow a similar pattern. Roger Thornhill must outgrow his mother's domination before he can grow into the requirements of his various roles in *North by Northwest,* and John Robie, at the end of *To Catch a Thief,* is clearly dismayed by Francie Stevens's closing line: "So this is where you live. Why, Mother will love it here!"

Mothers are comically or darkly threatening in Hitchcock's later films because they prevent the opportunity for the (typically male) hero's growth.[26] The world of unmarked visuals, moral values, and rooted sense of identity which they represent, and which had been so reassuring in the early films, finally becomes stifling as Hitchcock becomes increasingly suspicious that such a given, genetic background can release one's sense of identity. The most sympathetic mothers in Hitchcock's later films—Jennifer Rogers in *The Trouble with Harry* and Jo McKenna in the remake of *The Man Who Knew Too Much*—represent not the hero's own mother but his lover or wife.

The furthest implication of the transformation of Hitchcock's mothers from supportive to threatening figures is that one's home, and the sense of a stable and unquestioned identity which that home supports, is not only remote and unreachable, a relic of one's distant past, but downright dangerous, and that it is just as well that Hitchcock's principals can't go home again. The attempt to find or maintain a family home is often indicative of a case of arrested development, a longing for a sort of security that the world of the films can never provide. John Ballantine learns his own past identity in *Spellbound* only to begin a new life with Constance Petersen, and the return to home at the end of *The Paradine Case* marks less Tony Keane's affirmation of his identity through his home with his wife than a refusal to accept the implications of his doubling with the stablehand André Latour (Louis Jourdan) and a consequent retreat.

Hitchcock has come a long way from his implication in the Gaumont-British films that people need to come to terms with the children within themselves by learning to play. The heroes and heroines of the Selznick films are radically alienated from the children within, and attempting to overcome this alienation by returning home or cultivating a sense of their roots is always traumatic and usually disastrous. If Hitchcock begins the decade nostalgic for a home his orphaned heroines can never have, he ends it sharply critical of the very idea of home as a basis for one's identity, ready to commit himself to providing a kind of amusement that does not depend on resolving the tensions arising from homelessness but works to prolong them indefinitely. If he can no longer offer the reassuring pleasures associated with the stability of home and mother, he provides the more subversive pleasures, beginning in *Jamaica Inn* and *Rebecca* and intensifying in *Notorious,* of discovering through a critique of domestic values, faith in one's social and genetic identity, and the automatic assumption of a happy ending that there is indeed no place like home.

# FIVE

## CAT AND

## MOUSE

**W**ith the completion of *The Paradine Case*, Hitchcock fulfilled the terms of his last contract with Selznick and embarked on his career as an independent producer. Throughout his remaining years Hitchcock was to operate as in effect an independent producer-director like Howard Hawks whose films were released through Warner Brothers, Paramount, MGM, and Universal. In the two films immediately following *The Paradine Case*, however, Hitchcock functioned as a true independent, releasing through Transatlantic Pictures, the company he headed in partnership with Sidney Bernstein. Never entirely comfortable under Selznick's supervision, Hitchcock had particularly chafed under the constraints imposed on the production of *The Paradine Case* and clearly looked forward to the freedom to choose his own subjects and treatments.[1] In the years immediately following his break with Selznick, Hitchcock's anti-domestic impulse, his suspicion of homes and the secure genetic identities they confer, continues as a dominant motif in his films. But instead of emphasizing the pathos of homelessness, as he had done with such brilliant consistency in *Rebecca*, *Shadow of a Doubt*, and *Notorious*, Hitchcock's attitude toward home is more ambivalent, and his critique of domesticity more obviously ludic. Like the Selznick films, Hitchcock's work from *Rope* through *Dial M for Murder* explores the motif of homes as traps, but now the process of entrapment is treated more openly as a game whose object is to imprison characters in their homes or in their given roles and to put on the screws in ways that may be painful for them but are fun for the audience.

The typical strategy for making entrapment fun is to trap the characters in ways that are available to the audience alone, as in the famous sequence in which Hitchcock cuts back and forth between the hero of *Strangers on a Train* struggling to escape from his tennis match and the villain straining to retrieve the hero's stolen cigarette lighter from a storm drain. Since neither one knows what the other is doing, the sense of the competition between them is reserved for the audience, whose privileged information adds a witty edge to the suspense. Sometimes, however, Hitchcock's dramatic irony is available to characters whose knowledge that they are trapped in a game does not help them to break out of the trap. Goaded beyond endurance by the detective figure in *Rope,* one of the murderers says fatalistically, "Cat and mouse—cat and mouse. Which is the cat, and which is the mouse?" It is a perceptive speech, for it indicates not only that he is the victim of a punitive game but that this game is a transformation of an earlier game in which he played the cat.

In Hitchcock's game of cat and mouse, the slyly manipulative director is the cat, and his trapped characters are the mice, but the position of the audience, as usual, is more complex. In almost every case the audience is cast in a double role as cat and mouse, sympathetically identifying with the trapped characters yet perversely enjoying their sense of imprisonment. Sometimes this ambivalence is established by aestheticizing of the idea of entrapment, as in the rigorous visual strictures of *Rope* and *Dial M for Murder;* sometimes, as in *Under Capricorn* and *Strangers on a Train,* it is maintained by presenting characters whose mixture of innocence and guilt constitutes a trap they have built for themselves; sometimes, as in *Stage Fright,* it is developed by substituting a guilty prisoner for the intially innocent prisoner, inviting the audience to take a retributive pleasure in the very confinement that had initially seemed threatening.

The director's primary move in this game of cat and mouse is to drive a wedge between the heroes and heroines and the homes and domestic values they begin by taking for granted. The homes in the first three films of the period are parodies of homes. In *Under Capricorn,* the second of the three, the parody is melodramatic, and the principals' multiple layers of homelessness recall Mary Yellan's estrangement from two unsuitable homes in Hitchcock's last costume picture, *Jamaica Inn.* Homelessness in both of these films is a subject for pathos, a loss to be remedied or deplored. In *Rope* and *Stage Fright,* however, Hitchcock's parody of domestic life is affectionately or savagely witty, so that the breakup of a false home provides an equivocal new pleasure. The tension between the melodramatic desire for a secure home and the identity it confers and the subversive desire to parody and destroy home and the values it represents continues in Hitchcock's following three films for Warner Brothers—*Strangers on a Train, I Confess,* and *Dial M for Murder*—incarnated in the figure of the sympathetic adulterous couple betrayed by villains who align themselves with the institution of marriage. All the films of the period, like the concurrently flourishing genre of *film noir,* thus engage the postwar audience's anti-domestic sympathies in order to play with their assumption that there is no place like home.

Though Hitchcock's filmmaking throughout this period is so often tentative, there is nothing tentative about *Rope.* From its first shot following the credits—a close-up of David Kentley (Dick Hogan) being strangled by his old school friends Brandon Shaw (John Dall) and Philip Morgan (Farley Granger), it is the most baleful and emphatic film Hitchcock had made to date.

Critics have most often been drawn to *Rope* as an exercise in technique, and like its contemporary cousin *The Lady in the Lake,* Robert Montgomery's notorious 1947 exercise in storytelling with the subjective camera, it is an unquestionable technical tour de force. Hitchcock's desire to film Patrick Hamilton's play *Rope's End* using a single set and a running time corresponding to the elapsed time of the story (a technique Fred Zinneman adopted four years later for *High Noon*) eventually led him to a wish to film the entire story as if in a single take, a continuous camera movement lasting from 7:30 to 9:15 and compassing all dramatic action from David's murder to Brandon's and Philip's eventual confrontation by their former schoolmaster Rupert Cadell (James Stewart). But pairing *Rope* with *The Lady in the Lake* indicates the ways in which neither film is truly experimental conceptually; they are both essentially one-idea films, based on the kinds of inspiration that strike most people in the middle of the night only to be sheepishly dismissed next morning. The difference is that Hitchcock treats his idea frankly as a game by linking his manipulation of the audience to his villains' manipulation of their dinner guests. Brandon's histrionic playacting and compulsive witticisms are logical correlatives for the director's claustrophobic use of space and outrageous visual jokes.

Like Brandon's murder, *Rope* is an inventive technical exercise, and not only because of its ten-minute takes. It is Hitchcock's first color film and his first to have an entirely diegetic and post-synchronized soundtrack as well. Hitchcock's decision to shoot in color led to his well-known dissatisfaction with the sunset lighting in five shots which required retakes, but it also allowed him to light the film in a way whose expressiveness is motivated and naturalized by the gradual fall of night. The opening of the film is lit by cool, neutral evening light; the central section, beginning with the arrival of the dinner guests, is lit by the more brilliant and highly colored sunset light; and the guests' departure marks another change to nighttime lighting, so that Brandon's and Philip's growing desperation before Rupert is illuminated by the colored lights which flash on and off outside their window, giving the apartment a surrealistic glow. Hitchcock spoke repeatedly of his sparing use of color in the film, and indeed almost nothing has any strong color except the light.

The post-synchronized soundtrack, necessitated by the movement of props and walls which made live sound recording impossible, increases the stylization of the film by reducing ambient sound to a minimum and providing a television-like homogeneity to the voices. Hitchcock's soundtracks are never as dense or naturalistic as Renoir's or Robert Altman's, but the extreme auditory stylization here aptly reflects the film's leading concern: the claustrophobic sense of enclosure or entrapment created by the relations among its principals and reflected by its visual design.

Indeed each of Hitchcock's technical innovations in the film heightens the sense of claustrophobic interconnection among its characters. Even more pointedly than the Selznick films, *Rope* works by alienating most of the characters from their homes and inverting the values usually associated with home, so that home becomes a trap. This is most clearly true of the one home Hitchcock actually shows, the apartment of Brandon and Philip. Brandon regards his home as a theater in which he will stage a deceptive show for his dinner guests, David's friends and relatives. Accordingly, Brandon serves dinner from the chest in which he has hidden David's body, takes the opportunity to throw David's fiancée Janet Walker (Joan Chandler) together with her former boyfriend Kenneth Lawrence (Douglas Dick), chats solicitously with David's perturbed father (Cedric Hardwicke) about where David might be, and ties Mr. Kentley's bundle of books with the same rope he had used to strangle his son. By audaciously treating his home as a public place, Brandon apparently precludes the possibility that he could have any private life of his own.

Brandon's sense of his home as a theatrical setting for a game of cat and mouse is dramatically complemented by his lover and accomplice Philip's sense of his home as a place where he is trapped himself, helplessly on display in front of witnesses who are observing every slip that gives him away.[2] When Brandon first transfers the dinner furnishings from the dining room table to the chest containing David's corpse, Philip insists that "we have to have an excuse" for the housekeeper Mrs. Wilson (Edith Evanson) when she notices the change; he clearly feels under her thumb, as if his home were really hers. Later he tells Janet and Kenneth that "I'm to be locked up" at Brandon's mother's in Connecticut for piano practice. Throughout the film Philip acts trapped by his own guilt, and he is the one who awakens the suspicions of Rupert, who eventually pieces together the clues Philip has dropped.

Brandon's and Philip's home, which is a confining trap for both David and Philip, is set against another home: the Kentley home, which, although it is never shown, becomes more and more insistently present through Mr. Kentley's calls to his wife about David's failure to return home. David had been expected at Brandon and Philip's dinner party, but when he was delayed, Mr. Kentley assured the others that David would surely call his mother at home as soon as he could. He defines David in terms of ties to home and home values (devotion to his mother, impending marriage to a woman approved by his parents, consideration and punctuality), which Brandon and Philip systematically deny, and his home, even though it never appears and he never returns to it, shows Brandon and Philip's apartment up as a parody of home, an anti-home.

Hitchcock heightens the ironic contrast between onscreen and off-screen homes in several ways. He emphasizes the unnatural intimacy among the dinner guests both in his title, which suggests things bound together, and in his end credits, which list the characters in order as "David Kentley . . . His Friends . . . Their Housekeeper . . . David's Rival . . . David's Girl . . . David's Father . . . David's Aunt . . . and Rupert Cadell," suggest that David is the center of the film, the person on whom all the others base their identity.[3] David's central position in the film is reinforced by Hitchcock's constant reference to a third home, the chest in which his body is hidden and which serves, as Brandon remarks, as his burial ground. The film's most ironically complex framing shows a corner of the chest in the lower left foreground and the corridor to the kitchen door on the right. As the guests muse offscreen where David could have gone instead of coming home, Mrs. Wilson walks back and forth from the chest to the kitchen, carrying more of the dinner furnishings each time, until the chest is finally cleared. The guests do not realize that their speculations about David's offscreen whereabouts are about to be answered in a horrifyingly unexpected way; instead of wandering around offscreen, he has actually been present, in this visual and ceremonial home, all along.

Even Brandon regards David as the centerpiece of his dramatic production; he has organized the evening around David's unseen presence, just as stage productions of the play invariably organize the action around the incriminating chest at front center. But Brandon considers the chest a prop rather than a conceptual center; nor does he regard David as the center of the assembled guests. That honor, of course, is reserved in Brandon's mind for Brandon, who is using David himself as a prop in his shock-the-bourgeois theatricals. The tug-of-war between Brandon and David over the question of who is really at the center of the gathering not only gives the film its narrative impetus (who will finally set the agenda for the evening?) but dramatizes the fundamental conflict in the two would-be heroes' values. David represents the domestic values—academic excellence, filial consideration, sexual monogamy, punctuality—Brandon the values of charm, entertainment, and unfettered brilliance. The conflict between David's institutional loyalty and Brandon's unchecked play impulse links them to such earlier dual figures as the second Mrs. de Winter and the first, to Bob Lawrence and Abbott, and to Hitchcock the faithful adapter and stage-manager and Hitchcock the irrepressible joker, popping up in the antic setups of *The Skin Game* or as the target in a game of find the director. The split between Hitchcock the law-abiding citizen who is terrified of the police and who cleans the bathroom religiously after each use and Hitchcock the playfully sadistic manipulator of audience reactions—both carefully cultivated dramatic personae—would never be more clearly dramatized than in the first film he directed for his own company.

As in all but his earliest films, Hitchcock provides a mediator between his two would-be heroes, a figure who emerges as the hero himself. No audience who went to see *Rope* because of the names on the marquee, or who knew that twenty percent of its budget had been reserved for James Stewart's salary, could seriously entertain the question of whether Brandon or David would emerge as the hero.[4] Of course the hero would be Rupert Cadell, whose unannounced entrance when Philip begins to play the piano provides the film with one of its most carefully prepared and quietly effective moments. As a former teacher of both Brandon and David and as Brandon's acknowledged mentor, the resolutely independent publisher who baits acquaintances with an aplomb approaching Brandon's (when Janet says she hopes David's description did her justice, he asks, "Do you deserve justice?"), and the man who has supplied the playfully Nietzschean rationale for Brandon's exercise in homicide, Rupert is ideally placed to mediate between the claims of home and self, institutional and personal loyalty, piety and play. And the big scene to which the film builds—Rupert's denunciation of Brandon on the grounds that in carrying out the ideas Rupert has casually entertained, Brandon has gone further than Rupert would ever have gone—confirms Rupert's status as the mediator who can understand Brandon (he has been Brandon's target audience from the beginning, and a great deal of Brandon's behavior seems designed to drop hints to him) but who finally recoils from him in self-righteous horror. But Rupert's self-consoling pieties show just how difficult it is to mediate between the claims of David and Brandon, how much easier it is to dramatize the conflict than to resolve it without simply taking sides.

*Rope* is the first of Hitchcock's thrillers to leave an unmistakably bad taste in the mouth, and Brandon the first of Hitchcock's unmistakably malicious murderers.[5] Hitchcock's earlier murderers, when they had not been marginalized, as in *The Lodger,* had acted either self-protectively or reluctantly, often with a sense that they were victims themselves; except for Peter Lorre's grotesquely comic and disturbing General in *Secret Agent,* his spies killed people strictly in the line of business and were either disinterestedly dedicated or downright apologetic (as in Dr. Hartz's final line in *The Lady Vanishes,* "Jolly good luck to them!"). Brandon's violence is gratuitous—"We've killed for excitement and for the sake of killing"—and directed against a character who is structurally at the center of the film. His pervasive malice might make the film seem impossible to watch except as a pathological case-study.

But this malice is essential to the film's perverse appeal, for Brandon's cat-and-mouse game with the Kentleys prepares for Rupert's similar game with him, and sets the tone for the film's claustrophobic visual program as well. Unlike any of Hitchcock's earlier films, *Rope* is an exercise in dramatic irony. Since the audience sees the murder in the first minute of the film, there is no mystery, not even (for an audience wise in the ways of the Production Code) about whether or not the killers will be caught. Brandon's irrepressible witticisms about the crime and Philip's helplessly revealing gestures anticipate their inevitable confrontation by Rupert. But although Brandon and Philip are both monstrous and doomed, the film's dialogue is filled with jokes that establish a prevailing mode of black comedy. Asked by Kenneth if it's somebody's birthday, Brandon replies that it's just the opposite. Later, when Kenneth says that Brandon would like David to walk in on Kenneth and Janet in the bedroom, Brandon smilingly answers: "That would be too much of a shock." Other characters unwittingly get in on the act when Janet, hurt by Brandon's remarks about her fickleness, says she could strangle him, and when Mrs. Atwater (Constance Collier), an amateur palm-reader, tells Philip: "These hands will bring you great fame."

Hitchcock's visuals are as shriekingly obvious in their effects as his throwaway jokes. Since his decision to film in an apparently unbroken long take precludes cut-ins, he shows significant objects or gestures by emphatic pans or tracks.[6] When Mrs. Atwater mistakenly greets Kenneth as David, Hitchcock pans all the way to the far end of the room over the sound of breaking glass and tracks in to show a close-up of Philip's hand, bleeding from a glass he had crushed in a panic of apprehension. As Rupert, about to leave, takes off a hat that had been much too small for him, the camera tracks in to show the initials "D. K." inside. Later, as Brandon assures Philip there won't be any trouble as he prepares to let Rupert back in, Hitchcock shows his hand in the foreground opening and spinning the cylinder of a revolver. Each of these moments works like a visual joke, with the unsettling residual effect of assuring the audience that such pointed irony is so invariably the rule that it becomes perversely funny.

On the one hand, the film seems to establish the principle that entrapment can be fun, not because one anticipates escape from the trap, but because Brandon's heartlessness licenses the audience to enjoy the game of cat and mouse which is bound to turn on him; on the other, Hitchcock's inveterate dramatic irony shifts the focus away from David's murder to the perversely theatrical means by which it is simultaneously concealed and advertised. Brandon's and Philip's buffet, with its gruesome centerpiece, seems a more monstrous crime than the murder itself. Hitchcock would never again make a film in which he treated social betrayal as the material for black comedy—his later comedy of broken taboos, *The Trouble with Harry,* is precisely a comedy of social integration—but his fascination with entrapment and betrayal as images of alienation remain at the heart of his work until *Rear Window.*

*Rope* begins a new stage in Hitchcock's career less concerned with the crime of murder than with the crime of malicious deception—a deception that characteristically, in the films that follow, takes the form of betrayal. In *Rope* the betrayal is well-nigh universal—Brandon and Philip betray the ties of friendship and hospitality in killing David, the trust of David's friends in lying and joking to them, and the rituals of civilized behavior in turning a dinner party into a funeral—and the technique is one of strict, almost schematic concentration on mise-en-scène and action. Hitchcock's following film, *Under Capricorn,* explores similar conflicts more ruminatively and expansively; watching the film feels less like playing a game, and even the long takes which had enclosed the circle of Brandon's claustrophobic anti-home in *Rope* are used completely differently here.

*Under Capricorn* is a virtual anthology of different motifs of homelessness, as patterns of alienation multiply in wild profusion. Even though
contemporary reviewers of the film complained that, for a Hitchcock
movie, it was surprisingly devoid of incident, *Under Capricorn* has in
some sense enough plot for three movies, all three of which leave their
shadow on the completed film.[7] Hitchcock had overcome his distaste for
costume pictures—a distaste widely known and easily explained by his
inability, given a historical setting, to impart a sense of normalcy that
could be disrupted by the plot of intrigue—sufficiently to option Helen
Simpson's novel, evidently because its long-suffering heroine seemed so
promising a role for Ingrid Bergman, but also perhaps because it offered
so many perspectives on its isolated principals. Given the novel's premise—the mystery surrounding Lady Henrietta Flusky (Ingrid Bergman),
who followed her husband and former stablehand Sam (Joseph Cotten)
to colonial Australia after he was transported for killing the brother who
opposed her marriage—there are at least three different ways Hitchcock
could have treated the material in order to emphasize the condition of
homelessness. Australia in 1831 could be presented as a wilderness remote in place and spirit from the values which gave the colony birth; the
emphasis could be on the clash of two cultures, British and Australian;
or the film could focus on the Fluskys' home as a mysterious Gothic
mansion in the line stretching from Manderley to the Bates house, a
home whose secrets the film would unlock. The film features elements
from all three possible treatments.

Hitchcock's opening scene presents Australia as a rude land barely
controlled by British colonialism. The contrast between the official wel-
coming speech of the new Governor (Cecil Parker), attended by neat
rows of British redcoats, and the ragged response of the sparse crowd
for whose sake this pageantry is being displayed, is developed in Lady
Henrietta's tenderness for her cousin Charles Adare (Michael Wilding),
presented to herself, her cousin, and her husband as a nostalgia for her
home in Ireland. When Adare is asked how he likes Australian society,
he replies: "Is there any?" and when he goes to the Fluskys' for dinner,
he is surprised to see that not one of the guests Sam has invited has
been able to persuade his wife to come. (The overhead shot showing
every second seat at Sam's table empty is one of Hitchcock's most som-

berly witty surprises.) Similarly, Lady Hetty regards Australia as barren, though for different reasons: "When Sam came out, we lost each other." Australia is a frontier which offers no possibility of home, a perfect metaphor for Lady Hetty's estrangement from her own home ever since she allowed Sam to take the blame for her own crime of killing her brother.

In another film Lady Hetty's imprisonment in her own guilt might have been used to emphasize her betrayal of Sam. In this film Lady Hetty is more like Philip than Brandon, and Hitchcock emphasizes the circumstances of her entrapment rather than its cause. Other elements in the film, for example, define the colony not just in terms of its distance from Britain but as a place with its own opposed values, a culture to set against the culture represented by the Governor's troops and Lady Hetty's ties to Ireland. Australians have no personal history, Adare is repeatedly cautioned; they are what they have made themselves, and inquiries into their past are not encouraged. The conflict which develops from this contrast is not between British plenitude and Australian emptiness but between defining oneself in terms of a given homeland, its culture and ceremonies, and defining oneself in terms of one's actions, what one is doing and has done in recent memory. As *Under Capricorn* looks back ten years to *Jamaica Inn* and *Rebecca* in its wistful nostalgia for the characters' lost home, it looks ahead ten years to *Psycho* in presenting this conflict between genetic and dramatic conceptions of identity.

The conflict is dramatized by the Governor's repeated warnings to Adare not to go to Sam Flusky's house, his refusal to let him stay at the Governor's house once Adare has defied him, and Sam's furious disruption of the Governor's ball to take his wife home. This lacerating scene, in which Sam appears at his most callous, is balanced by an earlier, more quietly painful scene in which Sam's rough love for his wife is confirmed by a close-up, just before she leaves for the ball, of his hand secretly clutching a ruby necklace as Adare airily remarks that rubies would look gaudy with Lady Hetty's dress. Sam is turned against her by the hints of their housekeeper Milly (Margaret Leighton), a junior-grade Mrs. Danvers who hopes to marry him either by allying herself with him socially—she and Sam lack the gentility of Lady Hetty and Adare—or by driving his wife mad.

Hitchcock's focus on the Fluskys' home defines colonial Australia in still a third way. The unusually large number of exterior shots of the house not only serve as expository or narrative links but establish it as the film's unmarked setting, the place where most of the action will take place. When Adare first approaches the house, after the obligatory scene in which his coachman refuses to wait outside for him, Hitchcock begins the most elaborate shot of the film. Adare approaches the front door, then hesitates and moves toward a row of windows, the camera tracking along with him as he sees, through one window, a woman (not yet identified as Lady Hetty) being held down on the kitchen table (a blocking which echoes Adare's first glimpse of Sam, also through a window, in an earlier scene), then further along the row of windows, around a corner and through the back door, following Adare through three rooms to the reception for the guests, continuing on through the entrance of each unaccompanied male, back into the dining room as the guests take their seats, and finally cutting on Sam's face as he looks over his shoulder to see who has entered behind him. By using such a fluid long take instead of the usual sequence of re-establishing shots to enter the Fluskys' home, Hitchcock indicates the problematic relation between inside and outside (the moment when Adare actually enters the house is hard to detect) and provides a blocking or linking device which, unlike the architectural structure it to a certain extent replaces, is available to the audience but not to the characters. When characters stand around or even refer to a home, they are aware of its meaning for them and the loyalties it bespeaks. But this long take, like the first interior shot in the Governor's house, creates a frame, a visual context, and a series of connections that the characters are not aware of. The penetration of the Governor's foursquare establishment or the Fluskys' mysterious home thus becomes a metaphor for the secret, quietly ludic revelation of personality, as the audience is granted the privilege of spying on the Governor's bath or Lady Henrietta's sickness.

Unlike the long takes in *Rope,* which are interesting mainly as a technical device (how long can Hitchcock let the camera run without cutting away?) and a means of establishing the motifs of entrapment and claustrophobia, those in *Under Capricorn* are frequently more expressive visually.[8] What they express, however, is an equally profound ambivalence toward homes and betrayals of their values. If *Rope* presented three characters, one of them deceased, in keen competition for the position of hero, the different patterns of homelessness in *Under Capricorn* project three independent and largely contradictory villains. If Australia is conceived as a foreign land defined by the absence of civilized values, then the villain is Lady Hetty, who in killing her brother has alienated herself from her family and homeland and violated her own standards of truth, a violation which has driven her to a madness of guilt and sorrow. If Australia is conceived as a culture actively opposed to the colonial culture of Britain, then the villain is Sam, whose supposed crime has prevented his acceptance into the society he craves for his wife, who helps Adare launch her in society only to humiliate her in front of every important person in Sydney, and who finally wounds Adare with a pistol. And if Australia is conceived as a mysterious home whose mysteries have been set by a subtle manipulator, then the villain is Milly, who has encouraged Lady Hetty's drinking, poisoned her husband's mind against her, and resolved to kill her and marry him. Not only is Milly responsible for the Gothic apparatus ranging from hallucinations and poisoned cups to shrunken heads, but she alone, of all the characters in the film, has from the beginning the kind of awareness Hitchcock's long takes create for the audience; like Brandon until near the end of *Rope,* she is the setter of theatrical scenes rather than their victim. Yet only the last fifteen minutes of the film, after the extent of Milly's betrayal of her mistress is made clear, make any use of the dramatic irony Hitchcock had exploited so single-mindedly in *Rope.* The exchange of roles between cats and mice is so much more fluid and complete than in *Rope* that Lady Hetty's climactic revelation of her guilt makes it impossible to determine just who is preying on whom.

Given Hitchcock's different ways of conceiving the principals' homelessness—is their home a distant past in a faraway land, or an intolerably rough present which demands they live up to the consequences of their actions, or an enigmatic mystery to be resolved?—it is not surprising that the film has as much trouble as *Foreign Correspondent* or *Suspicion* in coming to an end. Milly's duplicity is discovered; Sam and Lady Hetty dedicate themselves to each other's happiness on a less deceptive footing; Adare swears on his honor as a gentleman that he wounded himself accidentally and prepares to return to Ireland. "It's a big country," he tells Flusky's secretary, who asks, "Then why are you leaving?" Glancing at Sam and Lady Hetty, Adare says, "Not big enough." Nor is the film finally big enough to resolve the different conceptions of home and homelessness Hitchcock explores.

*Under Capricorn* was the second and last film released by Transatlantic Pictures; its resounding financial failure ended Hitchcock's brief career as head of his own studio, and his subsequent pictures through *Dial M for Murder* were produced by Warner Brothers. *Stage Fright,* the first of these films, deals, like *Under Capricorn,* with homelessness, entrapment, and betrayal, and presents multiple perspectives on homelessness and several parodistic homes. This time, however, Hitchcock integrates these perspectives by means of the theatrical metaphor of his title. The film is a comic exploration of the inevitability of manipulative role-playing in a world whose homes, like Brandon's and Philip's apartment in *Rope,* turn out to be only more intimate theaters.

Jonathan Cooper (Richard Todd), on the run from the police for killing the husband of Charlotte Inwood (Marlene Dietrich), is forced to take refuge with the his friend Eve Gill (Jane Wyman), a dramatic student. The film opens with a curtain rising to reveal an extreme long shot of London, immediately followed by a series of shots showing Eve's car hurtling toward the audience. The pursuit of Jonathan will not end until the end of the film. Almost immediately, the police approach Eve for news about Jonathan, who becomes thereby dependent on her acting ability to fool them. In the meantime, she tries to get close to a policeman named Wilfred Smith (Michael Wilding) by pretending to a sensational interest in the murder, and close to Charlotte herself by acting the role of her new maid, having persuaded her former maid, Nellie Goode (Kay Walsh) that she is a reporter trying to get a newspaper story. For his part, Jonathan, although he has sworn his innocence to Eve and a flashback has illustrated his story, is only feigning innocence, since he really has killed Charlotte's husband after all, even though Charlotte encouraged him to commit the murder by falsely leading him on. None of this acting takes place on stage. In fact, every bit of acting that does take place on stage is immediately undermined, its artifice emphasized. Jonathan interrupts Eve's scene at the Royal Academy by dashing onstage and ad-libbing; Hitchcock shoots Charlotte's number "I'm the Laziest Gal in

Town" in long shots that show the stagehands, lights, and audience; and Charlotte's guest appearance at a garden party is interrupted when Eve's father Commodore Gill (Alistair Sim) has a Cub Scout show her a doll whose blood-smeared dress makes her unable to continue.

Acting, the film everywhere indicates, is the only possible way to define oneself in a world in which everyone is homeless and so has no identity to fall back on. Both Charlotte and Jonathan are made to feel trapped in her home: Charlotte by a loveless marriage, Jonathan by his fear of the police and his discovery by Nellie. Jonathan has to keep on the run because the police have staked out his home. Eve succeeds in placing herself in Charlotte's home, hoping to discover the secret life she keeps hidden from her public, only to discover that she is just as histrionic and insincere there as everywhere else.

*Stage Fright* has a great deal in common with *Murder!*: its flirtation, rare in Hitchcock, with a formal detective plot, its theatrical mise-en-scène and its corresponding emphasis on role-playing as the basis of identity, its universally deceptive characters, who are never truly off-stage (Eve comes closest when she is in her father's home, and later when she is in a taxicab with Smith, unsuccessful in implanting in his mind the idea that Charlotte killed her husband because he is distracted by his love for her). And like *Murder!* it treats alienation and betrayal as a universal condition to be endured by the weak—no one in the film is a heroically enduring character like Lady Hetty, since Charlotte's pose of endurance is outrageous—or a game to be played by the strong. But it differs from *Murder!* in one crucial respect: the theatrical roles its characters adopt as refuges from alienation or weapons against each other's hypocrisy are just as confining, just as treacherously imprisoning, as the homes they displace. Unlike Hannay's spontaneously assumed role as a political speaker in *The 39 Steps*—a role which kept him safe from his pursuers as long as he could sustain it—the characters in *Stage Fright,* like those in *Rope,* are at the greatest risk when they are acting a role. This danger is indicated early in the film, when Eve's acting teacher at the Royal Academy, annoyed by Jonathan's disruption of Eve's scene, announces, "We'll begin the rehearsal again—with the other cast. This cast seems to think that acting is all fun and games." Of course acting *is* fun and games, as the film will demonstrate, but very risky fun and games indeed. Eve acts the role of Nellie's cousin Doris Tinsdale in order to take Nellie's place as Charlotte's maid and dresser. But instead of putting her into a position of power, this masquerade becomes a threat to herself, since the minute Eve enters Charlotte's house, she sees Inspector Smith, who she knows can identify her as the actress Eve Gill. The comic mainspring of the plot is Eve's attempt to keep her different roles—she has pretended to Smith to be a weak-kneed girl fascinated with murder, to Nellie to be a newspaper reporter, and to Charlotte to be Doris Tinsdale—from colliding with each other; the harder she works to unmask Charlotte's duplicity, the greater the danger that she will be unmasked herself, especially after her brush with Jonathan at Charlotte's theater sets Smith on a hunt for Doris Tinsdale, actually the woman with whom he has just had tea. The ruse Commodore Gill uses to shock Charlotte out of her theatrical composure also unmasks Eve, whose identity as Doris is revealed when Charlotte's manager-lover Freddy Williams (Hector MacGregor) calls her from Smith's side to help Miss Inwood offstage.

It is no wonder that Hitchcock's characters have stage fright, since the stages whose conventions seem to sanction hypocrisy turn out to be the most dangerously revealing places of all. Charlotte, who wants her husband dead but does not want the trouble of killing him herself, is indeed, as her song suggests, the laziest gal in town. Eve's role as Doris Tinsdale makes her both cat and mouse, and Jonathan, the innocent victim of Charlotte's plotting, turns out to be both mouse and cat, since he not only killed Charlotte's husband but is finally prepared to kill Eve in order to pass himself off as deranged and escape hanging. But this final role inspires Eve to one last role of her own: she pretends that she will help Jonathan escape the theater where he has gone to ground, but traps him in the orchestra pit and screams for help. Jonathan has nowhere to run but the stage, where he is surrounded and killed by the falling curtain— an echo of the film's opening curtain-rising which shows that theatrical roles, though vastly more entertaining, are no safer than homes.

The conflict between pious endurance and playful audacity exploited so ruthlessly by Brandon Shaw, whose home becomes a trap for his guests and then himself, and so unconvincingly by Eve Gill, who cannot play a role without falling victim to it, takes a new form in *Strangers on a Train, I Confess,* and *Dial M for Murder.* In all three of these films, Hitchcock establishes from the beginning an equivocal attitude toward acts of betrayal by organizing each story around the betrayal of a pair of sympathetic lovers whose relationship itself constitutes a betrayal of marriage. Each film presents as part of its background a romantic triangle in which the audience's sympathies are enlisted against the institutional bonds of marriage and on the side of the lovers. Such a triangle involving Jonathan, Charlotte, and Charlotte's late husband had occupied a prominent place offscreen in *Stage Fright,* but now the triangle is at the center of the film. The hero of *Strangers on a Train* plans to allow his wife, who has been carrying on with at least one other (offscreen) man, to divorce him so that he can marry a senator's daughter. The heroine of *I Confess,* married to a rising young statesman in Quebec, is still in love with another man, now a priest. The heroine of *Dial M for Murder* considers her affair with a mystery writer a thing of the past, but the audience knows better even before they find that her husband is planning to murder her. Hitchcock had dealt many times before with romantic triangles but had seldom allowed the married characters in his thrillers to show any interest in other romantic partners. Lina Aysgarth's extramarital romance was excised from *Before the Fact* when it became *Suspicion;* Charles Adare's interest in Lady Henrietta Flusky is mostly non-amatory; Mrs. Verloc cannot take Ted seriously as a lover until her husband is dead.[9] The cat-and-mouse game in these films involves making the audience sympathetic to heroes and heroines whose adulterous desires prepare for their more complete betrayals by the villains.

Hitchcock's sympathy for his adulterous relationships does not amount to a critique of marriage as such, for it remains a valid ideal in all three films: *I Confess* ends with the heroine returning to her husband, and the other two clear the way for marriages between the lovers. Instead, the sympathetic lovers are used to play on the audience's anti-domestic impulses and equivocal feelings toward institutionalized romance and family ties, to prepare a bond between the villains and their victims—if the lovers can break social rules with impunity, why shouldn't the villains?—and to make give criminal betrayal a subversive appeal by rooting it in the appeal of forbidden romance. In all three films, the uneasy relationship between marriage and betrayal establishes a constant tension, since marriage does not domesticate the characters' desires but makes them lead to transgressions. But even though the principals' outlawed desires link them to the villains who prey on them, they do not make them outlaws, for the films encourage their forbidden love while ultimately providing a scapegoat for the consequences of their actions. Beginning with *Strangers on a Train,* the films place a successively greater and more reassuring distance between hero and scapegoat, confirming the general movement in the films of this period from the confrontational black humor of *Rope,* in which the intimacy between the principals becomes an oppressive joke, to the accommodating melodrama of *Dial M for Murder,* in which the intimacy between the villain and his victim turns out to be a sham.

Because the films are organized around the problem of betrayal, they emphasize both the attractiveness of the extramarital affairs they present and the dangerous consequences of unfaithfulness. Compared to betrayal, murder itself becomes a minor crime. As had been customary in all of Hitchcock's films except for the problematic *Secret Agent* and *Sabotage,* the characters who are killed are minor, unsympathetic, or only briefly shown. As in *Rope,* the focal crime in all three films, the crime for which the murder merely prepares, is that of betrayal. Unlike *Rope,* however, each of these later films works by setting the betrayal of marriage by a romantic affair against the betrayal of the sympathetic romantic lead by the criminal, and by establishing a close identification between the romantic lead and the audience, who are both released by the villain's climactic public confession.

All three films, in fact, use extramarital romance principally to motivate the frame-up of the hero or heroine. Since the frame-up is a cherished cliché of suspense fiction, it is surprising how seldom Hitchcock had used it before 1951. Ever since Ivor Novello's lodger, Hitchcock's heroes had been almost universally suspected of crimes of which they were innocent, but until *Stage Fright,* in which Jonathan cast suspicion on Charlotte in order to win Eve's sympathy, Hitchcock's villains had never maliciously implicated any innocent suspects in their crimes. They had never had to. Innocent suspects had invariably walked into rooms where corpses still lay, refused to answer questions or lied to the police, run away from investigations, or behaved otherwise suspiciously, providing the criminals with fortuitous red herrings. In films like *The 39 Steps, Young and Innocent,* and *Spellbound* the world is a place not so much of universal guilt as of universal suspicion, and it is in the nature of things for the hero to be suspected of wrongdoing. In the series beginning with *Strangers on a Train,* Hitchcock for the first time rationalizes his heroes' suspicious behavior through the villains' plotting. Guy Haines, Michael Logan, and Margot Wendice do not just fall under suspicion; they are betrayed to the police.

The three films taken as a group, in fact, could be called an anatomy of betrayal. The theme of betrayal which had surfaced in *Rope* and run beneath *Under Capricorn* and *Stage Fright* is treated in these later films much more rigorously, even formulaically. The criminal in each case frames an innocent person whom he doubles for his crime. But this pattern changes through the three films as the intimacy within each pair becomes gradually attenuated. The relation between betrayer and betrayed, which is central to *Strangers on a Train,* becomes less vital and less intimate in each of the succeeding films.

The intimacy between Guy Haines (Farley Granger) and Bruno Anthony (Robert Walker) is masked by the fact that they are, as the film's title announces, strangers; yet critics have unanimously seen Bruno as Guy's double.[10] The film insists on this intimacy in many ways: by its repeated use of terms like *double* ("The only kind of doubles I play," Bruno tells Guy about the pair of double Scotches he orders), *shadow* (the policeman who has been assigned to follow Guy), and *crisscross* (which refers not only to Bruno's plan for exchanging murders, but to the crossed tennis racquets on Guy's cigarette lighter, and by extension to Guy's relationship with his girlfriend Ann Morton [Ruth Roman]); by the scene in which Guy, learning from Bruno that his wife Miriam (Laura Elliott) is dead, stealthily joins him behind the barred fence outside his apartment rather than facing the police; by the later scene in which Guy, having knocked Bruno down at a party given by Senator Morton (Leo G. Carroll), helps him up and reties his bowtie; and by the film's famous opening sequence, in which floor-level shots cutting back and forth between the two men's feet finally show them meeting when Guy accidentally jogs Bruno's foot.

The theme of the sinister or diabolical double had already been well-established in Western fiction, in earlier films (particularly in German films of the 1920s, in Fritz Lang's American films, and in the *films noirs* so clearly influenced by the expressionistic visual style of the German films), and in Hitchcock's own work (*Shadow of a Doubt*). What is unusual in *Strangers on a Train* is the terms on which the relation between the hero and his double is established and the kinds of pleasure it offers. For Bruno shows no trace of the stock villain that even Uncle Charlie had revealed in his speeches about rich widows and about the world as a foul sty; he is always charming, polished, and even a little apologetic in his importunity—a much more attractive character than Guy himself. His attractiveness is rooted in the casting against type of Robert Walker, who plays him throughout as a spoiled child. Bruno's childlike charm, which is closely linked to his childish petulance and rage, sets the film apart from other treatments of its theme: Hitchcock has here presented a double who represents the repressed child in his hero.

Bruno's childishness is suggested even in Patricia Highsmith's novel, which, like the film, sets the murder of Miriam in an amusement park, a place where adults are expected to act like children. But Hitchcock makes this analogy much more explicit. In Highsmith's novel, Bruno talks like an adult and is capable for long periods of time of acting like an adult; Guy is ultimately destroyed not by Bruno's threats but by his inability to resist them. (In the book, when Guy goes to kill Bruno's father, he really does kill him, and finally, after Bruno's accidental death months later, is picked up by a policeman who overhears his confession to Miriam's inebriated lover.) Hitchcock emphasizes Bruno's status as child by returning to the amusement park for his final scene, where the carousel spinning out of control as one young passenger screams with delight provides a not merely an arresting image of uncurbed childish appetite but a powerful invitation to indulge such appetites oneself. *Strangers on a Train* is not likely to turn its audience into murderous psychopaths, but it appeals overtly to their destructive impulses by licensing those impulses as childish mischief and showing just how much fun they can lead to.

Children like Bruno are defined morally by their self-absorption. Bruno's petulance when Guy refuses to have anything to do with him after the murder and his patience in repeatedly explaining his position show his own inability, despite his friendliness to Guy, to see the situation from any point of view but his own. When he first sees Guy after the murder and tells him that they'd better talk when Guy isn't so tired— "I know I am. I've had a *strenuous* evening"—his egoism has an unnervingly comic edge. In adults, however, such moral self-absorption is the mark of the psychopath, the person who lacks any moral sense. Hitchcock had treated this problem before in the figures of Uncle Charlie and the General in *Secret Agent,* but most of the few children in his films are presented as innocents rather than cases of arrested moral development. As for the adults whose development has been arrested, both John Ballantine and Norman Bates have developed mental illnesses to protect themselves from a crippling guilt over their own deeds; their exaggerated sense of morality is the very opposite of psychopathia. Alone with Peter Lorre's charmingly murderous Abbott, Bruno dramatizes the connection between the charm of moral innocence and its potentially terrifying consequences.

This connection is confirmed by the pivotal figure of Ann's younger sister Barbara (Patricia Hitchcock), the other grown child in the film. Like Bruno, Barbara delights in flouting the conventions of adult speech and behavior: her speech is tactless, her sense of humor ghoulish, and several of her observations ("I think it would be wonderful to have a man so much in love with you that he'd kill for you!") uncomfortably reminiscent of Bruno. She is appropriately paired not only with Guy's childishly irresponsible wife—who, apparently recognizing Bruno as more completely a man than her two escorts, flirted with him at the amusement park until the moment he killed her—but with Bruno himself at her father's party. As Bruno playfully pretends to strangle a society woman (Norma Varden) who has several interesting ideas about killing her husband, he catches sight of Barbara, whose face and eyeglasses remind him of Miriam's, and begins to strangle her in earnest. Even as he seems to recognize Miriam in Barbara, the audience recognizes Barbara in him, for Bruno represents the little boy who, refusing to grow into any of the social roles offered an adult, appeals to the resentment, the antisocial bias, all adults share at being forced to act like adults. As he follows Miriam through the amusement park, Bruno is paired with the little boy who points a toy gun at him and says, "Bang bang"; in revenge, Bruno bursts the boy's balloon with his cigarette. There is something dangerously appealing in a villain who is willing to act as juvenile as the boy who is bothering him, even though the gesture of social defiance is petty, mean-spirited, and portentous of the violence to come.

Guy, the clean-cut tennis player who plans to marry the boss's daughter and launch his career in politics, is Bruno's natural prey because his own life leaves no room for the childish impulses which run wild in Bruno. He treats Bruno on their first meeting as a simpleton and thereafter as "a crazy fool" (one thing Bruno is certainly not), and like Bruno he never reveals any sense of humor about himself or any ability to see his situation from any point of view but his own. Hence Guy never appreciates the ways Bruno's murderous anti-domesticity is a parody of Guy's self-justifying anti-domesticity. Since Guy treats Bruno first as a child, then as a naughty child, threatening him but declining to exercise authority over him, it is fitting that Bruno behave more and more like a child intent on embarrassing his surrogate father, even to the point of planting his lighter at the scene of the crime. The figure of the misbehaving child suggests both why Bruno is charming and why he is so dangerous; since he has an adult's power without an adult's corresponding notion of moral consequence, he is liable to do things which make the analogy to a child woefully inadequate. When his mother (Marion Lorne) treats him literally as a naughty boy, her ignorance is both funny and appalling.

Bruno is dangerous because both he and Guy treat him as Guy's child, conferring on him a status that licenses his crimes as so much bad behavior. Like the 1934 version of *The Man Who Knew Too Much,* the film moves toward a resolution which shows the possibilities for accommodating the childish impulses that threaten to disrupt the social order.[11] At first it seems that Barbara's adolescent directness of speech is both childish and harmless, but Bruno's reaction to her at the party suggests that her childish impulses are potentially more dangerous than she realizes. The only safe way to release these impulses is under controlled conditions, in an amusement park whose boundaries are fixed, or, more obviously, within the context of a game. *Strangers on a Train* is the first of Hitchcock's films to make its status as a game whose conflict promises amusement (a notion essential to the Gaumont-British thrillers) into a theme which defines the primary relationship between his characters. In *The Man Who Knew Too Much,* games had been subversive, consistently threatening the social order; here they are metaphors for the social contract, for different ways of conceiving relations with other people and with society generally. The motif of games is organized around the first scene in the amusement park, which releases Miriam's dangerous sexuality and Bruno's murderous violence; Guy's crucial tennis match, which establishes the rules he must follow if he is to catch Bruno in time; and the return to the amusement park, which shows the two men struggling over a symbol of Guy's tennis game as they are spinning around on a ride gone mad and as a child pummels one of them in the belief that they are playing.

As sociologists like Huizinga and Caillois have shown, games are an especially valuable way of expressing one's childlike resistance to socialization because they establish a relationship between two adults which is at once competitive (and therefore expressive of a limited amount of hostility), controlled by rules which govern the participants' behavior, and inconsequential. The games in *Strangers on a Train* become dangerous only when their rules are broken. Guy's loss of his lighter, Miriam's flirting, Barbara's tactless witticisms, Bruno's pretended strangling of the society matron, and the final apocalyptic destruction of the merry-go-round all provide images of games or amusements run out of control. Guy gets into trouble in the first place because Bruno thinks they have made a deal and accuses Guy of breaking the rules, whereas Guy thinks that Bruno has broken the rules. The two are like competitors in a game each defines in his own way—an image that is brought vividly to life when Hitchcock crosscuts between Guy trying to win his tennis match and Bruno trying to recover Guy's lighter from the storm drain into which he has dropped it. Bruno betrays Guy (as he believes Guy has betrayed him) because they cannot agree what rules govern their play; the very relationship of parent and child that seals their intimacy ensures their isolation from each other's values.

Bruno becomes Guy's betrayer even though he likes him—likes him so much that he has done what he considers the favor of killing his wife. Guy, for his part, cannot acknowledge that the stranger he would prefer to have nothing to do with has released him from an intolerable marriage by acting out the child Guy has repressed. In *I Confess* the relationship between betrayer and betrayed is socially more intimate, since they are not strangers but members of the same household. Otto Keller (O. E. Hasse), like Bruno, does not begin as his friend's betrayer; just before he confesses to Father Michael Logan (Montgomery Clift) that he has killed the lawyer Villette, he thanks him for his help in taking in him and his wife (Dolly Haas)—they are German refugees in Quebec— and for realizing that they are "not ordinary servants." But Father Logan, even more pointedly than Guy, begins to act suspiciously because of his guilty knowledge, which makes him an accessory after the fact. In one sense, the story of *I Confess* is the story of Keller's changing attitude toward Father Logan: at first abjectly grateful to him, he later becomes self-justifying ("Hasn't God forgiven me, thanks to you? But the police never would. . . . You are so good. It's so easy for you to be good. Have you no pity for me?"), even as his wife begins to worry that Father Logan will turn her husband in. Later, Keller orders his wife not to wash the bloodstained cassock he has worn in his masquerade, and in his next meeting alone with Father Logan, who is trying to avoid him, he says, "Perhaps they'll hang you instead of me. That frightens you, yes?" It is only an hour or two later that Father Logan is arrested for Villette's murder.

The pattern of the criminal who begins as powerless and dependent on the hero's good will but gathers power from the hero's refusal to acknowledge him and ultimately becomes a threat who must be uprooted echoes the design of *Shadow of a Doubt,* but the specific threat—the criminal will set up the hero, arranging for him to shoulder the guilt—is peculiar to the Warners films. Yet this threat has a very different value in *I Confess* than in *Strangers on a Train,* for the relationship between Keller and Father Logan is not really at the center of the picture. Compared to Bruno, Keller himself is a comparatively minor character who serves mainly as the precipitating agent of Father Logan's ordeal rather than as his double. Keller sees himself as Logan's double, but the film presents their relation on quite different terms, for Logan's ordeal is complicated by two other moral problems.

The first of these involves Logan's own relations with the dead man, who was attempting to blackmail Ruth Grandfort (Anne Baxter) on account of the night she spent with Logan some five years ago, before he knew of her marriage. When Villette surprised the couple in his summerhouse the following morning, addressed Ruth as "Madame Grandfort," and made some unspecified suggestion about her behavior, Logan knocked him down. The prosecutor in his trial (Brian Aherne) therefore asks Logan how the jury can be sure Logan would not have killed Villette in a similar moment of anger, and asks Ruth whether their liaison really ended that night or continued without interruption to the present. Hitchcock makes a good deal of both these attempts to transfer Keller's guilt to Logan (who, according to this logic, might as well have killed Villette and therefore ought to suffer the consequences). Logan is moved to tell the prosecutor, "I'm not capable of murder." Later, as the jury is considering their verdict, the one bit of dialogue the scene presents concerns Logan's intimacy with Ruth: "They can't have spent just one night together. There must have been many more times." Both these attempts to make Michael Logan guilty of something have little to do with his relationship to Keller. Logan's and Ruth's first tête-à-tête reveals, even before Hitchcock presents the flashback showing the fateful night, that they have not continued their love affair; and whether or not Logan is capable of murder is beside the point, as both the prosecutor and the director must have realized.

Logan's distress stems not from his actual guilt, but from the appearance of his guilt, which leads to his moral condemnation. This universal condemnation is the second complicating factor in assessing the nature of Logan's ordeal. Almost from the beginning of the film he is the object of suspicious gazes—by Mrs. Keller as she serves breakfast, by Inspector Larue (Karl Malden) as he looks past Keller at Logan pacing the street outside Villette's house, by the policemen Ruth suddenly imagines to be watching them on the boat where they meet, by Keller as he follows Logan into the sanctuary, by the judge as he tells him that Logan personally disagrees with the jury's verdict, and finally by the mob which has gathered outside the courtroom to execrate him—a very rare representation in Hitchcock's work of the social order as a whole. Although these gazes carry different meanings (Mrs. Keller's gaze is clearly different from the judge's), they have a surprisingly similar force: the audience

feels each one as a threat to Logan's sense of himself, and therefore reacts with embarrassment and shame—not because Logan is guilty, but
because the scrutiny to which he is subjected is obscene.[12] The two most
important gazes in this pattern are Villette's gaze, when he first discovers
Logan and Ruth together (this is obviously the gaze which the others,
from Logan's point of view, all recall: the gaze that sees what Logan
would prefer to keep hidden, a gaze that will return with annihilating
force in *Psycho*), and Alma Keller's final gaze identifying her husband as
the murderer. After running through the mob to Logan's side and crying
"My husband!" she points directly at the camera, and Hitchcock cuts to
a shot of Keller firing his gun directly into the camera, in a violent sum-
mation of all the gazes thus far. But these last two shots warrant Logan's
innocence: the pattern of victimizing gazes, like the insistent parallels
to the stations of the Cross, establishes the pressure on Logan without
making him any guiltier. After *Strangers on a Train,* which focuses on
the relation between innocence and guilt, the desire to kill and the deed
itself, *I Confess* shifts its focus to the outrage visited upon its hero by
the circumstances which make him appear guilty and the priestly role
which makes him powerless to clear himself.

    Critics of the film have commonly remarked two problems it poses
but does not resolve: the coincidence of Keller's killing a man who just
happened to be blackmailing Ruth (Keller did not even know that Father
Logan knew Villette), and the melodramatic ending which vindicates
Logan before the police. Clearly, both these problems stem from the
film's insistence on Logan's essential innocence, for if his relation to
Keller and Villette were more intimate or equivocal, the conflict between
his urge to save himself and his sacramental duty would be less sharply
focused, and his return to a community which refused to accept his
innocence would be logically reasonable but emotionally frustrating, like
the death of Stevie in *Sabotage*.[13] The need, in making a film about a
Catholic priest, to gratify censors of all sorts—a need that delayed the
film, whose property Hitchcock had originally optioned while he was at
Transatlantic, until after *Strangers on a Train*—undoubtedly limited the
extent to which Father Logan could be implicated in Keller's guilt. Even
apart from this need, however, the final contrivance of Alma Keller's
breakdown and accusation, and the histrionic scene in which the dying

Keller tells Logan that "it would be better if you were guilty like me; then they would shoot you, quickly," suggest an imperative to distinguish innocence from guilt which is new to Hitchcock's American films—an imperative which for once takes precedence over the need to make Logan's persecution amusing to the audience. As Rohmer and Chabrol observe, "The just man assumes another man's guilt to the very extent that he himself is innocent."[14]

The focus on the outrage to an innocent principal by a scheming betrayer reaches a climax in *Dial M for Murder,* based on Frederick Knott's close adaptation of his play. Like Knott's play, the film is an exercise in turning the screws on its heroine, who is so resoundingly innocent that the film marks the greatest possible contrast between the scheming villain and his innocent victim, even though their relation is closer than that of Bruno and Guy or of Keller and Father Logan. The plan Tony Wendice (Ray Milland) makes to murder his wife Margot (Grace Kelly) depends on interposing one third party, his old ne'er-do-well schoolmate Swann, now called Captain Lesgate (Anthony Dawson), between them to commit the actual murder and another, Margot's old lover Mark Halliday (Robert Cummings), to provide him with an alibi. But Tony's murder by proxy turns out to be merely a preparation for his most insidious betrayal of Margot, his quick-witted and methodical framing of her for murder after she defends herself from Swann by killing him. When the police begin to question her story, it never occurs to Margot to doubt Tony's love and support; the very closeness of their relationship protects him from her suspicion. Since Tony has made it clear from his early conversation with Swann that he has married Margot, and intends to kill her, for her money, the film becomes, like *Rope,* an exercise in dramatic irony, and the pleasures it provides are principally those of watching Tony act out his suavely duplicitous role.[15]

The transference of guilt that bound Guy so closely and unwillingly to Bruno has all but disappeared in *Dial M for Murder.* Margot's affair with Mark is glossed over as an episode in the past; even when her guilt motivates her actions, as when she refuses to go to Tony about the letter from Mark that has been stolen from her, she is represented as a passive figure in Tony's game, since he has stolen the letter himself in order to encourage her to reveal the affair to him. And by this time—indeed, by his own account, the very night he first learned of the affair—he had already planned to kill Margot, using Swann as a cat's-paw. Later, when Margot is on trial, Hitchcock emphasizes her passivity still further by picturing only her but using the voices of the prosecutor, judge, and jury foreman rather than her own to recount the progress of the trial.[16]

Margot's innocence is a function of Tony's guilt. Guy hides Bruno's guilt because he is afraid of implicating himself more deeply in Miriam's murder; Father Logan shields Keller because of his priestly vows. But Margot covers up for Tony—telling the police, for example, the story he urges on her about why she did not call them immediately—for the most innocent reason of all: she has no idea that he is guilty. How could she, when she knows that she killed Lesgate herself? Nowhere in the film does Hitchcock touch on the question at the center of *Blackmail*— the guilt another woman might have felt over killing someone, even in self-defense—for in death, Lesgate is simply an object of horror and loathing to Margot, someone she rightly believes has nothing to do with her moral identity, her conception of herself. Because Margot, despite her technical implication in Lesgate's death and her marriage to her betrayer, remains untainted by Tony's villainy, the end of the film leaves no barrier to her reunion with Mark.

The dramatic irony that drives *Dial M for Murder* forward and makes Tony's duplicity so absorbing is not the only feature reminiscent of *Rope*, the other film bracketing this period. Both films are technical exercises as well, since *Dial M for Murder* is the third of Hitchcock's four one-set films (the others being *Lifeboat, Rope,* and *Rear Window*), and the only one of his films to be shot in the short-lived 3-D process. A widely remarked limitation of three-dimensional photography is that it does not create truly three-dimensional space but rather a series of flat planes at distinct apparent distances from the audiences, as in a diorama. But in *Dial M for Murder* Hitchcock brilliantly exploits this effect to turn the Wendices' London flat into a trap, first for Swann, then for Margot, and finally for Tony. Even audiences who have never seen the film in 3-D may well recall the moment when Margot's hand gropes frantically toward the camera to grasp the scissors she kills Lesgate with or the moment when Inspector Hubbard (John Williams) produces the latchkey which will incriminate Tony from beneath the stair tread and extends it toward the camera, but they are less likely to appreciate the ways Hitchcock exaggerates deep space at moments of emotional intensity. He marks the stages in Tony's cat-and-mouse game with Swann by placing Swann behind a lamp that looms menacingly in the foreground. When Tony casually chats with Margot while Swann rehearses the steps he will take in killing Margot, Hitchcock shows the action first in a steeply raked overhead shot, then in an eye-level shot that places Swann in a background whose focus is deeper than any interior space Hitchcock had shown since *Shadow of a Doubt*—far deeper than the relatively shallow focus of *Rope*. Later, when Margot, at Tony's request, tells her one lie to the police (she says that she delayed calling them because she assumed Tony would do so, not because he expressly told her not to talk to anyone), Hitchcock frames Hubbard in the foreground with Tony directly behind him, anxiously signaling Margot over his shoulder. In between these dramatic effects, Hitchcock favors compositions that place lamps, knickknacks, and pieces of furniture in the foreground, walls well in the background, and human subjects in a middle-ground clearly distinct from either, emphasizing the ways in which the mise-en-scène serves as a trap for Swann (whom Tony has enticed to the flat to blackmail into the murder), Margot (who, getting out of bed to answer Tony's phone call, is tantalizingly framed with Swann standing just behind her in the darkness), and Tony (who gives himself away by producing Margot's key to let himself into the flat). Even in 1953, 3-D was generally considered nothing more than a novelty whose only value was the competition it offered television—*Dial M for Murder*, along with *Kiss Me Kate*, was the only important film to use the process, and although shot in 3-D, it was first released in flat prints—but in Hitchcock's hands, this gratuitously aesthetic play with space, like the showy long takes of *Rope*, becomes part of the larger game of making entrapment fun.

# SIX

## HOME

## FREE ALL

**W**ith his move from Warners to Paramount in 1953, Hitchcock once again, as in the 1934 *Man Who Knew Too Much, Rebecca,* and *Rope,* broke the pattern of his most recent films and redefined the pleasures his audience could expect from his films. Audiences who had grown accustomed to watching expectantly as increasingly innocent victims of malicious betrayals were vindicated by plots which fixed the guilt on villainous scapegoats found the social polarities of the Warners films virtually inverted. The four films Hitchcock made at Paramount continue to set the isolated individual against the larger world, but that individual is no longer nearly so innocent or the social order so threatening. Instead the heroes themselves are guilty despite the audience's identification with them, and the world they fear so much represents their only hope for achieving a stable identity. The world of these films still represents a threat to the individuals' sense of themselves, but their resistance to this threat is now presented much more comically as paranoia, resistance to a social order which seeks to rescue them from themselves.

In a sense the conflict between self and world had always been at the heart of Hitchcock's work, particularly since his arrival in America. Since whole narrative genres like the novel have been organized around the conflict between the desires of the individual and the constraints of the social order, between perception as a function of individual vision and of social consensus (two conflicts rehearsed, for example, in *Don Quixote*), it is not surprising to find this conflict at the center of Hitchcock's earlier films, especially in the series beginning with *Rebecca* that treated personal identity, through the figure of the homeless hero or heroine, as a problem to be resolved. But the conflict between self and world appears exactly that in the films of the 1940s and early 1950s—a conflict which pits an uncompromising self against a hostile world. The new development in the Paramount films is the presentation of the world as a place which, although it may oppose particular desires of the individual, offers a context, indeed the only stable context, within which to define one's identity. The movement in each film is from suspicion of the social world as thwarting and threatening to a gradual acceptance of communal, as against naively individual, values as a means to self-definition. The four films of this period—*Rear Window, To Catch a Thief, The Trouble with Harry,* and the remake of *The Man Who Knew Too Much*—mark a climax of affirmation and optimism unique in Hitchcock's career, an optimism deeper than that of films like *The Lady Vanishes* because they acknowledge more fully the paranoia that such affirmations must overcome.

Such optimism is a startling development in the work of a director who had spent so much of his time in America casting aspersions on home and mother. But the source of this new development is no mystery. For one thing, *Rear Window* inaugurated a rare period of harmony in Hitchcock's professional life. When he moved to Paramount in 1953, he added a talented company of experts in production—assistant director Herbert Coleman, editor George Tomasini, camera operator Leonard South, costume designer Edith Head—to a staff that included his favorite cinematographer, Robert Burks, who had been working with him since *Strangers on a Train.* And he enjoyed the company of other, even more important collaborators: the actress Grace Kelly in his first two Paramount films, the composer Bernard Herrmann in the next two, and the screenwriter John Michael Hayes in all four. Hitchcock, who always preferred to work with the same actors and technicians and who regarded departures from his entourage as personal betrayals, seems to have found in this group of collaborators the security that had eluded him at Transatlantic. And his enthusiasm and optimism were sharpened

by the witty and affectionate screenplays of Hayes, whose work has a
relaxed confidence and humor unique in Hitchcock's films. Hitchcock
had worked from witty screenplays before, for example in *Secret Agent,*
*The Lady Vanishes,* and *Rope*. But the wit in the Gaumont-British films
typically bypasses the characters completely (when Hitchcock cuts from
Hannay's char to the train in *The 39 Steps,* neither Hannay nor the char
appreciates the joke), and the wit of the later films is generally ironic and
often punitive. In the four Hayes films, the principals constantly joke
among themselves, creating an atmosphere of high comedy that does not
simply involve the director and the audience but invokes a larger community of fictional characters. Though Hitchcock persisted in regarding
screenwriters as carpenters of dialogue to his visual and narrative speci-
fications, it is clearly Hayes who sets his seal, more completely than any
of Hitchcock's other screenwriters ever had, on the films of this period,
the only time in Hitchcock's career when the world around his principals is presented in an unequivocally positive light. The shift in tone
amounts to a reversal from the melodrama of betrayal and vindication
to the comedy of social integration.

This reversal is not as abrupt or treacherous as the reversals of *The*
*Man Who Knew Too Much* or *Rope,* then, because so many of Hitchcock's earlier films—from the time of *The Pleasure Garden,* which first
set public behavior against private lives—had dealt with similar subjects. What is unique about the four films Hayes wrote for Hitchcock at
Paramount is the lighthearted way they play with the characters, whose
expiation of guilt becomes softened from a matter of personal survival
to a ludic ordeal, and with the audience, who is invited at once to question and to affirm the pieties of middle America—the importance of a
stable home, the nurturing value of families, the need for conformity to
a social order—Hitchcock's earlier American films had treated, on the
whole, with cool skepticism.

The characters in the Hayes films are placed under the same kinds of
legal and moral scrutiny as earlier Hitchcock characters, but this time
the scrunity is less threatening. Just after leaving Francie Stevens's hotel
door still burning from her unexpected kiss in *To Catch a Thief,* John
Robie walks to the end of the corridor, briefly examines the building's
outside walls for ways a cat burglar might approach, then draws back

when he sees a policeman on the street below. The moment recalls a similar episode in *Strangers on a Train* when Guy, delayed from entering his home by Bruno's call to him, joins Bruno behind the wrought iron gate at the sound of a police car's approach, since both innocent heroes start to act guilty in front of the police. But the putative guilt of Robie, even though Hitchcock does not clear him conclusively until his film is nearly over, is a much lighter affair than the putative guilt of Guy, for even though the audience knows Guy did not kill his wife, the suspicion of complicity turns his life, like the lives of Father Logan and Margot Wendice, into a nightmare, whereas it just gives Robie a bad moment. In three of the Paramount films—*Rear Window, To Catch a Thief,* and *The Trouble with Harry*—the principals' essential innocence is so palpable, and their ultimate vindication so clearly and constantly portended, that the suspicion they fall under becomes, even to themselves, a game, like a game of hide and seek in which the threat of being tagged out is contained by the reassurance that the dilemma is only temporary and that arriving home will indeed free all. Robie and Jefferies and Sam Marlowe are all guilty of something, but compared to Devlin or Max de Winter or Rupert Cadell, they radiate reassurance. Even in the more melodramatic fourth film, Hitchcock's 1956 remake of *The Man Who Knew Too Much,* the threats to the kidnapped child and his family are contained by the frame provided by the earlier film, whose subversive shifts in tone give way here to a more opulent, soft-edged reworking of a now reassuringly familiar story.

It is precisely because his heroes' homes offer them a more stable identity—in effect, an escape from their private selves—that Hitchcock can play more freely with his audiences' associations with home. Each community in the Paramount films is presented as a center of value for its principals—precisely the sort of value Hitchcock's homes from *Rebecca* through *Dial M for Murder* had failed to offer their heroes and heroines. At the same time, the stories whose pull toward home and family is so strong play at any number of points on the audience's dissatisfaction with home. For the most part this play is comic, as in Francie's famous closing line as she surveys Robie's retreat in *To Catch a Thief:* "So this is where you live. Why, Mother will love it here!" As the Gaumont films indicate, however, Hitchcock's play is never more serious than when it is funny.

This play with the ideal of home is announced at the opening of *Rear Window* with the boldness of a manifesto, when housebound photographer L. B. Jefferies (James Stewart) tells his magazine editor that if the editor doesn't get him out of his apartment soon, he's going to do something desperate—like get married, a sentence Hitchcock underlines visually by the introduction of Lars Thorwald (Raymond Burr), whom Jeff will become obsessively convinced has killed his nagging wife. *Rear Window* is bold in other ways as well. It is the first of Hitchcock's films to use voyeurism as an explicit metaphor for the kind of male dominance based on male insecurity.[1] It illuminates the ways several earlier films have explored the same relation between patriarchal authority and the fear of insecurity even though they use different metaphors: the police in *The Lodger* and *Blackmail;* the problematic father-figure in *The Man Who Knew Too Much, Rebecca,* and *Shadow of a Doubt;* and the spy in *Notorious.* Finally, it suggests, for nearly the only time in Hitchcock's work, the possibility of conversion for the hero, who can become less authoritarian and disengaged by facing and overcoming his fears about himself. The film casts a retrospective illumination on Hitchcock's earlier work even as it shows a new path that work would take.

Hitchcock agreed with Truffaut that Jeff is a voyeur whose activity, which combines idleness, immobility, visual stimulation, and a keen imagination, serves as a metaphor for the audience's own. Since most of the camera setups are from inside Jeff's apartment, the audience is restricted until nearly the end of the film to his point of view as he pieces together the clues that will convict Thorwald. Despite this identification, however, the film is far from taking Jeff on his own terms as a man who just happens to be watching his neighbors. Both Jeff's girlfriend Lisa Fremont (Grace Kelly) and his nurse Stella (Thelma Ritter) chide him for snooping, and the way the camera isolates Lisa and Jeff in their conversations makes it clear from the beginning that Jeff is more interested in watching his neighbors than in pursuing his romance with Lisa.

It is not that the neighbors are more interesting than Lisa; one of their principal attractions, in fact, is that they offer Jeff a safe way of considering his relationship with her. Every set of neighbors Jeff watches is organized around a love relationship, and every relationship is somehow deviant or deformed.[2] The spinster Miss Lonelyhearts and the composer both dedicate themselves to absent or hypothetical lovers; the dancer

Miss Torso entertains groups of men Jeff considers potential boyfriends and Lisa wolves; the older couple treat their dog as a child; the sculptress expresses neighborly concern by meddling; and the newlyweds are comically at odds almost from the beginning, with the groom repeatedly opening the shade and looking out the window and his bride repeatedly calling him back to bed. The Thorwalds offer a more pointed analogy to Jeff's and Lisa's own situation. Since Hitchcock never shows why Mrs. Thorwald is confined to her room, as Jeff is, or why Thorwald has decided to kill her—only that she constantly complains about him and that he is carrying on with another woman—there is reason to fear that Lisa and Jeff, who disagree about everything, will end up as the Thorwalds, perhaps because she will become impatient of taking care of him or because he will grow restless with her domestic demands. As Jeff gazes around his courtyard, in fact, he is watching a kaleidoscopic prophecy of his future, a catalog of the number of ways love can go wrong.

The analogies between Jeff's position and his neighbors' lives explain why he should be so interested in them. But Jeff's interest is not merely predictive: he is so determined that Thorwald killed his wife that he becomes obsessed with demonstrating his guilt. Since proving Thorwald guilty would justify Jeff's reluctance to settle down with Lisa, he has a great deal at stake in his spying, and it is not surprising how despondent he becomes when his old police friend Tom Doyle (Wendell Corey) deflates his hopes by producing evidence corroborating Thorwald's story that his wife is away on a visit. But it is—or ought to be—surprising that he is joined in his depression by Lisa, whose stake in the case is originally the opposite of Jeff's. Although Lisa has no interest in impugning the promise of domestic felicity as such, she has by this time seized on Jeff's suspicions as an occasion for disproving his belief that the two of them are too different to share a life; hence she wants Thorwald to be guilty just because Jeff does.

This mixture of motives—Lisa wants to catch Thorwald as a way of trapping Jeff into marriage, Jeff wants to prove his guilt in order to justify his escape from marriage—which goes to the heart of *Rear Window* and the other Paramount films, is rooted in the audience's contradictory desires. On the one hand, Jeff's telephone speech to his editor constitutes a clear challenge to domestic values the film cannot leave unanswered, and numerous conventions of romantic comedy—the attractiveness of the leading couple, the man's resistance to marriage, the emphatic advice of Stella (whose happy marriage provides an effective counterweight to all the warped romances in Jeff's neighborhood)—are enlisted on behalf of the promised happy ending. On the other hand, Jeff's desire to prove Thorwald guilty echoes the audience's desire for something to happen in his neighborhood to justify all his watching. The most telling implication of the audience's identification with Jeff is that, despite wanting an ending ripe with romantic promise, the audience wants Thorwald to have killed his wife too, in order to make its audienceship—or snooping, as Hitchcock calls it—worth it.[3]

Jeff is not the first Hitchcock hero to fear emotional intimacy, but he is the first whose fear takes the form of preferring voyeurism to consummation, mediated to direct experience. Holding a wineglass Lisa has filled for him, he watches Miss Lonelyhearts share a toast with her imaginary lover and silently holds his glass up too. He is sharing her emotion, but she does not know that, because he is watching her without revealing himself, experiencing her vulnerability without making himself vulnerable to her. It is appropriate that Jeff, a free-lance photographer (that is, a professional watcher), prefers this kind of mediated, non-reciprocal relationship to the intimacy Lisa offers him. Mutual intimacy imposes a burden which spying offers a way to avoid—an avoidance not only of romantic entanglements but of membership in the larger community.

Jeff's sexual desires throughout the film are made symbolic of his relationship to the larger social community—a community defined more generally by his home and neighborhood. The restlessness Jeff expresses over the phone to his editor is essentially a reluctance to put down roots, as Lisa points out when she chides him: "Isn't it about time you came home?" This is an astonishing question to be seriously asked in the new film by the director of *Rebecca, Notorious, Under Capricorn,* and *Dial M for Murder.* But the film proceeds even more surprisingly to answer it in the affirmative by breaking down Jeff's voyeuristic sense of independence from Lisa and his neighbors, a sense which is tied by the photographic equipment he uses in his spying to his determination to retain control of the gaze: to define his relationships with others as those he controls by watching his partners without being watched himself. It is precisely this independence, on which he bases his identity, that precludes the openness to others, especially to Lisa, which would release his true identity and give the audience a kind of pleasure seldom associated with Hitchcock. Instead of waiting expectantly for the social order to recognize the hero's innocence and let him off the hook, the audience waits for him to emerge from his isolation and discover his identity through his relationship with the larger community. Although Jeff, like Hitchcock's heroes and heroines of the forties, can't go home again, he and Lisa can make a new home rooted in their acceptance of each other.

In order for Jeff and Lisa to earn their happy ending, they both need to prove they can act as in accord with each other's wishes. Lisa, who has disdained the active life Jeff leads, proves herself a worthy mate for him by sneaking into Thorwald's apartment to get the proof his wife is dead: her wedding ring, which she triumphantly displays behind her back to him across the courtyard as the police question her. The ring links the dead Mrs. Thorwald with the future Mrs. Jefferies, who is using it to force Jeff to propose, and so summarizes the film's profoundly equivocal attitude toward the project that brings Lisa and Jeff together and toward the ideal of marriage in general. And Jeff proves that he takes Lisa seriously when he forgets his own danger from Thorwald, who has seen Lisa's gesture, and sends Stella down to the police station to bail her out. Before this final episode, however, Jeff must confront the embarrassment of having Tom Doyle pair him with Thorwald when he interrupts Jeff's tirade about Thorwald's hidden life with a significant glance at Lisa's negligee (she had earlier announced her plans to stay the night) and asks, "Do you tell your landlord everything?" Jeff bridles at this remark, but he accepts its import, marking the first time in the film when he acknowledges that he, like Lisa, Thorwald, and the rest of his neighbors, is someone to be watched.

There might seem further perversion or irony in the fact that Jeff gets interested in Lisa only when she is put on display as an object to be watched in Thorwald's window. The scene is the opposite of perverted; far from regarding Lisa as merely an object, and therefore, finally, a legitimate object of attention, Jeff is now regarding her with frantic, self-forgetful concern; it is the first time in the film when his looking out his window has carried with it any of the emotional engagement normally associated with looking, and Lisa is the first person he has watched who knows she is being watched, who returns his look, and who is therefore an agent, not just an object. But there is irony aplenty in the scene. Jeff, who has counted all through the film on being able to watch his neighbors without the threat of involvement, now finds that he cannot share Lisa's danger, try as he may. He can only hope that the police officers he has called will rescue Lisa from Thorwald's apartment by arresting her for robbery. And when Thorwald intercepts the signal Lisa is sending with the wedding ring, Jeff becomes vulnerable himself—more vulnerable, more isolated and immobile, than Thorwald has ever been, as the film demonstrates by suddenly slowing and magnifying the sounds of Thorwald's approach to Jeff's apartment. Jeff tries to save himself by blinding Thorwald with flashbulbs—not only relying on the tools of his trade, but forcing Thorwald to assume once more the position of object of his gaze—but he can only delay him briefly; and his rescue depends on the police, just as his convalescence depends on the loving attention of Lisa, which he is now finally ready to accept.

Jeff's fall from his apartment makes him, naturally enough, the object of all his neighbors' gaze—it is evidently the first time most of them have become aware of his existence—and the film's final sequence ties up the various love knots in conventional repetitions, jokes, and romantic pairings. Like most of Hitchcock's films, *Rear Window* has an ending—the substitution of an ideal community of lovers for a pathological collection of deformed lovers—that does not really resolve the problems the film has posed. Jeff at least has overcome his crippling sense of voyeuristic independence by seeing himself in his neighbors and his neighbors in himself, and so accepting his necessary ties to his community; in the last shot of the film, he is finally, for the first time in the film, ignoring them, peacefully sleeping, while a pan over to Lisa, dressed in the height of casual fashion, putting down a copy of *Beyond the High Himalayas* and picking up a copy of *Harper's Bazaar,* might be taken as indicating that she has learned how to share Jeff's life without giving up her own.[4] But this ending, like the ending of *Suspicion,* could equally be taken in the opposite way, as indicating that Lisa has now snared Jeff by learning to get around him, and that the two of them are headed toward the

long, slow slide that ends at the Thorwalds'. The second sequence of
*Vertigo*, which shows another voyeuristic hero played by James Stewart
at the point of emerging from his medical confinement ("Tomorrow the
corset comes off," he tells his solicitous female companion) and bound
for catastrophe, suggests that the habit of spying may not be so easy to
overcome after all.

But *Vertigo* was still four years off as Hitchcock finished work on *Rear
Window*, and the ambivalence of the films that immediately follow at
Paramount is far more reassuringly comic. Although *Rear Window* has
unmistakable similarities with Hitchcock's forties films, its more accepting view of society marks a dramatic change in the relation Hitchcock
establishes with his audience. Instead of inviting them to identify with
an innocent hero or heroine who is threatened by a hostile environment,
a villainous double, or a treacherous intimate, Hitchcock makes their
identification here far more equivocal, since Jeff is anything but innocent. *Rear Window* is a comedy that makes the audience feel good by
encouraging the audience to distrust the hero's self-isolating impulses
and then rescuing him from those impulses. Such an optimistic ending
would have been unthinkable in the films since *Rebecca* because these
films typically double their heroes or heroines with mysterious figures
who represent their own darker side, but with whom they cannot be
reconciled. Hence the films end with the death or utter rejection of the
double, not with an integration of public self and shadow self. When the
conflict is between self and social order rather than self and double, as
in *Spellbound* and *Notorious,* the emphasis again is on the vindication of
the individual hero or heroine, not his or her reconciliation to a community, for the primary function of the community in these films is to cast
doubt on individual identity. What enables Hitchcock's earlier American films to arrive at happy endings, as almost all of them do, is their
selection of a scapegoat who is assigned responsibility for the antisocial
impulses of all the characters. This pattern is dramatized most straightforwardly in *Lifeboat,* but it operates in all the other films of the forties.
The emphasis of the films' endings is therefore not on the heroes' triumph but on the punishment of the villains, the diminution of the social
world, or a decidedly tentative or muted resolution. *Rebecca*'s apocalypse
neglects the second Mrs. de Winter in favor of the dead Rebecca and the

dying Mrs. Danvers; *Foreign Correspondent* presents an ending which concludes the plot without resolving the issues it raises; and *Suspicion,* that film of so many endings, concludes with a shot that is the most ambiguous of all.

The heroes' resolution of their problems in these films is often so tentative or incomplete that they become less important and interesting than their tempters or opposites, from the enigmatic Rebecca through Johnnie Aysgarth, Uncle Charlie, Willie the U-boat captain, and Lady Paradine to Charlotte Inwood. *Strangers on a Train* and *Dial M for Murder* present equally strong, though less mysterious, villains, but the villains in the other films of the early 1950s are either perfunctory, comparatively retiring, or altogether absent. These films, less often organized around a mysterious and equivocal figure, are themselves less mysterious; they continue a tendency begun with *Rope* to substitute dramatic irony for mystery, and struggles for power for struggles for knowledge. Although films like *Rebecca, Shadow of a Doubt,* and *Under Capricorn* might be said to be about their villains, the films of the early 1950s are, with one exception, about their heroes.

This exception is *Dial M for Murder,* the most backward-looking of Hitchcock's films of the period, as *Notorious* had been the most forward-looking of the Selznick films. *Dial M for Murder* is from beginning to end a display of its villain's virtuosity. Indeed a weakness of the film is that although its focus is on its heroine's peril, she takes center stage only briefly; before and after the attempt on her life, her husband's businesslike planning of her demise dominates the film, while she is kept offscreen. *Notorious,* by contrast, focuses throughout on its heroine, although, like the films of the 1950s, it masks its status as an exploration of her identity by concentrating on social roles and reputation rather than on the psychology of a principal whose identity is problematic but not mysterious (the audience always knows what Alicia, as against Rebecca, Johnnie, and Uncle Charlie, is like), an individual whose identity is ultimately stable and so capable of integration into the social order—although *Notorious* pointedly declines to show this integration.

Although Hitchcock continues to encourage the audience to identify closely with his threatened heroes and heroines, the social order in which they operate is represented in more attractive terms in the later films. In the Selznick films the police were the avatars of social will and social identity, who mistakenly pursued Barry Kane and John Ballantine, branded and exploited Alicia Huberman, arrested Lady Paradine, vindicated Max de Winter, and were heard arriving at the end of *Rope* as public figures who would confirm Rupert Cadell's assessment of Brandon and Philip. Charlie Newton, Alicia Huberman, and Eve Gill are given policemen as lovers who will affirm their identities by fusing social and romantic conceptions of them, and Charles Adare serves much the same function for Lady Henrietta Flusky without becoming her lover. In the films of the early 1950s, policemen become more and more marginal. Although Guy Haines is doubled not only with Bruno Anthony but with the policeman Leslie Hennessey, policemen recede in importance throughout the films that follow until they become simply avatars of power rather than certifiers of identity. This latter task is taken over by the closed community, already foreshadowed in *Under Capricorn,* which isolates its characters thousands of miles from the values that inspire them. In *Rear Window* and *The Man Who Knew Too Much,* this community is defined by the traditional group of lovers or family, a group common to Hitchcock's earlier films and many other stories. In *Rear Window* and *The Trouble with Harry,* the community is further specified, more surprisingly, to include a neighborhood of sympathetic people. These four films mark the only time in Hitchcock's career when he offers the pleasures of sympathetic self-transcendence; together they comprise his most thoughtful examination and affirmation of the possibilities of self-definition through social definition, the unity of self and world.

Most of Hitchcock's earlier thrillers had concerned the efforts of suspected criminals to establish their innocence. Each of the Paramount films, beginning with *Rear Window,* opens with characters who are obviously guilty of something, guilty precisely (as it turns out) by virtue of their individuality, their determination to define themselves as autonomous individuals in opposition to the social order, and offers them the opportunity to integrate themselves into a society that defines them more fully and compassionately than their individuality can. In Hitchcock's chase films, or in *Blackmail* or *Notorious* or *I Confess,* the function of society is precisely to fix individual guilt. But in the Paramount films, for the only time in Hitchcock's career, society offers, if not forgiveness or escape from individual guilt, the possibility of transcending guilt and so of a magical self-discovery unavailable to the isolated individual. But just as the Warners films had marked a gradual retreat from the unsettling intimacy *Rope* had established between the hero and the villains (who have merely been putting his Nietzschean social views into practice), the later Hayes films retreat from the sharpness of *Rear Window,* in which Jeff urgently needs to be rescued from his unhealthy isolation but fears entering a community he considers too compromised. These films consolidate Hitchcock's exploration of the possibilities of social integration for his heroes and heroines, but they make integration easier by making the principals less isolated and less fearful and the community less threatening.

After *Rear Window, To Catch a Thief* appears as something of a holiday for the director as well as the characters. The film might be described as a simpler, major-key version of *Rear Window,* since the hero's guilt is so manifest that it can for the most part be relegated to a barely remembered past. John Robie (Cary Grant), a former cat burglar, is roused from retirement on the Riviera by accusations that he is committing a new series of burglaries aping his style. In attempting to clear his name, Robie finds himself trapped by his past reputation. Can he establish a new identity based on his detection of the real thief? The film plays with the question of Robie's innocence in the same way *Rear Window* plays with the question of Thorwald's guilt: although both are technically in doubt until the closing scenes of the film, both films endorse the desires they predicate, so that audiences who assume that Robie is innocent and Thorwald guilty because of the conventions of their stories turn out to be right.[5] Hitchcock's success in making the audience take Robie on his own terms—I have never met an audience who did not believe Robie's protestations of innocence to his old confederate, the restaurateur Bertani (Charles Vanel)—leaves him free to take the issue of Robie's guilt or innocence as the basis for a series of increasingly complex games. The primary game which gives the story its shape is the romance between Robie and the demurely predatory Francie Stevens (Grace Kelly), whose company he cultivates, suitably disguised, as a likely victim of the thief but who turns detective on her own, identifies him as John Robie, and announces that she would like nothing better to share his next job and

the excitement of the life she takes him to be leading. Within this framework other games abound, two of particular importance: the masquerade
and the chase. In the film's second sequence Robie eludes the police by
turning his distinctive car over to his servant and later pretends to be a
vacationer; for Francie, he plays the role of the American lumber tycoon
Conrad Burns; after he is forced to leave her, he disguises himself as a
fisherman; in the film's final sequence, he assumes a double disguise,
appearing first as the blackface servant of Francie and her mother (Jessie
Royce Landis), then leaving that disguise to the insurance investigator
Hugheson (John Williams) so that he can wait in hiding for the real thief.

Chases are even more prominent, providing a structural model for
the film as a whole. First Robie is chased by the police; later Robie
and Francie are followed by the police; after they shake their pursuers,
Francie makes it clear that she is chasing Robie; as Robie chases the
real thief over the roof, he is in turn threatened by the police; finally
Francie chases Robie to his house. Most of these chases are logically inconsequential. Robie spends the first twenty minutes of the film trying
to escape from the police, but in the next shot after his capture he is
sharing a drink with Hugheson outside his villa; the police have chased
him only to let him go, as in a game of fox and hounds. When Hugheson offers to introduce Robie to the Stevenses, Robie announces that he
prefers to introduce himself in disguise and by means of a ruse, because
"in this business you can't do things the honest way." His wish to play at
being Conrad Burns from Oregon serves no purpose except to heighten
his own and the audience's pleasure.

Robie's masquerade is amusing rather than pointless because it takes
what would elsewhere be suspensefully serious threats—unjust accusations, apprehension by the police, imprisonment for life—and turns
them into the suspensefully inconsequential threats of unmasking by
Francie, an unsought romantic liaison, and imprisonment in an improbably glamorous and exciting marriage. Robie protests his innocence to
Francie, but whether she believes him doesn't really matter, because if
she catches him, he's simply fallen into a pipe dream of romance. Casting
Francie as Robie's principal pursuer charges the whole idea of pursuit
with such glamor and wit, in fact, that it makes every pursuit into a
game. When she takes him in her car, ostensibly to visit houses he is

considering renting, they are followed by the police to no purpose (as usual, Robie has nothing to lose if he is caught), and when Francie reveals her own suspicions of Robie by the announcement that they have shaken the police, her challenge seems no more or less threatening than theirs.

As it turns out, the game between Robie and Francie is played for higher stakes than Robie's pursuit by the police; Francie is determined to make Robie deflower and finally marry her, Robie is determined to maintain his independence by avoiding romantic commitments. Like other games, this one is less important for its propositional content than for the experience it affords the players, and in this case the audience. And like other games, it is fun only as long as it lasts. Although Francie is intoxicated by the idea of Robie's thefts, she sobers up the minute she thinks he has robbed her mother. Clearly it is more fun to pursue an elusive goal, to chase or search for someone, or indeed to be pursued, than to reach the goal or unmask the masquerader. Because the threatening game between Robie and the police is displaced but not resolved by the more high-spirited game between Robie and Francie, *To Catch a Thief* is structured as a series of attempts to prolong the dance of desire indefinitely by deferring the moment it must end in anticlimactic consummation, the consummation which gives the film its shape but which also signals the end of its enchantments.

The dance takes another form in Hitchcock's following film, *The Trouble with Harry,* whose principals' games of ritual self-accusation, romantic confession, and official dissimulation, like the games of *A Midsummer Night's Dream,* reflect a more generally comic ambivalence toward the social order whose principles they triumphantly exemplify by playfully flouting. The four principles spend the entire film alternately burying and exhuming the corpse of a man mysteriously dead in the Vermont woods in order to assuage their guilt and conceal their possible involvement in his death. The film's single obsessive joke turns on the extremely unsentimental, matter-of-fact attitude that everyone adopts toward the dead Harry Warp. Captain Wiles (Edmund Gwenn), who thinks he has shot him accidentally, chides him for coming so far from home to die. The absentminded Dr. Greenbow, his nose in a book, trips over the corpse, mutters an apology, and walks off in a new direction. A local tramp steals his shoes, and Sam Marlowe (John Forsythe) sketches his portrait. When Arnie Rogers (Jerry Mathers), having discovered the body in the film's opening scene, returns with his mother (Shirley MacLaine), and she tells him that the man is taking "a deep, wonderful sleep," and adds, "Come on, let's go home and get some lemonade," her response seems at once logically consistent and outrageous. The outrage presupposes the audience's reverence toward the fact of human death, especially concerning the necessity of ritual observances like funerals as a way of distinguishing people from animals. Treated as a nuisance, an obstacle, or a source of shoes or images, Harry seems comically less than human.

But this apparent diminishing or misplacing of Harry's humanity gradually reveals a deeper, communal idea of humanity, for Harry's death, unlike his life, has the power to unite the people around him into a community. At the beginning of the film, Hitchcock's standoffish New Englanders have little to do with each other, and especially with the apparent outsiders among them—Jennifer, who has lived in the village for only a few years, and Sam, a painter who has come for the summer. Miss Gravely (Mildred Natwick) and Captain Wiles have never been inside each other's homes or learned each other's first names. The gathering-place for the village has been the general store, run by Mrs. Wiggs (Mildred Dunnock), and its representative authority figure has been her son Calvin (Royal Dano), the deputy sheriff who forbids hunting on posted land "because I posted it." Calvin's rules allow the community to operate by stifling personal expression (e.g., hunting, the great pleasure of Captain Wiles's life) in the name of meaningless formalities. As the unobserved pieties toward the late Harry Warp come to seem more and more meaningless, Calvin gradually reveals himself as the true outsider. Although he has lived in the village all his life, his narrow concern with the law blinds him to everyone else's activities—the film ends just as he is finally about to discover the body that has been arranged for him to find—and his fondness for tinkering with noisy old cars introduces the one discordant note into the film's bucolic soundtrack, a note far more jarring than that of Captain Wiles's harmless three rifle shots.

The other outsider to the community is Harry himself, who has forced himself on his sister-in-law Jennifer Rogers (when his brother died shortly after their wedding, Harry insisted on taking his place, then abandoned her in the face of an unfavorable horoscope), followed her in order to take her back with him, and finally, dazed from her hitting him with a bottle, insulted and attacked Miss Gravely. Since Harry, like Calvin, represents the letter of the law estranged from its spirit, his death is aptly treated with a complete disregard for the letter of the law (everyone is willing to cover up for whoever may have killed him) in observance of its spirit. This spirit, a sense of compassion and concern for others, allows Harry's death to assume its proper importance, as a natural event entirely proper to the community.

The propriety of Harry's death is secured by the final revelation that he died of natural causes, but the film has intimated much earlier that Harry's death was not the outrage it seemed. The setting of the story at the height of the New England autumn emphasizes death as part of a natural cycle, a cycle that is echoed by the time frame of the story (it begins early one morning and ends early the following morning) and the low-angle shot of Arnie standing over Harry's body, its feet to the camera, as if he were growing out of the man later revealed as his uncle. Unlike Calvin Wiggs, who treats death as an outrage, an extraordinary event whose implications are inevitably suspicious, the other principals are drawn together by their ability to accept Harry's death as a natural event in the life of the community. In ignoring Harry's putative claims as a human being—his presumed individuality, the superstitious reverence due the very fact of his dying—it is precisely Harry's deeper humanity, his life in the community, that his survivors ought to be honoring. Since in Harry's case there is little such life to honor, their concern to shield each other from suspicion is doubly natural.

If the film's story emphasizes the importance of the community in releasing the energy and confirming the morality of its individuals, Hitchcock's visuals are equally important in establishing the community as the natural or unmarked unit of humanity, so that the isolated individual seems exceptional and deviant. *The Trouble with Harry* looks different from any other Hitchcock film. For the only time in his career, Hitchcock avoids close-ups entirely and works in the range from mid-shot to long shot. Individual compositions tend to balance figures against each other or against their surroundings, which thus achieve far more importance than in most Hitchcock films. The tendency to balance characters against their backgrounds within each shot—a tendency critics have typically associated with Howard Hawks as against Hitchcock[6]—had already been underway in *To Catch a Thief,* which marked the first time Hitchcock was shooting in a wide-screen aspect ratio, Paramount's new VistaVision process, which was designed to widen the screen's aspect ratio without sacrificing definition or depth of field. Robert Burks's decorative cinematography for the film, which won an Academy Award, set the standard for the rest of Hitchcock's color films through *Marnie;* in particular, Hitchcock took advantage of the wide-screen beginning in *The Trouble with Harry*'s opening credits, which are laid out in a horizontal line like a joke with Harry's corpse as the punchline, and continuing with a virtually unbroken series of shots balancing individual characters or groups with the autumn backgrounds within the frame, which marks a social unit from which the isolated individual deviates.

Within this broader visual field Hitchcock, like Hawks, places less emphasis on facial expressions than on physical acting. Since most of the characters remain resolutely poker-faced through most of the film, small changes of expression and gesture become disproportionately significant: when Miss Gravely extends an arm to Captain Wiles over Harry's corpse and thanks him for his support, her gesture has more impact than the firing of a machine gun in a Sylvester Stallone film. Hitchcock's preference for two-shots rather than shot-reversal sequences, particularly in the scenes between Jennifer and Sam, confirms the framed group rather than the isolated individual as the fundamental social unit. And the gradual movement of the visuals not only from day to night but from exteriors to interiors suggests the gradual building of a new social order whose center is Jennifer's front room out of the natural experience associated with the plot of land in which Harry is repeatedly interred.

The editing of the film is as unusual as its choice of camera distances. The fragmentary nature of the story in *Rear Window,* in which apparently unrelated and repeated events were separated by hours before the story returned to the same location, had led Hitchcock to use an unprecedented number of fade-outs to separate individual sequences. The fades slowed down the rhythm of the film, confirmed the ritualistic nature of the repeated actions outside Jeff's window, and emphasized the fact that with minor exceptions (the composer's progress on his song, the death of the dog), the Thorwalds' apartment was the only place in the neighborhood subject to change or development. *The Trouble with Harry* uses just as many fades, but for a different reason. Hitchcock's plan to shoot the film on location in Vermont was ruined by heavy rains which allowed only a few exterior shots to be made before the trees lost their autumn foliage.[7] In addition to process shots allowing the shooting of outdoor scenes indoors, Hitchcock also used some exterior extreme long shots—of a church, a meadow, and several groups of trees—as introductory shots for each episode. These shots, which are unique in Hitchcock's films, are reminiscent of what Noël Burch has called the "pillow shots" of Yasujiro Ozu[8]: they break the action into episodes and simultaneously provide a sense of the primacy of the non-human environment, so that human action itself is perceived as having an irruptive force. Both the camera setups and the editing of the film, in other words, tend to organize the story around the environment and its interactions with the characters, and so encourage the audience to take the long view of Harry's death. The emphasis is not on assigning individual guilt— although Calvin Wiggs is treated as a threat, he is never offered seriously as a moral authority—but in recovering from a trauma, and the best response to Harry's death is one which allows the community to grow in sympathy with the natural rhythms the film so carefully establishes. Nowhere else in Hitchcock's work is there such a consistent emphasis on the social order, and nowhere else is the triumph of the community as complete, as unruffled, or as joyously celebratory.

*The Man Who Knew Too Much,* Hitchcock's remake of his 1934 film, deals again with a community which must be created by the principals rather than assumed—a community whose power therefore is especially subject to scrutiny. In this case, the community is based not on the common cause strangers make in order to become friends but on a husband and wife's rediscovery of each other. Like Bob and Jill Lawrence in the earlier film, Ben McKenna (James Stewart) and his wife Jo (Doris Day) play at their relationship; together with their son Hank (Christopher Olsen), they joke about Ben's losses last year in Las Vegas, and Jo sings duets with Hank, dances with him, and tells him, "Oh, you're divine." When Hank is kidnapped to prevent Ben from passing on the message given to him by the dying agent Louis Bernard (Daniel Gelin), not only the McKennas' son, but their relation to each other, is at stake.

Even before this crisis, Ben and Jo McKenna had disagreed about everything, from whether Bernard was acting suspiciously to who should answer the door. Their disagreements, it turns out, are rooted in an unresolved problem: Jo has given up her stage career and moved to Indianapolis to be a doctor's wife, but neither she nor her husband has come to terms with the resulting tension. This tension appears as soon as she is recognized by the Draytons (Bernard Miles and Brenda de Banzie) as "*the* Jo Conway," and continues as an undercurrent when Jo asks when they will have another child, whether they are about to have their monthly fight, and why her husband is trying to give her tranquilizers when he has repeatedly complained about her taking too many pills. From the very beginning of his story, then, Hitchcock complicates his wide-screen version of *Father Knows Best* with a critique of paternal authority and a more general critique of the normal family life the McKennas end by yearning for.

Ben imagines himself chosen for no good reason for the misfortune that befalls him when Bernard makes him his confidant. The film makes it clear, however, that Bernard does not so much bring the McKennas trouble as reveal the trouble already present among them. After Bernard is killed and Ben is summoned to the office of the police inspector for questioning, he unwittingly aggravates Hank's danger by replying to the inspector's request for Bernard's message with a tirade about his unwillingness to comply, then self-righteously insists on taking the call that tells him Hank has been kidnapped (two minutes more and he would have handed over the message and been off the hook), and finally sends Drayton back to the hotel, from which the Draytons promptly disappear. This kind of egoistic self-reliance, which Ben has obviously been practicing for years at his wife's expense, is what he needs to outgrow in order to make common cause with her.

In one sense, Hank's kidnapping establishes that common cause, just as it did for the Lawrences in 1934. But unlike the Lawrences, who worked together comfortably by separating, the McKennas find it nearly impossible to work together at solving their problem.[9] Ben cannot even think of a good way to share the news with Jo except in a professional capacity (compare Jeff's dogged professionalism in *Rear Window*): he refuses to tell her what he knows about Hank until has given her a sedative ("I'm the doctor. . . . I make my living by knowing when and how to administer medication"). Later that night, as she lies unblinking on the bed and he packs their bags and tells her, "We're going to London," her point of view motivates several alienating low-angle shots of him, but the scene ends with their first real, albeit anguished, embrace.

Arriving in London (where Jo receives a bouquet labeled "Welcome home"), Ben suddenly finds himself recast from the head of the family to Jo's consort: a crowd of her admirers turns out at the airport to greet them, and one of her friends addresses him as "Mr. Conway." Although the Scotland Yard man Buchanan tells them that "we might find him quite soon indeed if we work together," Ben and Jo cannot even work with each other; Jo accuses Ben of acting "as if you're the only one concerned with this," and they are both close to tears on the phone. The most optimistic note is struck by the surprisingly sympathetic Buchanan, who says, "I have a son myself. I don't know what I'd do" (compare the admonitory Gibson in the 1934 version), as if his temperate attitude could impose greater family unity from outside.

Throughout their ordeal, the McKennas maintain an attitude of barely suppressed outrage and grief; there is nothing to suggest that they consider their experiences the adventures that befell Bob Lawrence in the more brilliant and mercurial 1934 version, just as "ordeal" would not have been an apt word for the Lawrences' experience. The treacherously shifting tones of the earlier version are replaced here by a single leading tone of domestic melodrama, which Hitchcock sustains with only minor variations. The earlier version focused less clearly on its central family, and most of its revelations about their relations among themselves were offhand or indirect; the later version, placing the McKennas squarely at its center, focuses on Ben's and Jo's estrangement from each other in order to trace the steps that will bring them together again. The Lawrences' story, however harrowing, keeps turning funny on them because of the improbable situations in which it lands them preparatory to leaving them as they were originally; the McKennas' story is never funny to them, but is dramatically justified because it brings Ben and Jo closer than they have ever been before.

The scene in Ambrose Chapel, an updated version of the scene in the Tabernacle of the Sun, shows how different Hitchcock's interest in his material has become. The earlier scene, in which Bob was accompanied by his brother-in-law, was played for swift alternation between melo-drama and farce; the later scene, featuring both Ben and Jo, is used to show the difficulties they have in working together. Jo, realizing that the Ambrose Chapel Bernard mentioned is a place rather than a person, goes there and calls Ben from a phone booth outside. When he arrives, she wants to call Buchanan, but he demurs, and they go in together. Even though Mrs. Drayton recognizes them, she is unable to make her husband understand their danger until Jo, at Ben's request, gets up to call the police. The McKennas' failure to recover Hank is laid to Ben's inability to stall for time while Jo is calling Buchanan, Jo's slight but painful delay in getting a promise of help, and the responding officers' skepticism about Jo's story. After beginning the scene united in pur-pose and plan, the McKennas end it widely separated, Jo en route to the Albert Hall, Ben climbing the bell rope to the cupola above in order to escape from the locked and otherwise deserted chapel. Everything—the villainy of the Draytons, the lack of support from the police, their own difficulty in cooperating—seems to work against the McKennas.

Now at last, however, the climactic moment of cooperation is at hand. When Ben follows his wife to the Albert Hall, Jo, who has already real-ized the assassination attempt will take place here, clutches him, tells him everything he needs to know (the music significantly masking the words of their reunion from the audience) to find the assassin, and screams at the moment the shot is to be fired; Ben, in the meantime, having unsuccessfully attempted to enlist the help of the police, chases the murderer to his death. At the end of this scene, having finally estab-lished their ability to work with each other, the McKennas are able to ask Buchanan for "that help you promised us."[10] In the final scene at the foreign embassy where Hank has been taken, Ben and Jo indeed require all the help the police can give them—without the police cordon sur-rounding the embassy, their plan would never have worked—but it is their plan, or more accurately Ben's plan, depending for the first time on his wife's talents and his acceptance of her own professional identity:

while she distracts the guests at the embassy by singing, he will search for Hank.

Nothing reveals Hitchcock's revision of the 1934 film more clearly than the new climax. Instead of shooting the assassin who is threatening her child, Jo rescues Hank by singing "Que Sera, Sera." In part the change reflects the temper of America in the fifties, since it relegates Jo to a traditionally feminine role and allows her husband to face the villain's pistol. Again, as in the Albert Hall sequence, Hitchcock seems intent on confirming the McKennas' solidarity by showing them working together. But the point of their teamwork is not really that Jo will front for Ben while he does the dangerous work; it is that Ben can finally accept his wife's status as a performer. The surrealistic overtone of the sequence is maintained and gradually amplified from the moment Ben interrupts the ambassador's request for a song with an impatient "I'm sure my wife would be delighted to sing for you, Your Excellency" to the third verse of the song, given a tone of comic desperation by Doris Day's labored performance. This climactic sequence marks the one point in the film in which Hitchcock plays with the tonal modulations so characteristic of every part of the 1934 version *except* for its melodramatic climax. Unlike Jill, Jo does not rescue her child by displaying an improbable skill; it is the unlikely cooperation between husband and wife that is being displayed. And it is not until the very end of the scene, when Ben, threatened by Drayton's pistol, tells Hank, "Do as he says," that Ben finally shows himself able to submerge his own ideas and emotions even for a moment—just long enough to catch Drayton off guard and push him down the stairs.

The film's final shot, which places Ben, Jo, and Hank together for the first time in the context of a supportive community—Jo's friends, who have come to represent her public and the public in general, are sprawled around the McKennas' hotel room in attitudes of exhaustion as the family bursts in and Ben apologizes for keeping them so long, explaining simply, "We had to pick up Hank"—is its most exultant affirmation of the link between individual identity, the family unit, and the larger community. It is a shot and a thematic conception whose uncomplicated optimism is quite outside the range of the far more problematic

1934 version. At the same time, it concludes Hitchcock's most socially sportive period with a reminder of how much more pointedly the melodrama of *The Man Who Knew Too Much* conflicts with its witty surface—for example, Ben's and Jo's discussion in the marketplace in Marrakesh of the diseases and confinements that have made their trip possible—and how completely that wit dries up in the face of a clear threat to the family's safety. Just as Hitchcock's whitewash of his put-upon heroine in *Dial M for Murder* had prepared for the more high-spirited social integration of the Paramount films, *The Man Who Knew Too Much* marks a transition to the paranoid nightmares to follow.

It would be a mistake to read a simple biographical significance—a leavening of the director's vision before the descent into the coming darkness—into the Paramount films, which were influenced by Hitchcock's continued ambivalence toward home and family, his playfully relaxed assurance in his own mastery, his use of the wide screen, his dependence on a team of congenial collaborators, and especially Hayes's distinctively lightsome dialogue. But there is no question that Hayes's refusal to follow Hitchcock to Warners for *The Wrong Man* marks the end of this period. The comedy of social ambivalence—undermining the accommodations of the social order even while acknowledging the triumphant integration of self and world it made possible—in the Paramount films was about to be eclipsed for good.

# SEVEN

## TAILS

## YOU

## LOSE

itchcock's return to Warners to make one last
film prompted his break with John Michael Hayes, who was unwilling
to follow Hitchcock's example of forgoing his salary, and led to the the
climactic period of his career. *The Wrong Man,* the film Hitchcock chose
to direct for Warners, is not a masterpiece, but it inaugurates a series of
masterpieces—*Vertigo, North by Northwest,* and *Psycho*—all organized
around the same subject, personal disintegration, which they all treat
as a nightmare. Surprisingly, Hitchcock had treated madness only mar-
ginally in most of his films. When he presented psychopathic killers like
Uncle Charlie or Bruno Anthony, he had always emphasized the contrast
between their apparently normal social behavior and the homicidal impulses this behavior conceals. But madness is at the heart of *The Wrong
Man* and the films that follow, as Hitchcock repeatedly focuses either on
a more graphic depiction of insanity or on the disintegration of a healthy
individual.

"Disintegration" is an especially apt word here because madness in
these films is always marked by two symptoms: the failure of any attempt
to mediate between the claims of self and world, leading to the subject's
complete isolation from everyone else, and a corresponding loss of self-

control, so that even the self this isolation throws one back on is felt as another being, another identity, whom one is powerless to control. The distinctive features of these four films are the heroes' experience of themselves as another, as someone else, and viewers' corresponding sense of themselves as being trapped in an identification figure's nightmare.

The experience of nightmare might seem remote from the games of Hitchcock's earlier films, and indeed the director's attitude toward his audience in these films is more challenging, more confrontational, than ever before as he works to engage his viewers in identifications with principals who will be painfully humiliated or psychologically distorted or shockingly murdered. If Hitchcock's identifications always extend the promise of harrowing pleasures, the identifications of the films beginning with *The Wrong Man* have a potentially devastating force because their subjects are so close to disintegration and death, and because the customary reassurances that make the audience's identifications pleasurable despite their dangers turn treacherous in these films. Even at their most malicious, however, Hitchcock's games are still games, and most of these films manipulate their audience through playing fast and loose with generic affiliations. Roger Thornhill's loss of identity in *North by Northwest* is treated frankly as a game, and the film, like a more well-upholstered version of the 1934 *Man Who Knew Too Much*, challenges its audience to keep up with the plot twists and shifts in tone, the way the film plays with different generic possibilities, that encourage such rapidly changing responses. *Vertigo* and *Psycho* play a more deceptive game, establishing a single specific set of generic conventions (the supernatural thriller, the domestic tale of theft and pursuit) they undermine with unprecedented ferocity. This bait-and-switch technique represents a logical culmination of the adversarial side of Hitchcock's game-playing, now presented in a series of films whose identifications are too seductive to resist but too painful to endure without a fundamental redefinition of the pleasure contract. The audience, first enticed into identifying with a sympathetic hero or heroine, is ultimately invited to admire the skill with which this identification has been nightmarishly transformed, and so to enjoy Hitchcock's latest game: heads I win, tails you lose.

The least obviously ludic of the four films is the first, *The Wrong Man*,

whose plot summary sounds like a recipe for suffering. How could anyone possibly enjoy a film about an innocent man mistaken for a thief,
arrested, arraigned, and imprisoned by the police, dogged by a run of
bad luck that makes him unable to produce witnesses to his innocence,
and forced to endure his wife's mental breakdown? Hitchcock's emphasis throughout that his story actually happened—the film begins with
a long shot of the director addressing the audience in his own voice,
telling them that what they are about to see is based on a true story; the
credits cite the *Saturday Evening Post* article, "The True Story of Christopher Emmanuel Balestrero"; the film ends with another title reminding
us that the story of Manny Balestrero (Henry Fonda) was true; and in
between the visual texture of Hitchcock's world emphasizes everyday
reality, especially Manny's orbit of Jackson Heights, in a way unique
among his American films before or since—seems to insist that reality
has caught up with the melodramas he has been purveying. The world
really is as dangerous as his outrageous stories have suggested all along.

Because the film is so firmly grounded in a sense of everyday reality—
much of it was shot on the locations involved, and even the Stork Club
looks drab—Manny's suffering becomes the audience's own, and his
degradation becomes the audience's vicarious humiliation. Manny is able
to look away as he is handcuffed to another prisoner while being transferred to the Long Island City Jail, but the audience has nowhere else
to look; although the audience never sees the prisoner, its members are
forced to share Manny's anguish. Hence the film makes its audience suffer in much the same way its hero does, and apparently to as little effect.
What kind of enjoyment does Manny's ordeal provide? Lacking the exhilaration or wit of the adventures of Richard Hannay or Guy Haines, it
would seem to have mainly an educational value: in watching what can
happen to Manny Balestrero, members of the audience may realize how
slender is their own grasp on the institutions that establish for them an
innocent identity. But this lesson is of no value in ordering their lives or
considering the actions of other people; it seems more simply a plausible
pretext for the imposition of Manny's nightmare, a nightmare which
can have no meaning for Manny and no resolution for his wife Rose
(Vera Miles), a nightmare the film simply asks the audience to endure

until awakening over the closing credits. It is, to say the least, a surprising kind of pleasure to get from Hitchcock, but it is the kind that will dominate the films to follow.

From *Blackmail* to *Suspicion* and *Rear Window,* many of Hitchcock's earlier films had rescued their principals from nightmarish landscapes by improbable plot twists or otherwise adopted an ambivalent attitude toward their own endings. *The Wrong Man* pushes this ambivalence to an extreme by incorporating two blankly contradictory endings. Rose has broken down after Manny's arrest because she takes his troubles as a judgment against her need to have her wisdom teeth extracted, which had sent Manny to borrow money at the insurance office where he was misidentified as a thief, and her inability to economize, which had put them in need of money in the first place. In the last scene of the film, she is still apathetically withdrawn (when Manny tells her that the police have caught the man he has been mistaken for, she says repeatedly, "That's fine for you"), but after she is led off and a nurse asks Manny to come again to see her, the scene is followed by a title announcing that "two years later Rose Balestrero walked out of the sanitarium—completely cured").

The dissonance between these two endings is too extreme to be resolved completely, but the closing title, which describes the Balestreros' present life in Florida as making their earlier experience seem "like a nightmare," suggests how both endings together mark the final move in an unusually baleful game. Nightmares are frightening experiences dreamers suffer without having control over either their circumstances or their reactions to them, and this is exactly the form that Rose's encroaching madness takes. The doctor to whom Manny takes Rose tells him, "She's buried under some kind of landslide of fear and guilt. She knows she's in a nightmare, but it doesn't help her to know. She can't get out." The feeling of being in a situation in which awareness and knowledge leave one still powerless to act, in which one's thoughts and actions have no impact on the world around one, is precisely the mark of Rose's apathetic despair. Her madness has other affinities to nightmares as well. In an earlier scene Manny, realizing that Rose has begun to withdraw from him and deeply concerned about proving his innocence, observes, "For the last few days, you don't seem to care what happens to me at the trial." Rose replies, "Don't you see? It doesn't do any good to care," and continues with a plan to keep her entire family at home in order to keep "them" away from the family, a sudden accusation of Manny ("How do I know you're not guilty?"), an attack on him with a hairbrush, and finally a weary acknowledgment of her illness: "You're right, Manny. There is something wrong with me. You're going to have to put me somewhere." This scene dramatizes the leading stages in her disintegration: the paranoid withdrawal from the social order, the treatment of her husband as another outsider, the refusal of intimacy with him (she attacks him when he attempts to touch her), and finally the sense of alienation even from herself. Rose's nightmarish experience is marked by rapid mental transitions that are only apparently illogical or unmotivated and a simultaneous sense of guilty responsibility ("this must be my fault") and resentment ("this can't be my fault") leading to paralysis ("how did we get into this?" is the question the film repeatedly asks and fails to answer). The film's final title, emphasizing the discontinuity between her breakdown and her return to health, suggests that after two years, Rose simply woke up from her nightmare, as if it were a game whose rules no longer applied and the film itself a game this final title brought to an end.

Manny's ordeal, not Rose's, is at the center of the film, and his faith in himself (his prayer for help dissolves into a scene showing the real thief's capture) is set against her disintegration. But in a more fundamental sense Rose's breakdown is simply the purest expression of Manny's own nightmare, a nightmare which is generalized in a way new to Hitchcock's work. Hitchcock had created a sense of nightmare in many other films: in Alice's walking the streets all night long in *Blackmail,* in Mrs. Verloc's reaction to Stevie's death and Elsa's reaction to the news that Ashenden has killed the wrong man, in Iris's attempt to recreate Miss Froy in her compartment, in Charlie Newton's trip to the library, in the climactic scene on the merry-go-round in *Strangers on a Train,* and of course in John Ballantine's dream in *Spellbound.* Most of these scenes are based on hallucinations or sensory distortions, moments in which one's senses are out of control. *The Wrong Man* introduces a new figure for madness: the scene in which Rose's perceptions are not distorted but her sense of her powers of action and response is pathologically diminished, so that the accuracy of her perceptions mocks her sense of herself as caught in a chain of circumstances which stifles action like a nightmare. This sense of disorienting paralysis is exactly what Manny shares as he is forced to endure the rituals of arrest, arraignment, and trial.

The evocation of nightmare is a hallmark of *The Wrong Man* and the three films that follow. Scottie Ferguson ends the opening scene of *Vertigo* dangling from a gutter high above the street with no apparent possibility of rescue; in the next scene he is nearly recovered from his ordeal, though Hitchcock never shows how he got down. In *North by Northwest,* Roger Thornhill finds himself trapped in an elevator with two men who are trying to kill him, a mother who does not believe his hints to her, and a highly amused audience of onlookers. Marion Crane spends much of the first third of *Psycho* in an attempt to escape the eyes of the police—an attempt she knows is futile, for the police officer she is trying to escape from is watching her as she trades in her car for another. Each scene dramatizes the breakdown of the connections between oneself and the world around one, a breakdown experienced not as sensory distortion (as in Hitchcock's earlier work) but as a sudden vertiginous sense of helplessness, a sense of life as a nightmare from which there could be no escape except simply waking up, as Scottie does sometime after the opening scene of *Vertigo* (and again, evidently, after Madeleine Elster's death) and as Rose does after the final scene of *The Wrong Man*. A particularly disturbing feature of each of these films is that the audience never sees the principals waking up. Hitchcock never lets the audience see Scottie getting down from the gutter or regaining his sanity or lets them hear the conversation at the airport in which Thornhill learns why the villains have been chasing him all over the map, and Marion's apparent recovery of her moral bearings after talking with Norman Bates is only a prelude to her violent and shocking death. In each case Hitchcock casts a spell, inviting the audience deeper and deeper into a nightmarish world, and then simply cuts away.

In Hitchcock's earlier films, the experience of madness communicated to the audience is always local, ascertainable, and marked as different from the normal, unmarked mode of perception. Even though viewers may believe for the moment Mrs. Verloc imagines she sees Stevie that he is still alive, they immediately realize they are mistaken and she is hallucinating, because the film provides a visual correlative for her madness, an impossible way of seeing, just as mental strain in *Secret Agent* is correlated with distorted sounds. In the series of films beginning with *The Wrong Man,* however, madness is not local, not so easily perceived, and not the exceptional case: it is simply the inevitable response to a world which is mad itself. "Don't you think we all go a little mad sometimes?" Norman asks Marion in his back room. The line is an ironic joke, since Norman is more than a little mad. But the joke has another dimension: Marion has also become more than a little mad; her plan to steal forty thousand dollars and join her lover in Fairvale has made her obsessively suspicious of everyone who approaches her (except, ironically, Norman himself); and everyone whom her life touches will in turn begin to act obsessively. (The few non-obsessional characters in the film, Marion's boss and Sheriff Chambers, are made to look ridiculous.) In these films, madness is not a deviation, but the norm.

In the work of other writers like Conrad or filmmakers like Polanski, the argument that the social order was based on madness might be treated in a despairing tone. But universal madness has even more often been a comic subject in films from *Bringing Up Baby* to *Ruthless People,* and Hitchcock is always alert to its ludic possibilities even when he is not making a comedy. The final title of *The Wrong Man,* coupled with its last scene, treats Manny's nightmarish ordeal, focused as it is on his wife's madness, as a throwaway joke. Even though Manny's own steadfast faith in himself is repeatedly contrasted with Rose's breakdown, Hitchcock makes it clear that he is using Rose's mental breakdown as a metaphor for Manny's own degradation, as his ordeal threatens to undermine his sense of himself as a rational agent, and so to unman him. The focus of Manny's torment is Rose's illness. When he is finally confronted with the real thief, the one thing he says is, "Do you realize what you've done to my wife?" By giving in to the despair Manny is resisting, Rose turns the dissolution of his individual identity into a dissolution of his social identity, the family whose support he has been. Even Rose's doctors are visual equivalents for the policemen who arrest Manny. In her first scene with the doctor, she is spotlit in the foreground while the doctor hovers, faceless and disembodied, in the background, in a medical version of the third degree Manny has already undergone. Later, when Manny takes her to the institutition he has chosen, she is escorted upstairs by two attendants flanking her as the policemen had earlier flanked Manny.

More and more, Manny is threatened with the despair which has already engulfed his wife. His experience has clearly left an indelible mark on his sense of everyday reality: on his first visit to his lawyer's office in the Victor Moore Arcade, he glances nervously toward the door of the insurance company he was accused of robbing in the same arcade, and on his return home he stares for a long moment at an empty space across the street where a police car had stood when he was first taken into custody. During the night he spends under arrest, Manny repeatedly and patiently affirms his innocence, and he continues to assure Rose that they will find the witness needed to establish his alibi. But when a juror's prejudiced outburst ("Do we really have to listen to all this, Your Honor?") causes the judge to declare a mistrial, and his lawyer (Anthony Quayle) tells him he will have to go through the whole procedure again and asks, "Can you take it, Manny?" his only response is, "I'll try, Mr. O'Connor." In the following scene with his mother, Manny says, "I've been such an idiot, you'd all be better off without me," echoing Rose's own descent into madness. But Manny's mother asks him to pray for strength, and as he does so Hitchcock dissolves to the real criminal attempting the robbery that will lead to his arrest.

Just as Manny's nightmare began because of forces that had nothing to do with him, his own descent into madness is halted, equally abruptly, because a mistrial is declared, because the criminal happens to be caught, because he prays for strength. In a Bresson film Manny's prayer would express something unique to him or would give him the strength to make him different from Rose or explain why he had always been different, but here the divine intervention it betokens is presented as something purely external, a deus ex machina Manny invokes as if it were the punchline of a particularly unfunny joke.

If divine providence seems to operate arbitrarily in the film, the representatives of earthly law are even more remote and unreasonable. Ever since *The Lodger,* Hitchcock's heroes had always been in danger from the police, but nowhere earlier had the police themselves been so gratuitously menacing, such legitimate objects of paranoia. When they are not the hero's allies or potential allies, Hitchcock's policemen tend to be either featureless, comically ineffectual, or compromised and humanized by their intimacy with the suspects. Only *I Confess* adumbrates the unbridled fear of the police which runs through *The Wrong Man*, and Inspector Larue is much less threatening than Manny's persecutors because he leaves his prey the dignity of his priestly office. As Manny is forced to visit the scenes of two robberies, answer probing questions about his finances and personal habits, empty his pockets, allow his fingerprints to be taken, and surrender his necktie as he is locked up, the camera seems to spare no opportunity to humiliate him—to strip him of his privacy, his dignity, and his individuality—before its final revelation: just kidding.

Each earlier period in Hitchcock's career has begun with a film (the 1934 *Man Who Knew Too Much, Rebecca, Rope, Rear Window*) which had challenged the rules of the Hitchcock game and offered the audience a new pleasure contract whose terms were then refined and explored in a series of less challenging or confrontational films. *The Wrong Man* begins a new period unlike all the others, for this is the only time in Hitchcock's career when subsequent films of the period will not back down from this initial challenge or mark a consolidation or retrenchment. Instead, each film will attempt in a different way to resolve the problem introduced in *The Wrong Man*: the question of how to make nightmare into a game. Each film works by immersing the audience in the hero's or heroine's nightmare, but these nightmares offer distinct pleasures. *Vertigo* gives its hero's nightmare the dignity of romantic tragedy, *North by Northwest* the exhilarating possibilities of romantic comedy, *Psycho* the corrosive power of black comedy. Hitchcock points his oppositional stance toward the audience in his two greatest films, *Vertigo* and *Psycho*, by misdirecting viewers' expectations about the kinds of pleasure they can expect. The somber, forthright opening of *The Wrong Man* warns them about the nightmare they are about to experience. But the effect of *Vertigo* and *Psycho* depends on the audience misreading the films' openings in preparation for later revelations of the true nature of his stories. In each case Hitchcock offers the promise of one kind of pleasure—the close identification with Scottie and Marion—only to turn pleasure to pain by breaking that identification and offering a new kind of pleasure: the fun of being expertly harrowed by a nightmare from which they can only wake up.

If *The Wrong Man* presents a clinically objective account of Rose Balestrero's descent into madness as a metaphor for her husband's ordeal, *Vertigo* presents a sympathetic hero disintegrating before viewers realize what is happening to him, or to themselves. The character is Scottie Ferguson (James Stewart), a detective whose fear of heights prevents him from saving the life of Madeleine Elster (Kim Novak), whom he has been hired to protect from the possessive spirit of her great-grandmother Carlotta Valdes. Scottie's melancholic despair leads him to another woman, Judy Barton (Novak again), who had actually played the part of Madeleine as part of Elster's plan to kill his wife, and whom Scottie is fatally successful in molding into a reincarnation of Madeleine.

The long, dreamlike opening segments of the film, with their ethereal music and seductive point-of-view shots, force the audience into an identification with Scottie so close that it masks his obsession with the unattainable Madeleine before his dream after her death signals his complete breakdown and his treatment of Judy indicates the depths of his obsession. The harrowing climax of the film shows Scottie's furious resentment of Judy for having played, as Madeleine, on his weakness, and in arousing his love for a person who never existed.[1] At the same time, however, Judy as Madeleine has presented Scottie with exactly the love he craves and deserves, indeed the only love he is capable of. Like the earlier Stewart hero L. B. Jefferies, whose situation he reenacts in so many ways, Scottie is at heart a voyeur who, fearing sexual consummation, prefers to avoid intimate and endangering involvements in favor of relationships he can control completely. Scottie thus shuns his sympathetic and available former girlfriend Midge (Barbara Bel Geddes) in favor of the equivocal Madeleine because Madeleine is by definition unavailable—married, possessed by a dead woman, and the object of his purely professional gaze—and therefore unlikely to demand a threatening reciprocal intimacy.

In the long series of shot-reversals that show Scottie following Madeleine to the flower shop, the Palace of the Legion of Honor, and the McKittrick Hotel, Scottie is already falling in love with her; after he rescues her from the bay, his first word to her is a passionate "Madeleine." But what is this love based on? Since they are not sharing any common experiences, his love seems based purely on his fascination by her mystery—he loves her *because* she is someone else, because she is not herself—and his specular gaze. She offers Scottie a feminine ideal which will never be tarnished because it will never be possessed, even by himself. What Scottie fails to realize is that by idealizing her he is already possessing her, abstracting certain qualities of her and ignoring the others. "No one possesses you," he tells Madeleine, "you're safe with me." But he is twice wrong, for Madeleine is possessed not only economically by Elster but psychologically by Scottie himself, who has internalized his ideal of her so completely that he will never recover from her death.

Scottie's lethal identification with Madeleine is clearest in his remaking of Judy to resemble the person she once pretended to be: he is dominating Judy just as Madeleine still dominates him. But this identification goes much deeper. Halfway through the film Madeleine describes to Scottie a dream in which she is walking down a long corridor lined with fragments of mirrors toward a mysterious darkness she always wakes up before reaching. Although Scottie is baffled by the description, he has been moving through a series of remarkably similar landscapes ever since he first saw Madeleine. When he first follows Madeleine at Elster's request, she leads him by car through a network of San Francisco streets whose sheerness boxes him in, then into a small, dark alley to the back door of a florist's shop, where he watches her, surrounded by brilliant flowers, from behind a mirror. From the florist's, Scottie follows Madeleine to the Mission Dolores through the back door of a darkened church to a graveyard of unearthly beauty; but at the end of this corridor Scottie finds, instead of a mirror, Carlotta Valdes's tombstone. At the palace of the Legion of Honor Scottie watches through a narrowing archway as Madeleine sits staring at the framed portrait of Carlotta, and at the McKittrick Hotel he uncharacteristically runs up a dark, steep, narrow staircase to Madeleine's empty room only to find himself staring at the window framing the space where her car had been parked. This progression of narrow passages leading to climactically framed images or artifacts—the mirror, the tombstone, the portrait, the window—will continue with the shot of Madeleine, apparently contemplating suicide, framed by the Golden Gate Bridge, with the cross-section of a giant redwood which Madeleine and Scottie will examine, and finally with Scottie's view through a window of Madeleine falling to her death.[2] The succession of darkened corridors, along with the film's emphasis on inward spirals, suggests a sexual penetration, and the progression of objects at the end of the corridor hints at the links between Scottie's idealization of Madeleine and his own death wish. More fundamentally, it shows the extent to which Scottie has from the beginning been living out Madeleine's dreams, submerging his identity in the object of his desire. His dream of Madeleine, which began so seductively at Ernie's with a track-in to her immaculately coiffed head, has turned into a nightmare which leaves him haunted by her image.

The doctor who diagnoses Scottie's breakdown attributes it to a combination of acute melancholia and a guilt complex, but Scottie's own dream after Madeleine's death makes it possible to pinpoint Scottie's malady more closely. Since the silhouette he imagines falling from the mission tower, like the open grave he finds, is clearly his own, the shock of Madeleine's death is inseparable from a horror of his own death, not a death impending (although the general fear of mortality underlies the effect the sequence has on the audience), but a death already accomplished. Scottie begins the film by watching a fellow policeman fall to his death in an attempt to rescue him; later he sees the woman he loves fall to her death because he could not save her. His identity is so caught up in both of these figures that he imagines himself dead, partly to avoid his shattering guilt, partly to punish himself, but partly (and most powerfully) because both policeman and lover comprehend so much of the way he has defined himself. Like Achilles after seeing the body of Patroclus, wearing his own armor, recovered from the fields around Troy, Scottie acts as if he were already dead.

The psychological basis of acrophobia is a fear of falling coupled with a longing to fall.[3] Although Scottie tells Midge that he has evidently had such a phobia for some time without realizing it, the opening sequence of the film in effect sets up an instant past, a clinical history for Scottie's neurosis. From that point on, Scottie acts as if he had no control over his own actions, as if his life were a waking dream which he could experience but not control. At first the dream is pleasurable. When Scottie follows

Madeleine to the church graveyard where he first sees Carlotta's grave, the combination of pastels, soft focus, late afternoon light, and Bernard Herrmann's otherworldly music for high strings, together with the unusually sparse yet precise texture of the diegetic sound—Scottie's every footstep makes a muffled but distinct fall—creates a dreamlike atmosphere appropriate to Madeleine's presumed possession by Carlotta and trancelike behavior but also to Scottie's possession by the remote and exotic Madeleine, and indeed to the audience's sense of this episode, and the sequence in which it is embedded, as somehow outside time or the characters' volition. Scottie's distance from Madeleine, and the halo of light which surrounds her at the end of the first scene at Ernie's and the beginning of her last scene at Scottie's apartment, heighten the sense of his experience of her as a dream to be enjoyed but not controlled. When she runs from him into the Mission of San Juan Battista, however, the dream turns to nightmare, as Scottie's inability to control his circumstances or even his responses has disastrous consequences. This nightmare, represented explicitly by the sequence that signals Scottie's breakdown, recalls Rose Balestrero's madness in that awareness of one's situation still leaves one powerless to act because one's possible reactions are experienced as external: the self has become someone else. In Scottie's case this other self is at first Madeleine. Just as Scottie idealizes her after his own desire, his own will and perceptions become inseparable from hers—he neglects Midge and does nothing but "wander," first following Madeleine, then accompanying her—and is unable to recover from her death because too little of his identity has survived her.

He does not really want to survive her, because his own vertigo, the fear of falling combined with the desire to fall, unites him to her too closely. As Scottie watches the policeman's body strike the pavement and attract a cluster of bystanders in the opening scene, he must surely be tempted simply to let go, since holding on is agony—the physical strain is intense, and there will be a painful inquiry even if he is rescued—and letting go, relinquishing control of his situation deliberately, would make everything agonizingly easy. But the film uses his fear of heights, marked by the contrary impulses toward self-protection and self-abandonment, as a metaphor for a more fundamental fear. After Scottie first finds Judy at the Empire Hotel and leaves her to get his car, she writes him a letter which begins: "And so you found me. This is the moment that I've dreaded and hoped for." The second sentence could refer to Scottie's clinical vertigo, his dread of falling and his longing to fall, if the context did not make its meaning unmistakably different: Judy is talking about the prospect of an intimate relation with the man she has fallen in love with.

The phrase "fallen in love" indicates the affinity between Scottie's pathological fear of heights and the common and natural fear of love. Why do people fall in love and not leap or step or rise into love? The metaphor presumably depends on a loss of control, a merging of one's identity with that of the loved one which is both desired and feared. Falling in love means relinquishing sole control of one's will and emotions for the sake of an ecstatic experience outside oneself, like the thrill of falling from an infinitely high tower. Although the word *falling* suggests a final catastrophe which lovers might fear, the initial experience of love is so intoxicating that it seems worth giving up one's self-control for an experience that allows one to transcend the limits of one's own appetite and will. Falling in love and consummating one's love are thus eminently to be desired and feared.

Ironically, Madeleine is a more appropriate subject for Scottie's affections than he can know. In seeking a relationship with a woman he can idealize freely because she is beyond possessing, Scottie fails to realize that Madeleine is nothing but an ideal whose carefully constructed artifice echoes that of his dream landscape's other feminine images— the bouquet, the tombstone, the portrait. He has fallen in love with a nonexistent woman, a woman who has been created purely in order to appeal to him, as products are marketed to create the appropriate consumer desire. Scottie's fear of commitment is thus abundantly justified. His vertigo, which stems from a desire for the release of falling combined with the fear of hitting the ground, aptly figures his desire for an idealized relationship combined with the fear of betrayal, of finding that his love is not as he imagined her. Midge embodies a benign version of this betrayal: their three-week engagement in college did not lead to marriage because Midge was only Midge, not Scottie's ideal woman, and he cannot bring himself to settle for less than his ideal. (Hence his disastrous withdrawal from Midge when she paints herself as Carlotta, offering herself as romantic object by suggesting that any woman can be idealized.) Madeleine's betrayal is far more devastating: after encouraging Scottie to fall in love with her, she vanishes, leaving behind only a dead body, as he first believes, or an ideal that was the result of malicious impersonation, as he later concludes. After an unprecedented step toward commitment, Scottie finds he has committed himself to a void, and to that extent—to the extent that he has submerged his identity in Madeleine's—he has simply diminished himself.

In a world in which romantic ideals are in constant danger of betrayal, idealists like Scottie will typically seek relationships that depend on distance and protect themselves when imprudent intimacy leads to betrayal by withdrawing. But there is another defense against betrayal, a more sinister and finally devastating defense: instead of opening oneself to love by revealing one's vulnerability and allowing oneself to be possessed by another, one can head off the possibility of being possessed by seizing the intiative and possessing the object. This is precisely what Scottie does with Judy. Instead of accepting her as only Judy, Scottie, who has been from the very beginning of the film singularly uninterested in being loved by anyone, sets out to dominate and possess her as Madeleine had dominated and possessed him. The relations among these different possessions—Carlotta's of Madeleine, Madeleine's of Scottie, Scottie's of Judy—which structure the film are sharply reordered by the realization that Elster, not Carlotta, is the original possessor, and that the domination at stake involves not a romantic, pathetic, historical obsession but a greedy present-day scheme whose idealistic obsession is bogus and whose sexuality is treacherous. Even before he discovers the link between Madeleine and Judy, however, Scottie has already begun to take unconscious revenge on Judy for what he takes to be Madeleine's theft of his identity by taking Judy's own. Hitchcock described this theft as a rape, and it is clear that Scottie is both victim and perpetrator of this rape.[4] Even though he is outraged about Judy's earlier transformation to Madeleine in order to deceive him (the focus of his accusations in the last scene is on this deception, not on her complicity in the murder of the real Madeleine Elster), he has already repeated this outrage himself, changing Judy's clothing, grooming, and hair coloring until she emerges from the otherworldly greenish glow of the hotel's neon sign as his ideal resurrected. Even before Scottie realizes he has been the victim of a monstrous deception, he has become a monster himself.

Scottie is doomed from the beginning of the film because he cannot reconcile his fear of falling with his desire to fall: his life, whether dream or nightmare, cannot be resolved, only endured until he awakes, because his vertigo amounts to a paralysis leaving him unwilling and unable to take responsibility for his own desires, his own ideals, his own love. His fear of consummation is matched by a longing to possess his ideal, a longing he finally acts on all unaware. Scottie embodies in a single personality the contrary impulses of Manny and Rose Balestrero: attempting to control a hostile or treacherous world by asserting an identity (here, an identity which acts by imposing itself on others), resigning one's identity to the control of others, and so relinquishing responsibility for a self perceived as other. But he also embodies the contradictory desires of the movie audience, whose ideal vicarious romance would allow both the delicious thrill of falling in love and protection from a disastrous landing. Most movies allow the audience this kind of enjoyment, but in *Vertigo* the promise of a fantasy romance is extended only to be betrayed.

Scottie's personality is from the beginning deeply split, but instead of perceiving or accepting this split, he prefers to attribute it to Madeleine, whose inacessability drove him mad, and Judy, whose treachery sanctioned his own betrayal of her. "You're my second chance, Judy," he tells her in a frenzy of self-absorption as they enter the Mission of San Juan Battista for the last time. Evidently he wishes to take her to the top of the tower and watch her not fall, so that his sense of reponsibility for Madeleine's death will be exorcised. But as they struggle at the top of the stairs it gradually becomes clear that he doesn't know what he wants to do: he is torn between a desire to save her—a gratuitous and illogical desire, since her only danger now is from him—and a desire to punish her and make her confess. Like *Rear Window*, *Vertigo* sets the audience's desire for affirmation of the social order (the normal household, punishment of the wicked) against the fulfillment of the identification figure's fantasies (eternal union with the nonexistent Madeleine). The film's ending, like the endings of so many earlier Hitchcock films, shows how Hitchcock has used these contradictory desires to paint the audience into a corner: no ending could possibly make everything come out right.

Scottie's success in wringing a confession from Judy leaves him more aimless than ever; as she pleads that she exposed herself to danger deliberately because she was in love with him (one more way of reminding him that although he continues to be obsessed with Madeleine, it is Judy who has loved him all along), he can only mutter, "It's too late." Judy wants Scottie to return her love, but Scottie is incapable of reciprocal affection because he defines love in terms of power. Throughout the film, in fact, male identity and male desire are defined in terms of power. Three characters—Elster reflecting nostalgically on old San Francisco, Pop Leibl telling the story of Carlotta's lover who stole her child, and Scottie expressing contempt over Elster's treatment of Judy—link the terms "power" and "freedom," and the subject in every case is men's power over women. Scottie believes he can secure his freedom from his obsession with Madeleine only by establishing his power over Judy: either he is Judy's dupe or her judge, or else—and this is the contradiction which destroys them—both at once. Despite his breakdown, Scottie continues to be presented as an authority figure. Earlier in the film his authority was established visually and sexually by repeated low-angle shots framing him with phallic towers (the landmark Madeleine uses to find his apartment is Coit Tower) which represent both his official and sexual authority and his domination by ideals beyond his control (as Norman Bates, sitting among his stuffed birds, will be presented at once as their analogue and their prey). Even though Scottie cannot accept or control his own potency, he continues to act like an ex-policeman after he meets Judy, cross-examining her, overriding her objections to the gray suit he buys her, and finally demanding that she acknowledge her guilt even though the acknowledgment will not help either of them.[5] He insists that Judy honor a moral, sexual, and institutional authority he cannot accept in himself. In forcing Judy to pay for his own inadequacies, his own inability to reconcile his conscience, his fear, and his desire, Scottie is not so much destroying his own identity as re-enacting a ritual that dramatizes the self-alienation Hitchcock has presented from the beginning. Judy, like Madeleine before her, is simply the agent of the realization that Scottie has never had a self to lose.

*Vertigo* is Hitchcock's most profound exploration of a sympathetic hero's descent into nightmare and madness. What is perhaps most re-

markable about Hitchcock's anatomy of madness, however, is his transformation of madness into a comic nightmare in *North by Northwest*,
whose title, an echo of Hamlet's reference to his own whimsical or
assumed madness, announces its subject—the problematic relation between madness and sanity in a world which is itself mad—and hints
at its final resolution through an anatomy of action.[6] The film's similarities to *Vertigo* are striking. Like Judy Barton as Madeleine Elster,
Roger Thornhill (Cary Grant) is doubled with a mysterious (in this case
nonexistent) person and pursued in mistake for that person. Like Judy,
Thornhill consents to the staging of his own (or his alter ego's) death
in order to confound his pursuers. But Thornhill's position resembles
Scottie's even more closely, especially since his film, like Scottie's, is
organized around his pursuit of the phantom which has come to overshadow his own identity. Both men are innocently involved in criminal
plots; both become entangled with women with whom they fall in love
but who betray them because of their complicity with the criminals;
both react to this betrayal with anger and disillusionment; and both ultimately find themselves in high places with the errant heroines, whose
lives they are called upon to save. The final scenes of the two films are
especially similar. *Vertigo* ends with Scottie's forcing Judy to return to
the Mission of San Juan Battista in order to relive the scene in which he
had earlier failed to follow her to the top of the tower; *North by Northwest*
ends with a scene presumably aboard the Twentieth-Century Limited
to New York, where Thornhill and Eve Kendall (Eva Marie Saint) are
re-enacting his climactic rescue of her. "Roger, this is silly," says Eve,
and she is right, because the game is so inconsequential in the light
of the perilous scene it recalls. *North by Northwest* recapitulates a great
deal of *Vertigo*'s material in a context which controls its consequences,
persuades the audience that it doesn't really matter, and so releases its
comic potential.

How can two films with such similar subjects adopt such radically
different tones? One way to put the difference is to note that whereas
Scottie believes Madeleine possessed by an incarnation that portends a
tragic end and himself becomes fatally obsessed by Madeleine to the extent of losing his own identity, Thornhill, despite the fact that practically
no one in his movie believes what he says about himself, never doubts

his own identity. His loss of identity thus concerns a commodity more like Alicia Huberman's reputation than like John Ballantine's formative childhood memories. *North by Northwest* has frequently been compared to *The 39 Steps* and *Saboteur,* two other films involving an innocent hero chased across the country by authority figures mistaking him for a killer. And the story Ernest Lehman wrote for Hitchcock borrows liberally from the structure of these earlier films, particularly from *The 39 Steps*. What is new here is the emphasis on madness, on a world whose time is out of joint. Although Richard Hannay and Barry Kane are powerless to clear themselves, they are not confused about what is going on: Barry knows from the beginning that Frank Fry is the saboteur, and Hannay learns almost as soon as he meets Professor Jordan, less than halfway through the film, that he is the head of the group of spies that has killed Annabella Smith. But Thornhill, even though he meets Philip Vandamm (James Mason), Leonard (Martin Landau), and the other criminals at the beginning of his film, and meets them as criminals, is at a loss to understand the nature of his involvement with them because he does not know that he has been mistaken for a phantom, someone whom the CIA has invented in order to draw attention away from Eve, Vandamm's mistress, whom they have recruited as one of their own agents.[7] Hence Thornhill maintains his faith in his own sanity but not in the rest of the world's.

But Thornhill's faith in his identity (unlike that of his predecessors in flight Richard Hannay and Barry Kane) is misplaced, because the identity he bears at the beginning of the film is dangerously thin, as is to be expected from a hero whose monogram is "ROT," and whose middle initial, like David O. Selznick's, stands for "nothing."[8] His attempts to assert an identity independent of Kaplan's—announcing his real name and agenda for the evening, offering a wallet full of identification, and turning his practiced sarcasm on the thugs who kidnap him from the Oak Bar at the Plaza ("Don't tell me where we're going," he says, "surprise me")—all backfire because there is nothing about the identity they project that is inconsistent with George Kaplan. Comically unable to prove that he is not Kaplan by his reference to the externals of social and institutional status, Thornhill attempts to ridicule his captors (when the Townsends' maid announces dinner, he asks, "What are we having for dessert?"), but they are impervious to the conversational skills that have made him so successful on Madison Avenue. Later, looking around Kaplan's hotel room with his mother (Jessie Royce Landis), he tries on one of Kaplan's jackets and concludes petulantly, "It's obvious that they've mistaken me for a much shorter man"—as if his height were an inalienable guarantee of a stable identity.

Thornhill's identity is at risk because the relationships which define it—"a mother, a secretary, two ex-wives, and several bartenders"—are so superficial, but for a more fundamental reason as well. The twice-divorced Thornhill, who is kidnapped when he gets up to send his mother a telegram, is clearly under her thumb, as Hitchcock shows when Thornhill uses his one call from the Glen Cove Police Station to call her and calls her again as he is fleeing New York to avoid being arrested for the murder of the real Townsend at the United Nations. And he is equally at the mercy of other mother-figures in the film, from his secretary Maggie, who organizes his appointments and reminds him when he's repeating material from his last tender note to a woman, to the false Mrs. Townsend, whose assumed solicitude for him completely allays the police officers' suspicions. Thornhill is indeed a mother's boy who prefers to delegate the decisions that control his activity and so his identity to the women around him. But he is dominated as well by a complementary force indicated by the film's color scheme.

The film's maternal figures are all associated with red, rust, and earth tones. Mrs. Thornhill's coat is the same rust color as her hair, a color repeated in the false Mrs. Townsend's hair. Maggie's hair is blonde, but her conference with Thornhill takes place in a red and yellow taxicab. Later, Eve will wear a red figured dress in Chicago and a rust-colored suit in South Dakota. The film's complementary hues, blues and grays, are associated with male figures. Thornhill himself wears the same gray suit through most of the film, and the CIA principals in Washington, including their chief, the Professor (Leo G. Carroll), all wear different shades of blue and gray; the criminals, like the police, wear navy blue, except for the assassin (Adam Williams), whose tan suit echoes his gardener's uniform. Viewers might expect the film to distinguish more sharply between criminals and police in visual terms, but after all their structural function is the same: they are all out to get the hero. Dark blue

and gray are the colors of masculine and institutional authority, represented by the world of Madison Avenue shown briefly at the opening of
the film and the twin bureaucracies of government and criminals. This
is the world of the paternal order, the displaced father (significantly,
Thornhill's father is never mentioned in the film) whose authority is
mediated through institutions. As Scottie clings to an identity based on
his obsessive memories of the dead policeman and the dead Madeleine
as stand-ins for himself, Thornhill is dominated equally by father-figures
and mother-figures. Besides allowing his life to be arranged by women,
he allows the terms in which he thinks of himself to be dictated by a
faceless male order. In his dedication to the "expedient exaggeration"
and superficial charm of the good advertising executive, Thornhill is the
organization man par excellence, the faceless son of an absent father, the
man defined so completely by parental authority that he has no identity
of his own.

There are many films about the difficulty of establishing an identity
apart from one's parents, but *North by Northwest* differs from the others
in two obvious respects: its hero is a grown man—in fact, his self-
alienating dependence on protective mothers and authoritarian fathers
is his true madness, a figure for the psychopathology of everyday life—
and his parents are not just unhelpful or unsympathetic but murder-
ously threatening. Vandamm, who consistently treats Thornhill like a
little boy ("Games, Mr. Kaplan? Must we?" he wearily asks on their
first meeting), is a homicidal father who gently insists that Thornhill
cooperate or be killed. The Glen Cove police are scarcely less paternal,
and the police in general, once Thornhill is accused of murder, scarcely
less threatening. Even the soft-spoken Professor is ready to "do nothing"
to save Thornhill. Nor are the leading women, whose aid Thornhill repeatedly invokes against the men as a child might ask mommy to keep
daddy at bay, any more trustworthy. Even though Thornhill is helplessly
dependent on women—the minute his secretary leaves him, he gets
into trouble—the women he depends on refuse to protect him from the
threatening male order. Thornhill's mother ridicules her son on his appearance in court and refuses to believe his story about two men trying
to kill him, even when she comes face to face with them in an elevator.
The false Mrs. Townsend does everything she can to undermine his story

to the police. The ultimate expression of female treachery disguised as maternal solicitude is the patly named Eve, whose protection Thornhill solicits and accepts from the moment he meets her. She misdirects the police on the train, hides him in her compartment, and arranges for his escape in Chicago. Her behavior on the train is consistently maternal. After she offers her help (indeed forces on him help which he is only too ready to accept), Thornhill, who has been hiding in a men's room, allows her to lock him in the upper bunk in her compartment, a giant womb from which he emerges with infantile impatience.[9] When they leave the train the next morning, Thornhill is masquerading as a red-cap—a disguise which simultaneously reduces his identity to a function of his apparel (a series of overhead long shots show the police rushing through the crowd after redcaps) and marks him with the color red as if with a female brand. Later, when he shaves in the men's room, the man next to him eyes him askance for using Eve's tiny razor—another mark of his acceptance of feminine authority. But this authority is dangerous, as demonstrated when Eve sends Thornhill to an isolated Indiana field to be machine-gunned by a crop-dusting plane.

Unlike the false Mrs. Townsend, Eve has not acted solicitous simply in order to betray Thornhill; her troubled open-eyed gaze in the last shot of them on the train and her discomfort in saying good-bye the next morning make it clear that she is genuinely attached to him. But whether she is more attached to Vandamm, as Thornhill thinks in Chicago, or to the patriarchal order defined by her loyalty to her job and her country, as he later decides, she has chosen intimacy with father-figures over intimacy with the son. Thornhill's middle initial, which stands for nothing, might just as well stand for Oedipus.[10] The scene at the auction in Chicago, in which Thornhill, Eve, and Vandamm are present together for the first time (together with another complicating figure, the homosexual Leonard, whose sexual jealousy of Eve is obvious), provides a nearly undisplaced moment of Oedipal rivalry between Thornhill, stung to adolescent disillusionment by the revelation that Eve prefers Vandamm to himself, and Vandamm, who retaliates with his usual condescension in an attempt to re-establish his authority but who is clearly equally uncomfortable about the possibility that Eve is in love with Thornhill. It is a moment very like the moment in *Vertigo* when Scottie realizes that Gavin Elster rather than Carlotta Valdes is the figure behind his obsession and reacts with rage, not toward Elster, but toward Judy.

But Thornhill, unlike Scottie, is ultimately able to outgrow this rage, allowing the audience a far more benign pleasure—itself perhaps a surprise by now—than either *The Wrong Man* or *Vertigo*. It is not simply that Thornhill's doppelgänger Kaplan merely threatens his reputation rather than his identity—for in *The Wrong Man,* Rose has a breakdown simply because other people do not believe her husband's story—but that the film develops a metaphor for Thornhill's comic nightmare which, like the principals' game-playing in the Gaumont-British films, predicts and motivates an affirmative conclusion. The metaphor for Scottie's loss of identity is obsession, the possession by another person which allows him to surrender control of himself and indeed to prefer to surrender that control, just as he continues to prefer the dead sham Madeleine to the live Judy. Scottie is incapable of overcoming his obsession because he is incapable of accepting love and so insists, paradoxically, on his own self-reliance. "I think I can lick it," he tells Midge about his vertigo, as if he could pull himself up by his own bootstraps. But the ego weakened by vertigo is incapable of healing itself. Just as John Ballantine found himself only through the love of Constance Petersen, Scottie would require an act of commitment to someone else's love for him (as opposed to his love for her), which he cannot make. Hence his malady makes him incapable of choosing healing love over tragically destructive idealism: the cycle in which he is trapped can only repeat in a descending spiral. The metaphor for Thornhill's loss of identity, by contrast, is parental domination, a figure which implies its own course of development from infantile identification with one's parents through stormy rebellion against them to an independence consonant with accepting them as fellow-adults who can be counted on without that dependence becoming absolute. In other words, Thornhill learns, as Scottie never does, to accept the help he needs in clearing himself because he finally learns to accept other people even when he has been disillusioned with them. This ability to cooperate with others is in turn based on Thornhill's acceptance of a contingent notion of identity. Eve is not simply a mother-figure, not simply a treacherous prostitute, not even simply a government agent, but a woman whose behavior sometimes seems incomprehensible because her personality, like his own, is contingent on the demands of specific situations.

The process through which Thornhill makes this discovery is the familiar motif of acting, in the double sense of playing roles in order to understand one's own identity better and as preparation for consequential action. Like Hamlet, Odysseus, and Huckleberry Finn, Thornhill is able to perform necessary actions (and thus establishes a new and stable identity based on his own deeds, not his given maternal dependencies and paternal credentials) by acting out various roles.[11] He begins by refusing the constraining role forced on him when he is taken for Kaplan, but in Kaplan's room at the Plaza, he gradually finds himself assuming the role in order to prevent embarrassment (a threat he seems to take more seriously than death) and find out more about Kaplan. When he pages Townsend at the United Nations, he gives Kaplan's name in the hope that Townsend will recognize it. After Townsend is killed, he begins by protesting his innocence, but then, realizing the unlikeliness of his being believed, plays the part of a mad killer, waving the murder knife and shouting, "Wait a minute! Get back!" at his would-be captors. None of these roles is completely successful. Masquerading as Kaplan involves Thornhill more deeply than ever with Vandamm's henchmen, and acting the role of Townsend's murderer confirms the witnesses' suspicion of him. In the meantime, however, Thornhill has already played his first successful, though unwitting, role: the drunk driver whose lack of inhibiting self-control makes his kidnappers underestimate him and so allows him to escape from them. Although Thornhill's intoxicated behavior is clearly regressive, it already expands his repertory of roles, and shows the practical utility of acting.

When Thornhill meets Eve on the train, he first tells her that the police are after him for seven parking tickets and later introduces himself as "Jack Phillips, western sales manager for Kingsby Electronics," but Eve is not fooled by either role. Their relationship involves another kind of acting—the kind associated more directly with games and play, and whose power here depends on the ambiguity between what is and is not a game. As they embrace in Eve's room, she asks him, "How do I know that you're not a murderer, and that you're not planning to murder me here, tonight?" Thornhill asks, "May I?" and she replies, "Please do." He is only playing at being a murderer, but she really will send him to his death the next morning. After he realizes that she has set him up, he returns to her hotel in a scene in which each tries to outplay the other. Eve attempts to reassert her maternal control over Thornhill by telling him, "You're a big boy now," but Thornhill wants to define their relationship in other terms: "Now, let's see. What could a man do with his clothes off for twenty minutes?" Up to this point the scene has closely echoed the episode in *Vertigo* in which Midge tries to awaken Scottie from his obsession with the idealized Madeleine by painting her own picture in the same pose as Carlotta, but Thornhill's reply indicates that his obsession is only situational, not pathological: even though he no longer trusts Eve to live up to the maternal ideals he has imposed on her, he still wants to go to bed with her. He will survive his film because his shallower idealism makes him far more pragmatic, and ultimately better able to mature.

In the following scene at the auction, Thornhill, realizing that he is about to be killed, plays his most successful role so far, reprising his drunk routine by making a shambles of bidding protocol in order to be escorted out by the police. Afterwards, he reprises his unsuccessful scene with his kidnappers by making conversation with the police in the role of the mad killer, another role which is far more successful in irritating his companions and finally goading one of them to respond to his self-accusations of homicidal mania, "You ought to be ashamed of yourself"—the film's most economical deflation of an authoritarian threat into comic paranoia as the faceless figure of authority turns out to be just another impatient father.

Thornhill's progress is arduous; for every step forward, he seems to take two steps back. After his initial unsuccessful attempts to deceive Eve, he allows her to dictate his identity on the train, with perilous results. Later, after he learns she is a government agent, he allows the Professor to dictate his identity—he will pretend to be Kaplan one last time so that she can pretend to shoot him—with the understanding that he and Eve will be free together. But the Professor betrays Thornhill just as Eve had done: he actually plans to have Vandamm take Eve abroad with him. The benign father would rather send Eve off with the malign father than turn her over to the son. When he tricks the Professor (again by acting alcoholic and asking for liquor) and goes after Eve, Thornhill learns what the Professor would never have known, that Leonard has seen through his masquerade and that Vandamm is planning to kill her. Thornhill's final interference in the world of adult affairs—whereby he helps the Professor and saves Eve's life—at last seals his own adulthood; although he needs the help of the Professor and the police to rescue Eve, he accepts that help as an equal. It is true that the image of Thornhill making Eve relive this final rescue, his definitive emergence into adulthood, is somewhat equivocal, but the film's famous last shot, a miniature of a train entering a tunnel, treats any suspicion of his lingering adolescence as a joke. Evidently his sexuality has become adult too.

The tragic nightmare of Vertigo turned comic in North by Northwest reappears in starker terms in Psycho in the unexpected mode of black comedy. Audiences whose idea of a black comedy is The Trouble with Harry might be outraged at this suggestion, but in fact Psycho's method is precisely outrageous, focusing as it does on the drastic, peremptory, and humiliating deflation of any claims to obsession concerning personal identity—and of the notion of identity as such. Unlike Scottie Ferguson's romantic obsessions, which wreak disaster but are treated seriously throughout his film, the obsessive paranoia of Marion Crane (Janet Leigh) is merely a pretext for Hitchcock's most monstrous joke on both her and the audience.

The title music to North by Northwest, Bernard Herrmann's lighthearted fandango, not only helps set the film's tone but indicates a thematic link between the moments when it returns: Thornhill's intoxicated escape through Glen Cove, his masquerade as a redcap, and his flight with Eve down the face of Mount Rushmore. In each case a paranoid flight is turned to comedy by the absurdity of the circumstances and the ultimate success of the escape: even if all the world is crazy, even if everyone is out to get Thornhill, he can escape through a series of increasingly improbable adventures. Herrmann's title music to Psycho bespeaks the same paranoia without suggesting either the buoyancy of North by Northwest or the romantic dignity of Vertigo. The music, which is associated exclusively with the flight of Marion Crane after she steals forty thousand dollars from her employer, Mr. Lowery (Vaughn Taylor), returns first when she is leaving town with the money after asking for the rest of the afternoon off to go to bed. Driving along a street, she sees Lowery walk in front of her car and absentmindedly waves to him. As his smile of recognition turns to a frown, the title music breaks in. Later, the music returns again as Marion continues to drive through Arizona, imagining what the reactions to her theft will be. In each case the music signals a break in the chain of ordinary social relations, a frenzy of isolation, and the specific fear of being watched. Stealing forty thousand dollars, the music suggests, does not alienate Marion from the human community; it is the prospect of getting caught, and her resulting sense of the world as a series of traps, that alienate her.

The self-alienation at the heart of *Psycho* is organized around the nightmarish fear of being watched. Although Marion feels alienated from other people without feeling crazy—as Roger Thornhill never doubts his own identity even though everyone else does—the broken rhythms of the title music suggest that her paranoia is precisely a sign of her disintegration because the person she believes herself to be is not consonant with the person other people *correctly* perceive her to be. Unable to accept the identity other people's gaze confers on her, she is yet unable to defend her own conception of herself, and so loses all sense of identity. Unlike Thornhill, but very much like Scottie, Marion does not have a strong enough sense of self to resist the temptation which will challenge and finally overwhelm her.

Like Rose Balestrero's madness, Marion's paranoia is used to illuminate the disorder of her film's main character, in this case Norman Bates (Anthony Perkins). Norman's psychosis is best understood through Marion's disintegration, which establishes a bridge between the presumably normal world of the audience's perceptions and judgments and the *grand guignol* of the Bates Motel and Norman's California Gothic house.[12]

Marion most resembles Norman in her fear of being watched. Her part of the film is filled with prying eyes: those of the oilman Cassidy (Frank Albertson), as he leans across her desk and tells her she needs a weekend in Las Vegas; of her boss as he sees her driving along the street; of the patrolman who questions her about sleeping in her car all night; of the used-car salesman who asks her if she can prove that car is hers;

and finally of Norman himself, as he spies on her through the peephole in the room behind his office. After killing Marion in the guise of his mother, Norman will be watched suspiciously by the detective Arbogast (Martin Balsam), by Marion's lover Sam (John Gavin), and by her sister Lila (Vera Miles), who will go through the house until she comes to his room and realizes that he has been permanently arrested in a state of preadolescence. Norman's real fears of being watched, however, concern not himself but his mother. When Marion suggests that he place her "somewhere," he goes into a tirade about "the cruel eyes watching" at such institutions; later, he will move his mother's corpse to the fruit cellar to hide it from prying eyes; and Hitchcock last shows Norman sitting rigid and alone at the police station watching a fly crawl on his hand as Mrs. Bates's voice-over gently insists that the whole thing has been Norman's fault and that she's not going to kill that fly just in case anybody is watching. Marion's fear of being watched, a fear that other people might surprise an identity she could neither conceal nor acknowledge, even to herself, expresses itself in Norman as a paranoia so intense that it suppresses all personality whatever and takes on the identity the presumed audience imputes. *Psycho,* which begins by teasing the audience to expect a story of romantic intrigue whose heroine is threatened by the alienating institutions of law and society, turns out to be structured by the contagious fear that we are the person others see. Like *Vertigo* and *North by Northwest,* its plot justifies its central fear: both Marion and Norman end by surrendering their own sense of themselves to the person their watchers think they are.

Marion and Norman attempt to deal with their fears in the same way, by externalizing the actions they cannot acknowledge as theirs. Norman's solution to the problem is psychotic: he creates an alter ego, his mother, who will be responsible for his crimes. But Marion portends this psychosis in her attempts to insulate herself from her crime, as if her actions were not her own. The mirror in her bedroom at home splits her, in typical *film noir* fashion, into observing judge and observed criminal, and she does everything she can to maintain this split. She puts the money in her handbag without looking at it, as if someone else were taking it. At the used car lot, she goes into the ladies' room to count out the seven hundred dollars she needs. At the Bates Motel, she registers under a false name ("Marie Samuels," both expressing her longing for marriage and claiming Sam's complicity in her theft). But the most telling image of Marion's attempt to treat her actions as external to her takes place just before her death, when, after writing down a list of figures on a sheet of paper (she has subtracted 700 from 40,000, trying to figure out how much money she has left), she flushes the scraps of paper down the toilet, as if putting the crime behind her were as simple as a flush. This image is part of a pattern of attempts to keep unpleasant experience at bay: Marion's friend Caroline's taking tranquilizers on her wedding day, Sam's elderly customer's insistence on knowing whether or not an insecticide is painless, and Mrs. Bates's shouted refusal "to speak of disgusting things [like his acquaintance with Marion] because they disgust me." The toilet flushing looks forward in its sound as well as its image to the shot of Norman sinking Marion's car in the swamp behind the hotel—the climactic event in his compulsive attempt to eradicate every trace of Marion's presence from the motel—and smiling in relief and satisfaction when she and the car finally go down the drain.

The image that ties all the others together, and the pivotal shot in the film, is the shot of the bathtub drain, with water and blood spiraling down into it, dissolving into an extreme close-up of Marion's dead eye. This is the climax of the film's melodramatic tease, the moment when its mode switches decisively from psychological drama to black comedy. On a first viewing the principal effect of the shot is pathetic: Mrs. Bates, treating Marion as a blight to be removed from her son's life, has cut off another human being, ending a life the audience has felt uncommonly close to. But the ironies of this dissolve become more complex once an audience knows that Norman is the killer. Norman's spying on Marion as she undressed reveals a voyeurism which, as so often in Hitchcock, constitutes an implicit rape, a assault on the object's privacy that already foretells another kind of assault. Marion has in effect been killed by an eye: her fears about being watched were all too justified. Ironically, she has not been killed for reasons having anything to do with her paranoia; indeed, the most brutal way her identity is thrown away is that everything she has considered so vitally important is inconsequential—savagely, comically inconsequential—in the film's scheme of things. "Someone always sees a girl with forty thousand dollars," Arbogast tells Lila and Sam, but he is wrong; once Marion stole the money, she died before anyone found out she had taken it.

Marion's paranoia, though misguided in its pretext, is accurate, for her attempt to split herself in two brought her very close to the true horror: the realization that the dangerous watcher is not outside, not one of them, but oneself, that one's identity is literally unbearable. Just as Madeleine is Scottie's ideal, though fatal, love, Norman is Marion's sought-for executioner, the person who makes her realize that she cannot flush her crime down the drain without flushing herself with it, since there is no difference between the eye that sees and judges and the drain that carries away filth—and life itself.

Hitchcock's camera lingers on Marion's dead eye as if it held some shocking secret. Over and over again *Psycho* raises the question of what is behind the threatening gaze that everyone fears, the gaze that compels them to acknowledge their identity and so their alienation. But there is never an answer. Marion can only imagine what the inquisitive patrolman thinks behind his sunglasses. Norman's eye as he watches Marion reveals nothing. Marion's eye is blank. The image of identity becomes, in the course of the film, simply a denial of identity, a weapon that kills by its gaze and a blank that undermines the watcher's own claims to identity. Indeed Hitchcock's use of prying eyes that reveal nothing about either the object or the subject of their gaze indicates that *Psycho* is his most annihilating attack on the very concept of human identity.

The philosophical basis for this attack is sketched during Marion's and Norman's conversation in Norman's back room, where they discuss the traps people can get caught in. Observing that "everyone goes a little mad sometimes," Norman suggests that "we're all in our private traps" that prevent people from overcoming their isolation. Marion agrees, and goes on to ask how people get into their traps. Norman claims to have been born in his, whereas Marion says that she stepped in one herself back in Phoenix. Although neither presses their disagreement, two opposed views of action and identity are at stake. For Marion, identity is a function of action, and action is freely chosen, at least up to a point: now that she realizes she has stepped into a trap, she intends to go back and see if she can get out. For Norman, by contrast, identity is a function of heredity or fate: free action is a contradiction in terms, because everything has been settled long ago by the traps everyone has been born into.

Marion's definition of herself in terms of an authorizing ego will be mocked by her absurdly unmotivated death, but her assumptions are called into question throughout the film by the story's ominous treatment, or non-treatment, of moments of decision. Marion thinks that she made a free decision to steal the money, but when did she make it? The film cuts from a shot of her leaving Lowery's office to a shot of her standing in her bedroom, half-dressed, with her bag half-packed. Throughout this scene she acts tentative about taking the money—she acts, that is, as if the decision were still before her. Yet the money is there on the bed all along; she has already failed to put it in the company's safe-deposit box. At what point does she actually decide to steal it, and at what point is it actually stolen? The second question is easier to answer than the first, since it is clearly Lowery's frown as he passes her on the street that makes Marion decide it is too late to turn back. But in a sense it has been too late from the beginning. Even as Marion debates whether or not to steal the money, she has already stolen it.

The question about decision will return later in another form: when did Norman decide to kill Marion? Sitting in the Bates kitchen moments before she is attacked, he seems to be thinking about something, but he has already been watching her through his peephole; perhaps his choice of cabin 1 for his guest (the film shows his hand hovering teasingly before the twelve keys before it falls on this one) sealed her fate still earlier. But even this is not the moment that makes Norman what he is to be, since the police later learn that he killed his mother years ago, and probably two other missing girls since then. Like Marion, Norman is treated as having a choice that he has actually made long since—a choice that has in some sense never been his to make.

Hitchcock makes his principals seem reactive rather than purposive by manipulating the audience's sympathies in favor of Marion from the beginning. Her lover is unsympathetic, unhelpful, and remote; her fellow secretary is irresponsible and inefficient; her boss, who keeps a liquor bottle in his desk, has air-conditioned his office but not hers; and the man whose money she takes is a lecherous braggart who probably cheats on his income tax. Given Marion's provocation, it is nearly impossible for anyone in the audience to perceive her as a thief; she is just an ordinary person who happens to go off the rails one day. This is of course the way Marion perceives herself, and since she continues to retain her old conception of herself despite her actions—like Bruno Anthony, who helps a blind man across the street just after killing Miriam Haines—she naturally resists, with growing panic, any accusation which might force her to redefine herself in accord with these actions. Being watched is a threat not so much to her liberty as to her very sense of herself as independent of her actions, and the audience accordingly shares her fear of being watched. Seeing oneself as independent of one's actions, however, is typical not only of Marion but of Norman, who has internalized a defense against having to take responsibility, or even cognizance, of his crimes as his own.

But Norman's fatalistic account of his identity is as fallacious as Marion's assumption that she is an autonomous agent in control of the actions which define her. My circumstances leave me no control over my actions, he is telling Marion, with the sinister subtext: I can't control myself, I'm possessed by my mother. The psychiatrist at the end of the film echoes Norman's explanation when he says that Norman no longer exists and only partly existed in the first place. Norman and the psychiatrist agree that Norman isn't really Norman, he's really Mrs. Bates. But the relation between the two is far more complex. Morally, the psychiatrist's monologue justifies the district attorney's comment that he's trying to lay the groundwork for some kind of plea, presumably insanity or diminished responsibility. As Mrs. Bates's voice suggests in the closing scene, she can now hide inside Norman, join the court in condemning him, and let him take her punishment. But this attempt to parcel out Norman's personality between himself and his mother merely continues the cycle that Marion began with her attempts to treat her theft as someone else's. When the film's audience watches Anthony Perkins in the last scene, are they watching Mrs. Bates (as the psychiatrist seems to suggest) or Norman himself? To say that Norman believes himself possessed by his mother's personality is not the same as saying that he has become her, any more than it is true that Scottie ever becomes Madeleine. What happens instead is the surrender of individual identity to something conceived and idealized as outside, but a willing surrender to avoid the intolerable burden of responsibility for one's own actions, the burden of being oneself. The stuffed birds framed with Norman in his back room, which present him simultaneously as victim and analogue of their unwitting violence, and the skull superimposed on his face in the film's penultimate shot, which presents him as at once his mother and himself, indicate that the uncomfortable or horrific reality that so many characters in the film try to shut out of their lives by narcotics, money, air-conditioning, bug spray, flushing the toilet, or flushing Marion down the swamp is simply the unity of their own experience, the fact of identity as such. The characters in *Psycho* are so revolted by their own experience that they prefer to keep it at bay even at the price of defining themselves as other. As the human eye unsuccessfully attempts to define identity in contradistinction to the other, the human I similarly fails, and the secret Norman reveals as he watches Marion undress, the secret Marion reveals through her dead gaze, is the secret Lila reveals when she whirls in panic before the mirror on Mrs. Bates's bureau to confront her own image: the impenetrable and unendurable mystery of oneself. Hitchcock's brilliantly treacherous rewriting of the narrative contract—his determination to make his nightmares amusing for the audience by finding engaging modes like romantic tragedy or black comedy or by enticing the audience with the promise of one kind of pleasure only to change the contract in the middle of the film—has not only put the audience in the impossible position of looking forward eagerly to being cheated but has made the cheat enjoyable as well. The wheel may be rigged, these films suggest, but it's the only game in town.

# EIGHT

---

# FILL IN

# THE BLANKS

*P*sycho was the most successful financially of all Hitchcock's films, and his friend Lew Wasserman was able to arrange a lucrative new contract for him with Universal that gave Hitchcock virtually complete control over his work. With his move to Universal Hitchcock entered the last phase of his career, a period which echoes his earliest phase in virtually dispensing with the psychologically complex identification figures who had dominated his American films, and in particular the series of films culminating in *Psycho*. The heroes and heroines of the Universal films are not only simpler but less compelling, more distant, than any of Hitchcock's principals since his silent films. The disintegration of personality which reaches a crisis in Scottie Ferguson and Norman Bates is presented as a given in Hitchcock's last films. The Universal films do not, on the whole, outrage the audience by dramatizing the disintegration of a figure of identification; they present a world in which identification figures simply do not appear.

The disappearance of strong identification figures might be taken as an indication of the director's philosophical despair, and the landscape of the Universal films is certainly bleak. But their bleakness in no way marks a turn away from the games Hitchcock had long cultivated; indeed in many ways these are the most ludic of all Hitchcock's films. In retaining so many of the narrative techniques that encourage identification while emphasizing the psychological inadequacy of the potential identification figures—in effect substituting identification as a figure for identity—Hitchcock adopts a playfully mannerist style reminiscent of his earliest films. The stylistic hallmarks of the Universal films are self-absorption, self-reflexiveness, and intertextual play. The director is no longer concerned with the leading problem of his earlier American films, his heroes' and heroines' problem of how to establish individual identity in a world inimical to identity, but treats his characters more frankly as relatively inexpressive game pieces that may have different values (as rooks and knights differ from pawns) but are all clearly subordinated to the relation they establish between the human players, the director and his audience.

This tendency in Hitchcock's work had been portended by the tendency of his heroes and heroines from Scottie Ferguson to Marion Crane to destroy their own identities. Scottie's vertigo shows the paradoxical relation between self-absorption and self-annihilation especially clearly. In order to maintain his independence, his sense of himself as autonomous, Scottie refuses the love which would offer his only hope for recovering from his obsession with the past and with his own inadequacies. His self-absorption, that is, rules out any possibility of self-renewal. But the self whose independence Scottie guards so jealously is only a displacement of other selves. At the beginning of the film he is obsessed by the policeman who fell from the roof; later he falls under the spell of Madeleine Elster and allows her to dictate his behavior and his concerns. Scottie thus defines his obsessively independent self in terms of another, and another who in turn seems a displacement of an absent self (Carlotta Valdes) and is actually the creation of a manipulating criminal (Elster). The more frantically Scottie asserts his independence, the more completely he defines himself in terms of his idealized vision of someone else—a person (Judy) whom he cannot love as herself but only as his ideal. The ego that Scottie so proudly guards therefore becomes a function of his vision of another, as Scottie's I becomes revealed as defined exclusively in terms of his eye. Scottie's rage over Judy's complicity in Elster's criminal plot is the logical expression of his disappointment with himself for failing to live up to his impossibly high expectations because he has become what he has beheld.

*Vertigo* and *Psycho* thus disturbingly suggest that the whole project of personal identity is misbegotten because the act of seeing merely destroys its objects without securing an identity for its subjects, as Scottie's and Norman's gaze endangers others without consolidating their own identities. Their disinclination or inability to integrate their perceptions makes their eyes function as weapons rather than repositories of experience. *Psycho,* which is structured as a series of penetrations behind façades or into hidden recesses, seems to promise to take the audience behind the eyes of Marion or Norman.[1] But there is nothing behind these eyes: Marion's gaze is dead, and Norman is only substituting for his mother, whose eyes are the hollow sockets of a skull.

If the self is only an eye, then not only the identity of individual characters in films but the whole notion of character itself is at risk. *Psycho* presents a world of people so obsessed with sanitizing their lives and denying their authorizing power over their experience or the consequences of their actions that it is virtually a world devoid of egos, a world without a self, and the only significant relationship left is the one between the filmmaker and the audience. Yet because the audience itself is no more than an eye, and an eye which *Psycho* works to make single and monocular (hence Hitchcock's pleasure in using the film to "achieve something of a mass emotion"[2]), this relationship is as problematic as any the characters themselves had dramatized in their earlier films. Hitchcock's films of the 1940s and 1950s had involved the audience in outrageous plots by means of the close identifications they established between the audience and the principals. *Vertigo, North by Northwest,* and *Psycho* similarly depend on forming close identifications between the audience and their surrogates in the film. But because each of these surrogates' identities is itself problematic, the films come to encourage identification as a substitute for a stable identity.

Hitchcock had long been fascinated with problematic characters, figures whose identity was unstable or open to question. The enigmatic figures at the center of his earliest American films—Rebecca de Winter, Johnnie Aysgarth, Uncle Charlie, John Ballantine—are designed as mysterious touchstones for the identities of his principals, touchstones whose identity it is precisely the function of the stories to reveal. But except for Alicia Huberman, these enigmatic figures never operate as figures of identification for the audience; they are always paired with more stable identification figures (the second Mrs. de Winter, Lina Aysgarth, Charlie Newton, Constance Petersen) whom they double. In the series of films ending with *Psycho,* Hitchcock makes the audience identify with the enigmatic figures themselves by calling his principals' identity into question in a more radical sense than ever before. The relationships between Uncle Charlie and young Charlie, Bruno and Guy, Thorwald and Jefferies, prepare for the relationship between Madeleine and Scottie, but in the earlier films, the principals, the audience's identification figures, all maintain a core of stability despite the ways their identities are complicated or compromised by their doubles. The good guys may resemble the bad guys, but they are still recognizably good. In *North by Northwest* Roger Thornhill is always clearly the hero, but Eve Kendall is only intermittently the heroine, and Thornhill's identity is called more completely into question than that of any earlier Hitchcock innocent—even that of Manny Balestrero, who is accused only of committing a series of robberies, not of leading a life which is simply a masquerade. In *Vertigo* and *Psycho* the line separating heroes from villains is erased, since both of the audience's identification figures define themselves in terms of obsessions (Scottie's with Madeleine, Marion's with the $40,000) that devastatingly weaken their identities even as they encourage the audience to identify with them.

The Universal films break Hitchcock's contract with the audience for one last time by encouraging the audience to identify with characters who have virtually no identity. The heroes and heroines of these films are not fascinating, glamorous, or psychotic; they are simply ciphers whose world is more interesting than they are. In a sense Hitchcock is completing his career by bringing it full circle: in losing interest in the investigation of personal identity that has marked his films since *Rebecca,* he is returning to the mannerist style of his silent films, whose visual effects often operate independently of his narrative. The director is not seeking to outrage his viewers by betraying their identifications; instead he is inviting them to a chilly complicity in contemplating the fate of his fictional pawns.

Hitchcock's final films are his most problematic, and the most problematic of all is the first and exemplary work of this period, *The Birds,* the only Hitchcock film to have generated radical discrepancies in interpretation. Critics may disagree about whether *The 39 Steps* and *Notorious* are great films, but they agree about what they mean. But there is no consensus about what *The Birds* means—or, more specifically, about why large numbers of birds of different species suddenly begin to attack the residents of the California community of Bodega Bay shortly after the arrival of Melanie Daniels (Tippi Hedren), who has brought a pair of lovebirds as a birthday present for Cathy Brenner (Veronica Cartwright) and a playfully malicious joke on Cathy's much older brother Mitch (Rod Taylor), whom she had met for the first time earlier that day when he teased her in a pet shop for her irresponsible pranks. The most striking feature of the bird attacks is their gratuitousness, but this summary is meant to indicate that the actions of the film's human principals are equally gratuitous, that in fact Hitchcock pointedly declines to provide adequate motivation for the actions of anyone in the film.

This omission has naturally encouraged speculation from all sides, at least on the subject of the birds. The speculation begins in a scene in the Tides Cafe, where Melanie and Mitch have gone to warn the community. Mrs. Bundy (Ethel Griffes), an ornithologist, insists that Melanie is imagining things because "birds are not aggressive creatures." Her observations have an ecological basis: since only humans make war on nature, any natural affronts to people take the force of retaliations. A drunk in the cafe offers another explanation: "It's the end of the world." Another man suggests that the aberration is temporary and limited and that the inhabitants of Bodega Bay "get yourself guns and wipe them off the face of the earth." The mother of two children begs the others not to talk about the birds, but later, after birds have attacked the area of the cafe itself and caused several deaths, she accuses Melanie of having provoked their attacks, which have coincided with her arrival.

Hitchcock's critics have pursued each of these lines and added others. The major alternatives were laid down by 1965, when Robin Wood summarized them under three headings: "1. *The birds are taking revenge for man's persecution of them. . . . 2. They are sent by God to punish evil humanity. . . . 3. The birds express the tensions between the characters.*"[3] Wood himself dismisses all three of these explanations (though the third has maintained a considerable following) and offers a fourth:

"the birds . . . are a concrete embodiment of the arbitrary and unpredictable . . . a reminder of . . . the possibility that human life is meaningless and absurd."[4] Other possibilities could be adduced. The attacking birds could be outlaw birds, or they could be maddened by some particular ecological outrage—noxious gas, an oil spill—or determined to take revenge on Melanie for caging a pair of lovebirds; or they could be massing in an attempt to free the lovebirds. All these explanations sound ridiculous. In fact, setting aside the trailer Hitchcock produced for the film, in which he delivers a monologue humorously emphasizing humans' longstanding exploitation of birds, and his repeated injunctions in interviews against disturbing the natural order, there is no suggestion in the film that the attacks can be explained at all. The question is raised repeatedly throughout the film, but all the answers the characters give are made to seem absurdly inadequate.

The pattern of unexplained and perhaps inexplicable violence is common to Hitchcock's films. From *The Lodger* to *Psycho* Hitchcock has delighted in undermining his characters' complacent explanations of the villains' murderous impulses or simply dispensed with these explanations altogether. The audience is rarely troubled by this obscurity because it is subsumed under a generic convention which provides for mysterious outbreaks of violence. (For many years "homicidal mania" was an adequate explanation of the behavior of Hollywood villains.) But this time Hitchcock suspends the convention of rational explanation (a convention he had broadly parodied in the psychiatrist's explanation at the end of *Psycho*) without indicating why. The film's only answer is another question: why *should* the attacks make sense? For that matter, why should anyone's behavior make sense?

Hitchcock generalizes the mystery of the birds by establishing a series of analogies between people and birds which have no explanatory power. From the film's opening scene it is clear that Melanie is like a bird. As she crosses the street to go into a pet shop, she turns in appreciative response to an offscreen whistle which sounds like the gulls' cries in the background. When Mitch, after pretending to take her for a salesperson, encourages her to take out a bird which promptly gets loose and flies around the shop, she flutters after it with birdlike movements. Mitch, capturing the bird at last, returns it to its cage with the remark, "Back in your gilded cage, Melanie Daniels," and in response to Melanie's pique, explains, "I was merely drawing a parallel. . . . I merely wanted you to know what it felt like to be on the other end of a gag." Later Melanie describes Mitch as wanting "to put everyone behind bars," and still later her identification with caged birds is made visually more explicit when she is trapped by attacking birds, first in a car, then in a phone booth.

If Melanie is like a bird, then birds are also treated like people. Mitch tells Melanie he is looking for a pair of lovebirds that are "not too demonstrative, not too aloof." Later, as Melanie drives up to Bodega Bay with the pair of lovebirds she has found, Hitchcock cuts in a shot of them swaying on their perch as Melanie rounds a tight corner, compensating for the centrifugal force just as people in movies are aften shown to do during car chases. After Annie Hayworth (Suzanne Pleshette), Mitch's old flame, who has moved to Bodega Bay to be near him, tells Melanie about her hopelessly thwarted love for him, the scene ends with the women's discovery of a gull which has killed itself by flying into Annie's door in an equally futile gesture.

Suggestive as these analogies are, they do not explain the birds' aberrant behavior. Nor is it logically clear why they should. Hitchcock had used the analogy between birds and people in *Sabotage* and *Psycho* to dramatize the relation between passivity and violence, but the analogy did not explain the relation, nor did it depend on any universally shared assumption that birds are both passive and aggressive. Just as birds did not simply explain human mysteries in the earlier films, the human analogy does not explain the birds' mystery here. It could scarcely have much explanatory power at any rate because the behavior of Hitchcock's characters, especially Melanie and Mitch, is so gratuitous itself. When Mitch pretends to take Melanie for a salesperson in the bird shop, she adopts the role for no good reason. After becoming unduly resentful, she tracks down a pair of lovebirds, evidently at some trouble, traces Mitch's address, and, when he turns out to be out of town, decides to spend several hours driving up to Bodega Bay to deliver them. Arriving in Bodega Bay, she goes to see Annie Hayworth just in order to ascertain Cathy Brenner's first name and insists on hiring a boat in order to sneak the birds into the Brenners' house through the back door. When Mitch discovers the birds and asks in some bewilderment why she has come so far to deliver them, she tells him untruthfully that she is up on a visit to her old school friend Annie Hayworth and almost immediately rekindles her quarrel with him (in fact, through the first half of the film, every scene between Melanie and Mitch begins amicably and ends in a quarrel). In the meantime, on her way to return the boat, Melanie has been struck in the head by a swooping gull. This first bird attack seems illogical, but no more so than the human behavior it interrupts. Hitchcock has simply undermined the well-known but unrealistic conventions of romantic comedy (the incessant bickering of hero and heroine, the consequent strong mood swings, the preposterously unlikely behavior, the exaggerated significance of trivial events and remarks) by substituting the conventions of mysterious violence without providing a rationale, or even indicating a preference, for either convention.

This does not mean that the characters' irrational behavior causes or explains the birds' irrational behavior, only that it casts doubt on the assumption that there is an explanation. To put it another way, the birds' attacks, and the film generally, make sense only in the context of generic conventions, conventions of the film available to the audience, not psychological conventions available to the characters. No matter what explanation the audience postulated for the attacks, the characters would never be able to understand it. But the characters' inability to understand their experience is precisely the point of that experience.

When Mitch says that he embarrassed Melanie in the bird shop because he wanted her to know what it felt like on the other end of a gag, it is eminently logical to take the sequel as providing that experience: Melanie, the carefree practical joker, is made the butt of a horrifying joke. But it does not follow that the birds represent Mitch's sense of sexual or institutional outrage or the world's revenge on a woman who has taken her experience too lightly because the attacks, like Melanie's original excesses of behavior, are unmotivated and gratuitous. Since the birds have no more reason for attacking than Melanie for driving to Bodega Bay, their attacks really are a gag and nothing more.

This conclusion is disturbing, for it emphasizes the discontinuity and irrationality in the film. But *The Birds* is a disturbing film—in conception Hitchcock's most disturbing film—precisely because it is a joke on its characters' lives and its audience's expectations, a joke whose point is precisely its irreducible outrageousness.[5] Critics have often attempted to rescue *The Birds* from its status as a gag by recasting it as satire or Freudian psychodrama, and the film provides considerable support for either reading. Hitchcock is clearly satirizing his characters' triviality, their obsession with business as usual, when Mitch's mother Lydia (Jessica Tandy), complaining on the telephone that her last supply of feed must have been bad, says, "No, they're not fussy chickens," or when the sheriff's deputy straightens from his investigation of a later attack and says, "That's a sparrow, all right," or even when Melanie is casually smoking in the schoolyard as the birds mass on a jungle gym behind her. In every case the response is so inadequate that the audience's response is comically condescending, even if their superiority is tinged with apprehension. Again, the attacks correspond so closely to ruptures between the characters, and the analogies between birds and people are so minutely elaborated, that the behavior of the characters seems insistently to promise an explanation of the attacks it never quite fulfills.

The satiric and psychoanalytic readings of the film, although they are inherently at odds with each other, are both rooted in the same impulse. The satiric reading trivializes the relations among the principals, the psychoanalytic reading inflates them,[6] but both agree that the fundamental problem in the film is the disproportion between the relatively inconsequential behavior of the characters and the magnitude of the threat they face, and both attempt to resolve that problem by establishing an intelligible relation between the two. It is the nature of the film, however, to resist any such resolution. Of course the characters' behavior can be seen as comically inadequate or psychologically portentous, but the very fact that it can be seen in either way, or both, suggests that it is not inherently one or the other; as Wood says of the birds' behavior, it just is, and any attempt to rationalize it will miss the point of the joke.

Throughout the film Hitchcock presents human behavior which supports any number of theories of human identity but resists definitive assimilation to any one. On the one hand, any audience who has sat through *Vertigo* and *Psycho* and who has considered the psychological reconstructions of Madeleine Elster (who was not obsessed by Carlotta Valdes but only pretended that she was) or Marion Crane (who is snuffed out and thrown away just as the film has penetrated her last mystery) will surely be skeptical of any psychoanalytic explanations of Hitchcock's mysteries. On the other, it seems almost an impertinence to psychoanalyze Mitch Brenner, as Hitchcock had invited viewers to psychoanalyze the false Dr. Edwardes, on the basis of such abbreviated clues as they are given here. The most interesting thing about Mitch and Melanie is that they are attacked by birds. The film therefore discourages explanations that operate on the characters' level and substitutes explanations that operate on the director's and the audience's. If the bird attacks are a gag, they are not a gag that Melanie Daniels could ever understand, but one that makes perfect sense to an audience that sees Melanie punished for wearing her hair in a bun, flirting with or condescending to everyone she meets, and acting generally as if she were in the wrong movie. Not only the characters but the plot itself (that is, the playful romantic intrigue the characters take to be the plot) is a study in futility; it is simply a pretext providing the audience with expectations that can be undermined. Instead of emphasizing the strong, generally sympathetic figure who mediates the relationship between his audience and himself, Hitchcock here inaugurates a period defined by the creation of a world in which the gap between human behavior and human identity is decisive, a world truly without a the possibility of a coherent self. The void at the heart of Mitch's and Melanie's characters is not presented as a reflection of existential despair but simply as an invitation to the audience to fill in the blanks as best they can.

More than any of Hitchcock's other work, the Universal films invoke a Hitchcock world as self-contained as the worlds of billiards or bridge. All the films abound in ludic set-pieces that often interrupt and even ridicule the development of an extended narrative (on this point marking a return to Hitchcock's earliest style), liberal borrowings from Hitchcock's earlier films, and references, for the first time in many years, to other specific films rather than to the audience's generic sense of Hollywood movies. Instead of consolidating or retreating from the affront to the audience of *The Birds,* Hitchcock's self-plagiarism amounts to a final manifesto: *le monde, c'est moi.* All these characteristics, especially the last, are particularly clear in Hitchcock's last two espionage films, *Torn Curtain* and *Topaz,* which present themselves as correctives to the James Bond films, whose popularity had by the mid-sixties reached a zenith.

If *The Birds* takes the form of a monstrous joke on the heroine's generic expectations, these two films, especially *Torn Curtain,* pose as specifically intertextual commentaries on the generic expectations evoked by the Bond mystique.

The Bond films, beginning in 1962 with *Dr. No,* had shown the polished, witty, omnicompetent, sexually attractive Sean Connery, armed with the latest technological hardware, vanquishing ever more ambitious and unlikely global conspiracies. Bond was an unvarnished figure of fantasy whose appeal was based on the myth of the power of personal style, the belief that individual charm, strength, and intelligence could overcome the most powerful and ruthless adversaries. The Bond myth was enormously appealing to an audience whose fears about global holocaust focused on their own impotent remoteness from the engines of destruction and their consequent inability to affect the fate of the world. Bond saved the world single-handedly every year, and had a fine time in the process.

*Torn Curtain* and *Topaz* are anti-Bond films which set out determined to show what espionage is really like. Against the myth of the solitary, omnipotent agent, they present a world in which spying is unheroic, indeed anti-heroic, in which the biggest risks are run by myriad unimportant characters, in which the individual is never as important as the organization, and in which the principals' private lives suffer accordingly. The conflict between public and private lives, in fact, is as important here as in Hitchcock's earliest work, but it is resolved very differently because the real point of both films is to deny the possibility of heroic individuality.

The principal agent in *Torn Curtain,* Dr. Michael Armstrong (Paul Newman), seems as unlike James Bond as an agent could be. An American physicist whose funding for an anti-nuclear device has been cut off by Washington, he pretends to defect to East Germany to continue his work with Professor Gustav Lindt (Ludwig Donath), but he actually is a double agent whose goal is to persuade Lindt to share his own knowledge. Armstrong's mission is being organized not by the American government but by a small German network which deplores his amateur status and offers him no advanced technology, no expense account, no beautiful women. Nor is Armstrong's personal power very great.

He is even unable to persuade his own fiancée, Sarah Sherman (Julie Andrews), to stay in Sweden; instead, unaware of his plan, she follows him to Berlin and begs him to return to America.

Hitchcock told Truffaut that his leading interest in the case on which his film was based was in the defector's wife: how did she feel about her husband's defection? The first third of Torn Curtain, Hitchcock continues, attempts to tell the story "from a woman's point of view."[7] Even here, however, Hitchcock seems less intent on dramatizing Sarah Sherman's bewilderment and grief than in making her fiancé look mysterious; every circumstantial detail of Armstrong's defection is handled portentously, even if Sarah is not present to react. Armstrong's opacity in the opening sequences, coupled with Hitchcock's sparing use of close-ups, keeps the audience at a distance.[8] After they arrive in Berlin, a pair of matched shots of Armstrong and Sarah sitting apart on a pair of settees perfectly expresses their mutual isolation without bringing the audience closer to them. Indeed, Hitchcock's use of color throughout this first third of the film, in which warm colors are associated with Sarah's anguished love and cool colors with the East Germans and their country, is so elegant and painterly that the film suggests the visual style of Antonioni, not a director from whom Hitchcock often borrowed.[9]

As in The Birds, Hitchcock substitutes his audience's identification for his characters' identity. Although he is interested in Sarah's point of view, he is not interested in her, and he no sooner establishes the centrality of her point of view than he abandons it to present Armstrong's murder of his watchdog Gromek (Wolfgang Kieling), who has discovered that he is not really a defector. After Armstrong and Sarah travel to Leipzig to meet Armstrong's German colleagues, the film briefly focuses on her again when Armstrong is prevented from answering his interlocutors' questions and she is asked to cooperate with them. By this time, however, the audience's identification with her is diminished, because she has been kept offscreen for so long and because the episode in which Armstrong persuades her to cooperate by revealing his true colors is so stylized: Hitchcock cuts from a long shot in which the lovers are talking but cannot be heard to a circling close-up around her, then partly around both of them, as she blissfully and silently embraces him. The sequence obviously recalls Judy's and Scottie's climactic embrace in the Empire Hotel, but this time the dreamlike camera movement cannot strengthen the audience's identification with anyone since it is detached from any particular character's perceptions.

Just as the scene at the farm resolved Armstrong's false position with respect to the audience, this scene resolves his position with respect to the heroine, and the second half of the film is mainly a tactical exercise: how can Armstrong get the information from Lindt and then escape from a country in which he is wanted for murder and in which every by-stander is a potential betrayer? Since Armstrong feels no scruples about picking Lindt's brain, and apparently none of the remorse Ashenden felt in *Secret Agent* about committing murder, the second half of the film focuses simply on his and Sarah's paranoia. During the extended sequence showing their escape, Hitchcock strengthens the audience's identification with his principals without making them any more dis-tinctive individually, for example by the liberal use of German dialogue to make both the characters and the audience uncertain about what is going to happen. Because everyone the couple meets is a presumed enemy, their paranoia has nothing of the figural power of Marion's and Norman's paranoia in *Psycho;* their fear, a sign of obsession and disinte-gration, defined them as individuals; Armstrong's and Sarah's fear is an entirely reasonable and morally uncomplicated apprehension. Hence the audience's identification with them is both close (because their fears are so plausible) and distant (because, like the principals of *The Birds,* they are so indistinct as individuals). Instead of focusing on its principals as moral agents, Hitchcock is more interested in subordinating them to the game he is playing with the Bond myth.

Because Hitchcock's running commentary on the Bond films is ludic, not realistic, his film is constructed as a series of anti-Bond set-pieces: the introduction of the principals in bed, where they have retired to escape the Arctic cold (and where Sarah tells Armstrong, "Now stop! This is supposed to be a serious congress of physicists"); their quarrel in a Berlin hotel room, filmed in one extended full-shot; the reunion of Armstrong and Sarah in a garden in the heart of Leipzig; the scene in which Armstrong's theft of Lindt's knowledge is dramatized by the equations they take turns writing on the blackboard; a charmingly ir-relevant turn by Lila Kedrova as an aging countess desperate to leave the country; and the recognition of Armstrong and Sarah at a climactic performance of *Francesca da Rimini* by a jealous *prima ballerina* (Tamara Toumanova), recalling similar scenes in both versions of *The Man Who Knew Too Much.*

Unlike *The Spy Who Came in from the Cold* and *The Deadly Affair,* *Torn Curtain* does not pose as a realistic corrective to the Bond films, since both its narrative structure and its visual style are even more artificial than those of the Bond films. Nor is it a further exploration of the relation between public roles and private desires, because Michael Armstrong, unlike the defectors on whom his story was based, is actually a double agent, and because the audience's perceptions of him do not finally depend on his fiancée's. Armstrong has no moral problems to speak of; he is simply a quieter, more diffident Bond after all. Hitchcock's real interest in the film lies in diminishing his characters to the vanishing point by adopting the conventions of heroic espionage (which are continually postulated by his inversions of them) without endowing his principals with heroic individuality, or even the nonheroic individuality of Elsa and Ashenden.

This drastically nonheroic view of spying reaches a climax in Hitchcock's following film, *Topaz,* whose story revolves around the Cuban missile crisis of 1962. American intelligence officers, speculating about a possible Soviet nuclear presence in Cuba, are concerned by revelations of the Soviet defector Kusenov (Per-Axel Arosenius) about a ring of Soviet spies called Topaz whose leaders, highly placed French diplomats, have been sending NATO military secrets to Moscow. Because they can get access to a crucial Cuban trade agreement only by bribing a Cuban official who hates Americans, Michael Nordstrom (John Forsythe), who had arranged Kusenov's defection, asks his French counterpart Andre Devereaux (Frederick Stafford) to take charge of the bribery. Devereaux finds himself more and more deeply implicated in the Cuban crisis until eventually he is asked to resign his post and can vindicate himself only by exposing the head of Topaz just as the Soviets remove their missile bases from Cuba.

The film dramatizes the split between public behavior and private desire from its opening sequence, which shows the escape of Kusenov with his wife and daughter during a family vacation in Copenhagen.

As they are followed through the streets and into a porcelain studio, the elder Kusenovs remain resolutely inexpressive despite their anxiety; only when their daugher Tamara (Tina Hedstrom) is about to be separated from them during their dash to Nordstrom's waiting car does she let out a wail of anguish. Asked by another American agent what the imperious Kusenov is like, Nordstrom replies in official terms: "He's a darling man. You'll see. He's just what you wanted. He's a big one." Later, Nicole Devereaux (Dany Robin) complains to her husband that he is leading a double life, masquerading as a businessman, and fooling no one, and when Nordstrom tells her after dinner, "You should be used to it by now—the intelligence work," she says, "A wife never gets used to it." When Devereaux has come with his wife to New York to see their daughter and son-in-law, visiting from Paris, Nordstrom's urgent request forces him to miss their dinner together. As the story develops, Devereaux's involvement with the Americans' mission endangers his relationships with his family more and more directly.

Unlike *Torn Curtain, Topaz* uses the conflict between public and private lives to cloud the moral terms and experience of its audience as well as its characters. Samuel Taylor's screenplay makes its heroes less sympathetic than they are in Leon Uris's novel. Kusenov himself, whose escape at the beginning of the film should make him an obvious identification figure, turns out to be arrogant and condescending as he calls the escape arrangements "very clumsy. . . . It wasn't the way we would have done it." The American agent who installs the Kusenovs at a safe house outside Washington insensitively insists on their sitting for photographs and questioning as soon as they arrive, and when Nordstrom protests, he says, "Didn't they relax on the plane? I always do." Devereaux himself is more devious than in Uris's book. Instead of responding to Nicole's accusation of an adulterous affair with the Cuban agent Juanita de Cordoba (Karin Dor) with a confession, he keeps it a secret. At the same time, Rico Parra (John Vernon), the story's stand-in for Fidel Castro, is made more sympathetic. Although Uris's Juanita calls him "a filthy beast" and sleeps with him only to save Devereaux's life, Hitchcock's Juanita is obviously his mistress from the beginning.[10] When he discovers that she is working against the Castro regime, Parra, in the film's most tender scene, shoots her to save her from torture. On the basis of such moral complications, John Belton concludes that it is "impossible to tell the good spies from the bad spies without a scorecard."[11]

The moral obscurity of Hitchcock's characters stems from their involvement in the political process, as the film's leading patterns of imagery suggest. Politics is essentially an adulterous rondelet. Devereaux's affair with Juanita de Cordoba is matched by Nicole's affair with his old friend Jacques Granville (Michel Piccoli), secretly the head of Topaz. Even nonsexual friendships are tainted by the need for political favors, as Nordstrom recruits Devereaux to help him and Devereaux in turn recruits his son-in-law, the journalist François Picard (Michel Subor), who is nearly killed.

This adulterous view of politics, in which intimacy is characterized mainly as an opportunity for betrayal, is reflected in Hitchcock's use of food and flowers to represent hypocrisy and the compromise of personal loyalties. When Rico Parra interrupts Devereaux's last night alone with Juanita, she offers him some dinner, and Devereaux praises the chicken, not mentioning that earlier that day it had been used to conceal a camera which took pictures of the Soviet military hardware. Later, as Devereaux explains his dilemma at a crucial lunch meeting with his French colleagues, the two men who begin to eat are the Soviet agents. One of these men, Granville, uses a floral code name, Columbine, which conceals his double status as diplomat and betrayer. Throughout the film other flowers are associated with hypocrisy and betrayal. When Devereaux and his wife arrive in New York, Nordstrom is waiting in their hotel room with a bright bouquet of flowers which indicates the favor he is about to ask. Devereaux arranges the bribe Nordstrom asks through an agent whose cover is a flower shop. When Parra kills Juanita, Hitchcock shows her death in an overhead shot that makes her fall look like the opening of a flower. This shockingly aestheticized view of violent death is motivated by the film's principal characters, who attempt to cover their involvement in politics under a more attractive façade.

Flowers are the most striking object in the film's color scheme, which for the most part returns to the desaturated colors of *Rope*. Except for the Cuban delegation to the United Nations, Hitchcock's diplomats all wear dark gray suits and move through neutral urban landscapes. Because most of the other characters wear equally neutral clothes, even moderately saturated colors like the red-brown of Tamara Kusenov's hair and coat stand out, indicating in this case warmth and responsiveness. Whenever bright colors, usually red, appear thereafter, they are, like flowers, associated with desire, intimacy, and betrayal. The film's whole color palette brightens on Devereaux's arrival in Cuba, where Juanita, unlike Nicole, always wears bright colors. The only man identified with such colors is Granville, who greets first his fellow-agent Henri Jarry (Philippe Noiret) and then, after he has left, Nicole Devereaux in a red smoking jacket. Bright colors maintain their traditional association with warmth and passion throughout the film, but this association is inseparable from that of treachery. It is as if the characters could form attachments to each other, or establish their loyalty to a political belief or institution, only at the cost of betraying someone or something else.

The film's most original and complex pattern of imagery deepens this paradox. In the second shot of the opening sequence, Hitchcock tracks in and down from an overhead shot of the Soviet embassy in Copenhagen to show a man's shot reflected in a tightly-framing mirror. The man turns out to be a security officer who is responsible for keeping watch on the Kusenovs. Later in the sequence, Tamara Kusenov creates a ruse by dropping a porcelain statue of a pair of lovers and so getting access to a telephone she uses to call Nordstrom. These two images—the mirror frame and the broken statue—begin a series of images including mirrors, paintings, drawings, framing enclosures, and objets d'art, all organized around the equivocal significance of the frame, which simultaneously aestheticizes, distances, and imprisons whatever it encloses.

Both Granville's apartment in Paris and Devereaux's townhouse in Washington are full of framed pictures and mirrors (though the characters avoid the mirrors as if deliberately). At the climax of François Picard's interrogation of Jarry, he is framed with a brightly colored print of Picasso's painting *The Lovers* on the wall behind. The print recalls François's status as a newlywed, his relative innocence and lack of political commitment, and therefore his danger in facing an adversary like Jarry, who has urged Granville to have Devereaux killed. At the same time, François, the willing victim of Devereaux's importuning, is still a powerful victim, like one of the birds in *Psycho,* who has made Jarry desperate, and whose charcoal sketches, for the second time in the film, will be used to identify a traitor.

If Tamara Kusenov's original gesture seemed to set the world of senti-
ment against the world of political expediency, these later images suggest
that no one can step outside the frame; Tamara, like all the characters
who follow, is both the destroyer and the victim of aesthetic artifice.
As Juanita de Cordoba lies dead in a perfect horizontal line, Rico Parra
walks away from her in a straight line across the checkerboard floor to
the double doors out front, whose shape echoes that of a framed picture beside them on the wall. Opening one door, he becomes part of a
frame within a frame, then passes outside. The frame makes him remote
in important ways—it makes him a less accessible figure of identification, ritualizes his emotions, and compromises his sincerity—but it also
emphasizes his own entrapment in the political structure whose agent
he has chosen to become. The moment looks forward to the moment
at the end of the film when Devereaux responds to the revelation that
Nicole has been intimate with Granville and that Granville is Columbine
by looking at a framed photograph of himself, Nicole, and Granville, a
photograph which suggests not only the multiplicity of their relations
and the betrayal of their friendship but also their imprisonment in a
political structure whose sides are meaningless.

The characters in *Topaz* are always, often unwisely, choosing to act
politically, but no matter how critically the film treats their motivations
or how pessimistic it is about the corrupting nature of politics, it never
suggests any alternative, because it uses the game of global politics as
a metaphor for the more general concept of community. In his early
films at Paramount, Hitchcock's characters had been able to establish
their identities by establishing their positions in small, enclosed communities, but *Topaz* offers no such communities, because everything
has become politicized. The film, whose credit sequence moves from an
extreme long shot of a May Day parade to tighter framings of trucks
carrying missiles before the opening sequence focuses on the mirrored
close-up of the Soviet security officer, presents its characters a choice
of framing groups—they can define themselves in terms of their marriages, their love affairs, their friendships, their professional contacts,
their institutional or national loyalties, their status as citizens of the
free world. But they can neither prevent their communal loyalties from
coming into conflict nor remove themselves from the corrupting network of relations. Hitchcock's characters need political relationships to

survive; without the forces that compromise and often destroy them, they would be wholly insignificant.

*Topaz* goes much further than *Torn Curtain* or any of Hitchcock's other films in analyzing the ubiquity of politics, which penetrates and corrupts every conceivable social relation. Like the other Universal films, it has virtually no interest in individual characters. Indeed as soon as a character threatens to establish an intimacy with the audience, Hitchcock drops him. The Kusenovs' escape, which the film, unlike Uris's novel, plays for suspense, marks almost the last time they appear in the film. Nordstrom emerges as the film's likely hero only to hand his assignment over to Devereaux. But Devereaux himself is a remote figure who has others do his work—the engaging florist (Roscoe Lee Browne), Juanita de Cordoba and her network of Cuban agents, his own son-in-law—and who therefore is never in any serious danger. This constant substitution of minor characters acting for potential heroes is characteristic of Hitchcock's latest subversion of the audience's expectations, as the director keeps creating situations demanding heroic behavior while withholding any individual heroes to whom the audience might feel close. His characters, who crave the attachments that corrupt and destroy them, inhabit a world truly inimical to individual agency and identity.

Between the dehumanizing gags of *The Birds* and these final anti-heroic espionage films, Hitchcock makes one last psychological study, the last of all his films to explore in any detail the identity of its principals. *Marnie* tells the story of the compulsive thief Marnie Edgar (Tippi Hedren), sexually alluring but frigid, who is hired, loved, and married by the masterful Mark Rutland (Sean Connery), who ultimately forces her to relive the traumatic experience that led to her kleptomania: her childhood killing of a sailor she thought was threatening her prostitute mother (Louise Latham). In these summary terms, the film sounds like a case history or a paperback romance, but in fact, although it is the most obviously psychologistic of Hitchcock's later films—and the only one of them to generate any considerable sympathy for its heroine and hero—both its Freudian view of the self and its romantic optimism are severely undermined.

An obvious point of departure for analyzing *Marnie* is *Spellbound,* which also deals with the therapeutic analysis of a withdrawn neurotic through romantic love. *Marnie* shares the earlier film's essentially dualistic model of personality, which sets psychological trauma and its associated threatening behavior against the public world of normative behavior and love.[12] In both films the audience's primary identification is not with the victim of this trauma but with the investigating therapist, who functions as the audience's detective surrogate.

But to say that the primary identification figure in *Marnie* is Mark Rutland raises immediate problems that indicate the extent of the differences between the two films, for Mark is a far more equivocal identification figure than Ingrid Bergman's Dr. Constance Petersen. He is less often onscreen than Marnie, whose subjectivity the film occasionally dramatizes directly, most clearly by the red suffusions which incapacitate her because they trigger her repressed memory of the bleeding sailor. Unlike Dr. Petersen, Mark is no paragon; as Connery plays him, he is as dualistic as Marnie, cultivated but brutal ("I'm fighting a powerful impulse to beat the hell out of you," he tells Marnie after she has cleaned out the Rutland safe), his sense of humor unflinchingly aggressive. After promising Marnie on their honeymoon that he will not make love to her, he breaks his promise in a scene whose mingled tenderness and brutality are deeply disturbing even before the film shows their sequel, Marnie's attempted suicide.

*Spellbound* begins with several scenes in which Dr. Petersen's authority is challenged by her patient Mary Carmichael and her lovesick colleague Dr. Fleurot. Her defense against them has the effect of moderating and placing her claims for psychoanalytic therapy from the beginning, so that the audience's acceptance of her authority thereafter remains secure. Marnie, by contrast, challenges Mark's authority more and more urgently as her involvement with him deepens—and no wonder, since his credentials are as equivocal as his emotions. Instead of sharing Dr. Petersen's training as a psychiatrist, he has a background which emphasizes social and economic power (he is a member of a prominent Philadelphia family whose members marry heiresses every other generation) and scientific curiosity (he is an amateur zoologist). Marnie correctly divines that he is drawn to her as to one of the predatory animals whose instinctual behavior he has studied; he wants to observe her, then master her, precisely because she is "really wild," just as he has tamed a jaguarundi to trust him and exercises mastery over horses without at all liking them.

Because Mark's status as therapist and the nature of his attachment to Marnie are so questionable, the film's investigation of Marnie's identity, although as pat psychologically as that of *Spellbound,* is again more equivocal. *Spellbound* directs its principals toward legal vindication and marriage, the two major conventions of Hitchcock's happy endings. But Marnie and Mark's marriage, halfway through the film, has no terminal or teleological force; it simply complicates Marnie's problems further by calling into question the institutional contexts which govern ownership (can Marnie steal money that belongs to her husband?) and sexuality (is Mark's attack on Marnie less a rape if she is his wife?). Nor can Marnie be whitewashed as reassuringly as John Ballantine, since she really is a thief, as the audience knows before they learn anything else about her, even the true color of her hair.

In fact, it is uncertain whether the audience ever does discover the true color of Marnie's hair, since her mother, on seeing her as a blonde, remarks disapprovingly that Marnie has lightened up her hair. As they watch the woman who has robbed Sidney Strutt (Martin Gabel) sort through a number of social security cards made out in different names and select one labeled Margaret Edgar, viewers may wonder which name is her own. Margaret Edgar is indeed Marnie's real name, but it does not certify her identity in at all the same way that the false Dr. Edwardes' name does in *Spellbound.* When Dr. Petersen learns that her lover's real name is John Ballantine, that name is attached to a lifetime's worth of memories and associations which his amnesia had obscured; learning his name restores his whole identity. But in learning Marnie's real name, Mark learns practically nothing; he does not even know until the film is nearly over that Marnie has a mother. Unlike Dr. Petersen, who allows John Ballantine to discover his true identity, Mark can only go beneath Marnie's façade, because her hysteria does not allow the same return to an integrated identity that Ballantine's amnesia does. At the end of her movie, therefore, Marnie is not restored to her true identity but wiped clean of all traces of adult identity, like a blank page. Even after she has emerged from the regression to her childhood killing of the sailor, she continues to behave, and Mark and her mother continue to treat her, like a child.

Feminist and psychoanalytic critics have had a field day with *Marnie* because it so clearly shows the institutionalization of patriarchal authority over a female subjectivity. Certainly the patriarchal institutions with which Mark is associated are treated throughout with much greater skepticism than they were in *Spellbound* (where the most serious criticisms of Dr. Petersen, Mary Carmichael's and Dr. Fleurot's accusations that she wasn't a real woman, were defused when she fell in love). But if the institutional authority, the Lacanian symbolic, Mark represents is presented with an irony that makes it impossible to take Marnie's regression as simply curative, Marnie's own pre- or extra-institutional self, the Lacanian imaginary, is defined just as critically. The independence from men conferred by Marnie's membership in her mother's "miniature matriarchy" is largely illusory.[13] Although the money with which she finances her mother comes not from her status as the employee nor the "girl" of the fictitious Mr. Pemberton, she depends economically on the men whom she entrances and robs. More ironically, her attachment to her mother frustrates her desires for happiness because Mrs. Edgar herself has embraced a puritanism which condemns not only her daughter's sexuality but her own earlier life. Mark's institutionalized values cannot be set against the authentic human values they have displaced, because these values are equally institutionalized. Even Mrs. Edgar's puritanism itself only displaces her original act of "degraded reciprocity," the barter of her virginity for the sweater of a young boy who impregnated and then abandoned her.[14] Behind social norms of behavior the film reveals not one's authentic identity but merely earlier generations of social behavior.

Since the film is so much more skeptical about what constitutes character, it is impossible to identify with Marnie as simply or wholeheartedly as with Hitchcock's earlier heroes and heroines. Even the moments in which Hitchcock encourages the audience to identify most closely with his heroine by placing her in a threatening situation maintain an odd detachment. When she is observed with Mark at the racetrack by a man who knew her in Detroit as Peggy Nicholson, the scene recalls the scene in *Notorious* in which Sebastian sees Alicia's meeting with Devlin. This time, however, Marnie's cool composure conveys no sense that she feels threatened; her composure will break down only when Mark forces his intimacy—legal threats, sexual domination, knowledge of her past—on her, because she does not take other men seriously as a threat to her self-sufficiency. When a cleaning lady interrupts her theft of the Rutland office and Marnie takes off her shoes and puts them in her pockets to make less noise, Hitchcock cuts in several shots of one shoe about to fall out of its pocket. The moment again recalls a scene from an earlier film, Psycho, when Marion's car momentarily stops sinking into the swamp behind the Bates Motel and Norman's face shows his anxiety. In both cases Hitchcock encourages the audience to share a criminal's apprehension. But the quality of apprehension in the robbery is quite specific. The audience takes Marnie's side, as it takes Norman's, in the sense of fearing for her—not wanting the shoe to fall and get the cleaning woman's attention—but not in the sense of exculpating her morally (the scene in Psycho plays an important role in persuading the audience that Norman is just a victim of circumstance, but the audience already knows that Marnie is really a thief) or in the sense of demanding that she escape (else the sequel—in which the shoe, falling without alerting the deaf cleaning woman, provokes a sense of relief which heightens the surprise of Mark's unexpected capture of Marnie in the following scene—would be intolerable). Hitchcock uses this scene, remarkably, to encourage the audience to respond strongly to Marnie's danger without giving her an identity to respond to.

Like the other Universal films, Marnie presents identification as a substitute for identity. Marnie follows Topaz, and to a lesser extent Torn Curtain, in undermining institutional authority without valorizing the individual whom earlier films like The Lady Vanishes and Notorious assumed was being compromised by that authority. In lifting the veil from Marnie's compulsive behavior, Hitchcock is returning to a story he has told many times before, but the search for Marnie's true identity turns out to be a labyrinth without a center.

The reduction of Hitchcock's strong identification figures to a series of blanks leads in Marnie to psychological impasse and in Torn Curtain and Topaz to a political disillusionment that is equally a disillusionment with individual identity. In Frenzy Hitchcock's turn from the psychological exploration of sympathetic principals reaches a logical extreme, for Frenzy reveals, more fully than any other film, the depths of Hitchcock's revulsion from his image of human nature and his remarkably consistent determination to frame this revulsion in ludic terms.

*Frenzy* is Hitchcock's most brilliantly unpleasant film. The story of Richard Blaney (Jon Finch), sought and eventually captured by the police for a series of sex murders including those of his ex-wife and current mistress, was sordid enough in the novel (*Goodbye Piccadilly, Farewell Leicester Square,* by Arthur La Bern) that Anthony Shaffer adapted for Hitchcock, but the film emphasizes this sordidness at every turn. The novel restricts itself to two murders; the film alludes to half a dozen, all committed by Blaney's friend Bob Rusk (Barry Foster). The novel presents Richard Blamey as a modern Everyman, a British war hero on his uppers because he cannot adjust to the institutional compromises of postwar England. The screenplay changes Blamey's metaphorical name to Blaney, treats his war record much more perfunctorily, gives his criticisms of England a throwaway truculence, strips him of supportive friends (La Bern's sympathetic and amusing Hetty Dring-Porterhouse becomes, in the film, Blaney's most savage detractor), and emphasizes his ungovernable temper, so that instead of ending a dinner with his ex-wife Brenda (Barbara Leigh-Hunt) by accidentally breaking a brandy snifter, Blaney shatters it in a fit of rage. Of all Hitchcock's heroes on the lam, Blaney is the only one who is clearly capable of murder.

Nor are the other characters much more attractive. Except for Brenda Blaney, her fellow-victim Barbara Milligan (Anna Massey), and Inspector Oxford (Alec McCowen), all Hitchcock's characters, even quite minor figures, are unappealing. Hetty's husband Johnny (Clive Swift) is spineless, Blaney's and Barbara's boss Felix Forsyth (Bernard Cribbins) selfish and high-handed, Brenda's secretary Monica (Jean Marsh) narrowminded and supercilious, the desk clerk at the hotel where Blaney takes Barbara suspicious and ignorant, and two men who discuss the case at a pub astonishingly insensitive in their comments that "we haven't had a good, juicy series of sex murders since Christie" and that they are "good for the tourist trade."

Hitchcock keeps his characters distant in another way which has by now become characteristic: by repeatedly, often obtrusively, framing his narrative in allusions to his earlier work. The film's story clearly embodies Hitchcock's desire to remake *The Lodger* more explicitly, and its most significant borrowings are from *Psycho;* but individual episodes and motifs direct attention to a wide range of his other films as well. The film's exposition, which strongly implies that the main character is a criminal, echoes that of *Sabotage* (and of *Marnie*). Blaney's situation is shaped not only by *The Lodger* but by *The 39 Steps* and *Saboteur*. The initialled stickpin Rusk must retrieve from Barbara's dead hand (in the novel it is a key to his flat, a far less intimate indication of his identity) recalls the cigarette lighter in *Strangers on a Train*. The scene looking into the courtroom in which Blaney is found guilty closely follows the opening scene of *Notorious,* and the sequence immediately following, showing Blaney returned to his prison cell, is borrowed from *The Wrong Man*. The film's final scene, in which Oxford and Blaney wait inside Rusk's flat for him to return and incriminate himself, is a reminiscence of *Dial M for Murder.*

It would be a mistake to see these self-plagiarisms as indications of laziness or flagging of invention, since they rarely have the same force they did in the original films. (A crucial distinction between the exposition of *Frenzy* and that of *Sabotage,* for example, is that although Blaney's guilt is as strongly implied as Verloc's, Blaney is actually innocent.) What they do indicate is Hitchcock's ever-increasing tendency toward a mannerist style. The world of *Frenzy* is not the audience's observed world, or La Bern's figurative postwar world, or the world of London (whose reviewers dismissed the film's settings as anachronistic), but rather the Hitchcock world, a checkerboard whose fixed and familiar pattern is requisite to the moves of each new game.

The first move in *Frenzy*'s game is made in the film's majestic opening shot. As the credits (beginning with an image of the City of London arms in the corner) roll over Ron Goodwin's flowing, diatonic orchestral fanfare, an aerial extreme long shot of the city moves in and down to the Thames and along the river toward London Bridge, which opens as the camera moves closer and closer, like an omniscient tourist on an official visit. But this shot, evidently so public and festive, is a setup line that establishes the visual pattern for the rest of the film. It is merely the first, broadest, and most public of a series of penetrations which structure all the principal action. *Frenzy,* like *Psycho,* presents itself as a series of movements from open to closed settings—outdoors to indoors, long shots to close-ups, public places to private—and toward the revelation of the secrets its characters keep locked up. This sort of visual penetration normally betokens a movement from detachment to intimacy, but in *Frenzy*, as in *Psycho*, penetration, operating at once as a metaphor for sexual aggression and a parody of scientific and psychological empiricism, produces a perverse intimacy whose keynote is horrified revulsion.

The film's opening sequence moves from an aerial shot of London to the discovery of a body, the latest victim of the Necktie Murderer, and then to an interior shot of Blaney knotting his own tie. After Blaney goes downstairs and helps himself to a brandy from the pub where he is working, the movement is again from outside (Covent Garden market) to successively closed settings: the fruit stall where Blaney meets Rusk, the pub where he drinks his lunch, Brenda's office (the glassed-in Blaney Bureau for Romance and Friendship), her club, the outside of her apartment (where presumably they spend some time together), and a Salvation Army shelter where Blaney spends the rest of the night. Thereafter the film emphasizes movement toward such enclosed spaces as Brenda's office, the staircase outside Rusk's apartment, the potato sack in which Rusk has hidden Barbara's corpse, and a steamer trunk over which the closing credits roll.

Any film could be divided into sequences in which interior shots alternate with exteriors, but the consistent movement of *Frenzy*'s visuals from outside to inside is more pointedly dictated by the desires of Hitchcock's hero and villain (who both characteristically seek sexual penetration), his police (who want to penetrate to the truth), and his audience (who are always, like L. B. Jefferies, looking for some further vicarious experience). *Frenzy* deauthorizes these penetrations by displaying their futility. Rusk's sexual rage clearly stems from his impotence, his inability to achieve sexual penetration. The police conscientiously pursue every clue in order to arrest the wrong man. And the audience too, penetrating to the heart of the characters, find not revelation or titillation but disgust, for in *Frenzy*, as in *Psycho*, the ultimate secret of human nature is that people are filth. The Thames is a repository for mutilated corpses. Blaney, showing not a trace of tenderness to either his ex-wife or his mistress, wants to sleep with them both. Rusk treats women as a meal to be consumed. Barbara ends in a truckload of potatoes which are on their way to be plowed back under. Blaney plots his freedom only in order to kill. Rusk hides the evidence of his secret identity in a potato sack, in a dresser drawer, in an empty trunk. The more closely the director focuses on this world, the more revolting and futile its revelations become.

Hitchcock's camera takes a special fascination in shooting down stairwells. In the first sequence at the Blaney Bureau, a newly united pair of lovebirds descending the stairs is presented as embarking on a life of comic exploitation and sexual servitude. The stairs down which Hitchcock cranes to the street outside Rusk's flat assume, in their banal neutrality, all the horror of the murderous assault going on inside. Hitchcock follows Blaney down a narrow flight of stairs from the courtroom to his cell and later shows him throwing himself down a staircase in order to get into the prison hospital. All these descents, like the penetrations from outside to inside and from long shot to close-up, are descents into hell, from the lower-middle-class nightmare of the Blaney Bureau's idyllic matrimonial unions to Blaney's annihilating obsession with revenge, so that the complacent street outside Rusk's flat inspires the same revulsion as Rusk himself.

This revulsion is expressed not only through Rusk's murderous sexuality but through a much broader range of sensory references. Hitchcock alludes briefly to flowers as rank or undisciplined growth when he has Rusk identify his mother (who appears in a cameo worthy of Hitchcock himself that momentarily irradiates the film with the genetic obsessions of *Psycho*) as living in "Kent, the garden of England," and tell Brenda, just before he rapes her, "I have my good points. I like flowers—and fruit." Fruit itself becomes a figure for what food generally represents in Hitchcock: the satisfaction of appetites, given that every appetite *Frenzy* presents is made to look revolting. Several hours after Rusk gives Blaney a bunch of hothouse grapes with the line, "Take one of these back to your girlfriend Babs—get her to peel you one," Hitchcock shows a close-up of Blaney crushing the grapes in rage and throwing the box on the ground. Rusk tells Brenda that his motto is "Don't squeeze the goods till they're yours" and kills her in between bites of an apple. Later, Oxford, referring to the killer's "appetite," pauses in discomfort before his dinner, quail with grapes.

Oxford's well-bred disgust is articulated much more fully by the other characters. Blaney's boss Forsythe tells Barbara that Blaney "can't keep his hands off you—he's always pulling your tits"—a judgment which is anticipated by Blaney's pulling moments earlier at the tap for a drink and echoed much later by Barbara's dismissal of his protestations of innocence: "Why don't you pull the other one? It's got bells on it." Since all appetites are equally suspect, Forsythe doesn't care whether or not Blaney was really planning to steal his drink; "A thief or a boozer, it's all the same to me." Hetty Porter (Billie Whitelaw) reminds Johnny that Brenda Blaney's divorce petition accused her husband of "extreme mental and physical cruelty." Brenda herself reacts to Rusk with disdain moments before he attacks her, and the porter at the Coburg Hotel, who had just asked Blaney if he'd like to send for something from the pharmacy, greets the news of the police search with the pronouncement: "Thinking about the lusts of men makes me want to heave."

This disgust would be simply morally superior rather than disturbing, and the film itself far less troubling and complex, if it were not so often laced with ghoulish humor. The desk clerk at the Coburg, realizing that the police are seeking their latest guest as a sexual psychopath, cries, "Not in the Cupid Room!" The two men at the pub who say that sex murders are good for the tourist trade respond to the barmaid's reaction— "They say he rapes them first"—by pointing out that "every cloud has a silver lining." The scenes in which Inspector Oxford tries to avoid his wife's unspeakable meals are played as high comedy. Even Rusk's feverish struggle with Barbara's corpse, which produces the same physical exhaustion in him as his earlier rape of Brenda, is horrifyingly funny, since she can no longer be hurt by his monstrous callousness, and she frustrates him far more completely dead than alive (he has to break two of her fingers to remove his stickpin). The film's perverse amalgam of humor and revulsion is established by its opening speech, in which a political speaker announces proudly that the Thames will "soon be clear of industrial effluents," that "there will soon be no foreign—" and is interrupted before he can add "bodies." *Frenzy* exploits this sick pun by treating the human body throughout as a foreign body, an excrescence on the natural order, something inherently disgusting to be gotten rid of as decently as possible.

There are precedents for this attitude in many of Hitchcock's earlier films, especially in *Psycho* and *Marnie,* whose heroine, so bourgeois in her values despite her profession, announces that "women are stupid and feeble, and men are filthy pigs." These two films establish the connection between self-loathing, paranoia, and disgusted revulsion from the world which provokes such horrified laughter in *Frenzy*. In Hitchcock's earliest films, the heroes' paranoia was justified, because authoritarian forces in their world were generally and unjustly opposed to them. In his films of the 1940s and 1950s, this paranoia becomes more and more closely associated with the (usually male) hero's sense of his or her own inadequacy. But the conflict was either resolved in an ending affirming one's sense of oneself (for example in *Notorious* and *Rear Window*) or presented as tragedy (in *Vertigo*). In the Universal films, the characters' sense of self-loathing renders them not only incapacitated but contemptible. Their contradictory attitude seems to reflect the director's own: a combination of disgust, moral posturing, condescension, and crude laughter in a desperate attempt to remove themselves from horrors which reflect their own, and a severe condemnation of any such attempt on the part of anyone else.[15] *Frenzy* makes the audience laugh but makes them ashamed for laughing, simultaneously allowing and condemning the release it encourages.

In its unappealing principals trapped by their own desires, its fascination with forbidden penetrations, its presentation of all appetites as aggressive and disgusting, its equation of the human body with filth, and its determination to outrage and horrify the audience, *Frenzy* marks the most extreme development of Hitchcock's ludic hostility toward his characters and his audience. Reviewers treating it as the master's final testament were taken aback by the equipose and geniality of his last film, *Family Plot,* which has frequently been described as a postlude or appendix to Hitchcock's career. But when *Family Plot* is grouped together with *The Short Night,* the last project Hitchcock had under development, it marks not so much a retreat from the series beginning with *The Birds* as one more recasting of the narrative contract, the beginning of a new, post-sadistic period. In some ways it suggests a return to the comic mode of the Gaumont-British films, but now Hitchcock's comic melodrama works without any attempt to maintain an identification with his principals, who are no longer repulsive but, like the spies of *Torn Curtain* and *Topaz,* blandly unengaging.

*Family Plot* concerns the efforts of the bogus medium Blanche Tyler

(Barbara Harris) and her boyfriend George Lumley (Bruce Dern) to collect a ten-thousand-dollar reward from Julia Rainbird (Cathleen Nesbitt) by locating her long-lost grandson. The film begins with Blanche and Lumley deciding to find the missing Rainbird heir, Eddie Shoebridge, then drops their story to show an apparently unrelated ransom pickup by Fran (Karen Black) and Arthur Adamson (William Devane), born Eddie Shoebridge. Hitchcock thereupon cuts back and forth more and more rapidly between the two stories until they eventually become one.

Family Plot diffuses the threats of Frenzy and the chill of the earlier Universal films. The sexual disgust of Frenzy is replaced by a series of comic double entendres (e.g., Lumley's complaint to Blanche: "I'm sick and tired of having you have me by the crystal balls"). The principals all joke about sex, but they also take it for granted in a way Frenzy never does. Since the villains are unaware of the heroes' existence for nearly half the film's running time, and the heroes do not meet the villains for even longer, the characters move through the story feeling largely unthreatened either by their own desires or by outside enemies. Instead Hitchcock focuses on the comedy of his raffish heroes, who are apparently even more disreputable than the self-possessed Adamson and Fran, and on the analogous relationships between the two couples.

This turn toward comedy, however, does not project anything like the communal resolutions of the Gaumont-British or Paramount films. The violence of Frenzy, as in Hitchcock's earlier comedies, is contained in Family Plot within the characters' sense of their activity as a game, but there is nothing inherently comic about their game-playing; it simply marks an attenuation of violence, its displacement by a good-natured diffidence which shows up in several ways. Adamson clearly regards his kidnappings as a game, and both Fran and Lumley refer to sex in ludic terms (when Adamson says that Fran will have to torture him to discover where he's hidden the diamonds they extort as ransom, she giggles, "Oh, I intend to," as they mount the stairs to the bedroom). More often, the film's mise-en-scène constructs a game available to the audience but not the characters, as in the famous overhead shot of Lumley pursuing Mrs. Maloney through the garden labyrinth at her husband's funeral. Hitchcock's double plot, which he evidently considered a new challenge in narrative construction,[16] works against the development of narrative tension, because in the absence of any other explanation for the kidnappers' presence in the film, the audience naturally assumes that Adamson must be the Rainbird heir and thus sees the film's principal surprise (a surprise telegraphed by Hitchcock's working title for the film, *One Plus One Equals One*) coming well in advance.

Once the audience has surmised Adamson's true identity, the film becomes an exercise in detection, a linear sequence of revelations, each link in the hermeneutical chain leading to the next. Ordinarily the interest in Hitchcock's films is never simply or primarily hermeneutical; even when he seems to be making a detective story, as in *Stage Fright,* his overriding interest in narrative is always expressed, however paradoxically, through particular moments, strong situations, or charged images. But except for the central sequence in which Adamson's henchman Maloney (Ed Lauter) doctors the brakes on Blanche's and Lumley's car and tricks them into a harrowing but amusing drive down a steep highway, *Family Plot* has no arresting situations, and its imagery is perhaps the least highly charged in any Hitchcock film. The director's preoccupation with circumstantial detail, a characteristic of all the Universal films except *Frenzy,* leads him to linger over the details of how the heroes follow each clue to the next, how Lumley breaks into a locked garage to rescue Blanche, and especially how the kidnappers go about their work without leaving any clues. Even the scene showing the kidnapping of a Catholic bishop in the middle of a church service, long a dream of Hitchcock's, is curiously disengaged, as if the director were more interested in showing how the thing could be done than in getting the audience to react to it in a given way. The pervasive air of benignant neutrality confirms the film's status as a ritualistic comedy whose characters wear masks with fixed, painted expressions. The expressions on the faces underneath, like the question of whether there are any faces underneath, remain inscrutable.

In setting his two couples against each other Hitchcock is on more familiar ground. The comedy of his heroes' relationship, whose appetite for each other operates on the same level as their appetites for food, drink, and information, is deepened by the sexual thrill Adamson gets from danger ("First it makes you sick," he tells Fran, "then, when you're done, it makes you very, very loving") and from dominating Fran (to whose protests about her possible involvement in murder he answers,

"That's what's so exciting about this. We move as one, nothing held back"). Blanche, who is clearly, by contrast, the dominant figure in the other couple, domesticates Adamson's criminal impulses. She too is a fake, though an opportunistic rather than a malicious one; she too has made a life for herself by dissimulating her identity—in her case, behind those of the spirits she pretends to be invoking. Adamson's sinister gamesmanship becomes, in Blanche's inexpert hands, a gift for improvisation that allows mutual respect and even tenderness between Lumley and herself.

The analogy between the two couples, however, is limited by the fact that the film tells so little about them, especially Fran, whose characterization is remarkably perfunctory.[17] Fran knows that Adamson is a kidnapper but not that he is a murderer (as Eddie Shoebridge, he had locked his foster parents in a closet while Maloney set their house on fire), and she wants nothing to do with murder. In forties *films noirs* like *The Killers* or *Out of the Past,* and in Noel Black's more recent *Pretty Poison,* the figure of the criminal who draws the line at murder is central, but Hitchcock is rarely interested in such figures (Mrs. Drayton in the 1956 *Man Who Knew Too Much* is the most prominent example), and his treatment of them is typically as perfunctory as here because they violate one of his cardinal rules: not to tell "a story in which the villains themselves are afraid."[18] This time, however, Fran's fearful subordination to Adamson simply emphasizes by analogy Lumley's comic subordination to Blanche—an analogy which takes precedence over either couple's threat to the other.

The film is remarkably devoid of any such sense of threat even though its leading couples both define themselves in a way that threatens each other. Because Adamson's menace is so vaguely defined—he does not commit an act of violence onscreen until the film is nearly over, and then his malignancy is largely neutralized by Fran's fear—the heroes never seem to be in much danger. Even after Adamson and Fran have caught Blanche and are planning to kill her, the danger remains oddly remote. While they are out collecting the ransom for Bishop Wood, Lumley tracks Blanche to their house and begins to search the upstairs rooms, but his search lacks the nervous edge of Lila Crane's search of the Bates house because Adamson and Fran are not nearly as threatening or as mysterious as Norman; despite the presence of the ransom diamonds hidden in a chandelier, there seems to be nothing for Lumley to find but Blanche. Nor does Hitchcock emphasize the suspense of Blanche's rescue; she escapes without any of the obligatory miscues.

The ways in which *Family Plot* departs from all Hitchcock's earlier work are best indicated by its refusal to explore the ironies of its title. The image of a family plot is full of the Hitchcockian resonances of buried secrets, family as fate, and a genetic conception of identity. But the film does not expoit any of these resonances because its characters live in a sunny, depthless present. Despite the fact that Adamson's past is full of guilty secrets and that Fran too alludes to a guilty past, the film takes no interest in the weight of the past; neither its characters nor their situations are invested with the tension characteristic of even Hitchcock's comic thrillers.

Clearly the Master of Suspense is not simply rehashing his old tricks in *Family Plot*. The film seems to be a demonstration of how to use the Hitchcock signature to evoke suspense, since its momentum is generated not so much from developments within its own story as from its play with the expectations of an audience whose last glimpse of a Hitchcock film was *Frenzy* four years before. Unlike the progression of Hitchcock's principals from Manny Balestrero to Richard Blaney, the characters of *Family Plot* are not trapped in alienating social roles or genetic fatality; they are free to cast themselves in whatever roles they wish. What makes Hitchcock's comedy so chilly here is that none of his leads settles into a constitutive role; all four of them end the film as blank as when they began.

The same pattern persists in *The Short Night,* an unproduced screenplay David Freeman wrote for Hitchcock based on Ronald Kirkbride's spy novel, which tells the story of Joe Bailey, whose search for a British agent, Gavin Brand, escaped from prison and bound to the Soviet Union, takes him to Brand's wife Carla, whom he intends to use as a lead but with whom he falls in love. Donald Spoto treats Brand's violence as central to the film, but in fact Brand's early killing of Rosemary, one of the agents who has helped him escape, is remote from the tone established by the film's optimistic ending, in which Joe lets Brand escape and remains instead with Carla and her sons.[19]

This optimistic ending, however, is as neutral as Blanche's rescue in *Family Plot* in one sense: it is nowhere clearly forecast by earlier developments in the screenplay. The story would have made just as much sense if Brand had learned of Carla's betrayal and killed her (an ending justified by the consistency in Brand's character), or if she had been accidentally killed in the cross fire between two men (an ending which would have echoed Brand's killing of Rosemary in another way). In allowing Brand to escape and letting Bailey and Carla off the hook, Hitchcock returns to the pattern of the melodramas—*Rebecca, Notorious, Rear Window,* both versions of *The Man Who Knew Too Much*—whose guiding principle is that characters can free themselves from the past because it's never too late to change. But since change and consistency seem equally arbitrary for the principals of *The Short Night* (although the completed film might well have portended its conclusion more explicitly than the screenplay does), the storyteller might as well be settling their fate by flipping a coin.

Hitchcock's optimism in these last projects may seem superficial because it cuts him off from the very source of his strength, the playfully adversarial/complicit relationship with his audience he had established and modulated over a period of fifty years. But he has not forgotten this relationship, as he shows in the famous final shot of *Family Plot,* in which Blanche, who has overheard Adamson talking about the diamonds' hiding place and then, pretending to be in a trance, has led Lumley to the chandelier, now for the first time including him in the audience for her psychic masquerades, looks directly into the camera and winks at the audience. The image has generally been taken as the director's Prospero-like valediction to filmmaking, but it fits as well into the pattern of apparent disruptions of the narrative illusion which had defined Hitchcock's ambivalent relationship to the audience for over fifty years. Coupled with Hitchcock's cameo in the film—the shadow of his profile, familiar from the years of *Alfred Hitchcock Presents,* appears behind a glass door labeled "Registrar of Births and Deaths"—the wink to the audience emphasizes Hitchcock's dual status as historical (and mortal) director and exemplary storyteller. The king is dead; long live the king.

# NINE

## ONLY

## A GAME

Although he continued working until well into his seventies and ended his career with hints of still a new direction in *Family Plot* and *The Short Night,* the principal legacy of Hitchcock's years at Universal is not the films he made but the portrait of himself and his work he authorized. Hitchcock's intention, and that of the executives at Universal, during this period was to secure the director's reputation with newly prominent film critics and theorists without endangering his reputation as a peerless entertainer and his commercial success. Although this attempt was not without its difficulties, Hitchcock scored a brilliant public relations coup with the publication of Truffaut's highly influential book of interviews, first published in French in 1965 and in English the following year.[1] Truffaut's book, whose English dust jacket modestly proclaimed it "a definitive study of Alfred Hitchcock," became known to a generation of film buffs as simply "Hitchcock/Truffaut" and indeed established its portrait of Hitchcock as definitive, the image in terms of which all later studies would define their own portraits.

Truffaut's Hitchcock is the quintessential raconteur, and Truffaut's book is in many ways the distillation of all Hitchcock's earlier interviews, or an anthology of the anecdotes and remarks the director most wanted to repeat. And nowhere does Hitchcock make his attitude toward his work clearer than in his remarks about *Psycho:*

My main satisfaction is that the film had an effect on the audiences, and
I consider that very important. I don't care about the subject matter; I don't
care about the acting; but I do care about the pieces of film and the photography and the sound track and all of the technical ingredients that made the
audience scream. I feel it's tremendously satisfying for us to be able to use the
cinematic art to achieve something of a mass emotion. And with *Psycho* we
most definitely achieved this. It wasn't a message that stirred the audiences,
nor was it a great performance or their enjoyment of the novel. They were
aroused by pure film. . . .

It's an area of film-making in which it's more important for you to be
pleased with the technique than the content. It's the kind of picture in which
the camera takes over. Of course, since critics are more concerned with the
scenario, it won't necessarily get you the best notices, but you have to design
your film just as Shakespeare did his plays—for an audience.[2]

The fascination Hitchcock displays here for the "technique" of "pure
film" and his dismissal of "performance," "message," "scenario," "content," and "subject matter" marks the point of departure for dozens of
critical discussions of his work. Truffaut himself indicates the response
of Hitchcock's admirers: "Hitchcock is universally acknowledged to be
the world's foremost technician; even his detractors willingly concede
him that title. Yet, isn't it obvious that the choice of a scenario, its construction, and all of its contents are intimately connected to and, in fact,
dependent upon that technique?"[3]

Truffaut's reference to Hitchcock's detractors is apt, for critics like
Charles Thomas Samuels and Charles Higham condemned Hitchcock on
exactly the grounds he named. Samuels described Hitchcock's films as
exercises in form devoid of content: "Intellectual emptiness and spurious
realism are preconditions for his effects. . . . Hitchcock's best films are
devoid of meaning, peopled by mere containers of stress, and set against
backgrounds chosen simply because their innocuousness counterpoints
terror." Higham more briskly dismissed Hitchcock as "a practical joker."[4]
How seriously could anyone take a director whose films were nothing
but games?

The battle over Hitchcock's reputation—was he to be seen as a serious artist or simply a successful entertainer and master manipulator of

audiences?—was eventually won by his supporters. Yet the debate over the nature of Hitchcock's achievement continues to define his place in film history.[5] Robin Wood's seminal study *Hitchcock's Films* begins with the provocative question, "Why should we take Hitchcock seriously?" and proceeds to a polemical defense of Hitchcock's films on the grounds of the particular experience they offer the audience, their "realisation of theme in terms of 'pure cinema' which makes the audience not only see but *experience* (experience rather than intellectually analyse) the manifestation of that theme."[6] Wood's Hitchcock is a moralist whose manipulation of the audience makes its members aware of the complicity involved in their own position as audience. Raymond Durgnat's contentious and freewheeling *Strange Case of Alfred Hitchcock,* by contrast, defines Hitchcock as an aesthete rather than a moralist in whom the audience's sense of penetration is still fundamentally superficial: "In his dramas, Hitchcock moves from a novelettish complacency to an uncertainty worthy of, but hardly deeper than, that of an ordinary middlebrow novel. . . . But if we are to promote Hitchcock to major artistic status, then he has to begin with a vision as sophisticated as ours is already, and lead us to a newer vision which at first we can grasp only partially and turbulently but which, as it steadily colours our outlook on the real world, vindicates itself by its clarification of reality." Lacking such a vision, Hitchcock remains a minor artist in the tradition of the fin de siècle "cult of pure sensation" of the aesthetes, decadents, and symbolists.[7] The debate over how seriously we should take Hitchcock, whether he is to be promoted to major artistic status, has colored Hitchcock criticism ever since. Hitchcock's defenders and detractors have often apparently agreed in defining artistic seriousness thematically and judging his work accordingly as the product of a major or minor artist. Durgnat points to the director's own repeated remarks about technique and his indifference to subject matter; Wood, who finds these remarks troubling, echoes D. H. Lawrence's dictum that we should trust the tale instead of the teller. But this disagreement is more political than substantive, for despite the different artistic status they accord Hitchcock's work, Wood and Durgnat actually judge Hitchcock's work in the same terms. So does Hitchcock. And these terms are not thematic but experiential; they have less to do with what Hitchcock shows his viewers about the world or themselves than about what he puts them through.

In support of his dismissal of Hitchcock's serious pretensions, Durgnat quotes another interview the director gave to Ian Cameron and V. F. Perkins of *Movie* around the time he described *Psycho* to Truffaut. In response to a question about distrusting the psychiatrist's explanation of Norman's madness, he volunteers the reminder that "*Psycho* is a picture made with quite a sense of amusement on my part. To me it's a *fun* picture. The processes through which we take the audiences, you see, it's rather like taking them through the haunted house at the fairground or the roller-coaster, you know. After all it stands to reason that if one were seriously doing the *Psycho* story, it would be a case history."[8] Hitchcock seems to agree here that his status as a carnival impresario precludes any claims to have made a "serious" film. But his assessment of the film itself is consistent with the satisfaction he expresses to Truffaut about using pure film to achieve a mass emotion. What emerges from Hitchcock's remarks about *Psycho*, and indeed about all his films, is that he is less interested, as Leo Braudy has noted, in each film as "a pure aesthetic object" than as "the medium for a relation between the director and the audience."[9] As both Wood and Durgnat observe, Hitchcock's emphasis on technique is not an emphasis on the logistical problems of filmmaking but on the most effective ways to arouse the audience. The director makes this distinction clear in the *Movie* interview, when he glosses his assertion (a staple of Hitchcock interviews) that "I'm more interested in the technique of story telling by means of film than in what the film contains" by explaining: "I wasn't meaning technical problems. I was meaning the technique of story telling on film *per se*."[10]

Durgnat and Wood both formulate their analyses as attempts to answer a question posed by Penelope Houston: Hitchcock is clearly a master, but of what?[11] Of the experience he provides the audience, they both conclude, although Wood emphasizes the moral and thematic aspect of this experience and Durgnat its aesthetic dimension. Hitchcock's remark in the *Movie* interview suggests another answer: he is a master of narrative, an exemplary storyteller. How seriously his critics take him depends largely on how seriously they take storytelling as such. But how seriously can they take him when he defends *Psycho* as a fun picture, when he clearly revels in his status as amusement park impresario, when he treats storytelling as a game? Hitchcock's commentators have typically addressed this question by taking sides: Hitchcock is a mere entertainer because his films are nothing but games, or he is something more in spite of himself.[12] But the choice between these two Hitchcocks is unnecessary if his films are conceived as serious games, like Iris's and Gilbert's play in the baggage car in *The Lady Vanishes* or Eve's masquerade as Doris Tinsdale in *Stage Fright* or the running competition between Guy and Bruno in *Strangers on a Train*. The salient feature of Hitchcock's films is the opportunities they offer their audience for serious play.

What makes game-playing serious? Hitchcock's games serve two contradictory but paradoxically interrelated functions. On the one hand, they reaffirm the audience's sense of themselves through the mastery they allow them to experience over their discourse. Audiences schooled in Hitchcock's games—audiences who can find the director, enjoy the shifts in tone from grave to gay, pleasurably identify with Hitchcock's odd men out, and follow each story—find in their experience of the films, their success in rising to each challenge, a confirmation of their sense of their own experience, and thus their own identity, as triumphantly unified. Jean Piaget's work on the role of play in childhood development leads him to conclude that "although play sometimes takes the form of repetition of painful states of mind, it does so not in order that the pain shall be preserved, but so that it may become bearable, and even pleasurable, through assimilation to the whole activity of the ego. In a word, it is possible to reduce play to pleasure-seeking . . . [if] the pursuit of pleasure is conceived as subordinated to the assimilation of reality to the ego. Ludic pleasure then becomes the affective expression of this assimilation."[13] Norman N. Holland, extending this assimilative argument to literary games played in maturity by arguing that "each of us will find in the literary work the kind of thing we characteristically wish or fear the most," concludes that the function of literary experience is to confirm each audience's "identity theme," so that "*unity* is to *text* as *identity* is to *self*."[14] Theorists like Piaget and Holland, following Freud, consider game-playing or listening to stories pleasurable because they

strengthen the audience's ego.[15] Hitchcock's audiences, like his characters, play games to discover and remind themselves who they are.

But Hitchcock's games serve another function quite contrary to this
one: they challenge, extend, question, undermine, and endanger the
sense of personal identity associated in Freud with the ego and in Hitchcock with the home and family. Before Hitchcock's strong resolutions
confirm his principals' identities, films from *The Lodger* to *Frenzy* spend
most of their running time calling them into question. Audiences can
enjoy this ordeal because they are confident that it will be satisfactorily
resolved, but it expresses in addition something of their own longing,
like Scottie, to let go of their complacent sense of themselves and to
fall endlessly through space. In the same way, Hitchcock's continual
subversion of the rules of his narrative contract, from his playful disruptions of his discourse in his cameos to his encouragement to the
audience to form identifications with characters whose identities are
void, is designed precisely as an assault on the audience's certitudes.
Being mistaken for a nonexistent CIA agent and plunged into danger
of death and acute embarrassment is the best thing that ever happens
to Roger Thornhill not only because it allows him a happy ending with
Eve Kendall, but because it rescues him from spending the rest of his
life as Roger O. Thornhill. In the same way, Hitchcock's films correct
the alienation of modern civilization by jolting his audience out of its
comfortable, stultifying routine.

Setting these two functions of Hitchcock's games against each other
helps explain why the critical response to his films has been so sharply
divided. Critics who ask whether we should take Hitchcock seriously,
no matter how they go on to answer the question, typically have in
mind a model of serious films as Platonic, Apollonian, or thematically
self-affirming. Commentators like Samuels and Higham are uncomfortable with Hitchcock because his games are meaningless in the specific
sense that they do nothing to confirm the audience's sense of its own
identity.[16] Hitchcock's defenders from Robin Wood to Lesley Brill, by
contrast, rescue the director from his antic reputation by recasting him
in a conservative mold, as if the primary function of his games were to
set up a resolution.[17] It is harder to make a case for Hitchcock's serious-

ness based on the subversive, Dionysiac power of his games, but critics like Raymond Bellour, influenced by Jacques Lacan's critique of ego psychology and Jacques Derrida's critique of logocentrism, have done much to make such an analysis, whereby Hitchcock's films break down the repressive mechanisms of politics and society, fashionable.

These are both compelling views of Hitchcock, but surely they are partial views as well. It is not merely that they oppose a Hitchcock who takes himself seriously against a more obviously ludic Hitchcock, for the essence of Hitchcock's games—of any games—is that they incorporate both these contrary impulses. Games are pleasurable both because they reaffirm institutional order and individual identity and because they challenge and subvert ideas of identity and order. In this regard Tania Modleski's Hitchcock, whose "strong fascination and identification with femininity . . . subverts the claims to mastery and authority not only of the male characters but of the director himself," best illustrates the dialectical appeal of Hitchcock's games, which entertain both highly conservative and radically subversive perspectives without definitively privileging either.[18]

Gregory Bateson's analysis of play illuminates the paradoxical nature of Hitchcock's games. Beginning with the observation that statements like "The playful nip denotes the bite, but it does not denote what would be denoted by the bite" violate Bertrand Russell's Theory of Logical Types "because the word 'denote' is being used in two degrees of abstraction, and these two uses are treated as synonymous," Bateson postulates play, together with threats, deceit, histrionic behavior, and spectatorship as marking a crucial step forward in the evolution of human communication (from unreflective reaction to a given behavioral sign to an awareness of the conceptual or circumstantial frames that give signs their meaning) and combining "primary-process" thinking (unconscious reactions to given stimuli) and "secondary-process" thinking (the kind of self-awareness associated with ego-formation). "In primary process, map and territory are equated," Bateson observes; "in secondary process, they can be discriminated. In play, they are both equated and discriminated" because players of a game, like movie audiences, routinely pursue goals or perceive implications disavowed by the frame of playing. The reminder " 'this is play' thus sets a frame of the sort that is likely to precipitate paradox" because it requires the audience to assume a position both inside and outside the frame of primary-process thinking. Playing is not, on this analysis, simply a function of the ego, as in Piaget, but a move toward defining and redefining the ego.[19]

Bateson goes on to compare psychotherapy to game-playing: "The process of psychotherapy is a framed interaction between two persons, in which the rules are implicit but subject to change. Such change can only be proposed by experimental action, but every such experimental action, in which a proposal to change the rules is implicit, is itself part of the ongoing game. It is this combination of logical types within the single meaningful act that gives to therapy the character not of a rigid game like canasta but, instead, that of an evolving system of interaction. The play of kittens or otters has this character."[20] Or, he might have added, of Hitchcock's audience. Since every signal in Hitchcock's films that a game is under way or that the rules are being changed becomes part of the game, the audience is required to maintain a double awareness of the game's boundaries that is not only logically indefensible according to Russell's Theory of Logical Types but also subject to endless oscillation between the poles of affirmation and critique of the ego that makes game-playing possible. At the same time, Hitchcock's films, unlike psychotherapy, characteristically pit primary-process thinking against secondary-process thinking, undermining the audience's sense of self through direct appeals to unconscious fears and desires that have the power to override rational identifications, the desire for narrative conclusion, conventional expectations, and other desires that depend on a conscious awareness of their discursive frames.

All Hitchcock's games, from his earliest irrepressible interruptions of his own faithful adaptations to his latest bait-and-switch games with the audience's identifications, reveal a fundamental duality between a conservative piety that accepts its framing premises—a deep respect for homes, families, the police, the law and its institutions, genetic and social ideals of identity, the moral dichotomy between good and evil, and the letter of the law or the original property—and a disruptive critique of those frames manifested most often in a tendency toward mischief, self-reflexiveness, self-advertising artifice, and the rejection of domestic and institutional pieties. This duality obviously takes different forms in different films: *The Farmer's Wife* and the 1956 *Man Who Knew Too Much* show Hitchcock at his most pietistic, *Rich and Strange* and *Frenzy* at his most radically anti-domestic. In every film, however, Hitchcock is still playing, however pietistically or maliciously. Find the director, his most distinctive game, merely expresses with unusual economy the conflict that runs through all the others as well.

These two functions of Hitchcock's games—to confirm and to attack social and institutional ideals of identity—combine in his films in several ways. They alternate within the diegesis of any given film not only through the narrative (Hannay is cut off from institutional support for his identity but then vindicated, Jeff expresses his fear of marital commitment by solving a murder that commits him to his fiancée) but through the discourse's address to the audience (Hitchcock undermines his faithful adaptation of *The Skin Game* or makes ironclad rules concerning his cameo appearances). They shape the principal phases of his career through their interplay, as unusually challenging or rule-breaking films like the 1934 *Man Who Knew Too Much*, *Rope*, and *Rear Window* are typically followed by a series of films consolidating the rules of a new game and so encouraging the audience successively to reinvent and recuperate their sense of themselves as the films alternately assault and affirm the idea of a self. Finally, they develop ever more intricate configurations through the process of rereading, which domesticates the films' radical impulses (so that eventually the shock of the murder in *Psycho* becomes reassuringly ritualized) while revealing new disruptions unavailable on a first reading. The ludic tendencies toward institutional recuperation and radical critique do not simply alternate in Hitchcock's films; they reinforce each other dialectically, both running in films like *Blackmail* and *Notorious* and *Vertigo* at full throttle. It is precisely this refusal to subordinate either tendency to the other, in fact, that makes the films so successful as play.

The debate over the nature of Hitchcock's films is not so much a debate over whether or not they are games—virtually all his critics agree they are and go on to judge or excuse or praise them on the basis of that observation—as a disagreement about the value of games as such. Critics who emphasize Hitchcock's conservative side take as their subtext the question, "What are games *for?*" assuming a functional character for games within a culture to which they are subordinate. Critics more sympathetic to his disruptive tendencies emphasize instead the question, "Why are games *fun?*" adopting the position that games express human tendencies more fundamental than culture itself. This split is at the heart of game theory itself, distinguishing Caillois's functional, cultural analysis of games from Huizinga's argument that culture itself is a game from which other games must periodically rescue its citizens.[21]

What is at stake in assessing the nature of games is thus the nature of culture as well. Mihai Spariosu, noting that "while in Plato, Aristotle, Kant, and Schiller, play/literature is subsumed, through mimesis, to Reason, in Nietzsche their relationship is reversed: appearance, falsehood, copy, representation, fiction, irreality, irrationality, become privileged over essence, presence (*ousia*), model, truth, reality, and rationality."[22] Nietzsche's work, like more recent deconstructions of modern culture, suggests, as Elizabeth Freund points out, that each of these positions, the Platonic faith in piety and rationality and the Nietzschean deconstruction of the stability of culture and identity as a function of culture, is the "repressed twin" that makes the other possible.[23]

These theorists posit a relation between two ludic impulses, culturally affirmative and culturally critical, in which both terms are alternately privileged but neither definitively or necessarily so. Hitchcock himself maintained that modern life was entirely too safe and predictable, and that his films were therefore designed to administer a series of salutary shocks to the audience. But his films do not maintain nearly so straightforward an opposition to the dominant culture. Nor could they be expected to do so, given their complicity in the mechanisms of capitalism—their eager adoption of generic conventions, their self-definition as popular art, the frank determination of their production companies and their director to use them as money-making commodities. Huizinga notes that the impulse toward games and play, which typically takes the form of social critique or social escape, often ends by reaffirming social institutions as the very activities designed to protect the players from the alienating powers of a capitalistic culture become commercialized and commodified themselves, as in bridge tournaments, Monday night football, and the modern Olympic Games.[24] And it might be argued that Hitchcock's films, although they begin as potentially subversive games, end as one more commodity marketed in the guise of games, providing an endorsement of cultural values masquerading as play. I hope my analysis of Hitchcock's films has shown, however, that although his films are indeed commodities, the conservative impetus represented by this commercialization is essential to the profoundly equivocal games Hitchcock plays.

# NOTES

## One. GAMES HITCHCOCK PLAYS

1. François Truffaut, *Hitchcock,* rev. ed. (New York: Simon and Schuster, 1984), pp. 158–59.
2. Truffaut, *Hitchcock,* p. 158.
3. Commentators do not agree where Hitchcock is to be found in *Rope.* Truffaut spots him crossing the street after the main title (p. 158), and Maurice Yacowar, *Hitchcock's British Films* (Hamden, Conn.: Archon, 1977) thinks he is present only in the citation of *Notorious* (p. 277).
4. Edward Branigan, *Point of View in the Cinema* (Berlin: Mouton, 1984), pp. 40, 41.
5. Ibid., p. 40.
6. See Yacowar, *Hitchcock's British Films,* pp. 270–78.
7. See Christian Metz, *The Imaginary Signifier: Psychoanalysis and the Cinema,* trans. Celia Britton et al. (Bloomington: Indiana University Press, 1977), pp. 94–95.
8. The bibliography of psychoanalytic (especially Lacanian) approaches to cinema could go on for many pages. The two most influential treatments remain Metz, *Imaginary Signifier,* and Laura Mulvey, "Visual Pleasure and Narrative Cinema," *Screen* 16, no. 3 (Autumn 1975): 6–18.
9. Gaylyn Studlar, *In the Realm of Pleasure: Von Sternberg, Dietrich, and the Masochistic Aesthetic* (Urbana: University of Illinois Press, 1988), p. 182.
10. David Bordwell, *Narration in the Fiction Film* (Madison: University of Wisconsin Press, 1985), pp. 30, 29, 62. Bordwell's model of film viewing is based most explicitly on the work of Helmholtz and the literary theory of the Russian Formalists, but it is closely related to the reader-response criticism of Wolfgang Iser. See Iser, "The Reading Process: A Phenomenological Approach," in *The Implied Reader: Patterns of Communication in Prose Fiction from Bunyan to Beckett* (Baltimore: Johns Hopkins University Press,

1974), pp. 274–94, and *The Act of Reading: A Theory of Aesthetic Response* (Baltimore: Johns Hopkins University Press, 1978), especially pp. 180–231.

11. Branigan, *Point of View in the Cinema*, p. 174.

12. Wittgenstein's best-known statement of this analogy is in *Philosophical Investigations*, 3d ed., translated by G. E. M. Anscombe (New York: Macmillan, 1958), section 492: "To invent a language could mean to invent an instrument for a particular purpose on the basis of the laws of nature (or consistently with them); but it also has another sense, analogous to that in which we speak of the invention of a game" (p. 137e). For the importance of the "point" of a game, see section 564 (p. 150e).

13. Lesley Brill, *The Hitchcock Romance: Love and Irony in Hitchcock's Films* (Princeton: Princeton University Press, 1988), pp. 56–57, 57–58.

14. Metz, *Imaginary Signifier*, p. 76.

15. Bordwell, *Narration in the Fiction Film*, p. 32.

16. David Bordwell and Kristin Thompson, *Film Art: An Introduction*, 2d ed. (New York: Knopf, 1986), p. 207.

17. Anthropologists have found that audiences unversed in the cultural and representational conventions of movies are not inscribed or "compelled" in at all the same way as audiences who have assimilated those conventions. See for example John Wilson, "Film Illiteracy in Africa," *Canadian Communications* 1 (Summer 1961): 7–14.

18. Branigan, *Point of View in the Cinema*, pp. 61, 62.

19. In "Psychology and Form," Kenneth Burke defines form as "the creation of an appetite in the mind of the auditor, and the adequate satisfying of that appetite." See *Counter-Statement*, 3d ed. (Berkeley: University of California Press, 1968), p. 31.

20. See Sigmund Freud, *Beyond the Pleasure Principle* (1922), in *The Standard Edition of the Complete Psychological Works of Sigmund Freud*, 24 vols., translated under the general editorship of James Strachey (London: Hogarth, 1953–74), 18:14–17.

21. Tania Modleski, *Loving with a Vengeance: Mass-Produced Fantasies for Women* (1982; rpt., New York: Methuen, 1984).

22. Studlar, *In the Realm of Pleasure*, p. 181.

23. For the distinction between "reading by error" and "reading by hypothesis," see Branigan, *Point of View in the Cinema*, pp. 50–56.

24. See for example "The World of Wrestling" and "Striptease," in Roland Barthes, *Mythologies*, selected and translated by Annette Lavers (New York: Hill and Wang, 1972), pp. 15–25, 84–87.

25. Bordwell, *Narration in the Fiction Film*, p. 37.

26. George M. Wilson, *Narration in Light: Studies in Cinematic Point of View* (Baltimore: Johns Hopkins University Press, 1986), p. 210.

27. Stephen Heath himself gestures briefly in this direction in the essay when he asks, "Does anyone who has watched, say, *The Big Sleep* seriously believe that a central part of Hollywood films, differently defined from genre to genre, was not the address of a process with a movement of play and that that was not a central part of their pleasure?" But he drops this line in order to consider more centrally "the question of that 'one' [for whom events in film take place] and its narrative terms of film space." See *Questions of Cinema* (Bloomington: Indiana University Press, 1981), pp. 44, 69.

28. Roger Caillois, *Man, Play, and Games,* trans. Meyer Barash (New York: Free Press, 1961), pp. 9–10.

29. Peter Hutchinson, *Games Authors Play* (London: Methuen, 1983), pp. 6, 7. See Bernard Suits, *The Grasshopper: Games, Life, and Utopia* (Toronto: University of Toronto Press, 1978), p. 41.

30. Caillois, *Man, Play, and Games,* p. 13; see also p. 29.

31. Ibid., p. 31.

32. Ibid., pp. 121, 120, 122.

33. The pleasure of following the rules for the sake of the rewards they promise is complemented by the pleasure of flouting the rules in order to experience one's own superiority and freedom. Both impulses are combined in Hitchcock's cameos, which break the rules of the storytelling contract but establish a new contract of their own. In Hitchcock's films as in most stories, however, the pleasure of flouting the rules is reserved for the storyteller and for frankly revisionary interpreters.

34. See John von Neumann and Oskar Morgenstern, *The Theory of Games and Economic Behavior,* 3d ed. (Princeton: Princeton University Press, 1953). The best introduction to mathematical game theory for nonspecialists is Morton P. Davis, *Game Theory: A Nontechnical Introduction,* rev. ed. (New York: Basic, 1983).

35. See Thomas Schelling, *The Strategy of Conflict* (Cambridge: Harvard University Press, 1960), p. 89.

36. For more on the world movies create, see Leo Braudy, *The World in a Frame: What We See in Films* (Garden City: Doubleday, 1976); and Stanley Cavell, *The World Viewed: Reflections on the Ontology of Film,* enlarged ed. (Cambridge: Harvard University Press, 1979).

37. See Braudy, *World in a Frame,* p. 48, for this distinction.

38. John G. Cawelti has argued that it is indeed a vital function of generic conventions to allow audiences to expose themselves to material that would

otherwise be too threatening. See Cawelti, *Adventure, Mystery, and Romance: Formula Stories as Art and Popular Culture* (Chicago: University of Chicago Press, 1976), pp. 17–19.

39. A representative assessment of Hitchcock as a sadistic manipulator, "a poker-faced tease who likes to pinch our nipples," is David Thomson, "The Big Hitch," *Film Comment* 15, no. 2 (March/April 1979): 26–29. See Donald Spoto, *The Dark Side of Genius: The Life of Alfred Hitchcock* (Boston: Little, Brown, 1983), for many examples of Hitchcock's non-cinematic practical jokes on friends and colleagues.

40. Contemporary theories of narrative have often approached the issue of cinematic pleasure in very different terms. Compare for example Roland Barthes's distinction between *plaisir* (rational, calculated pleasure) and *jouissance* (orgasmic bliss) in *The Pleasure of the Text* (1973), trans. Richard Miller (New York: Hill and Wang, 1975), and the psychoanalytic theory of pleasure adopted by Teresa de Lauretis in *Alice Doesn't: Feminism, Semiotics, Cinema* (Bloomington: Indiana University Press, 1984).

41. Hitchcock must have been fond of this auditory pun, for he had already used a similar pun for the discovery of the artist's body in *Blackmail* and would use another one at the corresponding moment in *Young and Innocent*.

42. See Hans Robert Jauss, "Literary History as a Challenge to Literary Theory," in *Toward an Aesthetic of Reception*, trans. Timothy Bahti (Minneapolis: University of Minnesota Press, 1982), p. 24. In developing the historical concept of a horizon of expectations, Jauss is attempting to avoid the charges of ahistorical reification leveled against such inscribed readers as the "implied reader" of Iser; the "super-reader" of Michael Riffaterre, "Describing Poetic Structures: Two Approaches to Baudelaire's *Les chats*," *Yale French Studies* 36/37 (1966): 200–242; the "informal reader" of Stanley Fish, *Is There a Text in This Class?: The Authority of Interpretive Communities* (Cambridge: Harvard University Press, 1980); and the "spectator-in-the-text" of Nick Browne, *The Rhetoric of Filmic Narration* (Ann Arbor: UMI Research Press, 1982). My own recourse to the perspectives of other audiences is designed to place my perspective, in Jauss's terms, as "the vanishing point—but not the goal!—of the process" of aesthetic history (p. 34).

43. See Michael Anderegg, "Hitchcock's *The Paradine Case* and Filmic Unpleasure," *Cinema Journal* 26, no. 4 (Summer 1987), for a detailed attempt to theorize a specifically unpleasurable response predicated "at least for some viewers" (p. 49).

44. Jauss, "Literary History as a Challenge to Literary Theory," pp. 23–24.

45. See Truffaut, *Hitchcock,* pp. 186, 209.
46. Truffaut, *Hitchcock,* p. 43.

### Two. FIND THE DIRECTOR

1. See especially Eric Rohmer's and Claude Chabrol's pioneering *Hitchcock: The First Forty-Four Films* (1957), trans. Stanley Hochman (New York: Ungar, 1979), whose case for the unity of Hitchcock's work rested on their discovery of a consistent thematic pattern—the "transfer of guilt" (p. ix) between heroes and villains—throughout his films.
2. Parenthetical page references in this and the following two paragraphs are to François Truffaut, *Hitchcock,* rev. ed. (New York: Simon and Schuster, 1984).
3. See for example Andrew Sarris's reference to *Juno* as a "literal transcription" in *The John Ford Movie Mystery* (Bloomington: Indiana University Press, 1975), p. 76. For better or worse, Hitchcock was immensely successful in establishing himself as a directorial personality; already in 1930, Paul Rotha calls him "the accredited pre-eminent director of the British school." See Rotha, *The Film Till Now: A Survey of World Cinema,* with an additional section by Richard Griffith, 3d ed. (London: Spring Books, 1967), p. 320.
4. The films Hitchcock directed were early but not universally recognized as Hitchcock films. Andre Sennwald, reviewing *The Man Who Knew Too Much,* observed that although the film might be expected to be important chiefly because it marked Peter Lorre's first reappearance since *M,* still it was "distinctly Mr. Hitchcock's picture" (*New York Times,* 23 March 1935, p. 11, col. 2). But B. R. Crisler's review of *Secret Agent* (*New York Times,* 13 June 1936, p. 13, col. 1), not exactly an assembly-line studio film, does not even mention Hitchcock's name. And although Frank S. Nugent, noting in his review of *The Woman Alone* (the American title of *Sabotage*) Hitchcock's radical departures from Joseph Conrad's novel, concludes that "Mr. Hitchcock's technique is its own excuse" (*New York Times,* 27 February 1937, p. 9, col. 2), Graham Greene, acknowledging Hitchcock's individuality in *Secret Agent,* still deplores his emphasis on obtrusive technique: "His films consist of a series of small 'amusing' melodramatic situations. . . . Very perfunctorily he builds up to these tricky situations (paying no attention on the way to inconsistencies, loose ends, psychological absurdities), and then drops them" (*Graham Greene on Film,* ed. John Russell Taylor [New York: Simon and Schuster, 1972], p. 75). Given these striking differences of opinion on the subject of what film directors were supposed to do, it is

not surprising that Hitchcock's early work so often sets these two sets of assumptions against each other.

5. For further discussion, see Edward Buscombe, "The Idea of Authorship," *Screen* 14, no. 3 (Autumn 1973): 75–85.

6. See in this connection Edward W. Said, *Beginnings: Intention and Method* (New York: Basic, 1975), on "style" as "a comparatively privileged *moment* in the life of a text" or career (pp. 257–58).

7. Maurice Yacowar, *Hitchcock's British Films* (Hamden, Conn.: Archon, 1977), pp. 145, 139.

8. See Robert Scholes, "Narration and Narrativity in Film and Fiction," in *Semiotics and Interpretation* (New Haven: Yale University Press, 1982), pp. 57–72.

9. Donald Spoto, *The Dark Side of Genius: The Life of Alfred Hitchcock* (Boston: Little, Brown, 1983), p. 89.

10. For this broader use of "exposition," see Meir Sternberg, *Expositional Modes and Temporal Ordering in Fiction* (Baltimore: Johns Hopkins University Press, 1978), pp. 5–8.

11. Despite contradictory reports concerning the closeness of Murnau's involvement with his cinematographers during the actual shooting of his films, his surviving colleagues interviewed by Lotte H. Eisner were unanimously agreed on his dedication to the visual design of his films. See Eisner, *Murnau* (1964), English-language ed. (Berkeley: University of California Press, 1973), pp. 71–77.

12. See for example the backstage sequences of *The Lodger, Downhill, Murder!,* and *The Pleasure Garden* (whose entire first half could be described as a backstage romance), the theatrical sequences of *Champagne* and *Murder!,* and the ironically debunked social rituals of *Downhill, The Farmer's Wife,* and *Rich and Strange.*

13. Hitchcock is right in calling Kendall an inadequate actor, but the film as written and directed would have reduced even Cary Grant to a stereotype of meanness. Joan Barry, on the other hand, is appealing in a difficult role.

14. Peter Bogdanovich, *The Cinema of Alfred Hitchcock* (New York: Museum of Modern Art, 1963), p. 12.

15. But Hitchcock routinely takes credit for adaptations in virtually all his British films from his move to British International in 1927 until his return to Michael Balcon at Gaumont-British in 1934. The list includes *The Farmer's Wife, Champagne, Blackmail, Juno and the Paycock, Murder!, Number Seventeen,* and *Rich and Strange,* the last based on a scenario by his

wife Alma Reville, whose name continues to appear regularly on adaptation credits for Hitchcock's films through *Stage Fright* (1950).

16. Robin Wood, *Hitchcock's Films* (London: Zwemmer, 1965), p. 20.

17. Nor were critics unanimous in using this title to describe or circumscribe Hitchcock. As late as 1941, Theodore Strauss could review Hitchcock's domestic comedy *Mr. and Mrs. Smith* (*New York Times*, 21 February 1941, p. 16, col. 3), discussing Hitchcock's distinctive contributions to the film at some length, without noting anything unusual about its having been directed by a specialist in suspense films.

18. Yacowar, *Hitchcock's British Films*, p. 32.

19. The final revelation that the Avenger, who is never shown, has been caught red-handed is an indication that in some sense the movie is pointless; the very existence of the Avenger, whom the Lodger neither equals nor apprehends, is a gigantic red herring in a movie which is really about the Buntings'—especially Daisy's—and the audience's perception of the Lodger.

20. Hence Yacowar's observation that *Champagne,* whose portentous narrative imputations have neither moral resonance nor even genuine narrative importance, is full of "false alarms" (*Hitchcock's British Films*, p. 84).

21. William Rothman is particularly unconvinced by this reassuring ending. See *Hitchcock—The Murderous Gaze* (Cambridge: Harvard University Press, 1982), p. 55.

22. The staircase is thus already, in Hitchcock's first sound film, firmly established as a transitional space between the normal world downstairs and the seductive, mysterious, dangerous world above, a pattern which was first suggested in *The Lodger* and is further developed in *Number Seventeen, Spellbound, Under Capricorn, Strangers on a Train, Vertigo,* and *Psycho,* among others.

23. See Bogdanovich, *Cinema of Alfred Hitchcock,* p. 13.

24. See for example Marsha Kinder and Beverle Houston, *Close-Up: A Critical Perspective on Film* (New York: Harcourt, 1972), pp. 52–58, and Tania Modleski, *The Women Who Knew Too Much* (New York: Methuen, 1988), pp. 29–30.

25. See Yacowar, *Hitchcock's British Films*, pp. 126–31.

26. Rodney Ackland and Elspeth Grant, *The Celluloid Mistress, or The Custard Pie of Dr. Caligari* (London: Wingate, 1954), p. 36.

### Three. GRAVE TO GAY

1. Hitchcock, "'Stodgy' British Pictures," *Film Weekly,* British Film Institute, Slide 1, Column 2, p. 14; quoted by Sam P. Simone, *Hitchcock as Activist: Politics and the War Films* (Ann Arbor: UMI Research Press, 1985), p. 23.

2. Edward Branigan, *Point of View in the Cinema* (Berlin: Mouton, 1984), p. 172.

3. See Elisabeth Weis, *The Silent Scream: Alfred Hitchcock's Sound Track* (Rutherford, N.J.: Fairleigh Dickinson University Press, 1982), pp. 80–82.

4. As Weis remarks: "Noise and talking reveal espionage activities and must be avoided at all costs" (Ibid., p. 80).

5. In *The 39 Steps* Hitchcock makes John Buchan's dying agent a sexually alluring female and introduces the character of Pamela to share his hero's hardships and triumph. In *Secret Agent* he follows Campbell Dixon's stage version of Somerset Maugham's stories in giving the solitary agent Ashenden a fake wife whom he ends by marrying. In *Sabotage* he turns Joseph Conrad's morally ambivalent Chief Inspector Heat, from *The Secret Agent,* into a conventional romantic lead who can console Mrs. Verloc, now saved from suicide, for the loss of her brother and husband. In *Young and Innocent* he changes Erica Burgoyne from the precocious adventuress of Josephine Tey's novel *A Shilling for Candles,* whose interest in Robert Tisdall has nothing to do with love, into a young woman who is forced to choose between her father and her lover. Finally, he takes the romantic relationship on the periphery of Ethel Lina White's novel *The Wheel Spins* and places it at the center of *The Lady Vanishes,* essentially reinventing the character of Gilbert in the process.

6. It is only fair to add that contemporary reviewers do not express any increased sense of reassurance. Andre Sennwald, reviewing *The 39 Steps,* observes: "Perhaps the identifying hallmark of [Hitchcock's] method is its apparent absence of accent in the climaxes, which are upon the spectator like a slap in the face before he has set himself for the blow. In such episodes as the murder of the woman in Hannay's apartment, the icy ferocity of the man with the missing finger when he casually shoots Hannay, or the brilliantly managed sequences in the train, the action progresses through seeming indifference to whip-like revelations" (*New York Times,* 14 September 1935, p. 8, col. 4). And Frank S. Nugent calls *The Girl Was Young* (the American title of *Young and Innocent*) "a taut skein of adventure and romance" (*New York Times,* 11 February 1938, p. 27, col. 2).

7. See William Rothman, *Hitchcock—The Murderous Gaze* (Cambridge: Har-

vard University Press, 1982), pp. 128–29. The implications of the shot are central to the argument of Rothman's book, motivating, for example, its title.

8. Frank S. Nugent's reaction to *The Lady Vanishes* is typical: "If it were not so brilliant a melodrama, we should class it as a brilliant comedy" (*New York Times,* 26 December 1938, p. 29, col. 1).

9. Maurice Yacowar encapsulates the audience's fascinated repulsion from the General when he observes that "the slimy, murderous General is part of the heroic center of the film" (*Hitchcock's British Films* [Hamden, Conn.: Archon, 1977], p. 194).

10. See Weis, *Silent Scream,* p. 63ff.

11. François Truffaut, *Hitchcock,* rev. ed. (New York: Simon and Schuster, 1984), p. 109.

12. Many critics have complained that the film radically simplifies Conrad's complex ironies by relying on such a melodramatic framework. Michael Anderegg begins his discussion of the adaptation in "Conrad and Hitchcock: *The Secret Agent* Inspires *Sabotage,*" *Literature/Film Quarterly* 3, no. 1 (Summer 1986), by acknowledging that "a Conrad enthusiast might be excused for feeling that *Sabotage* betrays its source on a rather fundamental level" (217). The Hitchcock film that most closely approximates Conrad in its lack of faith in action as the basis for human identity is not *Sabotage* but the much later *Topaz,* which was of course criticized on its first release as inexpertly melodramatic.

13. Or of *Marnie,* which, after an opening sequence which correctly imputes Marnie's guilt, goes on to mount a critique of the whole notion of Marnie "herself."

## Four. ODD MAN OUT

1. A well-nigh universal belief expressed by reviewers throughout the forties was that Hitchcock had lost his touch—that his American films were inferior to his British films because they were less identifiably Hitchcockian. See for example Lindsay Anderson's 1949 retrospective "Alfred Hitchcock," reprinted in Albert J. LaValley, ed., *Focus on Hitchcock* (Englewood Cliffs, N.J.: Prentice-Hall, 1972), pp. 48–59. James Agee, writing in 1943 in defense of *Shadow of a Doubt,* still concludes that "its skill is soft and that it is distinctly below the standard set by Hitchcock's best English work" (*Agee on Film: Reviews and Comments* [1958; rpt., Boston: Beacon, 1964], p. 66). Even Frank S. Nugent, in an enthusiastic review of *Rebecca,* agrees

that working in Hollywood had made Hitchcock's style less individual: "His directorial style is less individual, but it is as facile and penetrating as ever; he hews more to the original story line than to the lines of a Hitch original" (*New York Times,* 29 March 1940, p. 25, col. 2).

2. See *Memo from David O. Selznick,* selected and ed. Rudy Behlmer (New York: Viking, 1972), pp. 266–71; Donald Spoto, *The Dark Side of Genius: The Life of Alfred Hitchcock* (Boston: Little, Brown, 1983), pp. 212–14; and Leonard J. Leff, *Hitchcock and Selznick: The Rich and Strange Collaboration of Alfred Hitchcock and David O. Selznick in Hollywood* (New York: Weidenfeld and Nicolson, 1987), pp. 43–47.

3. The smuggler Salvation extends and generalizes this contradictory attitude by insisting that the whole lot of them will burn in hell, "me included."

4. See Raymond Durgnat, *The Strange Case of Alfred Hitchcock, or, The Plain Man's Hitchcock* (London: Faber and Faber, 1974), p. 165.

5. Maurice Yacowar contrasts Pengallan's sensuality with the "romanticism and despair" of Francis Davey, the inoffensive vicar who turns out to be the novel's chief villain. See *Hitchcock's British Films* (Hamden, Conn.: Archon, 1977), p. 252.

6. For a close analysis of the hysterical ambivalence at the heart of this fantasy, see Tania Modleski, *Loving with a Vengeance: Mass-Produced Fantasies for Women* (1982; rpt., New York: Methuen, 1984), pp. 59–84.

7. Daphne Du Maurier, *Rebecca* (Garden City: Doubleday, 1938), p. 10.

8. The ubiquity of Rebecca's initial, which appears on monogrammed stationery, on an address book, on a handkerchief, and on the embroidered pillowcase which is the last object to appear in the film, is one way the film compensates for its lack of an anonymous narrator by constantly reminding the audience that they do not know the heroine's name.

9. For a contrasting view of this exorcism, see Tania Modleski, *The Women Who Knew Too Much: Hitchcock and Feminist Theory* (New York: Methuen, 1988), p. 50.

10. The film emphasizes the tension resolved by their reunion by leaving the heroine alone with Mrs. Danvers at Manderley while de Winter goes with the others to see Dr. Baker in London, so that final drive is a race toward her; in Du Maurier's novel, by contrast, the de Winters make the trip to London and back together, and the climax is supplied simply by their realization that Manderley is on fire.

11. See for example Anderson, "Alfred Hitchcock," in LaValley, *Focus on Hitchcock,* pp. 52–53, 58–59; and William S. Pechter, "The Director Vanishes,"

in *Twenty-Four Times a Second: Films and Film-Makers* (New York: Harper, 1971), p. 176.

12. The conditions of Hitchcock's departure from England, which he had eagerly sought, were changed dramatically by the coming of the war, which prevented his return, and by the illness and death of his mother and the subsequent suicide of his brother William in England. Throughout this period, Hitchcock seems to have regarded himself as living in exile; unlike his wife, who filed for American citizenship immediately on arriving in California, he did not become an American citizen until 1955.

13. Spoto points out that Hitchcock introduced his leading actor and actress, who had not met each other before the first day of filming, in precisely this way, by handcuffing them together, pretending to lose the key, and then leaving them while he went off to photograph some insert shots. See *Dark Side of Genius*, p. 148.

14. William Rothman observes in *Hitchcock—The Murderous Gaze* (Cambridge: Harvard University Press, 1982), that "Hannay makes no declarations and has none to make. . . . He appears completely unselfconscious in the frame" and so "is not a character" (p. 119).

15. See François Truffaut, *Hitchcock,* rev. ed. (Simon and Schuster, 1984), p. 174.

16. His niece and nephew end up with his first bowler; he leaves his second in the cab he shares with Van Meer; his third blows into a puddle outside the mysterious windmill; finally, halfway through the film, he returns to his American fedora.

17. Orson Welles had been largely responsible for the wider popularity of deep focus through his enormously influential *Citizen Kane* (1941), but whether or not Hitchcock saw *Kane,* as presumably he did, his use of deep focus, which emphasizes relationships between characters and their backgrounds rather than relationships among characters within the frame, is consistently more like Wyler's than Welles's. Even in *Rope,* which is composed entirely in long takes, Hitchcock rarely stages conversations or other events in deep space and generally prefers to haze his backgrounds slightly in order to bring his characters into sharper visual relief. At any rate, he seems to have been unusually impressed by Wyler's casting of *The Little Foxes*—and Spoto emphasizes (*Dark Side of Genius,* p. 182n) that Hitchcock most often saw other directors' films for casting purposes—since both Teresa Wright and Patricia Collinge play similar roles in *Shadow of a Doubt.*

18. Hitchcock's reviewers were equally unprepared to accept the film's critique

of American home life. Agee notes that his own relatively high opinion of the film is "in disagreement with most qualified people" (*Agee on Film,* p. 66); and Bosley Crowther remarks, "We won't violate tradition to tell you how the story ends, but we will say that the moral is either anti-social or, at best, obscure" (*New York Times,* 13 January 1943, p. 18, col. 2).

19. See Truffaut, *Hitchcock,* p. 142; Spoto, *Dark Side of Genius,* pp. 245–46; and Gene D. Phillips, *Alfred Hitchcock* (Boston: Twayne, 1984), pp. 96–97.

20. The film's opening credits are followed by the epigraph, "The fault . . . is not in our stars, but in ourselves," and then by a brief explanation of how, through psychoanalysis, "the devils of unreason are driven from the soul."

21. The classic analysis of the distinction between *implicata* (implications of an utterance) and *implicatures* (acts of uttering) is in H. P. Grice, "Logic and Conversation," in *The Logic of Grammar,* ed. Donald Davidson and Gilbert Harman (Encino, Calif.: Dickenson, 1975), p. 65.

22. Evidently Hitchcock had long wanted to film the story of *Notorious*—"about a man who forces a woman to go to bed with another man because it's his professional duty"—and story conferences on the project began even before shooting on *Spellbound* was completed. See Spoto, *Dark Side of Genius,* pp. 283–86.

23. The MacGuffin is Hitchcock's term for the pretext that sets the plot in motion—the secret formula or the missing piece of evidence that the characters are determined to get, even though, from the storyteller's point of view, "it's beside the point," since its only importance is to give the heroes and heroines a goal to share with the audience (Truffaut, *Hitchcock,* pp. 138).

24. Ibid., p. 165.

25. Leff, *Hitchcock and Selznick,* p. 127.

26. Modleski has treated this situation at length in *The Women Who Knew Too Much* (see especially pp. 106–7).

## Five. CAT AND MOUSE

1. Leonard J. Leff reports in *Hitchcock and Selznick: The Rich and Strange Collaboration of Alfred Hitchcock and David O. Selznick in Hollywood* (New York: Weidenfeld and Nicolson, 1987), p. 272, that not even Bernstein was willing to veto any of Hitchcock's plans.

2. The film plays down the homosexual element of Hamilton's play but preserves the irony of Brandon's apparently nonexistent private life being very private indeed.

3. The tag for Warner's publicity campaign for the film was "Nothing ever held you like Alfred Hitchcock's *Rope!*"
4. See François Truffaut, *Hitchcock*, rev. ed. (New York: Simon and Schuster, 1984), p. 184.
5. Bosley Crowther observed in reviewing the film that "the emphasis on the macabre in this small story is frightfully intense" (*New York Times*, 27 August 1948, p. 12, col. 4).
6. The film is virtually unbroken, though Hitchcock made clean cuts at the end of the first three of the film's four double-reels for the convenience of projectionists.
7. Hitchcock told Truffaut that *The Hollywood Reporter* complained that audiences "had to wait a hundred and five minutes for the first thrill of the picture" (Truffaut, *Hitchcock*, p. 186).
8. For an extended analysis of Hitchcock's camerawork in *Under Capricorn*, see John Belton, "*Under Capricorn*: Montage Entranced by Mise-en-scène," in *Cinema Stylists* (Metuchen, N.J.: Scarecrow, 1983), pp. 39–58.
9. The most interesting exceptions are *Notorious*, in which the lovers' relationship enables what the audience perceives as a false and gratuitous marriage, and *Secret Agent*, in which Elsa flirts as a married woman with Robert Marvin even though she and Ashenden are only pretending to be married.
10. See most notably Eric Rohmer and Claude Chabrol, *Hitchcock: The First Forty-Four Films* (1957), trans. Stanley Hochman (New York: Ungar, 1979), pp. 106–12.
11. Leland Poague has urged that "the point of *Strangers on a Train*, at least as far as Guy is concerned, has little to do with whether or not Guy accepts guilt for killing Miriam. It is whether or not he takes Bruno, and the chaos which Bruno represents, seriously and acts in responsible accord with that seriousness." See Poague and William Cadbury, *Film Criticism: A Counter Theory* (Ames: Iowa State University Press, 1982), p. 126.
12. Compare the opening montage of one-way signs, labeled "DIRECTION," which prepare for these gazes by apparently pointing toward the murder scene and which have a similar air of breaking a taboo.
13. Raymond Durgnat, following Rohmer and Chabrol, suggests that Hitchcock is concerned here with the spiritual pride of martyrdom. See Durgnat, *The Strange Case of Alfred Hitchcock, or, The Plain Man's Hitchcock* (London: Faber and Faber, 1974), p. 232, and Rohmer and Chabrol, *Hitchcock*, p. 116. But in fact the film doesn't encourage such speculations; Logan's ordeal is presented perfectly straight, and the shots indicating Christian parallels

are not taken from his point of view but generally show views unavailable to him.

14. Rohmer and Chabrol, *Hitchcock*, p. 116.

15. This pleasure is increased by the film's making Tony less crass than in the play. Hitchcock's Tony does not give Swann a detailed account of his attempts to marry money, as in Frederick Knott, *Dial M for Murder* (New York: Random House, 1953), p. 37, nor does the film show him haggling over newspaper rights to Margot's letters (p. 141). And when he is finally caught, he is given a few chillingly good-natured remarks which serve as the film's conclusion.

16. Compare the corresponding sequence in *Spellbound*, in which Constance Petersen's image during John Ballantine's arrest, trial, and conviction is made more active by her voice on the soundtrack.

### Six. HOME FREE ALL

1. See Robert Stam and Roberta Pearson, "Hitchcock's *Rear Window*: Reflexivity and the Critique of Voyeurism" (1983), in Marshall Deutelbaum and Leland Poague, eds., *A Hitchcock Reader* (Ames: Iowa State University Press, 1986), p. 203.

2. Robin Wood first draws attention to this pattern in *Hitchcock's Films* (London: Zwemmer, 1965), p. 64. The analogy is emphasized by the film's music, which is entirely diegetic and consists almost entirely of love songs, including for example not only the composer's song-in-progress, "Lisa," but "Amore," "To See You Is to Love You," "Mona Lisa," and—as Thorwald is carrying parts of his wife's body out in his samples case—the Rodgers and Hart waltz "Lover." See Elisabeth Weis, *The Silent Scream: Alfred Hitchcock's Sound Track* (Rutherford, N.J.: Fairleigh Dickinson University Press, 1982), pp. 113–17.

3. François Truffaut, *Hitchcock*, rev. ed. (New York: Simon and Schuster, 1984), p. 216.

4. The last shot in prints currently available through Universal, that is. In its first release by Paramount, the film ended with a shot of the company's logo over the three shades over Jeff's window slowly coming down one at a time, in an inversion of the film's opening shot emphasizing, as Lisa had earlier remarked, that the "show's over for tonight"—and so reinforcing for one last time Jeff's status as surrogate audience whose story has now become the show the audience is watching. As a filmmaker's meditation on the essential theatricality of life and the resultingly contradictory nature of his own

work, *Rear Window* might profitably be compared to Renoir's *The Golden Coach,* made at the same time in France.

5. Bosley Crowther, who declines to say whether or not Francie is the burglar, hesitates only briefly before reassuring the audience about Robie himself: "We shouldn't even tell you that you may rest entirely assured Mr. Grant himself is not the slick cat-burglar he says he is out to catch" (*New York Times,* 5 August 1955, p. 14, col. 2).

6. John Belton, "Hawks and Co.," in *Cinema Stylists* (Metuchen, N.J.: Scarecrow, 1983), explicitly contrasts Hawks with Hitchcock on this point (pp. 232–33).

7. See Donald Spoto, *The Dark Side of Genius: The Life of Alfred Hitchcock* (Boston: Little, Brown, 1983), p. 355.

8. Noël Burch, *To the Distant Observer,* rev. and ed. Annette Michelson (Berkeley: University of California Press, 1979), pp. 160–61. In Hitchcock's case, the shots differ from establishing shots precisely in their failure to indicate just where the ensuing scene takes place.

9. The earlier film shows so little interest in the possibility that Bob and Jill might work together that their separation scene (in which Bob leaves Jill standing alone onscreen holding the handkerchief he pressed on her) is underplayed to the point of comedy.

10. Although declining to agree with Truffaut that the 1956 Albert Hall sequence was better than the 1934 version, Hitchcock emphasized a single difference he evidently considered an improvement: the presence of the husband, presumably in order to make the climactic set-piece mark the first time husband and wife had successfully worked together. See Truffaut, *Hitchcock,* pp. 93–94.

## Seven. TAILS YOU LOSE

1. This resentment has a specifically homophobic dimension, since Scottie finds that Madeleine's behavior has been dominated not by the mysterious Carlotta Valdes but by the manipulative Gavin Elster.

2. Cf. William Rothman's analysis of these "curtain-raising" shots in "*Vertigo:* The Unknown Woman in Hitchcock," in *The "I" of the Camera* (Cambridge: Cambridge University Press, 1988), pp. 153–54, 159.

3. Compare the treatment of a similar paradox in Poe's story "The Imp of the Perverse," whose murderer seems driven to confess his perfect murder by his uncompromising appetite for the *sensation* of confessing.

4. François Truffaut, *Hitchcock*, rev. ed. (New York: Simon and Schuster, 1984), p. 244.

5. Scottie has already echoed Hitchcock's earlier insecure and therefore bully-ing policeman in the scene at the McKittrick Hotel, where he obtained Carlotta's name by showing a police badge to which he was no longer en-titled, ignored the landlady's questions in pressing his own, and finally made her go upstairs to look into a room she had insisted was empty.

6. In *Hitch: The Life and Times of Alfred Hitchcock* (New York: Pantheon, 1978), John Russell Taylor points out that Hitchcock's and Ernest Lehman's work-ing title for the film was *In a North-westerly Direction*, credits the final title to Kenneth McKenna, of the MGM script department, and concludes that "any allusion to Hamlet's madness was entirely accidental" (p. 248).

7. Thornhill is confused for other reasons as well—for example, why Van-damm and his cohorts were using Townsend's house—that the film never bothers to clear up. Hitchcock delightedly reported to Truffaut (*Hitchcock*, p. 249) that Cary Grant found the story as confusing as Thornhill himself.

8. Thornhill's essential nonentity has been a commonplace of Hitchcock criti-cism ever since it was first remarked by Robin Wood in *Hitchcock's Films* (London: Zwemmer, 1965), p. 104.

9. For the connection between this "berth" and Thornhill's symbolic rebirth as Eve's child, see Stanley Cavell, "*North by Northwest*" (1981), in Marshall Deutelbaum and Leland Poague, eds., *A Hitchcock Reader* (Ames: Iowa State University Press, 1986), p. 255.

10. Much of the following Oedipal reading of the film is anticipated by Ray-mond Bellour's seminal essay "Le blocage symbolique," *Communications*, no. 23 (1975): 235–350.

11. In this regard Thornhill is more like Hamlet, who creates his own identity in the course of his play, than like Odysseus—or Richard Hannay—who are presented as complete when the audience first sees them.

12. Bellour argues a complex series of relations between Marion's mediat-ing neurosis and Norman's psychosis in "Psychosis, Neurosis, Perversion" (1979), in *Hitchcock Reader*, pp. 311–31.

## Eight. FILL IN THE BLANKS

1. Before it was included in *The Strange Case of Alfred Hitchcock*, Raymond Durgnat's chapter on *Psycho* was originally published in his volume *Films and Feelings* under the title "Inside Norman Bates."

2. François Truffaut, *Hitchcock*, rev. ed. (Simon and Schuster, 1984), p. 282.

3. Robin Wood, *Hitchcock's Films* (London: Zwemmer, 1965), p. 127.

4. Ibid., p. 128. For elaborations of the interpretations Wood dismisses, see Ian Cameron and Richard Jeffery, "The Universal Hitchcock" (1965), and Margaret Horwitz, "The Birds: A Mother's Love" (1982), both in Marshall Deutelbaum and Leland Poague, eds., *A Hitchcock Reader* (Ames: Iowa State University Press, 1986), pp. 265–78 and 279–87; and Raymond Bellour, "*The Birds*: Analysis of a Sequence," *Camera Obscura,* nos. 3–4 (1979): 105–34.

5. A great deal of commentary on the film, like these remarks themselves, adopts a tone of conceptual bravado, as if no one else had appreciated quite how unsettling the film was. See for example Wood, *Hitchcock's Films*: "The birds are not sent as a punishment for evil—they just *are*" (p. 147).

6. Horwitz, for example, argues in "*The Birds*: A Mother's Love," that "the bird attacks function primarily as extensions of Lydia's hysterical fear of losing her son" (p. 279).

7. Truffaut, *Hitchcock,* p. 309. For once Hitchcock's story was based on fact— the story of the Burgess-MacLean spy case, which Hitchcock wished to recount from Mrs. MacLean's point of view.

8. Cf. *Notorious,* in which Hitchcock takes pains to establish a close identification between his audience and his principals before unfolding his intrigue.

9. See Leo Braudy, *The World in a Frame: What We See in Films* (Garden City: Doubleday, 1976), pp. 43–44.

10. Leon Uris, *Topaz* (1967; rpt. New York: Bantam, 1968), p. 139.

11. John Belton, "The Perversity of *Topaz,*" in *Cinema Stylists* (Metuchen, N.J.: Scarecrow, 1983), p. 65.

12. Bernard Herrmann's musical score follows Miklos Rosza's score for *Spellbound* in establishing this duality over the credits and maintaining it throughout the film.

13. Kaja Silverman, *The Subject of Semiotics* (New York: Oxford University Press, 1983), p. 147.

14. Michele Piso, "Mark's Marnie," in Deutelbaum and Poague, *Hitchcock Reader,* p. 291.

15. Cf. Tania Modleski, *The Women Who Knew Too Much: Hitchcock and Feminist Theory* (New York: Methuen, 1988), on this oscillation or confusion (pp. 111, 113–14).

16. See Truffaut, *Hitchcock,* p. 341.

17. In *The Silent Scream: Alfred Hitchcock's Sound Track* (Rutherford, N.J.: Fairleigh Dickinson University Press, 1982), Elisabeth Weis quotes Ernest Lehman, who wrote the screenplay: "Here and there he sort of dropped

things in to pay lip service to who these people are, but he really didn't want the explanations in the script and shot them, then edited them out of the picture" (p. 164).

18. Truffaut, *Hitchcock*, p. 191. Hitchcock is speaking here of *Stage Fright*.

19. See Donald Spoto, *The Dark Side of Genius: The Life of Alfred Hitchcock* (Boston: Little, Brown, 1983), pp. 542–44. The complete screenplay for *The Short Night* is included in David Freeman, *The Last Days of Alfred Hitchcock* (Woodstock, N.Y.: Overlook, 1984).

## *Nine.* ONLY A GAME

1. On the attempt to sell Hitchcock as an artist, see Robert E. Kapsis, "Holly-wood Filmmaking and Reputation Building: Hitchcock's *The Birds,"* *Journal of Popular Film and Television* 15, no. 1 (Spring 1987): 5–15.

2. François Truffaut, *Hitchcock,* rev. ed. (New York: Simon and Schuster, 1984), pp. 282–83.

3. Ibid., pp. 16–17.

4. Charles Thomas Samuels, "Hitchcock" (1970), in Samuels, *Mastering the Film and Other Essays* (Knoxville: University of Tennessee Press, 1977), pp. 72, 73; Charles Higham, "Hitchcock's World," *Film Quarterly* 16, no. 2 (Winter 1962–63): 3.

5. Not necessarily within the academy, where prolonged critical scrutiny (witness the long shelf of books on Hitchcock) establishes a canonical status for the films that waives such debate. But the debate continues in the popular press, as in a commemorative article in the *Philadelphia Inquirer* for 26 April 1990 entitled "The Two Hitchcocks," and asking in its subhead, "Was he artist or entertainer?" (p. 1-E, col. 1).

6. Robin Wood, *Hitchcock's Films* (London: Zwemmer, 1965), pp. 9, 10–11.

7. Raymond Durgnat, *The Strange Case of Alfred Hitchcock, or, The Plain Man's Hitchcock* (London: Faber and Faber, 1974), pp. 31, 58.

8. Andrew Sarris, ed., *Interviews with Film Directors,* (1967; rpt., New York: Avon, 1969), p. 245.

9. Leo Braudy, "Hitchcock, Truffaut, and the Irresponsible Audience" (1968), in Albert J. LaValley, ed., *Focus on Hitchcock* (Englewood Cliffs, N.J.: Prentice-Hall, 1972), p. 119.

10. Sarris, *Interviews with Film Directors,* p. 243.

11. See Penelope Houston, "The Figure in the Carpet," *Sight and Sound* 34, no. 4 (Spring 1963): 159–64.

12. In her article on Hitchcock in Richard Roud, ed., *Cinema: A Critical Dictio-*

*nary,* 2 vols. (New York: Viking, 1980), Houston suggests one way out of the impasse produced by the assumption that "significance in art is related to moral concern": instead of assuming either that Hitchcock is simply "a master entertainer, limited by an inescapable triviality of theme," or that "his films consistently transcend apparent triviality by a moral complexity," critics might decide that "Hitchcock's self-definition should be taken seriously: that his work is much closer to abstract art, reflecting a continual fascination with the manipulation of the materials themselves, the placing and juxtaposition of moments of film to excite or affront or amuse" (1:501).

13. Jean Piaget, *Play, Dreams, and Imitation in Childhood* (1951), translated by C. Gattegno and F. M. Hodgson (New York: Norton, 1962), p. 149.

14. Norman N. Holland, "UNITY IDENTITY TEXT SELF," *PMLA,* 90 (October 1975): 817, 815.

15. For Freud's ego-oriented theory of fictional pleasure, see "Creative Writers and Day-Dreaming" (1908), in *The Standard Edition of the Complete Psychological Works of Sigmund Freud,* 24 vols., translated under the general editorship of James Strachey (London: Hogarth, 1953–74), 9:141–54.

16. In "The Director Vanishes," in *Twenty-Four Times a Second: Films and Film-Makers* (New York: Harper, 1971), William S. Pechter has expressed the resulting discomfort with particular openness in concluding his admiring analysis of *Vertigo,* whose hero and audience alike "are subjected to an ordeal of callous manipulation, expectations established only to be frustrated, hopes offered only to be shattered, and a final, pervasive impotence," that although "the experience of all this is enervating to exhaustion," still "the film actually *means* nothing, is *about* nothing beyond the exposition of its narrative. Or rather it is *about* suffering, the experience of suffering which the narrative engenders is its meaning. But we suffer, in effect, for the sake of entertainment; certainly not to the end of greater understanding; at best, to the end of beauty" (p. 179).

17. In *The Hitchcock Romance: Love and Irony in Hitchcock's Films* (Princeton: Princeton University Press, 1988), Lesley Brill argues, for instance, that "the artistic personality embodied in his films" suggests that "Hitchcock, far from being an exotic sadist, was deeply conventional, thoughtful, and rather soft-hearted. His dearest dreams were composed of nothing more remarkable than love and marriage, happy families, and a forgiving universe that allows such things" (p. xiii).

18. Tania Modleski, *The Women Who Knew Too Much: Hitchcock and Feminist Theory* (New York: Methuen, 1988), p. 3.

19. Gregory Bateson, "A Theory of Play and Fantasy," in *Steps to an Ecology of*

*Mind* (1972; rpt., New York: Ballantine, 1972), pp. 178, 185, 190. For the Theory of Logical Types, see "On Denoting" (1905), in Bertrand Russell, *Essays in Analysis,* ed. Douglas Lackey (New York: Braziller, 1973), pp. 103–19.

20. Bateson, "Theory of Play and Fantasy," p. 192.

21. See Johan Huizinga, *Homo Ludens: A Study of the Play-Element in Culture* (1944), translated anonymously (1950; rpt., Boston: Beacon, 1953), pp. 2–4.

22. Mihai Spariosu, *Literature, Mimesis and Play: Essays in Literary Theory* (Tübingen: Gunter Narr Verlag, 1982), p. 25.

23. Elizabeth Freund, *The Return of the Reader: Reader-Response Criticism* (Methuen: London, 1987), p. 127. See Jacques Derrida, "Structure, Sign, and Play in the Discourse of the Human Sciences," in *Writing and Difference,* trans. Alan Bass (Chicago: University of Chicago Press, 1978), pp. 278–93.

24. Huizinga, *Homo Ludens,* pp. 195–99.

# INDEX

Ackland, Rodney, 70
*Agon*, 16, 17
Aherne, Brian, 160
Albertson, Frank, 215
*Alea*, 16, 17
*Alfred Hitchcock Hour, The*, 1
*Alfred Hitchcock Presents*, 1, 255
Allen, Woody, 52
Allgood, Sara, 55
Altman, Robert, 139
Amann, Betty, 50
Anderson, Judith, 113
Andrews, Julie, 233
Aristotle, 265
Arosenius, Per-Axel, 235
*Ashenden, or The British Agent*, 96
Audience: capable of learning from experience, 14–15, 33–34; basis for theorizing, 31–32
Ault, Marie, 59–60

Balcon, Michael, 39, 74
Balfour, Betty, 48
Balsam, Martin, 216
Bankhead, Tallulah, 132
Banks, Leslie, 76, 79, 109
Baring, Norah, 66
Barry, Joan, 50, 51
Barthes, Roland, 4, 14

Basserman, Albert, 128
Bates, Florence, 112
Bateson, Gregory, 262–63
Baxter, Anne, 160
Beethoven, Ludwig van, 59
*Before the Fact*, 152
Bel Geddes, Barbara, 198
Bellour, Raymond, 262
Belton, John, 237
Bentley, Thomas, 70
Bergman, Ingmar, 52
Bergman, Ingrid, 125, 127, 145
Bernstein, Sidney, 136
Best, Edna, 76
*Birds, The*, 1–2, 8, 12, 134, 225–31, 232, 234, 240, 250
Black, Karen, 251
Black, Noel, 253
*Blackguard, The*, 44
*Blackmail*, 8, 36, 37, 38, 50, 59, 62–66, 67, 80, 99, 105, 116, 118, 119, 125, 133, 163, 169, 176, 192, 193, 264
Bogdanovich, Peter, 55
Bordwell, David, 7, 12, 15, 33
Boreo, Emile, 90
Boyer, Charles, 5
Branigan, Edward, 4, 5, 7, 12, 75
Braudy, Leo, 259

Brill, Lesley, 10, 261
Brisson, Carl, 46, 55
British International Pictures, 39, 40, 63
Brooks, Mel, 50
Browne, Roscoe Lee, 240
Bruce, Nigel, 128
Burch, Noël, 183
Burks, Robert, 166, 182
Burr, Raymond, 169

Caillois, Roger, 8, 16–18, 158, 265
Calhern, Louis, 125
Calthrop, Donald, 64
Cameo appearances, Hitchcock's, 2–3, 4, 6–7, 10, 75, 264; effects of, 3–7, 255; paradigm for narrative pleasure, 7, 13, 21, 22, 30, 264
Cameron, Ian, 259
Carey, Macdonald, 124
Carroll, Leo G., 154, 208
Carroll, Madeleine, 86, 96
Cartwright, Veronica, 226
Casson, Ann, 71
Cervantes, Miguel de, 34, 166
Chabrol, Claude, 162
Champagne, 47, 48–49, 52, 54, 119
Chandler, Joan, 140
Chaplin, Charles, 4, 21, 33, 44
Chapman, Edward, 42, 67
Chekhov, Michael, 133
Chesney, Arthur, 59
Children, and play, 80–81, 83, 84, 135, 155–58
Chimes, The, 128
Cinderella, 5
Clift, Montgomery, 159
Coleman, Herbert, 166
Collier, Constance, 143

Connery, Sean, 232, 240, 241
Conrad, Joseph, 101, 102, 195
Cooper, Gladys, 133
Corey, Wendell, 170
Cotten, Joseph, 124, 145
Coward, Noël, 52, 53, 54
Cribbins, Bernard, 245
Crime and Punishment, 38
Cummings, Robert, 122, 162

Dall, John, 138
Dano, Royal, 180
Dawson, Anthony, 162
Day, Doris, 183
Day, Laraine, 128
Deadly Affair, The, 235
De Banzie, Brenda, 184
De Marney, Derrick, 85
Dern, Bruce, 251
Derrida, Jacques, 262
Devane, William, 251
Dial M for Murder, 4, 136, 137, 138, 149, 152, 153, 162–64, 168, 171, 175, 188, 246
Dick, Douglas, 140
Dickens, Charles, 128
Diderot, Denis, 34
Dietrich, Marlene, 149
Discours, 5–6, 10
Disney, Walt, 5, 104
Dr. No, 232
Donat, Robert, 86
Donath, Ludwig, 232
Don Quixote, 166
Dor, Karin, 236
Dostoevsky, Fyodor, 38
Double, as Other, 108–9, 129–30, 132, 135, 154–55, 174
Downhill, 37, 49, 55, 59, 119

Du Maurier, Daphne, 107, 109, 112,
    114
Dunnock, Mildred, 180
Durgnat, Raymond, 110, 258–59

Easy Virtue, 8, 37, 43, 44, 47, 52–55,
    59, 61, 72–73, 116, 127
Elliott, Laura, 154
Esmond, Jill, 41
Evanson, Edith, 140
Exposition, narrative, 36, 38, 43, 48,
    75, 111–12

Family, critique of, 108
Family Plot, 9, 250–54, 255, 256
Farebrother, Violet, 53
Farjeon, J. Jefferson, 70
Farmer's Wife, The, 37, 39, 47, 52, 55,
    264
Father Knows Best, 184
Fathers, displaced, 208–9, 213–14
Film noir, 138, 155, 216, 253
Finch, Jon, 245
Fonda, Henry, 191
Fontaine, Joan, 112, 125
Foreign Correspondent, 9, 37, 107,
    123, 128, 148, 175
Forsythe, John, 180, 235
Foster, Barry, 245
France, C. V., 41
Freeman, David, 254
Frenzy, 2, 29, 30, 101, 244–50, 251,
    252, 254, 261, 264
Fresnay, Pierre, 76
Freud, Sigmund, 13, 260–61
Freund, Elizabeth, 265

Gabel, Martin, 242
Galsworthy, John, 39, 40, 41, 42

Gainsborough Pictures, 39
Games, in Hitchcock's films, 8–10,
    20–28, 36, 74–76, 84, 104–5, 136–
    38, 152, 157–58, 167, 231, 251–52,
    260–62; played by characters, 8–9,
    80–81, 88–90, 104–5, 137, 140,
    141–42, 150–51, 157–58, 163, 168,
    177–79, 206, 251, 253; rules
    subject to change, 17–18, 26–28,
    35, 106–8, 165–66, 190, 221, 225,
    261; adversarial vs. complicit, 19,
    25, 34, 66, 75–76, 90–92, 105,
    197–98, 250; and narrative
    contracts, 19, 30, 73; socially
    meliorative vs. subversive, 30–31,
    158, 188, 261–62, 263–66
Game theory, 8, 16, 18–19, 158
Gaumont-British Pictures, 38–39, 74
Gavin, John, 216
Gaze: as weapon, 52–53, 160–61,
    171–73, 199, 224; fear of, 215–16,
    218
Gelin, Daniel, 184
Geraghty, Carmelita, 43
Gershwin, George and Ira, 39
Gielgud, John, 95, 96
Gill, Maud, 52
Godard, Jean-Luc, 52
Gone With the Wind, 20, 107
Goodbye Piccadilly, Farewell Leicester
    Square, 245
Goodwin, Ron, 246
Granger, Farley, 138, 154
Grant, Cary, 32, 125, 126, 128, 177,
    206
Grey, Anne, 71
Griffes, Ethel, 226
Griffith, D. W., 41, 44, 72
Gwenn, Edmund, 40, 55, 179

Haas, Dolly, 159
Hall-Davies, Lilian, 55
Hamilton, Patrick, 138
Hamlet, 68, 102, 206
Hammerstein, Oscar, 39
Hardwicke, Cedric, 3, 140
Harker, Gordon, 48, 52, 55, 56
Harris, Barbara, 251
Hasse, O. E., 159
Hawks, Howard, 10, 21, 136, 182
Haye, Helen, 40
Hayes, John Michael, 166–67, 177,
    188, 189
Head, Edith, 166
Heath, Stephen, 15
Hecht, Ben, 130
Hedren, Tippi, 2, 226, 240
Hedstrom, Tina, 236
Herrmann, Bernard, 166, 214
Higham, Charles, 257, 261
High Noon, 138
Highsmith, Patricia, 155
Histoire, 5–6, 10
Hitchcock, Alfred: appearances in
    television shows, 1; in trailers,
    1–2; in films, 2–3, 4, 6–7 (see
    also cameo appearances); self-
    advertising style, 10, 21, 37–38,
    42–43, 45–46, 231; as auteur, 32–
    33, 34, 38, 39; as adapter vs.
    creator, 32, 36–40, 45, 46, 142; as
    Master of Suspense, 38, 59, 254;
    as artist vs. entertainer, 257–60; as
    storyteller, 259–60
Hitchcock, Patricia, 156
Hitchcock's Films, 258
Hogan, Dick, 138
Holland, Norman N., 260–61

Home: as thematic center and ludic
    topos, 25–26, 140–41, 168;
    alienation from, 108–35 passim,
    145–46; as basis for identity, 118,
    147, 171; as trap, 124–25, 139–40,
    150, 163–64
Homolka, Oscar, 99
Houston, Penelope, 259
Huizinga, Johan, 8, 158, 265
Hume, Benita, 54
Hunter, Ian, 55
Huston, John, 4
Hutchinson, Peter, 16

Ibsen, Henrik, 118
I Confess, 138, 152, 159–62, 163, 176,
    197
Identification: as basis for games,
    108–9, 190; equivocal, 174, 199–
    201, 203; vs. identity, 222–24,
    244
Identity: public and private, 52, 67–
    70, 76, 116–17, 167; as per-
    formance, 69, 117, 150–51, 212–
    14; as problem to be resolved,
    115–18, 130–32, 166; genetic basis
    of, 135, 218–19, 248, 254; loss of,
    202–5, 215–16, 217, 222–25;
    contingent on actions and situa-
    tions, 211–12, 218–19; function of
    perceptions, 218, 221, 223–24. See
    also Self
Ilinx, 16, 17
Imputations, narrative, 20–21, 44;
    and moral, 24–25, 61–62
Irony, dramatic, and suspense,
    143–44, 148, 162
Irvine, Robin, 53

*Jamaica Inn*, 109–12, 115, 122, 130, 135, 138, 146
James, Henry, 118
Jauss, Hans Robert, 32, 34
Jeans, Isabel, 53
Jokes, 45, 75, 143–44, 195, 196–97, 214, 228, 229–30, 257. *See also* Games
Jourdain, Louis, 135
*Juno and the Paycock*, 37, 55, 127, 129

Kahn, Florence, 97
Kant, Immanuel, 265
Keaton, Buster, 4
Kedrova, Lila, 234
Keen, Malcolm, 46, 60
Kelly, Grace, 162, 166, 169, 177
Kendall, Henry, 50, 51, 55
Kieling, Wolfgang, 233
Kirkbride, Ronald, 254
Knott, Frederick, 162
Konstam, Phyllis, 40, 67
Konstantin, Leopoldine, 125

La Bern, Arthur, 245, 246
Lacan, Jacques, 243, 262
*Lady in the Lake, The*, 138
*Lady Vanishes, The*, 8–9, 75, 85, 86–87, 89–90, 92, 93–94, 99, 104, 105, 117, 120, 127, 143, 166, 167, 193, 244, 260
Landau, Martin, 207
Landis, Jessie Royce, 178, 208
Lang, Fritz, 107, 155
*Last Laugh, The*, 45, 57
Latham, Louise, 240
Laughton, Charles, 109
Lauter, Ed, 252

Lawrence, D. H., 258
Lee, Canada, 127
Leff, Leonard J., 132
Lehman, Ernest, 207
Leigh, Janet, 2, 214
Leigh-Hunt, Barbara, 2, 245
Leighton, Margaret, 146
Levy, Louis, 99
*Lifeboat*, 2–3, 6, 7, 107, 119, 122–23, 127, 132, 163, 174, 175
Lion, Leon M., 71
*Little Foxes, The*, 124
Lloyd, Norman, 127
Lockwood, Margaret, 86
Loder, John, 101
*Lodger, The*, 3, 8, 29, 36, 37, 38, 43, 45, 51, 55, 59–62, 66, 67, 68, 73, 74, 75, 80, 105, 116, 118, 119, 120, 143, 153, 169, 196, 227, 245, 246, 261
Lombard, Carole, 123
*London Wall*, 70
Longden, John, 42, 63
Lorne, Marion, 157
Lorre, Peter, 76, 80, 83, 95, 143, 156
Lubitsch, Ernst, 27, 44, 107
*Ludus*, 16, 17

*M*, 80
McCowen, Alec, 245
McCrea, Joel, 123
MacGregor, Hector, 151
MacGuffin, 278 (n. 23)
MacLaine, Shirley, 180
Malden, Karl, 160
Mamoulian, Rouben, 39
Mannheim, Lucie, 88
Mannoni, Octave, 11

*Man Who Knew Too Much, The*
(1934), 8, 9, 35, 59, 74, 75, 76–84,
85, 87, 95, 98, 99, 107, 116, 117,
120–21, 142, 143, 156, 157, 158,
165, 167, 169, 184, 185, 186, 187,
188, 190, 197, 235, 255, 264
*Man Who Knew Too Much, The*
(1956), 9, 79, 80, 135, 166, 168,
176, 183–88, 235, 253, 255, 264
*Manxman, The*, 37, 46–47, 54, 119,
127, 129
Marmont, Percy, 50, 85, 96
*Marnie*, 182, 240–44, 246, 249–50
Marsh, Jean, 245
Marshall, Herbert, 5, 66
Mason, James, 207
Massey, Anna, 245
Mathers, Jerry, 180
Maugham, W. Somerset, 5, 96
Maxwell, John, 39, 70
Mayflower Productions, 109
Metz, Christian, 6, 7, 11
MGM Pictures, 136
*Midsummer Night's Dream, A*, 179
Miles, Bernard, 184
Miles, Vera, 191, 216
Milland, Ray, 162
*Mimicry*, 16, 17
*Mr. and Mrs. Smith*, 51, 107, 123–24,
133
Misreadings, encouraged by
Hitchcock, 24–25, 27, 30, 42, 49,
60–62, 76–79, 197–98, 221
Modleski, Tania, 13, 262
Montagu, Ivor, 43
Montgomery, Robert, 123, 138
*Moon and Sixpence, The*, 5
Morgenstern, Oskar, 18

Mothers, distrust of, 133–35, 208–11,
248
*Mountain Eagle*, 59
*Murder!*, 36, 37, 45, 66–70, 71, 75,
76, 117, 150
Murnau, F. W., 44–45, 107

Narrative, models of:
communications, 3–4; empiricist,
4–6, 12–13; psychoanalytic, 6–7,
11, 13, 14; constructivist, 7; ludic,
7–8, 10–35 *passim*
Natwick, Mildred, 180
Nerval, Gerard de, 34
Nesbit, Cathleen, 251
Neumann, John von, 18
Newman, Paul, 232
Newton, Robert, 110
Ney, Patience, 109
*New Alfred Hitchcock Presents, The*, 1
Nietzsche, Friedrich, 265
Nightmare, as game, 189–90, 191–92,
193, 195, 197–98
Noiret, Philippe, 237
*North by Northwest*, 9, 17, 118, 121–
22, 134, 189, 190, 194, 197,
206–14, 215, 224, 225, 261
*Notorious*, 9, 72, 107, 122, 125–26,
130–32, 133–34, 135, 168, 169,
171, 174, 175, 176, 207, 224, 226,
243, 244, 246, 250, 255, 264
Novak, Kim, 198
Novello, Ivor, 45, 49, 55, 60, 68, 74,
120, 153
*Number Seventeen*, 9, 36, 59, 66,
70–72, 76

Oates, Cicely, 81

O'Hara, Maureen, 109
Olivier, Laurence, 4, 112
Olsen, Christopher, 183
Ondra, Anny, 46, 63
*One Plus One Equals One*, 252
Ozu, Yasujiro, 183

*Paidia*, 16, 17
*Paradine Case, The*, 107, 108, 123, 132, 133, 135, 136, 175, 176
Paramount Pictures, 136, 165, 166, 167, 174, 182, 239
Parker, Cecil, 145
Peck, Gregory, 127, 133
Percy, Esme, 67
Perkins, Anthony, 215
Perkins, V. F., 259
Perrault, Charles, 5
Phillpotts, Eden, 39
Piaget, Jean, 260–61, 263
Picasso, Pablo, 238
Piccoli, Michel, 236
Pilbeam, Nova, 76, 85, 89
Plato, 265
Pleasure, as basis of narrative contract, 11–12, 13, 14–15, 19, 34, 35
*Pleasure Garden, The*, 43, 59, 67, 127, 167
Pleshette, Suzanne, 228
Polanski, Roman, 195
Police, representations of, 65, 81, 169, 176, 196–97, 205
Pommer, Erich, 109
*Psycho*, 1–2, 12, 13, 14–15, 16, 17, 19, 25, 27, 28, 29, 30, 100, 125, 134, 145, 146, 156, 161, 189, 190, 194, 195, 197–98, 205, 214–21,
222, 223, 224, 225, 227, 228–29, 234, 238, 244, 245, 246–47, 248, 249, 253–54, 256–57, 259, 260, 264

Quayle, Anthony, 196

Radford, Basil, 89
Rains, Claude, 125
Randolph, Elsie, 50
Raymond, Gene, 124
*Rear Window*, 4, 25, 144, 166, 167, 169–74, 176, 177, 182, 185, 192, 197, 198, 204, 225, 250, 255, 264
*Rebecca*, 8, 25, 107, 109, 112–15, 116, 118, 122, 124, 125, 129, 130, 132, 133, 135, 142, 145, 146, 165, 166, 168, 169, 171, 174–75, 176, 197, 224, 225, 255
Redgrave, Michael, 87
Reed, Carol, 13
Renoir, Jean, 4, 107, 139
*Rich and Strange*, 37, 43, 44, 49–51, 55, 76, 119, 264
Rigby, Edward, 91
*Ring, The*, 8, 37, 38, 43–44, 47, 55–59, 61
Ritchard, Cyril, 38, 63
Ritter, Thelma, 169
RKO Pictures, 32, 128, 130
Robin, Dany, 236
Rodgers, Richard, 39
Rohmer, Eric, 162
Roman, Ruth, 154
*Rope*, 3, 9, 11, 19, 23–24, 25, 31, 45, 136, 137, 138–44, 146, 147–48, 149, 150, 151, 153, 154, 162, 163, 164, 165, 167, 168, 176, 177, 197, 237, 264

*Rope's End*, 138
*Rosita*, 44
Russell, Bertrand, 262, 263

*Sabotage*, 9, 28–29, 30, 75, 76, 94,
    99–104, 105, 113, 117, 118, 120,
    124, 127, 152, 153, 161, 193,
    194–95, 228, 246
*Saboteur*, 107, 119, 121–22, 123, 127,
    129, 133, 176, 207, 246
Saint, Eva Marie, 206
Samuels, Charles Thomas, 257, 261
Sanders, George, 114
Sarris, Andrew, 38
Schelling, Thomas, 19
Schiller, Friedrich, 265
*Secret Agent*, 9, 75, 76, 94, 95–99,
    100, 101, 104, 105, 117, 120, 124,
    153, 156, 167, 193, 195, 234, 235
*Secret Agent, The*, 101
Self, vs. world, 165–66, 171–72, 174,
    175–77, 189–90
Selznick, David O., 94, 106, 107, 109,
    130, 136, 207
*Shadow of a Doubt*, 2, 25, 107, 118,
    124–25, 129, 132, 133, 155, 156,
    159, 164, 169, 175, 176, 189, 193,
    224, 225
Shaffer, Anthony, 245
Shakespeare, William, 257
*Short Night, The*, 250, 254–55, 256
Sidney, Sylvia, 99
Sim, Alistair, 150
Simpson, Helen, 145
Sirk, Douglas, 55
*Skin Game, The*, 37, 39, 40–43, 47,
    51, 55, 59, 129, 142, 264
Slezak, Walter, 127

South, Leonard, 166
Spariosu, Mihai, 265
*Spellbound*, 107, 118, 119, 123, 127,
    129, 130, 132, 133–34, 135, 154,
    156, 174, 176, 193, 207, 211, 224,
    229, 240–41, 242, 243
Spoto, Donald, 43, 254
Stafford, Frederick, 235
*Stage Fright*, 3, 8, 49, 66–67, 68, 137,
    138, 149–51, 152, 153, 154, 175,
    176, 252, 260
Staircases, 273 (n. 22)
Stannard, Eliot, 54
*Stars Look Down, The*, 13
Stewart, James, 138, 142, 169, 183,
    198
*Strange Case of Alfred Hitchcock, The*,
    258
*Strangers on a Train*, 8, 9, 14, 19, 22–
    23, 28, 46, 134, 137, 138, 151–52,
    153, 154–59, 161, 162, 163, 166,
    167, 175, 176, 189, 191, 193, 224,
    246, 260
Stuart, John, 70
Studlar, Gaylyn, 7, 14
Subor, Michel, 237
Suits, Bernard, 16
Suspense films. *See* Thrillers
*Suspicion*, 25, 32, 107, 119, 128–29,
    132, 133, 148, 152, 173, 175, 192,
    224, 225
Swift, Clive, 245

Tandy, Jessica, 230
Taylor, Rod, 226
Taylor, Vaughn, 215
Tester, Desmond, 99
*39 Steps, The*, 8, 17, 19, 20–21, 23,

27, 31, 46, 59, 74, 75, 85, 86, 87–
89, 90, 91–92, 92–93, 94, 103,
104, 105, 116, 117, 118, 121–22,
127, 131, 150, 154, 167, 191, 207,
226, 246, 264
Thomas, Jameson, 48, 55
3-D process, 163–64
Thrillers: paradoxes of, 14, 17–18, 20,
26–27; and moral engagement, 28–
29, 61, 63; as Hitchcock's chosen
genre, 14, 36, 72–73
To Catch a Thief, 8, 19, 23, 25, 31,
134, 166, 167, 168, 177–79, 182
Todd, Ann, 133
Todd, Richard, 149
Tomasini, George, 166
Topaz, 99, 231, 232, 235–240, 244,
250
Torn Curtain, 2, 9, 99, 118, 231–35,
236, 240, 244, 250
Toumanova, Tamara, 235
Transatlantic Pictures, 136, 149, 161,
166
Triangles, romantic, 58–59, 152–54
Tripp, June, 60
Trouble with Harry, The, 51, 134, 144,
166, 168, 176, 179–83, 214
Truffaut, François, 3, 4, 34, 36, 37,
38, 39, 43, 169, 256, 257, 259

Under Capricorn, 25, 45, 119, 137,
138, 144–49, 152, 154, 171, 176
Universal Pictures, 55, 136, 222, 256
Uris, Leon, 236

Valli, Alida, 123
Valli, Virginia, 43
Van Druten, John, 70

Vanel, Charles, 177
Varden, Norma, 156
Vernon, John, 236
Vertigo, 17, 47, 118, 174, 189, 190,
194, 197–205, 206, 209, 210–11,
213, 214, 215, 218, 220, 222, 223,
224, 225, 228, 233–34, 250, 261,
264
VistaVision, 182
Von Alten, Theo, 48
Voyeurism, 64, 169, 171–72, 173–74,
198–99, 217

Wakefield, Hugh, 77
Walker, Robert, 154, 155
Walsh, Kay, 149
Waltzes from Vienna, 76
Warner Brothers Pictures, 136, 138,
149, 165, 188, 189
Wasserman, Lew, 222
Watson, Lucile, 133
Weis, Elisabeth, 96
Welles, Orson, 4
Whitelaw, Billie, 249
Whitty, May, 87
Wilding, Michael, 145, 149
Williams, Adam, 208
Williams, John, 163, 178
Wilson, George M., 15
Wit, as stylistic hallmark, 43, 74–76,
84, 85; distinguished from humor,
94, 131
Wittgenstein, Ludwig, 7
Woman of Paris, A, 44, 45
Wood, Robin, 59, 226–27, 228, 258,
259, 261
Wright, Teresa, 124
Wrong Man, The, 24–25, 29, 31, 188,

*Wrong Man, The* (*continued*)
   189, 190–98, 204, 211, 215, 225,
   246, 254
Wyler, William, 124
Wyman, Jane, 149

Yacowar, Maurice, 4, 40, 60, 67

Young, Robert, 97
*Young and Innocent*, 8, 75, 85–86, 87,
   89, 90–91, 99, 104, 105, 116, 117,
   118, 120, 127, 154

Zinneman, Fred, 138